A Tour of Japan in 1920

A Tour
of Japan in 1920

An American Missionary's Diary
with 129 Photographs

by Wilson P. Minton

EDITED BY DAVID W. CARSTETTER

McFarland & Company, Inc., Publishers
Jefferson, North Carolina, and London

British Library Cataloguing-in-Publication data are available

Library of Congress Cataloguing-in-Publication Data

Minton, Wilson P. (Wilson Parke), 1888–1969.
   A tour of Japan in 1920 : an American missionary's diary with 129
photographs / Wilson P. Minton ; edited by David W. Carstetter.
     p.   cm.
  Includes index.
  ISBN 0-89950-593-7 (lib. bdg. : 70# Sterling gloss alk. paper)
  1. Minton, Wilson P. (Wilson Parke), 1888–1969–Diaries.
2. Missionaries–Japan–Diaries. 3. Missionaries–United States–
Diaries. 4. Japan–Description and travel–1901–1945. 5. Japan–
Pictorial works. I. Carstetter, David W., 1937– . II. Title.
BV3457.M55A3 1992
266'.58'092–dc20
[B]   90-53511
                                           CIP
                                           r92

Manufactured in the United States of America

McFarland & Company, Inc., Publishers
 Box 611, Jefferson, North Carolina 28640

*I lovingly and gratefully
dedicate this book
to my mother and father,
Ruth and Fred Carstetter.
—D.W.C.*

Contents

Preface

by David W. Carstetter

Wilson Parke Minton, D.D., my grandfather, was the newly appointed foreign missions secretary for the Christian Church of America when he traveled to Japan in 1920 and compiled the diary and photographs from which this book is made. He was born in Covington, Ohio, in 1888, attended Moody Bible Institute in Chicago, and was ordained a minister in the Christian Church of America in 1910. His first churches were in Goshen, Indiana, where he served as pastor of both the First Christian Church and the Elkhart Riverside Church.

He moved his family in 1916 to Defiance, Ohio, where he attended Defiance College and served as pastor for three rural churches. It was in 1920, when he was 32 years old and completing his last semester at Defiance College, that he received his foreign missions appointment. The family then moved to the church headquarters in Dayton, after which he was immediately sent to Japan to study the condition of the missions there and to attend the World Sunday School Convention in Tokyo. Upon his return to the United States, Defiance College awarded him an honorary doctor of divinity degree for his work in Japan.

The diary which follows shows that he kept a detailed record of his tour, not just as to the study of the missions in Japan, but as to every aspect of the Japanese people and their country which he encountered. Particularly noteworthy is the long interview which he had with Toyohiko Kagawa. Although Kagawa is not well known in America, his influence in Japan and with scholars of Japanese social history is immense. Kagawa, because of his pioneering work in improving the lot of the poor and the laboring classes in Japan, has been hailed by historians as the most influential leader in developing the thought and conscience of early twentieth-century Japan. The creative and compassionate methods which Kagawa used to help the desperately poor in the slums of Kobe are detailed by Dr. Minton in this diary.

Following his trip to Japan, Dr. Minton continued his work with foreign missions and took several inspection trips to the missions in Puerto Rico. In 1929, he was instrumental in the formation of the union between the Christian and the Congregationalist denominations. He subsequently wrote a book about this aspect of church history, *Some Little Known Aspects of the Congregational Christian Church Merger*, which can be found in the Library of Congress.

Dr. Minton was elected superintendent of the Conference of Congregational and Christian Churches of Pennsylvania in 1934. He served as superintendent of the churches in Pennsylvania until 1952 when he retired from the position following the death of his wife, Bertha. According to church authorities, when Dr. Minton was elected to the superintendency, the Pennsylvania Conference had little organization and was on the verge of disintegration, but through his personal qualities, he effected a fine organization that became a living tribute to his many sacrifices, untiring work, and faith in the church.

At the time of relinquishing his duties as superintendent, Dr. Minton expressed to his family that while he was grateful for the opportunity to serve in senior administrative capacities within the church, his primary desire as a minister had always been to work directly with church members in an individual capacity to improve their personal lives. He therefore became the pastor of Springbrook Congregational Church, a small, struggling church in a rural area outside Scranton. After he had built the Springbrook church to a level of activity and prosperity satisfactory to him, he left in 1958 to work as a voluntary visitor and social worker in the ghetto areas of Philadelphia. From then until his retirement in 1969 he concentrated on public welfare and housing, primarily in the Powelton Village section of Philadelphia, and was also active in the civil rights movement.

In 1969, Dr. Minton had retired from full-time church work and was living with his daughter, Ruth, and her husband, Fred Carstetter, in Reedsville, Pennsylvania, when he passed away at the age of 81.

Upon Dr. Minton's retirement as superintendent of the Pennsylvania church, a written tribute in the *Pennsylvania News*, the official paper of the Pennsylvania church, praised him for his foresight, tact, wisdom, energy, practical good sense, and rare judgment. It is hoped that those qualities have produced in this book something of value for all those who have occasion to read and use it.

Facts About the Diary and Photographs

All of the photographs in this book were reprinted from a collection of 159 three-by-four-inch glass slides, which were popularly known as Magic Lantern slides. Most of the photographs, as described by my grandfather in his diary, were taken by a Kodak folding-bellows camera, using 130A roll film. These were then developed by various shops in Japan by means of the glass-slide process, and many of them were handpainted through a process known only to the film developers.

The glass slides were placed in wooden and cardboard boxes, and remained in storage until Dr. Minton gave them to his daughter, my mother, Ruth Minton Carstetter. After his death in 1969, my mother gave them to me, along with his ancient Magic Lantern projector. The slides and the projector again passed into storage in my home in Florida until March 1989. At that time, I was at home recovering from an operation when my wife, Linda, encouraged me to occupy my time trying to get the ancient projector working so that we could take a look at the slides. Finally one night after many popped circuit breakers and much tinkering and manipulation, we got it working and used it to view the slides. We were immediately awed by the scope and content of the slides, and we began cataloging and sorting them.

Some of the slides had suffered from water damage. Many of them had gummed labels attached on which Dr. Minton had typed a caption for the scene in the slide.

I prepared a 12-page descriptive listing of the slides with his captions and provided my descriptions where no caption existed.

Acting on a hunch, I called my mother in Pennsylvania and asked her to go through the great mass of documents that Granddad had left behind to see if there might be a diary of some sort describing the slides. After an exhaustive search through the documents, which had now become rather musty, my mother found a 308-page document entitled "My Japan Trip Diary." The diary contained numerous references to the photographs and was a detailed account of Granddad's 1920 tour of Japan. In his usual frugal style, he had used a small-print typewriter with typing on both sides of each page. The diary was difficult to read because of its cramped typing. My sister, Romaine Carstetter, painstakingly typed the diary into manuscript form, thus filling 475 pages. In addition to the text, the diary contained 15 pages of hand-drawn maps of the various small towns he visited in Japan.

Granddad Minton, to those of us who knew him, was the keenest and most thoughtful of listeners. He was genuinely interested in all people in all levels of life and the way people lived their lives. Most people who talked with him instinctively trusted him and therefore tended to open up and speak freely. Fortunately, as this manuscript shows, he was also able to record these conversations and his impressions of people and places with clarity, detail and concern.

Jacksonville, Florida
February 1991

I. Voyage to Japan

Spent a busy day in the office and packing. Left the house at 9 P.M. in a downpour of rain to take the 10:05 train to Chicago. After reaching the station, we discovered that the new time had fooled us and we were an hour too early. While waiting, I bought $5,000 of accident life insurance for six months' duration. Also remembered that I had not had any supper, and Mrs. Minton hustled me off to a restaurant. Left on the Pennsylvania RailRoad train at 10:05, taking my family with me as far as Chicago because of the illness of Birdie's mother. It was the first experience of all three of them in a sleeper.

Arrived in Chicago at 7:20 A.M. Secured my ticket for San Francisco, had breakfast, and called on Elmer at his office. Went to the MBI where I bought a new Scofield Bible. Went out to Grace's for lunch. Visited Mother Siebrecht in the afternoon. She has not long to live. We talked and prayed with her, and she seemed to appreciate it so much. Spent the evening at Fox's.

Took the Chicago and Northwestern train "The Pacific Limited" at 10:30 A.M. for San Francisco. It was mighty hard to leave Bertha and the children for four long months, and yet we feel we are doing the right thing.

Met a maiden schoolteacher in my section, also a young man who was traveling with her for the day. They are from Kearney, Nebraska, and have been attending Teacher's College at Columbia for the summer. They were quite companionable and helped to dispel the gloom of starting. Passed through the cornfields of Illinois, and they looked fine. The great state of Iowa is a veritable national commissary with its rolling fields of wheat, in-the-shock corn coming to maturity, and great pastures dotted with thousands of fine cattle. If the cattle and hog cars passing us almost in a continuous stream are any indication, surely we shall not soon starve in America. The Iowa sunset is most beautiful. As a ball of fire a yard wide in appearance, the sun dropped behind the hills studded with trees in an indescribable manner. Retired at 9:30.

Monday, August 16 ——————— ◆ ———————————

Up at 6:30. Cool night, but warming up this morning. Have passed through Clinton, Cedar Rapids, and Marshalltown, Iowa, and in the night through Omaha, Nebraska. Changed time at North Platte where I attempted to get a picture of our train, the Pacific Limited, now running over the Union Pacific lines. Fear my attempt failed as I found the film torn when I took it out. A good part of Nebraska is level, but as we go on, it becomes more rolling. Very dry, and crops do not look so good. See great stacks of hay and straw indicative of a good harvest, however, and there are great fields of alfalfa. My change at breakfast included two silver dollars, the first I have seen for a long time. I understand the government is buying them up at $1.16 each. They are more plentiful in the West than in the East.

Find more cattle as we go west. See great herds of the famous white-faced steers. The houses are small and are widely separated; the barns are quite small as the crops are stacked in the field and fed there, even in winter. As we leave Cheyenne, we begin to climb the mountains with an oil-burning engine, thus avoiding the smoke in the many tunnels through which we pass. The section men along here are swarthy Mexicans with broad-brimmed hats. One sees an occasional prairie schooner camped by the roadside, but many transcontinental autos seek in vain to beat us. As we climb, we note great beds of granite rock. The Union Pacific has its own quarries and gravel pits, and the mountain road bed is exceptionally well ballasted. The Mexicans live in little uninviting huts by the railroad. I noticed a little girl standing upon one step of a little hut. What will be her life and future? There is no doubt a story behind her. I also noticed a number of wooden doors in the mountainside, showing where men had been digging for gold. I wonder how many of them are symbols of useless lives and blasted hopes, made so by greed. What is our life?

Long stretches of snow barriers indicate that the UP has a snow fight on hand each winter. We are running over a high plateau with distant hills on every side. The green and brown fields framed in the darker hills beyond make a very pretty picture as the sun sprays them with her departing rays and disappears from view, leaving the pink-tinted sky to indicate her pathway. Retired at 8:30.

Tuesday, August 17 ——————— ◆ ———————————

Up at 5:30. Great mountain sunrise. We are in the midst of masses of granite rock. When the sun shines upon it, the color scheme is marvelous. The roadbed is very winding, and it is not unusual to see the engine and several coaches disappear ahead of us in a tunnel before we reach it. At Castle Rock we are 6,240 feet above sea level. The air is brisk and fresh. We can see several other railroads on either side of us. The formation of the massive rocks have every appearance of castles of medieval days. At nine o'clock we passed the famous "Devil's Slide"—a great double column of rock running hundreds of feet down the mountainside with a smooth surface between. It looks much like the modern children's slide on a school playground, except that it is of ragged stone and hundreds of feet long. We are now coasting down the mountain, and as we go, a mountain stream races along with us. There are nicely laid-out small farms here, raising potatoes, cabbage, sugar beets, alfalfa, wheat, oats, etc. A large pea cannery at Morgan, Utah, indicates that pea raising is quite an industry. As we go, I notice on the great mountainside long stretches of brown interset with green like little islands, studded with white and granite rocks. There are no trees up here but many green shrubs. In a half hour we will be at Ogden, Utah. Our highest point was at Sherman, Utah, 8,009 feet.

Spent half hour at Ogden. Took several pictures and got some supplies. Left Ogden and started some 50 miles across the lake. The mountains are quite deceiving, as it seems every moment we would reach the other side but the trip was some 50 miles.

After crossing Salt Lake, we traveled nearly all day through alkali plains. It was hot and dry. Saw several auto tourists plowing along in the dust. When the wind strikes these plains, the salty dust flies. Saw several gangs of Japanese workmen on the railroad. The houses along the road are painted yellow, presumably by the R.R. Co. They are laying a pipeline for oil through these plains. It is dusty work. There is a young lady from Virginia going to China as a missionary. I noticed her a while ago utterly absorbed in a game of cards. Is she right or wrong? A young man is in my section who has just joined the Navy and is going to Frisco to be assigned. Father and mother both dead.

It is some cooler tonight. I shall retire early, as we go through some pretty country in the morning.

Wednesday, August 18 ——————— ◆ ————————————————

Up at 5:00 A.M. in the mountains of California. Saw a beautiful mountain sunrise. The lady missionary whom I met yesterday is an Episcopalian. Took several pictures in the mountains. We passed through innumerable snowsheds, much to our disgust. Just as we would get set to take a picture, we would be plunged into the darkness of another shed. The hills are covered with cedar and pine trees. The morning air is very cool.

Took a picture of the American River Canyon and also of a great bend. Wonderful scenery. Train is about two hours late. Just passed a mammoth grove owned by the Sugar Pine Fruit Co. There are orange groves everywhere over the hills, set out in patches so that at a distance they look like great crazy quilts. Sacramento was a disappointment—so hot and dry and lifeless. Saw the capitol building at a distance. The hot, parched fields sure do make California look like a golden state. They tell me it is better farther south.

Finally reached Benicia where the train was run on a large ferry and ferried across the bay. It is wonderful how they can manage some 16 cars and 2 engines on such a craft. Rolled onto Oakland Pier some three hours late. Transferred to ferry and landed at Ferry St. station to find no Mr. Fry awaiting me. Went to the Argonaut, got a room, took a bath and went out for supper. Later, on returning, I found a note stating that Mr. Fry would be in at eight, and he was. We talked quite late and in the course of the evening went out to see what looked like a bad fire but what proved to be not so serious. Brother Fry feels that the board did even more than could be expected in allowing the $500 year-end grant. He also feels that our great need in Japan is an established school but that the next best thing is the dormitory system.

Thursday, August 19 ◆

Brother Fry and I had breakfast at 8:30 and then began to make my final sailing arrangements. Got my passport visaed by the Japanese Consulate at 22 Battery St. Then got my sailing permit at the U.S. Revenue Office, 870 Market St., 505 Flood Building. Then secured my ticket, paying $5.00 war tax. My certificate from Cook and Son was all that was necessary for the ticket. Also got baggage labels and left word with the Union Transfer Co. to have my trunks at the wharf on time Saturday. Mr. Fry complimented me on the fact that I managed it all so quickly. It took about two hours.

We took the Berkeley Ferry at noon, eating lunch on the boat, and went to see the University of California. It is a wonderful place, and there were many normal students then on the grounds to enliven things. We went to the top of the Slather Tower commanding a fine view of the campus, the city and bay. Came back, and Mr. Fry took a train for San Jose at 3:30, leaving me alone. After doing a little shopping, I came back to the hotel and walked right into Frank Steiner, of Lima, Ohio—an old Moody friend of mine. Imagine our surprise and pleasure to find that we are to occupy nearby staterooms on the *Korea*, he going to China for his second term. This will lighten the monotony of the voyage. Spent the evening writing postcards.

Friday, August 20 ◆

After breakfast I did a little shopping, getting some things necessary for the long trip. Then took a Lincoln sightseeing tour through the Golden Gate Park, the Cliff House, Seal Rock, and Presidio. Went down Market Street four and a half miles long and the principal street of the city, 120 feet wide. Went through the $9,000,000 Civic Center showing the Red Cross buildings; Public Library, costing $1,000,000; the City Hall building, costing $2,000,000; the Exposition Auditorium, seating 12,500 where the Democratic National Convention was held; over Van Ness Ave., the widest street in Frisco, 132 feet, which stopped the Great Fire following the earthquake of 1906. The fire destroyed 4 7/8 square miles, with a property loss of $170,000,000. Passed the Masonic Temple. Market Street has four tracks; the outside tracks are the Municipal lines, and the others are owned by a private company. Saw Twin Peaks, 916 feet above sea level.

Passed the Southern Pacific Hospital and entered Golden Gate Park at the Panhandle. It is the largest artificial park in the world, 1,013 acres. Every plant in it was planted by man within the last 38 years. John McLaren has been superintendent for 32 years and has done much to improve the park. There are 5,000 varieties of plants, shrubs, trees, etc. in this park. Statues of Gen. Halleck, Garfield, a ballplayer, Rodin's "Thinker," Bobbie Burns, are located within it.

Passed Concert Valley where Tetrozini made her first public appearance in America. Passed the Academy of Sciences, Memorial Museum, and the Art Galleries, also Japanese Tea Gardens.

Turned into South Drive and followed the ocean. Saw the elk in their paddock. Stopped at the stadium, seeing Prayer Book Cross, erected in commemoration of the first church service held on the Pacific Coast by Sir Francis Drake and his party, 1529, when they discovered Drake's Bay, 30 miles north of the Golden Gate.

Saw the largest Dutch windmill in the world, having a pumping capacity of 40,000 gallons per hour. Stopped 20 minutes at Cliff House and Seal Rocks. Took a picture of Seal Rocks. Saw the *Cjoa*, the boat Capt. Admundsen used in making the northwest passage from the Atlantic to the Pacific Oceans. Saw the buffalo in their paddock. Passed Mirror Lake and "Portals of the Past," all that was left standing of S.N. Towne's beautiful house on Knob Hill after the great disaster of April 18 and 19, 1906.

Entered 14th Ave. Blvd. through the Richmond residential section, into the Presidio, the largest military reservation inside city limits in the world. Saw entrance to the Golden Gate and Alcatraz Island, the U.S. prison. Saw the site of the World's Fair of 1915. Saw batteries of 12-inch mortars protecting San Francisco. Golden Gate was named by Gen. Fremont in 1848. Passed Letterman General Hospital where the returned soldiers are recuperating.

Took in Chinatown after supper. Visited a joss house full of Chinese gods and especially idols of Buddha and Confucius. Listened to the strange music(?) of a Chinese orchestra. The climb up to the joss house covered some three long flights of stairs. There were a lot of curios here, also. Then went to a typical Chinese home of father, mother and six children. The older children sang for us in both English and Chinese. They passed the hat and sold postcards. Later we went through some of the dark alleys where many raids on opium joints were formerly made. After going the rounds of the stores, we ended up at Mon Yuen's, the musician's. He is the oldest Chinese musician in the United States and is past 70. He plays a large variety of instruments made of teelwood and lacquer. We also visited Sing Fat Co., the greatest Oriental bazaar in Frisco. Later we went back to the hotel in our bus. Lost my cap en route and had the distinction of stopping the whole party in the heart of Chinatown until I got it. In the high wind, it was carried nearly a block. Chinatown has 20,000 inhabitants in 30 blocks.

Wrote a lot of cards and letters and also my annual report as Foreign Mission Secretary, which I sent to Miss Smoot to copy.

Saturday, August 21 ——————— ◆ ———————

Wrote a number of letters and cards. Went to the dock at 10:15 and spent an hour getting my baggage checked, etc., for the *Korea Maru*, which is to carry me to Japan. Had a time finding my trunks as they were separated widely. But it was great fun, after all, and worth the trouble. It is intensely interesting to see the masses of people hurrying excitedly here and there hunting baggage. I managed to get mine located and checked. Then came aboard and located my stateroom, 115-A on B Deck. Deposited my baggage and strolled the decks.

It is a most interesting sight to see them deposit the trunks in the hold by means of a great derrick. A cable net is laid on the dock, and a half-dozen trunks are run on it. It is then caught up and carried swiftly to the hold. I also watched the steerage passengers getting their luggage. Boxes and bundles galore. One little bag—presumably a hat bag—fell overboard but luckily landed on the brake beam on the side of the tug where it swished back and forth until rescued by an employee of the tug. The way the baggage is handled is a shame, as it is thrown and knocked around uselessly.

The call for tiffin sounds. That is the new name for lunch. A Japanese boy hammers loudly on a big tin affair resembling a tenor drum. Nobody goes this time, for it is too near the time of departure. As the time draws near, last goodbyes are said, the passengers hurry aboard, and the last frantic efforts to finish loading on time are made.

My stateroom trunk was not on board, and I discovered at the last moment that it was still on the dock. A hurried trip and a few words gave me the satisfaction of seeing it go into the hold, though it should have gone into my stateroom. Mr. and Mrs. Steiner and their little girl came aboard just before we pulled out. We made a wild scramble for deck chairs and managed to locate four in a good position, though we had to hang on to the deck steward until he came across with them.

While this was in progress, the gangplank was raised mid shouting of orders and goodbyes intermingled, and we found ourselves slipping away from the dock. A strange feeling comes over one as the water space between the boat and shore grows larger and the goodbyes of the waving mass on shore grow fainter. I shall not soon forget the sight.

We moved off at 1:05 P.M. and noted that the *Columbia*, of the Pacific Mail S.S. Co., bound for the same port, was ahead of us. She did not remain so long, for the *Korea* is not only larger but much swifter, and in 30 minutes we were ahead. I took a picture as we passed through the Golden Gate, and the *Columbia* was not even in sight then. The *China* also sails today for Yokohama. As we went out of the harbor, the sky became overcast with clouds, and the wind increased. Sitting on our deck chairs, we found an overcoat comfortable and a steamer rug in addition not to be despised. We had tiffin at 2:00 P.M. as we left the harbor entrance. It was a very palatable meal, but I ate sparingly, fearing later consequences. After tiffin, we went to our deck chairs, having reassured ourselves that our baggage was all aboard.

Spent a delightful hour with Steiner getting some of the details of his work as an evangelistic missionary having 12 native workers under him at Hainan, China. He tells me the natives get from 6 to 14 dollars a month as pastors, depending upon their ability. This is about what they would get in other occupations according to their ability. He also said their mission as a whole, the Presbyterian, discourages sending native workers to this country because it often unfits them for their work. Too often it outclasses them, and they do not wish to go back on the same basis as before. The Presbyterian has its own seminary in China.

The salaries of missionaries in China under the Presbyterian board are on the two-to-one basis of the Mexican dollars used there. For example, Mr. Steiner receives $1,050 plus rent and travel expense in the field. This $1,050 means $2,100 Mexican dollars. He is in the interior where living is not so high. He has to furnish his own horse and motorcycle, however. The mission has a doctor paid by the board, and medical attendance for missionaries is free. In case of the death of a missionary, a retiring allowance is given the family, usually running about a year. The Presbyterian board has abolished the idea of increasing the salary with years of service, and all missions, regardless of age of service, receive the same salary. Children's allowances are $200 each now.

There is a tendency on the part of the Chinese workers to want to handle their own work, but this is not permitted.

At 4:30 we received our assignments of seats at table. The Steiners and I are together at table 3C. The sea is rolling and the wind constantly raising. I am confident I haven't my sea legs yet. It is four o'clock, and we had a little tea to tide us over to dinner at seven. Don't know whether I'll need any dinner or not. Will stay up as long as I can. Mrs. Steiner went to bed at five o'clock. No land in sight now — we are surrounded with a heavy gray mist.

My cabinmates are Mr. Strecker, of the First National Bank of Marietta, Ohio, and Mr. Louis Forner, of I don't know where. He is rather noncommittal and noncommunicative.

Nearing dinner hour. Wonder if I can make it. Oh, for a pair of good sea legs for the asking! Later — had a fine dinner and feel good over it. Shaved and ready to retire at 9:00 P.M.

Sunday, August 22 ◆

Arose at 6:30 and after a good bath went out on deck and took a mile walk by encircling the same some 10 or 12 times. Had a good breakfast, thoroughly enjoyable. The sea is quite calm, and I am feeling good except for a slight headache. We had a church service at 10:30. Dr. Beatty, of a Kansas City Presbyterian church, preaching. Sunday school followed, with Mr. Strecker of Marietta, Ohio, as superintendent.

Tiffin at 1:00 P.M., consisting of soup, chicken, baked sweet potatoes, bread and butter and pineapple ice. Fine. Still feeling good, in fact better than this morning.

Mr. Steiner tells me that Presbyterian missionaries on furlough have travel expenses for deputation work paid to and from the presbytery where the work is done. Then it is paid by the local presbytery. All offerings taken can be used as the missionary sees best. He also states that the Presbyterian church stands ready to give some financial help to the extent of about $100 to missionaries who wish to study while on furlough.

Spent the afternoon reading, writing a letter to my wife (to be mailed at Honolulu), and snoozing in my deck chair. Hungry as a bear at dinner and enjoyed California turkey with cranberry sauce, bread and butter, celery, potatoes, peach pudding, ice cream and cake and assorted nuts. The Filipino orchestra of some eight pieces plays at all meal hours excepting breakfast. The waves have been rising all afternoon, and tonight we are rolling quite a bit. Waves wet the deck three feet from our chairs. Am retiring at about nine o'clock.

Monday, August 23 ——————— ♦ ——————————

Bath boy called me at 6:00 A.M. Had a dandy saltwater bath. It is interesting to me and somewhat novel to have a boy prepare water (temperature always exactly right), towels, etc. for early-morning bath. After my bath I took a dozen turns around the deck, then dropped into my deck chair for morning devotions, *John's Gospel*, by Speer. As I came on deck, I sighted a large ship passing on our starboard side. It seemed quite nice to realize so vividly that other folks are afloat on the great sea. Saw a large drove of seadogs yesterday. They have a way of jumping through the water that brings their bodies into view as they leap. Breakfast at 8:30, just as I have been accustomed to whistle it for the children. I am wondering how they are at home today. God bless them and the dear wife. Their sacrifice in this undertaking is greater than mine.

The sun is shining today and seems to mellow the indigo of the sea to a dark blue, if you can sense the distinction. As the sun shines on the foam cast up by the ploughing boat, one is greeted with a continuous rainbow—a beautiful sight—and it reminds the Christian of God's never-failing promise to protect and care for his own.

Breakfast consisted of raspberries and cream, grapenuts, fried fish and potatoes, parker house rolls, coffee and an apple. Phew! What would that cost on a RR diner? And my appetite is becoming more and more alarming at each meal. Now for some reading on deck.

After reading some, had another talk with Steiner. He told me of their quarterly letter used by the mission to advertise their work. He also said that their board pays all expenses to Mayo brothers for operations—the operations being performed free.

Went to the top deck and played a game of shuffleboard—a lot of numbered squares into which you attempt to shoot disks by means of a specially made stick. Great sport. Also saw some of the fastest gambling I have yet seen. A half-dozen men were throwing dice, and the money was changing hands rapidly.

Tiffin at one o'clock—vegetable soup, fried fish, bread and butter, Waldorf salad, peas, pineapple ice, cake. Very good. Wrote several letters after dinner and read considerable in Terry's *Japanese Empire*.

Had a shower this morning, but the sun shone most of the day. Saw a beautiful sunset at sea tonight just before the call to dinner. Our waiters ("table boys") are Chinese. It seems to be beneath the dignity of the Japanese to act as table boys on a Japanese boat, though they do so for Japanese passengers. The Chinese boys wear long blue garments, for all the world like nightgowns, when serving breakfast and tiffin, but they wear short white coats and black trousers at dinner.

Our table boy is a young fellow named Wong Cheong. He is the most imperturbable I ever saw—always polite and never ruffled. Ask for anything, and he repeats it and goes after it, brings it back without a word. He serves four of us and has a knack of putting the menu card before you at just the right time. The bugle is blowing, so here goes. No babies or children are allowed to eat at the regular hours, and for some it is quite a hardship. After supper we had a moving-picture show on the boat. It was a daredevil affair of the West. I didn't see it through. Retired at ten o'clock.

Tuesday, August 24 ◆

Up at six for my bath and deck walk and devotions. Had a talk with Mr. Whalon, a Presbyterian missionary going out for his second term in China. He favors sending some select natives to America, but the policy of the mission is against it. He goes for an eight-year term but thinks it is too long.

Breakfast at 8:30 — prunes and cream, grapenuts, bacon and eggs, toast and apple.

Sat on deck nearly all morning, too sleepy to read most of the time. At eleven o'clock, the deck steward brings beef tea and crackers to keep us from getting hungry. Tiffin at 1:00. A very quiet morning. Spent some time this P.M. on deck, reading and sleeping. Went to the prow of the boat and watched her cut the water. The sun shone brightly, and the water was a beautiful blue, which churned into a snowy, fluffy white as the boat ploughed ahead. As one looks out in every direction, one can see nothing but water touching the sky in every direction. I know of no better way to describe it than to suggest yourself in the center of a great blue saucer with a blue rim rising above you on every side.

Fine dinner tonight. Went on deck a few minutes but will retire early. There is a dance on board, but I am not interested. Good night.

Wednesday, August 25 ◆

Bath at 6:00 and the usual morning walk. Have had an interesting time watching the flying fish. I notice that they have varied-colored wings. In a few minutes I noticed four or five different colors — purple, black, blue, gray, and red. They spring out of the water and fly for long distances along the water crest, sometimes dipping their tails in the foam as the wave rises to meet them. Flying is their means of protection from the big fish that try to swallow them. Sometimes when they drop to the water and dart away again, it is because they see some big fishmouth ready to catch them if they drop into the water.

Read S.D. Gordon's little booklet, *Prayer Changes Things,* also Cleland B. McAfee's *His Peace.* Very fine.

We made 385 miles since yesterday noon and have about 600 miles to go before we reach Honolulu. At 2:30 a meeting was called to arrange for a series of deck sports after we leave Honolulu. They put on a tournament and offer prizes in the various contests. After dinner tonight, the members of the Japanese crew put on an extensive wrestling tournament. I watched them for a while and found some very good wrestlers among them. Went to bed and read awhile. Sea is most rolling it has yet been.

We have on board a barber shop, a clothes-pressing establishment, a printing shop, etc. Have to get laundry done at Honolulu, though. As we will stop there some hours, it ought to be possible.

Thursday, August 26 ──────── ◆ ──────────────────────

Up as usual. The flying fish are out in force today. The weather is bright and the air warmer than when we left Frisco. Everybody wrote postcards today, preparatory to landing at Honolulu tomorrow. Wrote quite a number myself; also some letters. Played two games of shuffleboard and got beaten in both.

After tiffin, I took the picture of our table boy, Wong Cheong, a young Chinese boy, who tells me his home is in Hong Kong. He is the most imperturbable fellow I ever saw. He moves slowly and deliberately. If you order something, he simply repeats it and goes after it. He seldom smiles and says little. We have some little difficulty making him understand.

Wrote some more cards. Also watched the doctor examine all the steerage and second-class passengers preparatory to making Honolulu tomorrow. There were a great number of babies. Played a game of golf with Steiner and a Japanese young man. Steiner won the first and the Japanese the second. We then played partners, the Japanese and I against Steiner and a Mr. Cole. It was a most interesting and exciting game. Mr. Cole reached home first, and I followed, but neither scored in order to help our partners. All of us eventually reached the home hole, and for an hour we fought over it, they finally winning. A close, exciting game.

We held a prayer meeting on board tonight. Mr. Francis, connected with the U.S. Industrial Commission, spoke. Moving pictures and a dance also held. No land in sight when I retired.

Friday, August 27 ──────── ◆ ──────────────────────

Arose at 5:30 and found that we were lying just outside the harbor at Honolulu. It seemed good to see land after six days at sea.

It was a very beautiful scene we looked upon as we stepped out on deck. The hills of beautiful Hawaii were fresh and green from the intermittent showers, and they looked unusually beautiful in the sunshine with the city of Honolulu stretching up their sides from the harbor below. From the harbor, Honolulu looks very much like any American city, and such she proved to be. Everybody was anxious to go ashore, but before breakfast we had to pass quarantine.

A little gut boat brought out the gray-haired harbor pilot, who stepped aboard and soon started into the harbor. Another tug brought the U.S. doctor. We were all assembled in the dining room, and as our names were called, we had to march upstairs and pass the doctor, who checked our names off as we passed.

As we came into the dock, about 25 native Hawaiian boys in bathing suits swam out to meet us, begging us to throw money into the water. These boys dive for coins and seldom fail to get them. It is interesting to see a dozen of them go down together after a coin, only one of them, of course, coming up with it. The coins are put into their mouths as they get them. Their black eyes sparkle with the light of greed as they watch for coins. Some of the boys dive from the highest deck on the boat, and they swim about in the water for long periods at a time. It seemed to me I could distinguish Japanese, Hawaiians, and half-breeds. Some were quite young. If they see a coin coming, they catch it before it reaches the bottom.

Went ashore at nine o'clock, and after mailing a lot of letters and postcards, I cashed my first American Express Co. check at the First National Bank of Honolulu. I then struck out alone for a sightseeing tour. For beauty of color and variety of plant life as well as its profusion, I have never seen any place to equal Hawaii. Going down a street in Honolulu is like walking in an elegant, well-kept summer garden. The houses are usually small, square structures with the siding running vertically. Each home is a veritable flower garden itself, both inside and out. Palms, various fruit trees and shrubs grow about the houses, and within one can see small palms set about the rooms. A peep into the homes shows that the Hawaiians are no mean housekeepers, though their houses are so small.

I took a Fort Shafter car on King Street and went to the end of the line where I saw the regimental army post, Fort Shafter. Returning on this line, I stopped at the Kamehameha Schools and the Bishop Museum, containing a fine ethnological collection. Could have spent a day here if I had had time. Came back to Fort Street and transferred to the Nuuanu Valley line, which took me out past the Royal Mausoleum where former rulers lie and on to the end of the line. I then walked some five minutes to the country club. Here I had the most beautiful view I have seen. The building is standing on a hill overlooking a most beautiful valley, gorgeous with all kinds and colors of tropical growth. Behind the clubhouse and overlooking it on both sides are still higher hills rising up into the clouds that gleam with remarkable freshness when the sun shines. Looking toward the sea, one is charmed by the long ridge of hills on either side of a long valley sloping from above the clubhouse gradually to the sea, out over which one can see for miles as it stretches forth dotted with all kinds of watercraft set in the blue patches of the cloud-dotted sky and the still bluer sea. I shall never forget this most beautiful spot.

Returning on the car to Beretania Street, I transferred to the Punahow line, which took me through a fine suburban district and out to the Oahu College, founded in 1841 as a boarding school for children of missionaries and now a high-class preparatory school fitting pupils for American universities. Five years ago, it is said, children came from California to Oahu for their early education.

The fruits of the early missionaries are seen in the numerous and well-kept churches of Honolulu. A number of Mormon churches are also noticed, and that church is entrenched in the island. In going out to the museum, I noticed one Evangelical Church called a Union Church. At another time I noticed a very fine Christian Science church.

At Oahu College I transferred to the Manoa Valley line and enjoyed a most remarkable ride through a picturesque valley and another fine suburb. The verdure of the island is accounted for by the fact that it rains and the sun shines alternately many times a day, and sometimes both go on together. The natives never mind the rains as they usually do not last long.

Returning, I transferred to an eastbound Punahou-line car and proceeded to

Pawaa Junction where I transferred to an eastbound King Street car and went to Wai-
kiki Beach and Kapiolani Park. Here I saw the surf riders on their little boards having
the time of their young lives in the water. Also saw the new but already famous
Moano Hotel, a very fine place. Then I went into the aquarium where I saw many of
the most beautifully colored and odd-shaped fish in the world. All are natives of
Hawaii except one specimen imported from Japan. There were sturgeon fish, goatfish,
squirrelfish, swordfish, butterfly fish, and many others. Returning from this park, I
had lunch downtown, after which I made a few purchases of curios and with the
Steiners had some soda. Then we took a ride on a Leliha Emma streetcar up the
slope to the "Punch Bowl." Returning, we went to the post office to send a package
home and finally returned to the boat, which was to sail at 6:00 P.M.

At the boat we found a large number of Japanese steerage passengers coming
aboard. There is a custom among the Japanese that when one goes away, his friends
buy strings of seeds and flowers, and put them around his neck. Some of these folk
were loaded down in that way with bright-colored beads and flowers.

As we watched, a Japanese came on board who looked above the ordinary in intelligence. I noticed a Japanese lady and three children at the dock near where he
had stood. The little girl was crying as though her heart would break. He turned to
me and said, "Those are my kids." I asked him how long he would be gone, and he
replied, "Four months." I told him I had just left my wife and two little girls for four
months too.

The little girls are not thought much of in Japan. This man threw some of his
beads and flowers to them, and all were put on the two boys, while the little girl got
none. We have on board a prosperous-looking Japanese family of a man and wife
and daughter, but the wife is quite unhappy because the child is a girl. Some of the
other Japanese of poorer standing laugh at her because she has a girl and they have
boys.

Returning to our stay in Honolulu, a group of Japanese baseball players came
aboard to spend a few weeks in Japan.

The swimming boys reaped a harvest as they dived for coins tonight. Some of
them followed us quite a way out from the dock. Just a few minutes past six a tug-
boat began to pull us out amid the shouts and goodbyes of many. As we started,
two Japanese got into a fearful fight on the forward deck. They were separated two
or three times before they finally stopped.

Honolulu was a beautiful sight as we pulled away. It cannot be described. Later
on in the evening the sight was even more beautiful as the lights began to appear in
the towns at the base of the mountains. I noticed, too, the faithful light at the harbor lighthouse flashing twice in rapid succession at intervals of five seconds to warn
of dangerous rocks and at the same time to give hope to the lost. I was reminded of
the constant, never-changing light of the Son of God, who is even more to the soul
than a lighthouse to a ship.

Saturday, August 28 —————— ◆ ——————

Bath as usual. Read some this morning. We are out of sight of land again, but
birds following us show that it is not far away. Saw a large island this morning.

Played several games of shuffleboard today and some deck golf. A swimming tank was constructed on board, and a number have availed themselves of the opportunity to swim a few feet.

Sunday, August 29 ◆

After my morning bath, I spent some time reading and studying my SS [Sunday school] lesson. At breakfast I presented Steiners and Miss Hewitson, a Scots lady at our table, with pictures of Wong Cheong, our table boy. I also gave him one, and he seemed very pleased. He is quite a boy. The other day, our Scots friend wanted to know whether she was drinking Ceylon or China tea. She asked Cheong, "What kind of tea is this?" He replied, "Hot tea."

The Reverend Dr. Ham, pastor of the Baptist Tabernacle, Atlanta, Georgia, spoke this morning. He gave a very good exposition of I John, presenting God as light, righteousness, and love. SS followed, Dr. Beatty of Kansas City teaching the women and Mr. Cole of the East teaching the men. After tiffin, four of us got together and ran over a couple of male quartet pieces. Met a Mr. Hackett, who is going to Japan as treasurer of the Congregational mission. Also met Mr. Wicks, going out to North China for his second term as teacher in the Pekin University. His board unites with the Presbyterian, M.E. Baptist in this union enterprise.

The teachers are selected by the trustees from missionaries in the field, the respective boards caring for their salaries. The expenses are prorated to each denomination. The Congregational board pays as the Presby. board does in China— $2 Mexican for $1 gold.

There is continual strife between North China and South China, each section having mortgaged itself heavily to Japan. The latter country, of course, is willing to advance them money and is anxious to keep them at war with each other to keep China weakened and thus make it easier to exploit her.

Steiner and I took some of his records up to the lounge this afternoon and played them. Here is where you see the highlivers on the boat. Men and women playing cards and drinking. I was sorry to see the leader of the SS Convention party smoking in the smoking room. Just after dinner tonight I noticed Miss Hewitson, the Scots lady, at one table smoking a cigarette. There are a number of women on board who smoke.

At eight tonight we sighted a steamer passing us fully lighted. It was a beautiful sight and inspiring to realize that others are sailing the high seas. By the use of a light, the ships signaled each other until they had passed. It proved to be the Pacific Mail ship *Buenos Aires.*

At 8:30, a crowd of us went to the second-class deck where we held a song service. The Japanese matron interpreted for those who spoke and did it beautifully. She is a college woman.

Monday, August 30 ◆

Deck sports began this morning and continued all day. I lost in shuffleboard and deck golf and quoits, which I consider a very good showing. Had there been opportunity to play more, I feel sure I would have lost more. Sighted a freighter this afternoon and are scheduled to pass the *Tenyo Maru* at midnight.

A million-dollar film, *The Mask*, being carried to Japan by the manager of the Japanese Cinema Co., was shown tonight through his courtesy. It is not to be released in New York until September 15. I watched this film as I did several last week, and after seeing it, I pledged myself not to go to another. All that I have seen bear out my earlier convictions that nine-tenths of the films shown are of inferior and even disreputable quality and that since the corporations producing them are seeking to make money by catering to the demands of public taste, the institution of moving pictures as such is rotten. While I recognize that there are some good films, I also recognize that the good films do not pay. The public has come to demand films of blood and thunder, holdups, distorted affections, divorce, suggestive immorality, and the like, and consequently the whole plane of film production has been lowered so that I am convinced it cannot be raised by a few good people patronizing the select films.

The most of our so-called intelligent people have dishonored their good sense by allowing themselves to be led into desiring low and suggestive films under high-sounding titles.

Had a long talk with Mr. Donald Roberts, professor of English Literature at St. John's University, Shanghai, China. This is an Episcopal school with some 500 students. Mr. Roberts rather agrees with me that to attempt a large school undertaking in Japan under present conditions when the government supervises them so closely would be a risky thing to do.

Tuesday, August 31 ——————— ◆ ————————————————

Announcement was made at breakfast that today is the birthday anniversary of the emperor of Japan. It is also my sister Lillian's birthday. At breakfast, we gave three *banzais* for the emperor. At 10:00 A.M. the Japanese had a program. I am sending the only copy I could find to Mrs. Minton and a copy of the menu at tiffin to my sister.

Deck sports continued. I refereed one very exciting game. I have found the Japanese most agreeable sportsmen. They are very exact in following the rules, but fair, so far as I can see, in every respect. They are very proficient, too, and in the progress of the deck sports, the Americans have most worthy opponents in the Japanese. The characteristic politeness of the race does not desert them in their play, no matter how badly the game goes against them. When the game is over, they shake hands all around and thank both partner and opponent for the privilege of playing. They thanked me most profusely for my work as referee.

I have met on board a young engineer from near Tokyo by the name of M. Takamatsu, 2300 Sanno, Omori, Tokyo. Omori is a village near Tokyo and is a fine residence section. He is a fine fellow and invited me to come to see him. He has a factory making cylinders for rolling mills and has been in New York buying up-to-date machinery for it. He seems to be a very fine gentleman. In a conversation this afternoon, he mentioned the Japanese-American difficulty in California and Oregon, and expressed the opinion that it was due to misunderstanding and ignorance on both sides. He says most of the Japanese who come over are the ignorant laboring class.

At dinner tonight, the dining hall and tables were profusely decorated with flags of many nations, the Japanese flag predominating, in honor of the emperor. At each place was a menu card headed with a beautiful Japanese scene or a picture of the Golden Gate. At each place was also a favor, a bon-bon, consisting of a roll of Japanese paper that when opened, gave up a tissue-paper hat, which was to be worn as a tribute of the day, and some little trinkets. As we sat down to eat, we were brought to our feet by the playing of the Japanese anthem, which was sung by the Japanese present. The captain then led in three cheers (*banzais*) for the emperor, who is 43 or 44 years old today and who is suffering from nervous trouble. Rumor has it from better than rumor sources that the officers have imbibed quite freely today. If dinner tonight is a sample, it is no longer a rumor.

After supper, we went to the back of the ship to witness a Japanese play. The scenery was typically Japanese, as was the play itself. The first part was a drama depicting some historical event, but of course I could not catch it. During the entire scene, a musician somewhere in the background played on some kind of an instrument, a monotonous strain consisting of the repetition of just four notes. It sounded for all the world like my old mandolin used to sound after I had let it stand a month or two and then would strike the four strings in succession. To say it was a mournful sound is putting it mildly.

In the midst of the scene, one of the actors had to be knocked down, and as he fell, a little Japanese girl on the front row became so frightened and cried so, that her father had to take her out. Whether Japanese or not, that was certainly human.

The Japanese have the characteristic of being good listeners. I noticed in our Sunday night meeting and again last night that they give themselves heart and soul to the thing before them.

The second act tonight was a comedy. A man comes forth carrying several packages and proves to be a country lord on a trip. He conceives the idea of disguising himself and frightening his friend who is following some distance behind. He slips behind a bush and puts on his disguise while his friend comes on the stage and laying off his heavy load, tells the audience how very tired he is. The disguised man then jumps out and frightens him terribly. He then commands the tired man to carry the loads of both of them. As he is about to do so, however, his friend throws off the mask, much to the relief of his friend, and to the delight of the audience. Everybody has a good laugh, and the two comedians decide to assist each other in their journey. A pole is secured, and the combined load is hung between as they lift the pole to their shoulders and start off the stage, not by a rear exit but right out through the audience, making the little Japanese boys get out of their way as they go.

I was impressed with the marvelous patience of the Japanese audience between acts. The stagehands were exasperatingly slow, but the Japanese portion of the audience sat quietly and orderly. I did not stay longer than the second act, but I am quite sure the Japanese stayed until it was finished.

Today was really Meridian Day, the day we cross the 180th meridian and by which we drop a day from our calendar. This being the emperor's birthday, we decided to drop tomorrow instead. So tomorrow will be Thursday instead of Wednesday.

Thursday, September 2 ——— ◆ ————————————

'Wednesday is buried somewhere in the Pacific, and this is Thursday, September 2. It is not really lost, but the change was necessitated by the fact that our days on the boat have been longer than 24 hours.

Geneva Steiner, 4 years old, daughter of Rev. and Mrs. J.F. Steiner, missionaries to Hainan Province, China, was born in China, and is coming back after her first trip to America. Last night during a lull in the performance she looked up at the moon and called loudly to her mother, "Momma, will we have a moon in China?" Since leaving Honolulu, she has been singing the chorus of "Revive Us Again" as "Honolulu, thine the glory, Honolulu, Amen."

Professor Yamasaki, of a Tokyo university, gave a talk this morning on "How to Tour Japan." It was quite instructive. I did considerable writing today, arranging some material for use in Japan and also securing some valuable information from Steiner concerning the methods of work of the Presby. church. After tiffin, games were in order. First of all, the Japanese wrestlers gave an exhibition to the second-class and steerage passengers. Then came the potato race, sack race, and three-legged race. I entered the potato race and won first in the first heat, second in the second, and lost in the third and finals. It was interesting and exciting.

Saw a gorgeous sunset tonight. Yesterday I saw a lot of large fish jumping out of the water. They were either dolphins or porpoises.

Friday, September 3 ——— ◆ ————————————

After breakfast, I read awhile and watched some more deck sports, refereeing a golf match. Entered with Mrs. Steiner in the bottle race. A double row of bottles is set some two feet or so apart in each direction, and the lady must drive the gentleman blindfolded around each bottle. I lost without any difficulty. There were some very exciting races. Some of the missionaries on board spoke at the prayer meeting tonight.

Saturday, September 4 ——— ◆ ————————————

Spent some time copying the report of the special commission appointed by the Presbyterian church to report on mission work. Also secured a number of excellent missionary squibs. Deck sports continued and are nearing the finals. We passed a freighter bound in the same direction.

I met a Major Lansing from Scranton, Pennsylvania, who is a SS worker. He is trustee of the Pennsylvania SS Assn. and knows Herman Eldredge very well. Also met a Miss Wells, who is from Erie, Pennsylvania, and who knows Mr. Eldredge.

The fancy-dress ball came off tonight, and some of the dresses nearly did the same. At dinner, the fancy-dressed couples came down the main stairway. Some were really gotten up, but many were a disgrace. After dinner they went to A Deck where they voted for the winners and held a dance.

Some of the Episcopalian missionaries were a disgrace to their calling. One young woman, Miss Smith of Virginia, going out for the first time, was dressed as a young Negro sport (man's clothes) and was in company with a young man of most unsavory character, dressed as a young lady flirt. After dinner, I went to my room in disgust and did not witness the carnival and carousal on A Deck. Sent a wireless to McKnight today, stating I would arrive September 7. Dr. Woodworth had wire-lessed to see if I was aboard, and the purser had replied.

Sunday, September 5 ————— ◆ ————————————————

We are encountering the heaviest swell of the voyage. Some say the waves are as high as 40 feet. With a great many tons of coal used up, we are lighter and are pitching tremendously. Sighted another freighter at 6:30 and passed it at 8:30 A.M. It was lying very low in the water and pitching greatly. Officers say there is rough weather ahead.

Yesterday I had a talk with Miss Ignatia Schoch, who is going to China as a teacher under the United Evangelical Board. She is well acquainted with Herman Lambert, my close friend of MBI days. She goes to central China. Her expenses are paid to the field and are to be $650 the first year, the same the second and third years, and $700 after she passes the language examination. She is to have her tuition at the language school paid but must furnish her own board and lodging. She is to have $100 outfit allowance. She said children's allowance in the United Ev. is $50 up to 18 years, except when the child is sent to America for schooling, in which case the travel is paid and the allowance is increased to $100 a year.

Church and SS this morning. A Mr. Cunningham, of Scotland, a member of the Ex. Com. of the International SS Assn., spoke. Mr. Strecker led the SS, and Mr. Cole, the banker from Salem, Massachusetts, taught the men's class. We are rolling more and more. I have just read in Sec. 18d, page 18, of the *Presbyterian Manual*, "The Board cannot assume the responsibility of bringing missionary families home to the U.S. on account of the health of children." "To a missionary remaining at his post while his wife returns to this country, the salary of an unmarried missionary is allowed." "No medical allowance can be made for missionaries on furlough in the U.S. except in circumstances of extraordinary necessity."

Spent the afternoon reading, writing and conversing. Visited the steerage. It is terrible. One goes to the lower deck, then descends a stairway into a large room. On one side is the baggage, and on the other two tiers of bunks, looking very much like large wooden trays, set one above another. Mats are laid in this for beds, and men, women and children pile into them. There are no curtains and no means of privacy whatever. They eat at long tables between their bunks and the baggage. A Filipino died last night in the steerage, of tuberculosis. His friend told me he would take him to Manila for burial. We have on board 196 cabin passengers, 21 second-class and 641 steerage. Quite a number were affected by the pitching and rolling today. After dinner tonight, we held a service for the steerage passengers. I had the privilege of speaking through an interpreter for the first time.

Monday, September 6 ——————— ◆ ————————————

    Spent most of today packing, writing and loafing. We are only about 100 miles from land tonight and hope to be outside Yokohama by morning. Sighted several sailing smacks this P.M. Had a long talk with Y. Takahashi, a young man who belongs to one Oji church near Tokyo and who is freight clerk on this boat. His father is pastor at Oji. He is 24 years old, used to teach in our SS, has a high school education and several years in business college.

    He said he would like to continue with this boat several years, then take some more schooling and conduct kindergartens. He thinks it would be very difficult for our church to attempt a school.

    I also talked with my manufacturing friend of Omori, Mr. Takamatus. He has about 2,000 in his employ. I asked him if he was a Christian, and he replied that he had no religion, that most of the Japanese had none and cared for none. He said he believed the universe was created by a great force but there was no personal God. We talked a long time, and he was positive in his views as to religion. He said he read in the *Literary Digest* that attendance of boys in SS in America was falling off and asked why. I replied that it was materialism and that the religious life of the United States was endangered. He asked if the SS movement as represented by the Tokyo Convention had a political aim. I showed him it did not but that the aim of the SS was to get people to study the Bible. He promised to get a Bible and read it as he has read other philosophy. He said they were teaching ethics in the Japanese schools. I told him the best ethics could be found in Christianity. Saw a shark today. Also watched the doctor examine the steerage.

    Tonight we had a farewell dinner for the captain. After this, the prizes were awarded for the deck sports. Some $680 was raised, and the prizes amounted to $445 all told, the balance going to the deck hands, etc. It was a shame to spend so much money in such a way. As I retire, we are passing what seems to be a lighthouse on our left.

II. Meeting the Japanese

In the early morning I was awakened by much shouting and singing, and upon looking out of my porthole, I discovered the lights of Yokohama very near us. Arose early and went through inspection. It was quite simple. The morning was misty so we could not secure the coveted view of Fuji, but it was a very interesting sight to see the numberless fishing smacks start out on their hunt for fish. They are small boats with usually only one large oblong sail. As I watched, the sun came up and cast its yellow light upon the water. As we lay in the harbor, a freighter flying the American flag pulled in. She was from Seattle and looked mighty good to us.

After breakfast, we were quickly towed to the dock. Y. Takahashi was by my side and quickly spied his father waiting for him. Before he could point him out to me, I recognized him from pictures I had seen.

It took some time to dock, and after we did so, I waited for a while, hoping to see Dr. Woodworth or Mr. McKnight so I could get my baggage cleared at once. Just before breakfast I had presented my passports to the proper officials who had come aboard. The Reverend Matsuno was next to appear on the scene. He is pastor at Azabu, Tokyo church, and speaks very excellent English. It was a real pleasure to meet these two brethren. We decided to wait for a while on board for the other men. I enjoyed watching the natives at the wharf put up the gangplank and unload the baggage. All sorts of dress seemed to be in vogue. After a while, I got my grips and ordered my trunks ashore. Tips were as follows: Cabin boy $1.50, table boy $1.50, bath boy $1.00, bootblack 50 cents, Y. Takahasi for help with baggage 25 cents.

The trunks and bags were opened on the dock and my goods inspected. I found the lock on one trunk broken and have not been able to ascertain if anything was taken. The officials were very courteous and the examination brief. We then went out to the *jinrikishas*, which I saw for the first time. They are quaint-looking little buggies drawn by coolies. My trunks were loaded into them together with my grips (it took two rickshas), and since the electric station was not far, we walked along beside the rickshas. It was a most interesting walk, part of the time in the street but with no fear of being run over. Once in a while one would hear the familiar toot of an automobile and a little more often see a horse with a rickety wagon, but there was an endless stream of rickshas and carts drawn by men.

We passed the Yokohama courthouse, the National Bank and the Yokohama Specie Bank. Upon coming to the station, we met a Dr. Davie of the Disciple church, stationed at Tokyo, and a few moments later Dr. Frank L. Brown, Gen. Sec. of the

This photograph of lifeboats on the S.S. Ponce is believed to have been included in this collection by the author because the ship was involved in a late leg of his journey.— *D.W.C.*

SS Assn. He is a very fine fellow and urged that I join in a SS meeting at Sendai as soon as possible to work up interest in the coming convention.

Also met Mr. Beam of the Friends church and Mrs. H.E. Coleman who is working with Mr. Coleman, the SS Secy. of Japan in the interests of the convention. We waited long for McKnight and Woodworth, but they did not come, so we boarded an electric train for Tokyo.

(On the boat before we landed I noticed a ragpicker in a little boat picking up discarded boxes, etc. from the *Korea*. He sure was busy.)

We took second-class passage, the Rev. Matsuno explaining that they always travel third class, but my trunks were too heavy. I found the second-class coach very clean and comfortable. We rode around a number of hills, nestled among some of which we saw a big Buddhest temple. The houses are quite small, and the natives often appear scarcely half dressed. The streets are very narrow, and wide walks are scarcely noticed, even where they do exist. I noticed, however, some very up-to-date factory buildings. We passed endless little rice fields and saw the natives working. Also passed Japan's large aviation field.

After a ride of nearly an hour, we reached our station, had the trunks checked to 26 Kasumi cho, and took a tiny streetcar full of Japanese people, for the above-named address. We had to change cars once, and on this change we encountered a group of Japanese schoolboys and schoolgirls. The boys wear bluish-gray uniforms

The sign next to a double track railroad.

and the girls quaint, many-colored dresses. It was a brilliant sight as they came streaming out of the school building. We finally left the car and walked some few blocks down a narrow street, then turned off on Kasumi cho.

The house at Kasumi cho is a large English house set well back from the street, a good precaution, I fancy. After much ringing, Mr. Zendo Takahashi, a young ministerial student, and his dainty little wife appeared. They announced to our surprise that neither Mr. McKnight nor Dr. Woodworth was there. Miss Stacy is to come Thursday; Mr. McKnight, Friday. Dr. Woodworth wrote that he would be in last night, but he did not arrive. It is 3:00 P.M. as I write, and he is not here yet.

I was ushered into a large officelike room that is really the headquarters of our Japanese work, where Mr. Garman takes care of the treasureship and all of the many other details of his extensive work, where mission meetings are often held, and where the McKnights and Miss Stacy are staying while in language school.

A few minutes later we were taken to the dining room. The noonday meal was past but Mrs. Takahashi had very graciously sent out for a combination American-Japanese meal. The American part was grapes and bananas and bread and butter; the Japanese part (and this proved to be most of my dinner) was a Japanese pickle

Means of transportation in northern Japan. It developed rapidly but as late as 1920 this was a typical scene. The engine was always hitched up backwards to the freight cars with one or two passengers' coaches at the other end.

and a big bowl of rice, egg and small pieces of chicken cooked together. It is called *oyako domburi*, meaning mother and child, the mother being the chicken and the child the egg. A pair of chopsticks lay by us. Mr. Matsuno, who dined with me, picked up a fork and with a feeling of relief, I did likewise while the chopsticks lay idle until he later showed me how to use them. The meal was very palatable.

I was then shown to my room, a large airy one on the second floor where I proceeded to make myself comfortable. Between Yokohama and Tokyo I noticed many thatched cottages as well as some with tile roofs. At the stations along the way, guards on the platforms, not in the coaches, shout the name of the station. The name is also printed in English on boards. As the train stops, the peculiar clatter of many feet in wooden shoes (*geta*) greets one's ears. At some points along the way and in the narrow streets, the odors are stifling. At the dock, a man laid out a large supply of sandals of soft material, and Japanese visitors to the boat exchanged their wooden shoes for these softer-soled ones.

I checked up expenses and found it had cost me as follows to get to Kasumi cho: exchange for $10.00 gold into Japanese money, 50 cents; two rickshas for baggage Y1.80; tip for handling baggage at station, 40 sen; three tickets to Tokyo Y2.00; baggage transfer 45 sen; carfare 8 sen. Total Y4.73.

Yokohama is the third largest city in Japan, with a population of 444,039 in 1913. *Yoko* means "side," and *hama* means "beach" (where the first treaty port was opened through the efforts of Commodore Perry in 1854).

Tokyo, formerly called Yedo, is the largest, wealthiest, and finest city in New Japan, with a population in 1913 of over 2,000,000.

Dr. Woodworth came in at 4:00 P.M., stating he did not expect me to arrive

Picture of W.P. Minton and Japanese elder in traditional dress.

until Thursday, on the *China*. We talked over many things and then went out to look over the Azabu section. I sent a cable to Dayton telling of my safe arrival and also mailed some letters.

Passed the Siamese legation, which is quite near 20 Kasumi cho. A beautiful place.

We passed the Azabu Middle School, which is a private school with some 800 boys between 14 and 20 years of age. Mr. Ebara, the principal, is a man above 70 years old and very highly respected by the government. He teaches Christian principles, and although the government does not favor it, they hesitate to stop him. We are to visit this school tomorrow when I shall get further information concerning it. We passed the church of our denomination, the Azabu Christian Church, of which the Rev. Matsuno is pastor. The church is well located, but the surrounding community is very indifferent to it. The attendance is quite small. The pastor lives entirely too far from the church and cannot under the circumstances give proper attention to the work. There seems to be a need for a very unusual awakening. The community is thickly populated and, I think, not overchurched.

Later we passed down Juban Street (Tenth St.), a very, very busy place, at night especially. It was about 7:30 as we passed down this street, and it was almost impassable as we went, with many sandaled feet moving nosily about hither and thither. There were some bicycles and an occasional auto, but for the most part the people clattered along in their *geta*. The many and varied shops were brilliantly lighted and displayed their wares to good advantage right out on the ground in front.

Dr. Woodworth, in his unique way, explained that if we should stop before one of these stores, the owner might not like it, but if we went to a side street, it would be all right, and almost before I realized what had happened, we had stepped to a side street and were singing in English "Jesus Loves Me." When we had finished the third stanza, a hundred Japanese crowded about us, blocking the street so that a cart could scarcely pass. Dr. Woodworth introduced me and interpreted while I spoke. Later he gave a considerable message in the Japanese tongue. They listened attentively all the while and seemed loath to have us leave.

We then went to a Japanese teahouse for supper. We were ushered to a tiny room upstairs, having left our shoes below. Here we squatted on the floor on two mats while the neat Japanese girl served us a plate of *sushi*, consisting of rice prepared with five different styles of fish. There was tea, of course, and the meal was very good. I used chopsticks for the first time and got along very well.

After supper, we visited the YMCA where some 60 boys receive food and lodging at Y25 a month. The grounds cover about a quarter of an acre. After buying some ice cream and a Japanese pear that looked like an apple, we went back home. I neglected to mention, however, that we called on a Mr. Ando, who lives next door to a very nice M.E. church that he built in memory of his mother. He was a very nice old gentleman.

When we came home, we found the McKnights had arrived, and we were delighted to see them. Mr. Hirzell, who works for the American Trading Co. as expert accountant and rooms here, came in. It was quite an American reunion. Went to bed under my mosquito net and slept fine.

Wednesday, September 8 ———— ◆ ————————————

Arose at 5:30, and at 6:30 we were on our way to the Azabu Middle School. At 6:45, the teacher in charge clapped together a couple of sticks, and at least 100 boys assembled in the lecture room to hear me speak. I gave them a short message, which they seemed to appreciate. I then met Mr. Ebara, the principal, who had entered as I spoke. He is a fine old gentleman. He enjoys great freedom in his work, being a

Street scene in fairly affluent neighborhood.

member of Parliament. He receives no salary from his school but is supported by Parliament and other sources. His teachers receive only part pay from the school and do other work to help out.

I had an opportunity to question one of the teachers, Mr. Shimizu, who is well informed. This school is self-supporting. There are about 800 boys, who pay Y5 a month tuition for 11 months a year. This is twice the amount of tuition in a government school, but parents prefer to send their children to this noted educator, Mr. Ebara.

Last year there were 1,080 applicants from which he could choose only 180 children, which is the limit for new pupils. The school teaches Christianity and is a great power since it is possible to pick the students from the best families. I asked Mr. Shimizu what he thought of a church establishing a school. He said there would always be need for them but that the question of meeting the government standard in teachers and equipment was a big one. This school employs 31 teachers at an average salary of Y93.5 a month, while government schools pay salaries averaging Y120.

The principal of the government school receives Y3,800 and the highest-paid teacher Y3,100 a year. The annual budget of the Azabu school is Y47,550. The land comprises 4.5 acres—5,400 *tsubo*—a *tsubo* being 6 square feet.

The Toyko Prefecture plans to build three more middle schools at an avergae cost of Y550,000 each for buildings, land, and equipment. They will, of course, be supported by taxation, the tuition of Y2.5 per month not covering it.

The Baptist is building a school at Yokohama to cost about a million yen. The

Dr. Woodworth with his Japanese bicycle.

great questions to be considered in school building are location, equipment, land purchasing and building, and ability to finance and furnish satisfactory teachers. The school should aim to surpass the government school in order to offset the higher tuition required and to bid for students.

I asked for a copy of the latest government regulations regarding schools, which they agreed to translate for me.

After breakfast, I did some writing and at ten o'clock started down town. We first took Bro. McKnight to the dentist, then took some of Dr. McCord's pictures to N. Arai, on the Ginza (main business street), phone 2041, to have them framed for the missionaries and Japanese pastors. Later we visited the Methodist Book Concern. This concern has been laboring under a heavy debt for years (Y180,000 at a very recent date), but under the management of an efficient Japanese, they are getting on their feet.

The Woodworths and McKnights with four Japanese Bible students.

We next visited a number of mission homes, most of which were in crowded sections with practically no yards. The prices of these buildings have very materially increased recently. We passed the house where our first missionary, Rev. D.P. Jones, and his wife lived when they were in Tokyo. Walked along the Sumida River, upon which many boats carry cargo from the city to boats in the bay. It is a most foul-smelling place. In fact, we went through street after street of all sorts of shops, and the odors were almost unbearable at times. The streetcars are very small and crowded. The electric trains are very ill-smelling.

Had a long talk with Dr. H.V.S. Peeke, who is managing the business of the Christian Literature Society during the absence of Dr. S.H. Wainwright, who is on furlough. Dr. Wainwright was loaned to this work by the Southern M.E. Church in America. The CLS has quite a building and equipment, and is doing very excellent work. The property covers 492 *tsubo* of land at No. 8 Akashi cho (Tsukiji) Tokyo. Over 10.5 millions of pages were printed in 1919. Many books, booklets, tracts, and periodicals were printed. The *Myojo*, a monthly periodical, is sent to the students of 1,430 academies and the teachers of 989 primary schools and has a usual edition of 67,000 copies. The *Ai-no-Hikari* is a four-page paper for women not of the student class. The property purchased in 1919 cost Y78,000. The sales of books and papers in 1919 amounted to Y23,557.95.

Mr. Peeke has had a long term of service in Japan and is one of the best-informed men here. He says a mission home should be built American-style and

A beautiful structure (possibly a church) nestled in the trees.

would cost Y25,000 plus Y10,000 for land. He thinks 200 *tsubo* and a small house better.

Mr. Peeke gave some information concerning the Presbyterian School in Tokyo, called the Meiji Gakuin. It enrolls 660 in the middle school, 100 in the higher school or college, and 29 in the theological. The annual budget of this school is Y65,000, not including the support of six foreign missionaries. It does not have a high standing because of an inferior teaching force.

A small mission, Mr. Peeke thinks should keep out of middle school work. He advises evangelistic work along three lines: (1) loaning a missionary to such work as the Christian Literature Society, (2) newspaper evangelism, (3) ordinary methods of evangelistic work.

From here we walked through street after street of poorly kept shops and finally went into a tiny teahouse and ordered a *gyunabe*, small pieces of beef cooked in soy. Three pretty(?) Japanese girls waited on us. They live a horrible life at night in these cheap restaurants.

We then went to the great Buddhist temple called Kannon Temple in Asakusa Park. It is the vanity fair of Tokyo, and such an array of bright-colored shops leading to the temple gates I have never before seen. The temple is an imposing structure sitting well back in a large enclosure. As you approach, many old men and women line each side selling seeds that the people buy and scatter to the sacred pigeons as an act of worship. The pigeons enjoyed the feast, as did a bantam rooster and hen that had somehow gotten in. On each side of the entrance are huge hideous-looking

Street scene in Japanese town with trolley car.

images supposed to be frightful enough to frighten the devil away. Inside, many old priests are selling things.

For example, one old man was selling rolls of Japanese paper, which the people bought and pushed into an incense burner, after which they prayed to Buddha. Before the large shrine were eight or ten priests monotonously chanting some sacred music. Just back of them and immediately before the people as they come up the stairs is a large offering box. I should guess it to be ten feet square. Sometimes the crowd is so large that they throw their offering against the large screen back of the offering box from which it is deflected into the box.

A number were worshiping as we came up. They pay first, then pray.

The Obinzuru is the god of healing. The people come to this wooden god and rub the spot that hurts, then rub the corresponding spot on the god, then pray to it. The entire face is rubbed away, and the hands are gone. A woman with several children came up, dropped in a coin, rubbed her little boy's head, then the head of the god.

There are hundreds of immoral places in the close vicinity of the temple. There is a sacred horse in one of the stalls. It is a beautiful cream color. The Japanese buy grain and feed it as a sacred rite. It was quite busy eating.

We had lemonade, consisting of shaved ice over which was poured some kind of liquid with about as much of a lemon flavor as horseradish.

From the temple we took *jinrikishas* through the segregated district of Tokyo. It is called Yoshiwara. There are finely built houses, and fine pictures of the girls are displayed in front, and at night the girls sit out and solicit trade. There are about 3,500 girls here in seven acres and some of them receive as high as 20 guests a night. The keepers pay a license fee and are protected by the government. There is a guard in front of each house to prevent the girls escaping, and at night these guards act as secretaries, keeping a record of each guest and receiving the fee.

We then went to the city YMCA—a very nice building full of very polite Japanese. We found a reception in progress for a group of Americans. We became a part of the group. Met Mr. Matsumoto, gen. sec. of the YMCA; Dr. Kozaki, pastor of the Independent Cong. Church; Dr. Axling, supt. of the Baptist Tabernacle of Tokyo; Dr. Gary, pres. of Pekin University; Congressman Campbell of Pennsylvania; and Dr. Takami of the Methodist school here.

From here we started across the city to Miss Penrod's for supper. This was a very long ride, with change of cars three or four times. It took us past the emperor's palace—a most imposing place. The palace itself cannot be seen, and a foreigner can get only to the large moat surrounding it. Inside the moat is a high stone wall entirely surrounding the grounds, which comprise a number of acres beautifully laid out. The palace is in the midst of this. The approaches to the grounds are wide paved streets not unlike the streets of our national capital but so very, very different from the narrow, sidewalkless, dirty, ill-smelling streets found almost all over Tokyo.

It was nearly dark when we reached Miss Penrod's. She is a fine elderly lady of very sweet spirit. She is supt. of a large rescue home for girls and lives on the place. The tract of land is only 60 feet wide but quite long. There are quite a few buildings—an office building at the entrance, a number of smaller houses for the girls, a fine bakery, a maternity ward, a hospital, etc.

There are now 67 girls in the home from dens, teahouses, etc., and Miss Penrod's story of the work was fascinating indeed. She said the girls sometimes run away. Sometimes men help her get them out of dens, not to help the girls but in the hope of getting the girls themselves. It is often hard to do anything because the police do not help.

A large family is visited by the procuress of a house. The parents are told that easy employment can be found for their girl at good wages. The parents sign some papers, some of which are blank, and later on these blank pages are filled in, and the police say they are legal and do nothing to protect the girls.

Miss Penrod has an annual budget of about Y10,000 a year, and the work of the girls brings in about Y700 to apply on that. The girls conduct the bakery and make very fine bread, which is sold in large quantities not only in Tokyo but in outlying regions and towns and cities. They also do knitting.

The buildings are owned by the WCTU now, but they are expected to sell them to Miss Penrod soon. The work is supported by faith. There is a man in England who helps interested people in the work, and at present it is supported largely by English people.

Thursday, September 9 ———— ◆ ————————————

We started for the Baptist Tabernacle this morning. On the way, we passed the Russian Embassy, the Foreign Office, and War Office, the Navy Office. Also passed Cherry Tree Gate, typical of old-style walls for protection. Passed the Imperial Palace. Also many government buildings.

The Baptist Tabernacle is an institutional work with a church combined. Dr. and Mrs. Wm. Axling are in charge. There are 15 native women workers, only part of whom are paid. A young lawyer gives free advice to the poor people.

The kindergarten cares for 80. There are two paid kindergarten teachers and two helpers. The head kindergarten teacher receives Y35, the other Y30 a month. They must care for their own board and lodging. There is a fine roof garden for the children. The night school is always full. The summer Bible School had over 100.

See sheet of facts. [See pages 33–34.]

The central church is located in the building and is independent, with a membership of 200. The pastor received Y100 a month and a parsonage. The welfare department ministers to people up to the point of baptism and then turns them over to the church. The president of the Baptist Theological Seminary receives over Y200 a month, but he is American-trained. Mr. Axling's colleague, a graduate of Brown University, receives Y135 but should receive Y150. Ordinarily, according to Mr. Axling, a Western-trained native should not be put on the same basis as an American missionary. The Baptists have only one such among 60 native workers, (Mr. Shiba, the Pres. of the Theol. Seminary.) Some of the workers, depending upon their training, receive as low as Y50.

The budget of the Tabernacle is Y120,394 from the women's society and Y131,202 from the men's society.

This is administered by a committee of six Japanese and six for. missionaries and does not include salaries of foreign missionaries. To the above must be added income from tuition and local churches, and salaries for for. miss. [foreign missionaries]. This tabernacle would now cost Y200,000 to build. There are 320 *tsubo* of land at Y150 a *tsubo*, making the land cost now Y48,000. This is located, however, in the heart of Tokyo.

SALARIES

Foreign missionaries under the Baptist church receive a basic salary of $1,400 plus house rent, medical bills, income tax, and children's allow. A special grant of $460 was made this year, but the salary schedule has not yet been permanently raised.

When children are in the field, the allowance is 10 percent of the field salary when they are under ten; from 10 to 12, 16 percent; 13–16, 20 percent; 17–20, 25 percent. Children in America receive 6–12, $200; 13–16, $250; 17–20, $300. The salary of single men is $1,200 and for single women, $950. The salary for married men the first three years is $1,330, being raised to $1,440 after that, with the special allowance for this year applying to all. Outfit allowance is $300. The woman's board sends only women workers, recommending them to the general board at home.

Central church baptized 25 last year. Many others go to other churches. The tabernacle ministers to some 40,000 people; 2,000 were inoculated for cholera last year. Physicians give their services.

At Yokohama, the Baptist Middle School is headed by a Japanese principal and dean. Two missionaries teach English in the school. A board of trustees of three missionaries and three Japanese control. The board is self-perpetuating.

Saw the national YMCA and met Mr. Phelps, one of the secretaries. Took pictures of the Baptist Tabernacle. Also of the YMCA with a beggar sitting in front of it. Dr. Woodworth tried in vain to bribe him into sitting with his face toward me for his picture.

Went to the Salvation Army headquarters. Met Col. Beaumont. The land and building cost Y222,000, the 178 *tsubos* of land costing Y50,000.

SA SALARIES

The first two years, the salaries of native recruits are very small. The third year, single men, called captain, get Y30 a month plus house rent (Japanese house). This will need to be augmented by 50 percent if possible. The staff captain, four ranks above a captain, receives as a married man, Y60 a month, with Y3 per month for each child, a foreign captain, married, receives Y65 per month plus Y8 for each child under school age, Y16 for each child of school age, plus house. The foreign captain receives the same from the office in Japan as the native pastor but receives a supplemental allowance from the British office, making his total salary Y65.

The SA has 320 Japanese and 13 for. workers, including their wives. They register about 5,338 professions a year, of which, of course, some fall; 1,008 were actually enrolled as soldiers, corresponding to church members, last year.

Met Maj. and Mrs. Wilson of the Sal. Army. Had lunch at a Japanese teahouse. Dinner was called *nikunabe* (*nik* = meat, *nabe* = stew). It was some stew. We took our shoes off and went up to the third floor into a neat-looking little room—one of many separated by partitions. A neat-looking Japanese woman placed mats on the floor for us and sat by us while we ate, filling our rice bowls as often as we emptied them and pouring our tea. The one big dish contained beef cut small and cooked in soy with onions. There was also another vegetable dish. A meal of this kind for two ordinarily costs Y1.28, but Dr. Woodworth was hungry and ate all the onions (because I did not want them) and then ordered another dinner for himself. The bill for the three dinners was Y1.90.

We next visited the Disciple School. Met Miss Clausen, a teacher. There are nearly 200 in the girls' high school and 70 in the kindergarten. Over 200 boys in the boys' school. The tuition in the girls' school is Y3.50 and in the boys' school Y4.50. There is a theol. school, a domestic science school, and several homes for missionaries in the compound.

DISCIPLE SCHOOL SALARIES

Mr. Hirai, dean of the girls' school, receives Y100 per month, plus house rent up to Y25 per month, plus Y5 for his child of high-school age and Y3.50 each for three children under high school. There are 17 teachers in the girls' school, all Japanese, and their combined salary is $6,060 a year.

Miss Clausen believes there is no other agency to compare to that of school work, especially for girls, since the government is not so particular to put up girls' schools. Thousands of girls are crowding into schools. This girls' school comprises 3,900 *tsubo*.

Budget of the Girls' School

Salaries of 17 teachers	$6,060
Office girls	180
Janitors (4 of them)	498
House rent Prof. Hirai	150
Books	180
Heat and light	600
Incidentals	475
Ten scholarships	900

Total	$9,843	[sic]
Less fees received	2,750	

Balance of budget	$7,093
Added to this are salaries of three missionaries at $850	2,550

	$9,643

Bible School Budget

Dean Watanabe	$780
Prof. Inuieno	600
Lecturers	450
Head of dormitory	240
Office Sec.	180
Rent for Dean	150
Rent for Assistant	150
Janitor	270
Books	400
Ten scholarships	1200

Total for Bible School	$4,420

Middle School Budget

Pres. Ishigawa	$900
Children's allow.	240
Teachers and office help	5,640
Rent for Pres.	150
Heat and light	590

Total	$7,520
Fees received	4,118

Budget to be raised	$3,402
Salaries of 2 Mission families	

Kindergarten

Total expenses	$839
Fees	400
Outlay	$439

Salaries of Missionaries

Missionary families		$1,500
Bonus for this year		100
Children's allowance	1– 5 yrs.	100
	6– 9 yrs.	150
	10–16 yrs.	200
	17–18 yrs.	250
	19–21 yrs.	250 if in school

Up to a few years ago, nearly all the girls were Christians when they graduated. Lately, with a much larger class, there are more who do not become Christians. In the boys' school the number of Christians is not so large because the govt. regulations apply and limit Bible work.

Pastor's Salaries, Disciple

	Mission	Church	Total
New graduates	Y50	Y 5	Y55
After 2 years	50	10	60

The increase from the mission depends upon the increase from the church. The church on the campus is self-supporting. Membership is 300 and 400, mostly students. Pastor is paid Y25, his salary being supplemented by work in the school.

Pastor of Hongo Church, their best mission church, gets Y75 a month from the mission.

Schedule of salaries

	Mission	Church	Total
New graduates	Y50	Y 5	Y55
After 2 years	55	10	65
After 4 years	60	15	75
After 6 years	65	20	85
After 8 years	70	25	95
After 10 years	Y60	Y35	Y95
After 12 years	50	45	95
and so on			

For married men, add Y10 to amount received from mission. Children's allowance, Y5 a month up to middle school, then Y10. Women evangelists receive Y30 per month from graduation; after two years, Y35; after five years, Y40; etc. Met Mr. Wilson as we came out.

Made the long trip home by car across the city, making several changes in the dinky cars crowded with people. Met a Mr. Grant at 26 Kasumi cho. He takes his suppers there regularly. Teaches in a commercial school in Tokyo. Had a very pleasant evening with Dr. Woodworth and the McKnights.

Friday, September 10 ────── ♦ ──────────────

Met Mr. Oishi, who is Mr. Garman's helper. He is about half through the Imperial University and is trying to put himself through and at the same time raise a Y1,000 debt for his father and mother. He would go into Christian work were it not for raising this debt. A fine bright-looking fellow. Mr. and Mrs. Z. Takahashi also work in the mission home, and he attends a theol. school. There is also another maid.

Got a haircut this morning and packed my grips for Karuizawa in the mountains. It is 88 miles from Tokyo by rail. Rode clear across the city to the Ueno depot and missed the train by three minutes, so Dr. Woodworth and I settled down in the second-class waiting room until 2:30 P.M. I wrote for an hour. Then went out for a Japanese dinner. As we sat down to the table on the floor, we noticed a Japanese young woman making her toilet at the other end of the room. She was stark naked to the waist. Got some postcards after dinner. Took the 2:20 train, third class, and rode six hours through rice fields. I learn that a good field produces 200 bushels per 2.5 acres, which sells at Y8 per bu. to the middleman and is retailed at Y19 per bu. Two and a half acres of such land is worth Y8,000. A farmer makes a living on from 1.5 to 2.5 acres. Third-class cars are not bad riding. The seats are smaller than those in America. There is a cushion, but the back is straight wood. The tracks are narrow-gauge. I did this typewriting on the train and sure had an interested and interesting crowd of onlookers about me a good share of the time. The schoolboys and girls were the most interested.

On the train coming to Karuizawa I met a Miss Leigh, from England, who told me she was the only English-speaking person in a leper colony. There are about 350 people there, all lepers. A few years ago, a Japanese man became interested in the work, and later Miss Leigh came. The work has developed greatly. The lepers carry on certain kinds of town work, such as banking, stores, shops, etc. There is a men's society, a women's society, kindergarten, etc. A trained nurse is now giving her services to these helpless people at Y35 a month, and a medical doctor is giving her services at Y50 a month when she might get Y200 or Y300 in town. They do it for love of the work, and God is richly blessing it. Miss Leigh is enthusiastic. None but the Japanese language is spoken, but she says she is never lonely. She loves her "children," as she fondly calls them. About 85 of them have become Christians. On the train we noticed a young man with a folding wooden pillow. Dr. Woodworth said it might be bought. I wanted it, and he got it for 70 sen. It is most unique, being made of mulberry wood, of one piece but in two parts to fold up without separating the parts, which cannot be separated.

The trip is 88 miles from Tokyo into the mountains. We arrived at Karuizawa at 8:00 P.M., and after a long walk along a narrow and dark but very good road, we came to Woodworth's summer cottage. The ricksha man had already brought the baggage, and we were soon comfortable. When the ricksha man at the station began to load my suitcases, it was with a great deal of grunting. They were heavy. A Mr. Petrie and a Miss R.M. Francis, of the Christian and Missionary Alliance, came in for a chat. Miss Francis was at one time a student at Defiance, and we had a fine visit. After prayers, we went to bed, expecting to climb Mt. Asama, an active volcano, on the morrow.

Saturday, September 11 ——————— ◆ ———————

Arose at six to find a steady rain falling, which continued until nearly noon, so we could not make the trip up the mountain. Got my first view of this beautiful place. Karuizawa is about 2,000 feet above sea level and is a basinlike plain with beautiful green mountains on every side. The train changes engines for two electric locomotives eight miles from here and passes through 27 tunnels in the climb. Even in the rain, the view was beautiful as the low-hanging clouds shut off the many mountaintops. Near here is a range of peaks called the Alps. Karuizawa is a picturesque village, typically a summer resort for Tokyo and other residences and for missionaries for long distances around, some coming even from South China. The houses are mostly Japanese with sliding doors and paper windows. There is a Union Church, a junior building for children's work, and a Japanese Church, besides stores and curio shops. The missionaries are contemplating locating a hospital here.

After lunch, we called on the Rev. Norman, of the Canadian Methodist church, who is in charge of evangelistic work in this section. He says an ordained married native pastor receives about Y60 a month all told, including children's allowances. This is for pastor of a country church. The pastors are usually graduates of a middle school and a theological school. A native church is considered organized when it has 20 members, cares for its own heating and lighting, pays the conference assessments and one-seventh of the pastor's salary. The conference assessment includes expense of moving pastor, superannuated ministers' fund, conf. expense fund, quadrennial general conf. fund, and office expense, and amounts to about Y1 a member.

A theological student must be recommended properly and must be a Christian at least a year before entrance. When necessary, he is supported by the Canadian board. Expense of the student for the third year is about Y20 a month. The first two years, they have to shift more for themselves, and the expenses seem to be less. This shifting is done to test them out. The Canadian board sends the best young men to America for study. Sometimes the results are not satisfactory. The board pays the expenses of such a trip and an allowance of $300 a year. They travel second class.

We later visited Seldon Spencer, of South China. Mr. and Mrs. Spencer

A group of Christian Church missionaries and Japanese helpers. Miss Stacy, Miss Fry and adopted son, Maki.

and Mr. and Mrs. Pratt are in charge of the Presbyterian mission at Sheklung via Canton, China. Mr. Pratt's work is evangelistic, and Mr. Spencer is in charge of the educational work. There is a boys' school, enrolling 52 boys between 11 and 16 years of age. It is a boarding school. The tuition is $10 gold a year. (Mexican and gold are about equal now.) The tuition is usually provided by a native church or an American church or society. The food amounts to $3.80 a month, which the boys usually manage to provide. There are four Chinese teachers, getting $20 to $25 a month Mexican. Native preachers get $30 to $35 per month. Nearly all the graduating class are Christians; nine out of ten this year were Christians. There are about 2,000,000 in the district with two foreign missionary families.

Later we called on a Japanese woman who has just recently become a Christian. She was in a Tokyo hospital when the Rev. Matsuno talked with her and she decided to become a Christian. Dr. Woodworth has been helping her along while here.

We passed through a field, jumped a ditch or two, and emerged on what Dr. Woodworth called the road. It was to me a narrow bicycle path. Winding along this road for some three-quarters of a mile, we reached the neat summer home and, leaving our shoes outside, were ushered into a nicely arranged room. Dr. Woodworth wears a pair of shoes with no buttons or strings that slip off easily. He has been remarking about how long it took me to get my shoes off, but today the joke was on him, for his hurry to get into the house, he slipped off not only his shoes but one sock as well.

This Japanese house had wicker chairs and a stand, quite contrary to Japanese custom. In a few moments a neat little Japanese woman appeared, and it seemed to me the light of Christianity shone in her face. After I was introduced, the maid brought us tea and delicious cake, and later some Japanese pears. The cake was exceedingly fine.

As we sat together, though I could not understand a word, I soon surmised that Dr. Woodworth was leading this young Christian toward a deeper experience in Christ. They sat with their Japanese Bibles in hand, and certainly a radical antagonist to missions would have been persuaded could he have seen the look of intense interest and hunger in her face as she took in the truth. Dr. Woodworth told me what he had been speaking of and interpreted a few words of encouragement from me. She was quite interested and wanted to know how long I had been preaching and especially what led me to become a Christian. We then knelt in prayer together, and I prayed in English, after which both of them prayed in Japanese.

Here again, the truth came home to me that God can understand all languages. It is not necessary to Americanize or Occidentalize these Orientals to make them Christian, but it is necessary, by whatever way possible, to preach to them Jesus the Savior. I wish you could have heard her prayer. Though I could not understand the words, the earnestness of it was unmistakable.

After the prayer, with many bows we separated, and as we left, I could not help feeling that after all this is the type of missionary work that is most sure, most permanent, and in the long run the quickest way to bring a nation to a real knowledge of Christ. I had seen a missionary at his real task of winning the lost to Christ, and my heart burned within me with a new desire to go back to America and hunt for young men and women who know the Christ intimately and who have a real passion to talk with dying men and women face-to-face about a Christ who can save to the uttermost. There is no greater work in the world. That is why Dr. Woodworth said as we walked down the road, "I would rather sit down and talk with an individual about the matchlessness of Christ than to eat."

Sunday, September 12 ———— ◆ ————————

Took an early morning walk through the winding paths of Karuizawa. Attended church in the morning, and after dinner, Mrs. Woodworth, Miss Francis, and I went out for a little walk that ended in a long climb up the mountain called Usui. It was a most beautiful walk, along a path of lava. At one point we saw a three-faced god, one face smiling, one angry, and one sad. The Japanese think that to put a stone at the foot of this god will mean good luck. There was a great pile of stones around this god.

A little further up the hill we saw the entrance to a shrine, and Miss Francis and I decided to find the shrine. We followed a winding path for a long distance up the hill and at last came upon a Shinto shrine on a promontory offering a fine view of the valley and mountains. The shrine was locked, but we looked through the bars and saw a big drum and gong used to sound the call to worship. Over the door was the name of the ancestor worshiped here, and just outside was the grave, together with half a dozen stone images. There was also a wooden prayer wheel. I plucked a flower.

Another big climb brought us to a teahouse with a superb view of the mountains and valleys, with Karuizawa nestling below. From here we climbed higher and higher, finally reaching an old, old sacred place on the summit of the mountain. This is the famous Usui Pass Festival Kumano Temple. As I looked upon the beautiful scenery, Mrs. Woodworth called attention to the fact that in the Old Testament most of the places of worship were high places. Surely such points of vantage are conducive to worship.

This was another old Shinto shrine, Kumano Temple. A long flight of stone steps led from the path to the temples, of which we found six. Great stone lions guarded the entrance. At the top of the stairs are two hideous figures supposed to keep away evil spirits. Miss Francis learned from one of the natives that the ancestors worshiped here are Izanagi and Izanami. He was noted for having brought peace to the country. At this particular shrine the woman, Izanami, is worshiped. There is a mirror, a bell and a stone here over 700 years old.

As we stood on this high place looking down on the houses below, I noticed that the shingles are held on by a row of stones for each row of shingles. From here we went down a winding path to a famous spring called Usitoge Spring, in a pass by the name Usui. Foreigners call it the Hog's Back. A few years ago, the present emperor came and drank right at the spot where the water bubbled out of the mountain. It was absolutely pure here, but as we drank, a Japanese woman came up a little below us and began washing some clothes in the flowing water.

The view here was excellent, showing the other side of the ridge from which we had climbed, and we could look for miles over the hill and valley. Going back to the temple, Miss Francis talked to one of the natives while Mrs. Woodworth sat down to rest. I stood up to get a better view, and a Japanese woman came out and said something in Japanese that I discovered later meant "Hang your hips on the rock," meaning "Please be seated." I sat down. The lady was working with a wooden hoe in the garden.

Coming down was almost hard as going up. When we arrived at the house, we found the Christian Japanese lady whom we had visited on Saturday visiting Dr. Woodworth. She had been brought by her servants in a big touring car. Her husband is a prosperous businessman of Tokyo. They are living out here in order that she may recuperate from a series of operations. She said that the first was very painful but that in the others she kept praying and it was much easier. She said that she was trying to win her servants to Christ. She left as a gift to Mr. and Mrs. Woodworth a magnificent basket of fruit. Before she left, she said she hoped I would go back with a good report to help keep Japan and the United States from war. We went to bed at 7:30, planning to climb the active volcano Mt. Asama tomorrow.

Monday, September 13 ———— ◆ ————

Arose at 5:00 A.M., and after a good breakfast, we prepared our lunches (two for each of us), secured bicycles, strapped our lunches, a teapot for water, and raincoats

Picture of W.P. Minton and bicycle on front of torii on mountain side.

and umbrellas with camera swung over my shoulder, and were off for Mt. Asama, an active volcano, 8,230 feet high. It is about seven miles to the base of the mountain and upgrade most of the way. We planned to ride our wheels as far as possible, push them to the base, then leave them to use in coasting home.

On the way, we passed a small village. I had the tea kettle on my wheel, and it sounded like a cowbell as we went along, causing the natives to stare in wonderment. I stopped on the way and snapped a picture of two waterwheels, one of which had an overhead shot. Also snapped typical farmer's hut. These are typical of Japan country life. We passed a great many one-horse two-wheel carts, lumbering up the mountain pass hauling cement and other things. The drivers explained that the railroad had broken down. At one place we counted 17 resting before a teahouse.

We tried to strike a bargain with the boss to haul our wheels to the base of Asama for one yen. He agreed, and we accepted only to find that he meant a yen for each wheel. So we decided to push them ourselves. It was the most beautiful winding path, and except for the inconvenience of pushing the wheels and having to get out of the way of the carts, it was a most enjoyable walk. Dr. Woodworth taught me a new word or phrase to add to my two phrases already known. It was *konchiwa*, "How do you do." I used it successfully several times.

The road was quite winding and hugged the mountain on one side while on the other a deep gorge dropped straight away, with a dashing stream at the bottom. If Japan could harness her waterpower, she could turn the wheels of thousands of factories. The noise of the flashing streams is always a welcome sound to the traveler. We passed a new summer resort being opened by a land company. It was in the midst of a woods, with Japanese houses beautifully laid out. In the midst of the new village stood a stately and elegantly built stone bank building. The numerous banks

A stream with hills and mountains in background. Location unknown.

of Japan are indicative of the prosperity of a certain class but not of the common people, who in this section seem in utter poverty.

After a very, very long climb, we pushed our wheels up to the Japanese teahouse at the base of the mountain. I took a picture of Dr. Woodworth and had him take one of me, with Asama in the background. We ate some lunch, filled our water kettle, and with stout sticks started up the mountainside. It is a long, hard climb of about three miles, I should judge. At first it was not so hard; then it became more steep and rugged. We would walk awhile, then take a short rest, then start on.

As we climbed, we went round the base of Ko Asama, or Baby Asama, which looks the part when compared with Giant Asama, with its forbidding height. We finally left the timberline and emerged in the bleak bare slopes rising hundreds of feet. It afforded a wonderful view of the surrounding ridges in the sunlight as the clouds flitted about among them and green valleys looked up from below. The shadows of the clouds, combined with the varying green patches of the valley, some darker, some lighter, looked for all the world like a giant frog pond covered with patches of moss and the lighter green water lillies so often seen in ponds. The scene was simply beyond description. One new range after another came into view as we climbed higher and higher.

Japan is seven-eighths mountains, leaving only one-eighth tillable land to feed its 60,000,000 people, who are increasing at a rate of 700,000 a year. Japan really does have a problem. Think of a plot the size of Ohio, Indiana and Illinois, and only one-eighth of it tillable, supporting half as many people as the whole United States. No wonder the Japanese farmer has to cultivate every inch of his little plot.

A pony pulling a large load of telephone pole–sized poles on a two-wheeled cart.

As we passed hundreds of feet up the mountain, we discovered a party following us, but, oh, so far below us that we pitied them as we thought of their long climb. There were literally hundreds of pairs of worn-out sandals along the path, lying where they had been discarded by weary climbers. Some were stained with blood. As the climbers below moved, they looked like specks, and yet each one in God's sight is greater than the mountain. After passing ridge after ridge, we finally came to the last one, rising almost straight above us.

We were in the clouds, some of which dropped below us, the wind strong and cold, and it was with the greatest of difficulty that we reached the edge of the crater after a climb of three and a half hours. At first we could see nothing, for a cloud had dropped into the crater, but finally it lifted, and I looked for the first time into the yawning mouth of a volcano—not an extinct one, but an active one, for as we looked, we could see the hissing steam and the molten lava in great boiling quantities. Every little while it breaks forth in all its fury and throws great rocks fully the size of a house high into the air. I picked up many and varied-colored pieces of what was formerly red-hot lava. On the return trip, we had a good view of the great lava beds with their huge house-sized lava lumps just as they were vomited up by the volcanic fiend. It was a most impressive sight.

The descent was more tiring than the ascent, though it required an hour less time. We finally reached the teahouse at the base, ate our lunch, and mounting our wheels, started to coast four miles down the slope. But it was quite steep, and before long, my brake failed to work, and I found myself in a heap by the side of the path. I had a typical Japanese wheel; the pedals were so adjusted that one could not hold back, but there were two handbrakes on the handlebars, controlling the front and back wheels. After my first fall, I was more cautious, but almost before I knew it, both brakes gave way, and I found myself speeding headlong down the mountain.

About halfway up the volcano Asama Yama. Note the lava beds in the distance.

But it did not last long. My front wheels struck sand; then I followed. Dr. Wood-worth's brake was showing signs of weakening, so we led our wheels upon which we had counted so much for a delightful spin down home meekly back to level ground.

We pulled in at 6:00 P.M., took a hot bath, ate a hearty supper, and were ready for bed. But I could not retire until I had written some kind of a description of the day's trip. Coming home, we passed a lot of carts returning, and often the driver was singing a merry song as he ambled along.

Tuesday, September 14 ———— ◆ ————————

Arose early and prepared to start for Sendai by way of Utsunomiya. Got some postcards of the mountains. The lady who sold them to me could not speak English, so she wrote the price. The amount was 72 sen. She wrote it *702*. Took a picture of Dr. and Mrs. Woodworth before their cottage. At nine o'clock, our baggage was loaded on a two-wheel cart, and we started for the station three-fourths of a mile away. It was level all the way to the station and a beautiful walk down the road, with towering mountain peaks lifting their cloud-capped heads on every side.

At the station, under the direction of Dr. Woodworth, I bought three third-class tickets for Sendai. I said, "*Sendai santo.*" Have almost forgotten the formula already, but I got the tickets. In a few minutes we said goodbye to Miss Francis, entered the dirty, smoke-filled, littered-floored third-class car and were off. I admire the spirit of

This picture was taken with one foot on the inside slope of the crater of Asama Yama (8200 ft.), an active volcano in Japan.

the missionary who, like these two, takes third-class cars because second class costs twice as much and first class four times as much. Third class on a fairly long journey (it varies with length) is a little over 2.5 sen a mile.

One man on this car had stretched himself full-length and was enjoying a delightful sleep. We had to hunt for seats. The railroad makes 90 percent of its profits on third-class passengers and gives them the poorest service. On such a train as we took, it is not uncommon to see the second-class coach with only two or three people in it. The man who sat by me smoked several cigarettes and puffed great volumes of smoke in my face. A little later, the man across from him (the seats face each other like a Pullman) puffed in his face, and he didn't like it, so he made the other throw his cigarette out of the window. "Oh, consistency, thou art a jewel." I feel good over my trip up the mountain, but have a stitch in my back. The Japanese are great on bowing, and I am having my troubles with my back. HA!

The scenery through here is wonderful. A pair of electric locomotives pull us, or rather hold us back, as we glide for miles down the mountainside. Two engines are used so that if one breaks, we have another to fall back on. After we pass the 27 tunnels, we change to a small steam engine. As we ride, a Japanese lady decides to eat her lunch, so she turns her back upon all of us, folds her white-stockinged feet under her, and falls to. Having finished her *bento* (lunch) she resumes her former posture in apparent satisfaction. A Japanese man, desiring to smoke but having no pipe, borrows from his neighbor and enjoys a few puffs.

At Omiga we changed cars for Utsunomiya. As we drew into the station, I

A large lake and the surrounding mountains.

noticed a number of section men at work with picks. They were swinging their picks at exactly the same time, one man singing something in perfect rhythm with the swing of the pick and keeping it up with apparently no faltering.

As we boarded the train, a young Japanese invited me to sit with him. He could talk a few words of English and evidently wanted me to sit with him in order that he might pick up a few more. I learned that he was a dental student studying in Tokyo. His home is in or near Nikko. His name and address are Binko Wakatabe, c/o Kamazawa, 90 Aoyama onden, Akasaka, Tokyo. His home address is 2585 Sano, Tochigi-ken, Japan. He gave me his picture and took two snapshots of me at the station where he left the train. He said he believed in God, could see Him in nature, and that he read the NT, but he did not seem to have quite grasped Christ. He is evidently pantheistic in his belief. I told him I would see him at Tokyo in October.

We came through some beautiful farming land framed by distant mountains on either side. The Japanese are surely intensive farmers. It must be hard work with their simple tools.

Arrived at Utsunomiya at 4:30 P.M. A riksha man piled the following into his riksha: traveling bag, two suitcases, two baskets, and my briefcase. He charged us 50 sen (25¢) to take them a mile to Mrs. Fry's. We walked through the streets to her house, and on the way I noticed a Japanese man and woman coming toward us on the other side. She smiled in a familiar way and rushed out across the street to meet us. Imagine my surprise and delight to greet Kiyosha Awana, a graduate of Defiance, now teaching in Mrs. Fry's school. She was taking her husband to the train. We expect to see her again in the morning.

Mrs. Fry, Maki, their Japanese boy, and the Rev. Kimura, pastor of our

Young lady playing Japanese stringed instrument.

Utsunomiya church, met us in the street. It was a royal welcome. The Fry home is quite large, there being some seven rooms with a number of small closets and side rooms. It sets in a beautiful lawn of about 300 *tsubo*. There are many trees and shrubs, most of which were planted by the Frys during their past 13 years. I picked a ripe persimmon and a ripe fig, which I ate for supper. There are beautiful rose-bushes, chestnut trees, bamboo trees, etc.

After a good supper, we rested and talked. The Rev. Kimura is a very fine gentleman, the son of a nobleman. He has a wife and three children—1, 3 and 5 years of age. The middle one is a boy. The Rev. Kimura had to leave early to attend a meeting in the interests of the coming Sunday school convention.

There are a million people in Tochigi-ken, of which Utsunomiya is the capital. The city has about 50,000 population with the following mission churches: Salvation Army, M.E., Episcopal, Holiness, Catholic and Christian. There is a commercial school, an agricultural school, middle school, primary school, girls' school and Mrs. Fry's private girls' school. Mrs. Fry has this year seven girls in each of the four classes and three teachers besides herself. The girls living in the dormitory get board at about Y7 a month. They do their own work and are quite happy. Ten of the girls live in their parents' homes in the town. Mrs. Fry has 12 Sunday schools in operation in Utsunomiya with an average enrollment of from 20 to 100, or about 1,000 in all. The girls assist in this work, as all of them are Christians.

After supper we discussed the visit of the U.S. congressmen to Japan. It seems that last Sunday these men made a trip to Nikko, the seat of Buddhist worship in Japan, and praised the trip very highly. On another occasion they had a group of *geisha* (dancing girls) perform before them. Of course, the Japanese would see to it that nothing indiscreet was done, but the fact remains that the *geisha* are immoral women who are even more dangerous than the brothel type because they move in high society, spreading immorality and disease wherever they go.

The visit of the congressmen may produce glowing reports of the prosperity and high morality of Japan, but the reports are not founded upon the facts. One needs only to go into the low places of the cities and the humble homes of the country to realize the facts as they are. One must remember too that many businessmen regularly support several women besides their wives and that a girl who goes into a teahouse or factory to work virtually throws her virtue away. We retired early, intending to start early the next day for Sendai.

Wednesday, September 15   ———   ◆

After breakfast we visited the Utsunomiya church of which the Rev. Kimura is pastor. I took a picture of it. It is a neat little building with a parsonage next door. A kindergarten is in operation here.

Before we started out, we had morning prayers, Kiyoshi's mother, who is Mrs. Fry's servant, coming in. We next went to the school, where the girls were lined up on each side of the walk to greet us. I met Miss Yoshio Sato, who lately returned from America to fulfill her teaching engagement with Mrs. Fry. She is doing excellent work and is a credit to Elon, from which she recently graduated with high honors. I had the privilege of speaking a few minutes, with Mrs. Fry interpreting.

We then hurried to the station and took third-class passage to Sendai. Talk about a slow train through Arkansas—this was one. The coaches were not nearly so nice as those from Tokyo. There was no spring in the seats, and the cars were short and stuffy.

The floor was littered. At Fusijimura we changed to another train. Here we had plenty of room, but the seats had no springs, and the back was simply a straight board that took you amidships. On this type of coach the seats extend entirely across the car, and there are doors at each seat. There is no watercloset, so the train has to wait for passengers to relieve themselves at certain intervals.

We left Utsunomiya at 9:30 A.M. in a drizzling rain, and we had covered around 200 miles. I bought a pair of rubbers at Y5.50 but had to have them. We were met at the station by Pastor Kitano of our Sendai church. He is a most agreeable man of about 50. After supper at Woodworth's, he came around and helped plan the itinerary. We are to take a two-day trip, beginning tomorrow, going to Narugo first. I sat up and wrote late.

At Utsunomiya I slept in Maki's room. Maki's dog has fleas—so have I. Enough said. But I think I have conquered them tonight by shaking everything out the window.

Thursday, September 16 ———————— ◆ ————————————————

Took train for Narugo at 10:10 after failing to secure any Kodak film in Sendai. Have several exposures in my camera and wired McKnight for more. Took third class again. Cost Y2.74 for the two of us, while second class would be twice as much. After a tiresome ride of four hours through many villages with no preaching at all, we arrived at Narugo (pronounced "Narungo").

Mr. Koichiro Sumita is pastor here. He is a young man 26 years old and a graduate of Takinogawa Bible College, the Disciple school in Tokyo, in April 1920. Has middle school diploma. He preaches at Narugo every Sunday night and at Iwadeyama every other Saturday night and Sunday morning. He preaches on the street once a week, Sunday school at Narugo every Sunday, Sunday school at Iwadeyama every other Sunday morning.

Narugo is 60 miles north of Sendai. Both are on the railroad. Population of Narugo is about 2,000, with three other nearby villages making a total population of 9,063 and no other preaching in any of them. This total is increased by several thousand people who come every year to the 60 hot-spring baths. There is no church building here, but the Christians, of whom there are ten members of the organized church, meet in a private home, while Sunday school is held at the home of the banker, Mr. Takanashi, who is a Christian. The house can only accommodate 25, but 100 would come if there were room. There are two schools—Onichi Primary school, some distance out, and with 700 students, and the Narugo primary school nearby with 600 boys.

This organized church of 10 members has raised Y400 toward a building and lot. Land near the center of town but on a slope costs Y15 a *tsubo*, and as 100 *tsubo* are needed, the cost would be Y1,500. They estimate the cost of the building at about Y3,000, making the total cost to build a church here Y4,500. The Rev. Sumita desires to include kindergarten work, and if he does, the town authorities will help. But this would not be satisfactory to me as it might involve us in controversy with the authorities. The same would be true of rented land to build a church on.

The hot springs make this a very popular place. There is a river on one side and a mountain on the other, so land is scarce and high. They think it will take Y5,000 for both building and lot. It seems that Narugo is the center of a string of several villages here at the springs, none of which have preaching except Narugo.

The work here was started by Mr. Yokoyama, an old Greek Orthodox Christian. He is an interesting character.

Mr. Takanashi, the banker, has two children in Sendai school, and a daughter, Shinko Takanashi, in Mrs. Fry's school.

But to get back to my story. As we stepped from the train, we were met by the Rev. Sumita and a large crowd of citizens and schoolchildren. The children had made Japanese and American flags for the occasion. We were marched through this line of waving flags, and one boy at the end made a speech of welcome to me in English. He said, "Mr. Minton, we are glad to welcome you to Narugo." We then marched up town to the bank of Mr. Takanashi. Here we rested while Dr. Woodworth got a haircut and I secured some of the above information from Mr. Sumita while a streetful of young and old looked on. When Dr. Woodworth came back, I

A group of young people at Narugo with Dr. Woodworth greet Foreign Mission Secretary Minton. The group of children are holding American flags mixed with Japanese flags.

took a picture of the SS children with their flags. Here I was waited upon by a delegation of citizens who requested that I speak at the middle school on the American-Japanese question. We then marched to the school, which was up a large hill.

We left our shoes at the door and met the staff of teachers. After having tea, we were ushered into a room where were gathered over a 100 – not boys, as we expected, but largely men who were vitally interested in the question at hand. After my introduction by Mr. Sumita, I spoke, with Dr. Woodworth interpreting. I emphasized just one way to solve the problem, and that by making both Japan and America Christian.

Dr. Woodworth spoke a few minutes, and Mr. Sumita followed. Each of us was applauded vigorously. We went to the office of the school and had more tea, then went back to the bank for a further conference.

The Japanese present were attentive to our every need, carrying our baggage and securing a room for us at the hotel. The Narugo Hotel, where we were compelled to go because the others were full, is a fine new hotel, with electric lights but otherwise strictly Japanese, with no chairs or beds or tables. We simply had to live Japanese-fashion. We were conducted to a very nice room on a corner of the second floor, overlooking the town, with a fine view of the mountains nearby. The mountain Hanahuchi is said to be full of monkeys.

Before the evening service, we called on a very fine-looking young Japanese woman who is interested. Dr. W. talked with her. We then went to the home of Mr. Yokoyama where about 20 boys and men and women were gathered. Both Dr. Woodworth and I spoke. The boys sang "Jesus Loves Me," in Japanese and

A group of guests at a town reception are shown with Dr. Minton and another unidentified Occidental person seated in the center.

English. After the service, we were served watermelon. The boys presented me with one each of the Japanese and American flags they had made in my honor.

Went to the hotel for the night. There are hot baths in this hotel. I saw five women and three men taking a bath together. This is a sample of the moral status all over the island. They gave us the best room in the house and served us a big Japanese supper and added two fried eggs and ham. When we returned from the meeting, our beds were made on the floor, and I found mine quite comfortable.

Friday, September 17   ◆

After breakfast, two boys, 12 and 13 years old, called and said they had decided to become Christians. The pastor says they had not expressed themselves before last night. Young Mrs. Yokoyama, upon whom we called last night, also sent word that she had decided to become a Christian. So the efforts were not in vain. We paid our hotel bill, which amounted to Y5.00 each, including all the service and two meals. This is considered by Dr. Woodworth rather high. To show their goodwill, the hotel keeper presented each of us with a flimsy towel, as is their custom with prominent guests who pay a good price. The hotel boy carried our baggage to the train and insisted on sticking around until the train pulled out. Several of the prominent members of the church also went to the station with us, and as we pulled away from the station, there were many bows in saying goodbye.

As we boarded the train here, we noticed a young bride being taken by either her people or the groom's people to a nearby town. They came to the station in the rickety coach, and I noticed that the young lady was literally covered with powder, the kind that is palmed off on these people and ruins their skin. She covered her face continually with a cloth to avoid our gaze.

We went to Iwadeyama, 29 miles from Narugo, south toward Sendai. This town has a population of 5,000 and there is no other preaching than Mr. Sumita's on Saturday night and Sunday morning every two weeks. Kowatable is three miles south of Narugo with a population of 1,000; Izekuki is nine miles south of Kowatable, with a population of unknown numbers, and the next town south of Izekuki is Iwadeyama where we alighted. I just learned that *sumita* means "living in the rice field," and it is quite appropriate. He is living in a field white for the harvest.

Iwadeyama has a population of 5,000 and is 29 miles from Narugo toward Sendai. We have no church here, but services are held in the house of Mr. Ito, a banker. The mission rents the house for Y5.5 a month, and Mr. Ito lives in it free. The house is good-sized; the lot is 100 *tsubo*, and Mr. Ito says he thinks the house and lot can be bought now for Y2,000. There are ten members and several inquirers in this church. Another town seven and a half miles south from here is about the same size and has more business but no preaching. Have had preaching here for 28 years, and at Narugo about 12 years. At Iwadeyama we have been unfortunate in having had two preachers who were not only very ordinary in intellect but fell into sin. One of the church members also became immoral, and the town has lost confidence in the church. There is one middle school. Our Sunday school has an enrollment of ten. There is room for more, but Mr. Sumita says they will not come. Took picture of the house used as a church, with Mr. Sumita and the Ito family. Visited several families, and at one place, the husband was drunk on *sake*, and the wife was half drunk. Dr. Woodworth tried in vain to talk to them, and Mr. Sumita, supposing that he did not know the trouble, finally exclaimed in desperation, "Doctor, he's drunk." I got a good view of the evils of *sake*.

We visited the city hall and came back to Mr. Ito's. His house faces the post office. We had brought some lunch, which we ate, and started for the train. Left at 12:30 for Wakuya, about 19 miles from Iwadeyama and on a railroad.

Passed through Nakaruida, with 5,000 population and no preaching. It is seven and a half miles from Iwadeyama and is more flourishing than the latter. Also through Rikuzen Fruikawa, where two prisoners were brought aboard. They were closely handcuffed, wore dirty orange suits and straw hats, looking much like overturned wastebaskets, which entirely covered their faces. There were narrow slits for them to see through. Next station still going south toward Sendai was Kogota where we changed to another train for Wakuya. Arrived at Wakuya at 3:00 P.M. and was met by the Rev. Sakurai, the ordained pastor at that place.

WAKUYA

Wakuya has a population of 7,000. There is a Greek church and a Congregational church here, the former practically helpless, and the Cong. church having no

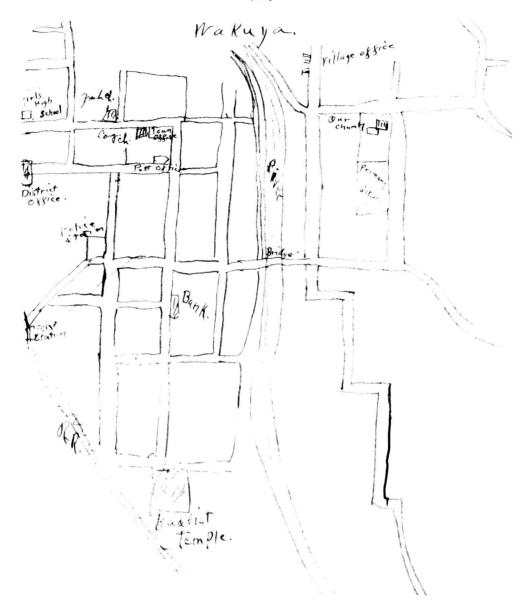

Map of Wakuya (by the author).

pastor in the field for nearly eight years. The Cong. has SS every Sunday, with an enrollment of 50. About ten members of the Cong. church now live in the town. They began work there in 1887, the same year that Bro. Jones came out for our church. They have not put as much into the work as we have. The pastor of the independent Congregational church at Sendai comes out once a month and gives them a weeknight service.

In our Wakuya church there is a resident membership of 20 and a SS enrollment of 50, with an attendance of 40. Many have been converted here and then moved away. Most of the converts are students, who scatter when they leave school. The Rev. Sakurai found that by having SS just after the primary school next door closes, he could have a full house, so he had SS on Saturday last year and intends to do so again this year. He has regular SS on Sunday besides. Shortage of teachers in winter, for SS is a problem. Four girls from here attend Mrs. Fry's school in the winter but teach in this SS in the summer. There have been five conversions during the past year. Mr. Sakurai has not been making an effort to make conversions among the children because he felt they could not understand, but I tried to show him that they could become earnest Christians. They have prayer meeting on Wednesday, with an attendance of about ten.

He is 47 and has preached for us 22 years. Schooling under Dr. Woodworth at Kasumi cho and at Sendai in the Tohoku Gakuin, the Presbyterian school. Also studied under Mr. Fry. Mr. Sakurai has seven living children, one having died. He receives from the mission Y61.64, Y3 being paid by the church extra. He preaches twice a month at Tajiri, a town of 600 ten miles northwest of Wakuya. There are about 20 Christians at Tajiri but no organized church and no buildings. They meet in the home of Mrs. Yoshida.

Sakurai also holds SS at Samine once a month. About 50 are enrolled here. Samine is a town of 3,500 fifteen miles northwest of Wakuya. No other services are held in either of these places. The people of Wakuya are indifferent to the church. He said, upon my suggestion, that he might try street preaching at the time of the annual festivals. The membership of Wakuya includes farmers, merchants and schoolteachers. The schoolteacher receives Y105 a month, Y35 being a special grant during the present high prices. It is impossible to tell how much the farmer and merchants receive. The community, as Japan goes, is considered not so good financially as Iwadeyama and Nakamida because of floods here. Mr. Sakurai goes to Nakamida once in two months for SS and to Ikezuki the same. The latter is small.

Two young men came to Mr. Sakurai's house with us. The elder is Uchiyama ("in the midst of the mountain"), and the younger Mr. Sakurai's son Masao. Both have recently graduated from the Sendai middle school. The former has poor health. They drew me an excellent map of the town of which this is a poor reproduction. [See p. 52.]

We have here a church seating perhaps 150 and a large parsonage on a fine corner lot of about three-fourths of an acre.

We called on an old man who has been considering Christianity for years. We pled with him to accept Christ, but he said he could not be sure Christ was the right one. His son, who spent 22 years in America and became a Christian at the Independent Japanese church in Los Angeles, was a steerage passenger on the *Korea Maru* upon which I came to Japan. I did not know it.

The Wakuya church is a memorial to the Rowell sisters of Franklin, New Hampshire. At seven o'clock, we went to the church, where about 30 people had gathered. Pastor Sakurai announced the hymns, and Mrs. Sakurai played the organ. It sounded good to hear the old hymns of the church sung, even though in a different tongue than mine. I was introduced and spoke on "The Water of Life," John 4:29. Dr. Woodworth interpreted and followed with a few words pressing the invitation as I had done. The interest was excellent throughout.

Dr. Woodworth, Pastor Sakurai and family (Wakuya).

Pastor Sakurai then announced there would be a reception for me, and while they made preparations, Dr. Woodworth did personal work. All seated themselves on the floor in the SS room, and I was invited to take a chair at the end of the room. I declined the chair and sat on the floor. Tea was brought, and paper bags full of all sorts of cookies. As these were passed, Pastor Sakurai made a speech of welcome in Japanese in which he said they were glad to welcome me and he believed the best way to show it was by their Christian testimony. There were several non–Christians present, among them a schoolteacher.

Dr. Woodworth spoke, and I responded to the welcome by stating how glad I was to be present and that I knew the welcome was genuine because of the good supper I had had at Sakurai's, but above all because of their interest at the service. I urged them to seek to win others to Christ and to pray for a revival.

After the reception, another schoolteacher arrived, and Dr. Woodworth spent an hour trying to bring them to the light. They then wanted to ask me some questions about the ever-recurring Japanese-American problem. It is a sensitive question, calling for very careful handling, but I mean not to compromise my position that Christianity is the only solution. Retired at midnight, tired but feeling that some good had been done.

Saturday, September 18 ━━━━━━━ ◆ ━━━━━━━

After an early breakfast, Pastor Sakurai gave me some postcard pictures. I took two pictures of the family and the church, and we were off to the station. A ride of 31 miles brought us back to Sendai. Arrived at 9:30, and I soon fell to writing up my notes. After lunch, a young man came in who said he was living in a dormitory of the YMCA near the Sendai High School and the Sendai University; 20 boys between 18 and 21 live here and attend these schools. Board, room, electric lights and bath are furnished for Y23 a month. They control the club themselves, and only Christian boys are allowed. They study the Bible together on Wednesday night. They hire a cook. The plan seems to work pretty well.

In the afternoon we visited the Filatures Katakura Co. Silk Factory. The manager, Mr. Oguchi ("Big Mouth"), met us at the door and very kindly and even eagerly consented to show us through the factory. We found him to be a most interesting talker and a most congenial guide. Leaving our shoes at the entrance, we were given a pair of sandals each. These were the kind that have the string between the toes, and I confess I walked with some difficulty and part of the time with real pain as the string rubbed the skin. But we got along somehow, and I saw a most interesting factory.

We were first ushered into the office, or rather reception room of the office, where tea was set before us. Then we started in at the very beginning where about 20 girls were sitting on their feet on the floor by large piles of white cocoons, sorting the good from the bad. A cocoon with a hole in its side, of course, has many broken and short threads, and these are second and third class. The manager told us that the silk from the best cocoons was sent to America, the inferior grades being sold in Japan. I do not know how many factories follow this policy. Eight and one-half pounds of the cocoons are worth Y7.

During the time they work, the girls receive about 90 sen a day (40¢). A pound of cocoons makes about one-tenth of a pound of silk when spun. The cocoon is received with the insect alive, and it is killed by being subjected to steam heat at 500 degrees, then at 200 degrees for five minutes.

From this room we went down a long hall to one of the rooms where the girls were soaking the cocoons in hot water, catching the thread, and starting it off on the winding spools. The length of a thread from one cocoon is about 1,800 feet. Before they can start the unwinding and rewinding process, they must put the cocoons in water at a temperature of 500 degrees for a few minutes to melt the wax. Then they are put into water at 190 degrees where the thread is caught and put on the spools. Four cocoons are spun off at one time onto each winding spool.

The dead worms are used to make soap, and from the residue is made a fertilizer to fertilize mulberry groves, upon the leaves of which the worms are fed. By mixing *ajinomoto*, a kind of Worcestershire sauce, with these dead worms, the manager said they were sometimes eaten. The worms are also used for fish bait, especially for catching eels.

One hundred twenty girls, in rows of 60 each, work in each of the six winding departments of this large factory. The factory employs all told about 800 girls and 200 men. They work 12 hours a day, at 50 sen (25¢) a day, or Y15 a month ($7.50). Sunday is not recognized in this factory, and the only two rest days the girls have each month are on the first and fifteenth. The work looks exceedingly tiresome and monotonous. Four or five years ago, the girls got about Y7 a month, but the cost of rice has made the increase necessary. The girls live in dormitories near the factory.

There are many times when they are allowed to have entertainments, the manager explained. They have a large hall for the purpose. He has spoken to the Rev. Kitano, our Sendai pastor, inviting him to conduct religious service for the girls. Here is opened up a fine opportunity to reach a large number of hardworking and underpaid girls with the gospel of comfort and help. But Rev. Kitano is already working to the limit, and Dr. Woodworth is absolutely unable to accept all the opportunities that come to him for service. The need for more workers is once more emphasized.

The Rev. Kitano says he has baptized some of the girls. They all come from the country and live in nearby dormitories. They are from 14 to 35 years of age, but the majority are 19 and 20.

Next we went to another long room where the thread is rewound on larger spools. These spools are so constructed that they move back and forth as well as round and round, so that the thread is crossed and recrossed to keep it from breaking or tangling. The small spools must be kept slightly wet during this process, so the silk will unroll easily, but if they are too wet, the silk will be injured. These larger spools are sent to an inspector before a large window, and he inspects them with the naked eye to see that there are no tangles or broken threads. The skeins taken from the spools are next wound like a braid of hair so the silk will not break.

From here we went into the weighing room where more girls weigh the skeins. From here it goes into a room for final examination. The first class goes to America; the second and third class stay in Japan. Some cocoons are yellow (Italian), and some white, making two colors of silk. A record of the tenacity, elasticity and length is kept; also of gross weight, deduction for sack container, and net weight. The manager graciously gave me a small skein of yellow and white silk thread and two of the cuplike threaders used in starting the silk on the spools.

The climate of Japan is especially well adapted to the silkworm industry. Too much rain or too little makes a great difference in the mulberry leaf and hence in the cocoon. The leaves are fed to the young worm in fine pieces. They have to be protected day and night. Can hear the rustling of the worms as they feed. While they are growing, they must be fed ten times a day. Once in two weeks they sleep a couple of days, then wake up and eat for two weeks. It takes about 35 days for them to get their growth. The worm will eat nothing but mulberry leaves and cannot be deceived into eating anything else. It takes a week or ten days to spin the cocoon, depending on the weather. They are put into straw and weave the outer layer first, then gradually hem themselves in. The manager gave me two yellow European, and two each of the white European and Japanese cocoons, which he said were perfect samples. The yellow cocoons are the best; the Japanese kind are much smaller than the others.

Dr. Woodworth tells me there are 2,000,000 working girls in Japan. It requires 200,000 fresh girls each year to take the place of those who fall by the way. Of the 200,000 who go out from their homes each year, 120,000 never see their homes again. Fifty percent of them lose their virtue within a year. The close confinement of their work causes much consumption. Outside this factory we saw where they swing a large log clear of the ground, and on this log the girls swing back and forth for exercise.

Went to bed early for a good rest looking to three services tomorrow.

Miss Imhoff, of the Sendai Orphanage, called before Sunday school time and invited me to see the orphanage. Her visit delayed us in getting started, and we reached the church at 20 Nijunimachi just as the little folks were coming out. There was an attendance of 70 at the morning service, and most of them were young people. I spoke on "Christianity, a Choice of Service." The attention was fine. This church certainly has a very fine future if the young people are any indication. Of course, they have little means to support the church now.

After lunch, I wrote a couple of letters and at three o'clock went to the regular service of foreign missionaries held in the building of the Reformed Church in America. It is sometimes called the Reformed Presby. Church, with headquarters in Pennsylvania. I preached on "The Reinforced Life." The attention was good. After the service, the company consulted as to how to revive or change their prayer meeting service. It seems that it has not been successful as it has been conducted.

At seven o'clock, we went again to the Sendai Christian Church. There were only about 30 out. Kitano says 20 is the usual evening attendance. He spoke first on the California-Japanese question, and I took it up from where he left off and said that I felt the best thing they could do as Christians was to pray and read the Bible and strive to win their fellow citizens to Christ as the only way to solve it. I said that would prompt better treatment by Japan of Korea and China. One man got up and went out. Dangerous ground.

After the service Sunday morning, Pastor Kitano told the young people we wanted them to sell pencils, which he had with him, to help build a memorial SS building to H.J. Heintz in Tokyo. This is part of the program of the world's SS convention. The pencils are worth 7 sen each but are to be sold at two for 10 sen. I questioned Dr. Woodworth as to wisdom of introducing such a moneymaking scheme in the church. He had just bought and paid for a box of them. It seemed to me that the principle of the whole thing was wrong and that it would serve to introduce into the Japanese church such methods for moneyraising as would spoil the spiritual life. I am coming more and more to feel that mission work is being conducted more and more on a plane of materialism that will in the end be disastrous. The average missionary I have met seems to me to be looking at the work far too much from the materialistic viewpoint. The old-time zeal and enthusiasm to win souls seems to be dropping out. I am glad to note, however, that Dr. Woodworth makes soulwinning his chief aim in every sermon he preaches and in every one of the many talks he has with these people. His type of personal work seems to be the right sort.

At the afternoon service I met Dr. Faust, of the Reformed church; Mr. Reed, a teacher; Mr. Nicodemus, another teacher; and quite a number of missionaries. Some of these seemed very fine-spirited. Later on, I shall call at their missions and secure statistics.

After the evening service, I had a long talk with Pastor Kitano of the Sendai church. Takaya Kitano, pastor of the Sendai church, is 54 and has a wife and five children. He has preached here 18 years, one year in Tokyo, one year in Koochi, and a year and a half in Yokohama. He became a Christian at 18 years of age on the island of Shikoku, being a schoolteacher at the time. He was led to become

Dr. Woodworth, the Rev. Kitano, pastor Sendai Church, and Secretary Minton.

a Christian through the preaching and personal work of a native pastor. He is a graduate of the Meiji Gakuin (Presby. Theol. School, Tokyo). He did some preaching while he studied.

The population of Sendai is 100,000. It is 214 miles north of Tokyo and is the capital of Miyagi ken.

Other churches in Sendai are the Episcopal, four Reformed churches, Baptist, Congregational, Disciple, Methodist, Holiness, Greek Catholic, Roman Catholic, Salvation Army and the Christian Orphanage. The Christian Orphanage here was formerly conducted by the Methodists but was given up by them and is now supported by contributions from several denominations, the M.E. still paying the salary of the supt., Miss Imhoff.

The Reformed church has both a boys' and girls' middle school and a theological and commercial school; and the Roman Catholic also has a girls' school. There is a government university, called the Northwestern Imperial Univ., a high school, two middle schools, one private middle school, two commercial schools besides that of the Reformed church, one normal school, two girls' middle schools (ages 14 to 18), one private girl's school, one agricultural school, and one technical school.

Our church and parsonage were built about 12 years ago at a cost of Y3,300 and Y700 additional for ground. Mrs. Fry built the church and parsonage, and gave it to our mission. The parsonage is a neat one, back of the church. The church will seat 300 or 400. It has a baptistry and SS room.

The church is located in a store district, the silk factory being the only factory near. It employs 1,000 people, and gospel services can be held in the hall set apart for recreation of the employees.

Sendai church has, all told, 110 members in the city. The SS enrolls 150, with an average attendance of 120. Prayer meeting is held Wednesday night, with an average attendance of 12. Fifteen new members were added to the church last year, and Kitano is working for 100 converts this year, having already secured 65 decisions. He thinks many of these will come into the church later, but most are young people who are unsettled and often leave town just after conversion.

The church property embraces 240 *tsubo* of land. The land is worth at present Y25,000, and it would cost Y20,000 to build the church now. Our church is fifth in the city in respect to membership. The church pays Y11 a month on the pastor's salary. The balance of Y73.25 is paid by the mission, making a total of Y84.25. Most of the members, being students, are not well off financially.

Pastor Kitano preaches at Iwagasaki once a month, at Kannari once a month, at Hirobuchi once a month, at Takota once a month, and at Hanayama, Kowaguchi and Miyama several times a year.

Monday, September 20 ————— ◆ —————————

Wrote to my wife, parents and Thomas, continuing letters begun yesterday. Packed up in the morning for the long ten-day trip through the churches of the northern field. Left at 12:35 with wheels and baggage on the train for Tajiri where we are to hold evening service. Arrived at 2:00 P.M. after a ride of 30 miles. The town is about a mile and a half from the railroad station. Pastor Sakurai met us at the station with two of the Christian boys of the place. As we brought our wheels out of the station at Tajiri, my back tire blew up. Dr. Woodworth loaded all my baggage on his wheel and started off, leaving Pastor Sakurai, the boys and me to come on by foot.

We came to the town of 2,500 and stopped at the home of Mrs. Yoshida, a widow lady, where meetings are held since there is no church organization and no effort to secure one; the pastor feels they are doing such good work, there had better be no effort made along this line. I wonder if he is not correct. There are about 20 Christians, the most devoted group I have yet seen.

Mrs. Yoshida reminds me vividly of Lydia in the NT. She lived in Sendai formerly, then moved with her husband to Tajiri where he died. She supported herself and daughter by means of a sewing school she started. Mr. Sakurai came here to preach but found no preaching place. No place could be rented, so he held little meetings in his room at the hotel. Later he was able to rent a little place for meetings. To the meetings in this place Mrs. Yoshida came about six years ago. She has been the center of the work ever since, her house becoming the preaching place. Under the blessing of God, 22 people are now Christians, though there is no church organization. Mrs. Yoshida says she has some kind of religious service at her house every day, but sometimes only a few come, as the people of the town are not interested. But there is a fine group of young people coming regularly.

Wrote an article for Dr. Morrill while Dr. Woodworth and Sakurai went to do some personal work. Several boys sat and watched me work the typewriter, and when I had finished, I showed them how to work it. Each one quickly and easily wrote his name in full. They were Makoto ("true") Kato, Ginjiro ("silver boy") Ito, and Seiichi ("Upright") Oka. Kato and Oka accompanied us to the hotel, carrying all the baggage. We were shown to the guest room, a very nice room at the rear on the ground floor. As we entered the hotel, I thought it looked much more like a stable, but the farther back we went, the nicer it looked.

The outdoor bath was heated for us, and robes brought out. Tea and wafers were set before us. As we sat, Dr. Woodworth talked to Kato, who then and there became a Christian. We prayed together, and I was impressed with the way Oka worked with his friend. Dr. Woodworth says, "We go out after people, and we expect to get them." This afternoon he visited a millionaire and talked to him and his wife about being Christians. Young Oka would like to preach but has no middle school education. Our mission as such objects to taking on a boy for Bible preparation for preaching unless he has a middle school education, and if possible, higher than that.

In the absence of the pastor here, the Christians take turns in leading the meeting. They seem to be a very spiritual people. The Christians are merchants, officers in companies, bankers, clerks, farmers and one schoolteacher. They pay Y1.5 a month on the pastor's salary. I suggested that he teach them to give. They pay the expenses of the work, and they also bring out special speakers from Sendai and have day meetings, which are evangelistic in nature. They say such meetings cost them about 20 yen a month. These meetings are held in a public hall rented for the purpose. No rent is paid Mrs. Yoshida for our meetings there.

At the evening meeting we found a room full of young and old. Dr. Woodworth spoke to the children, and they were dismissed. Enough older people came in later to fill the room again. There were at least 50 present during the evening. I spoke on "The Great Invitation." The interest was fine. The spirit of these people is the best of any I have yet seen. The people know how to pray. After the service, refreshments were served and a jolly time enjoyed. The young people entered into it with a zest and freshness that was good to see. We closed with a prayer meeting, and young and old really prayed. When we said goodbye, they wanted to shake hands—a thing I had not enjoyed since coming to Japan. The boys lighted us to our rooms at the hotel with a Japanese lantern.

Tuesday, September 21 ———— ◆ ————————————

Shaved without a mirror, as usual. Before breakfast, Kato was around to see us. He had to leave soon to go to work in the post office. Breakfast consisted of octopus slices, rice, raw egg, a mixture of vegetables, etc., served on lacquer trays.

After breakfast, I asked Rev. Sakurai what he thought of our work in Japan. He says we are small now but that we are planting the seed that will later produce a real harvest. The heads of the people are so filled with Buddhism and Confucianism that the new religion is confusing to them. He feels that the great need is earnestly to preach Christ and His glorious gospel. He has no objection to the schools but says we must not get away from preaching the gospel. He has not thought far into our general policy in Japan.

I asked him what kind of enlargement he would like to see in the Sendai field.

He doesn't feel that the church building at Wakuya is so essential, but it would be convenient. He feels that the main thing is to get people converted. At Tajiri (where we now are) the house used is not the best, but the people are right, and the work is progressing in a fine way. He says the *preachers* are too few. He feels we must try to get young men into theological schools for training. But now there is only one young man in training, Zendo Takahashi at Tokyo. He believes personal work is the most effective kind of work. He suggests we might combine a middle school and a theological school. He says nothing of the cost and has given it little thought.

After breakfast, we visited a sawmill run by waterpower. The wheel is an immense affair. On the shaft is a large flywheel of iron, very heavy. There is also a belt wheel. The logs are pushed into the saw as it revolves. I noticed that the larger logs cause the wheel to slow up perceptibly.

Our hotel bill for supper, night's lodging, and breakfast was Y2.13 each. Repairing my bicycle cost 10 sen (5¢), but it blew up again this morning. The tire seems rotten, so I had a new inner tube put in at a cost of Y3.00. We packed our baggage on the wheels and were off for Tsukidate at 10:00 A.M.

We passed through several villages of large size with no preaching whatever. I wondered how they lived. The houses looked so poverty stricken, and there seemed to be no enterprises to keep them going. Japan spends Y600,000,000 a year for drink, which is a sufficient amount of money to run the government for a year. She spends Y150,000,000 for a tobacco pouch and pipe on the person of nearly every Japanese man. They fill the tiny pipebowl with tobacco, light it, take a few puffs, then put it away again. Many, many cigarettes are also used.

At 12:30 we rode into Tsukidate, having covered the 12.5 miles by walking up hills a good share of the way and coasting down the balance.

Tsukidate is a town of 5,000, and ours is the only preaching place. Recently we bought a lot and house, and put it in repair at a total cost of Y3,300 ($1,650). The house is set a little to one side of the town, but in a good location. See map [p. 62]. There are 179 *tsubo* in the lot, and the house is so arranged as to be admirable for a parsonage and church combined. See plan [p. 64].

More than 100 can easily be seated in the rooms used for the church, and there is ample room in the one-story part for a good-size family to live Japanese-style. Dr. Woodworth thinks that perhaps in the initial stages the combined-house-and-parsonage idea is best suited to Japanese work. He says such a plan might well be followed at less expense and until the Japanese themselves feel the desire for a church and erect it themselves. There is some argument in this, I believe. It does not seem necessary to make the Japanese worship in exactly the same manner as Americans do, and perhaps it would be much better to allow them to continue in their usual manner. I feel quite sure it is a mistake to try to Occidentalize them. The main thing is to make them comfortable and to give them real worship. The Rev. Naruse is pastor here.

PASTOR NARUSE

He is 48 years old and a graduate from the Tsukidate Middle School, 1886. He taught in the Shiwashime Primary School some, then studied four years in the

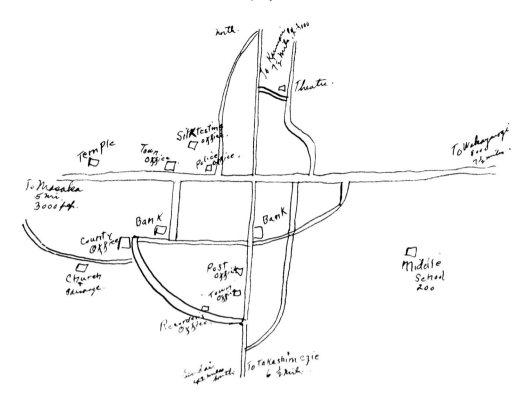

Map of Tsukidate, population 5,000 (by the author).

normal school at Sendai, where he graduated. For ten years after graduating from the normal school, he was principal in the middle schools at Iwagasaki, Wakayanagi and Sendai. Was baptized in 1908 by Matsukawa at Wakayanagi. In 1909 he entered the Bible school of Dr. Woodworth and Miss Penrod at Tokyo for a year, leaving his family at Tsukidate, they coming to Tokyo after the first year, for two and a half years, living in the small house at Kasumi cho. Naruse took another half year in the Bible school and two and a half years at the Aoyama theological school (M.E.) at Tokyo. He took the *bekkua* course, which is "Bible study" in the vernacular. While there, he acted as pastor at our church in Oji, a suburb of Tokyo. Following his graduation at Aoyama, he continued three years longer as pastor at Oji. He was ordained by the Japan Christian Conf. in 1909 and came to Tsukidate in 1911. Studied one year while living here, at the Sendai theol. school, Tohoku Gakuin (Reformed Presby.).

Naruse has a wife and seven children—boys are ages 3, 6, 17, 19, 23; girls are ages 9, 11.

The Tsukidate church was organized by Bro. McCord but was started by Bro. Jones and Woodworth earlier. The first convert was made in 1906 at midnight by Woodworth. His name was Shirotori Massaji ("white bird"). Later he lost faith and left the church, due largely to lack of shepherding.

There are now 13 resident members and two nonresident. Twelve boys from this place became Christians in January, but they scatter in schools. They became

A group of Japanese women manipulating a pile driver. The work is accompanied by singing; the leader carried the story with the group joining in as an intermittent chorus.

Christians in Sendai. There was one convert on the field last year and three baptized.
Since the church was started, there have been 44 converts. The present membership
embraces one doctor and his family, (pillars in the church), schoolteachers, pupils,
pastor and family.

The church raised Y94.47 last year. Paid on pastor's salary Y1 a month. Mission
paid on pastor's salary Y65.10 a month, including children's allowances. The town is
somewhat indifferent to the church, and Pastor Naruse feels the great hope is in the
children. They come to SS out of curiosity. The average attendance in SS is 70.
Preaching is held every Sunday evening, with an attendance of only seven or eight.
Prayer meeting is held on Wednesday evening, but the attendance is only three or
four.

Pastor Naruse preaches at Wakayanagi twice a month. The population at

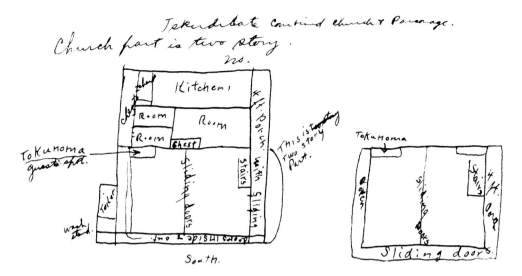

Diagram of the Tsukidak church (by the author).

Wakayanagi is 8,000, and there is no other preaching done here. There is, of course, no church building as yet. They meet in a room rented at Y1.20 a month, which is paid by the mission. The SS here averages 20. Only one church member, but there are some who are Presbyterians and Disciples who attend. This congregation pays 50 sen a month on Naruse's salary. The pastor says the people here are covetous and very much interested in trading. He has no plan to reach the older people but says the young people may be reached by the fact that they come through curiosity. Naruse feels that a Bible woman would be a help to his work.

As to our general work, he feels that a middle school would be desirable if it can be properly financed. He says the influence of the Woodworth-Penrod school lives strongly with him. Most of our preachers, it seems, got their start at this school. They lived in the dormitory that Dr. Woodworth had bought and were given practical Christian work in Tokyo. The school was stopped because preachers were turned out too fast and did not have as much education as the mission thought necessary. But when it was put into operation, it was done because of the shortage of preachers.

Naruse thinks the Tsukidate property is worth Y5,000. He feels that the late distinction made by the mission between *honkkua* men (theol. graduates) and *bekkua* men (men of lower education standing) is unfair, coming as it does after years of service on the part of some of the *bekkua* men. If it should be started from now on with new students, it would be all right as they would know in advance which group they would be in, depending upon the work they completed.

KANNARI, POP. 4,000

Information furnished by Kahei Nikaido, an old resident of Kannari, who attended the conference of Tsukidate.

Kitano is pastor. The population of Kannari proper is about 4,000. Sawabi is only a half mile from Kannari and has 5,000 with no preaching.

Our work began at Kannari in 1887 by Bro. Jones. There are about 20 Christians here, but no organization. They meet in Nikaido's house. Nikaido gave to the church sometime ago, 300 *tsubo* (¼ acre) of garden land, the income of which is used by the church. The land belongs to our mission. (The Shadan holds it, according to Japanese custom. The Shadan is composed of three missionaries, Woodworth, Fry and Garman, who hold all mission property since the government will not permit the title to be held in America.)

Nikaido also gave to the church Y2,200, which is not in the bank. His family is using the interest on Y600 of this, the church being entitled to interest on the balance. The church is anxious to have a building and has promised Y100 on the same. The mission board has already appropriated about Y1,400 for this, but as yet, no suitable land can be had. The garden land is not properly located for this purpose. This plot is worth about Y400 now, but land prices here are falling because of the fall in the price of rice and silk.

The average in the SS at this place is 40 to 50. The town is not on a railroad now, but a road is proposed that will practically connect by railroad all our mission stations.

Pastors Abe, Sakurai, Matsukawa, Ogata, Kitano, and Mrs. Watanabe arrived during the afternoon. We spent some time getting facts concerning the work here and looked over some of the maps of this section.

Later we had a fine Japanese supper. To my surprise and delight, they gave Dr. Woodworth and me some sugar and milk for our rice. It set the meal off in great shape. The Japanese are very fast eaters. Ogata ate four dishes of rice and all the other things while I was getting away with my first. They gave us some spoons to eat with too.

At seven o'clock, we held a prayer meeting, and at 7:30 the regular service began. There were about 40 present, a most interesting audience. Among them were three teachers and a number of middle school boys, a doctor's family and a number of others. I spoke first on "The Glorious Gospel." The Rev. Abe interpreted and did it beautifully. I had the closest attention throughout. The Rev. Kitano spoke next on the Japanese-California question. He said the newspaper articles were often written by men who misrepresented the facts, so that most people did not understand the problem at all. He concluded by saying that the only solution was to be found in Jesus Christ.

Announcement was made that I would speak to the ministers in the morning, then speak to the middle school at eleven o'clock. At 3:00 P.M., the town officials are to give me an official reception. Refreshments were then served, and we went upstairs to bed. Two large rooms were filled with ten mats, and ten men were soon lost in sleep.

Wednesday, September 22 ——— ◆ ——————————

At five o'clock we were awakened. There was to be a sunrise prayer meeting, and whether you intended to go or not, you were at least made to know that something was going on. I wanted to go. The Rev. Abe and I started off together, leaving Dr. Woodworth to his little bed. We climbed a large hill and passed a large Buddhist temple in a beautiful grove, commanding a view of the town. Here we found the little group of pastors who had preceded us in very earnest prayer in which we heartily joined. It was a most delightful service, made more helpful by the beauties of the rising sun in the east. Though I could not understand the words of the songs or prayers, yet I could not fail to catch the spirit of those present.

After the service, they took me over to the side of the hill, commanding a superb view of a beautiful valley with large mountain ranges on all sides, the rice fields, just turning a golden yellow, stretching out in little square patches completely filling the valley. We walked along through the trees to the large Buddhist temple located on this hill. The grove is full of large and stately trees, and like most temples I have seen, the spot upon which it stands is conducive to a spirit of worship of something.

There are numerous small buildings about this temple and of course a cemetery. Several small buildings stand before the temple proper. In one of these is a large iron bell, in another two images of Buddha. We mounted the temple steps, and just at the top hung two large disks of sheet iron facing each other much like cymbals. They were about 3 feet across and were hung a few feet from the ceiling some 15 feet overhead by means of large chains. Just before this gong arrangement was suspended an immense rope about 8 inches thick, made by plaiting together half a dozen inch-and-a-half ropes. It dropped past the center of and about a foot from the gong, and reached from the ceiling to the floor. The priest swings the rope in such a way as to strike the gong and call the people to worship.

Pastor Naruse tried to ring it but could barely produce a sound. It looked quite easy to do but was really difficult. I succeeded in producing a fairly good sound, but a few attempts were sufficient. Walking beyond the temple, we passed the priest's house and grounds. These were very much better kept than the temple grounds. As we descended the steps, we passed a very large old tree called the *sugi* (cedar). This particular tree is said to be 1,500 years old, and it looks it.

As we left the temple grounds, I noticed a row of very long boards much like American signboards except that they were not painted with signs, and the large boards proved to be made up of numerous small boards placed vertically side by side. Each board had Japanese writing all over it, and I learned that these were the names of the Buddhist followers who had made contributions to this temple. The boards also contained the amount contributed. Wonder what our American church members would say if their names and the amount of their yearly contribution to the church were thus posted? I also learned that the larger boards contained the names of those who gave the largest contributions and that the characters spelling the names and giving the amounts were very large and imposing, while those giving small amounts had their names and amounts in very small letters. All the boards showing the large contributors were at the head of the list, and so forth. I noticed another interesting thing about this contributors' list. In the midst of the large and small boards were left vacant spaces so that if any others wished to contribute, boards bearing their names might be set in. It was a rather unique affair, but perhaps a little too up-to-date, shall I say, or prominent in character for the American church.

The morning was spent in a long conference with the pastors of the northern field. I found it exceedingly difficult to conduct such a conference since it had to be done through an interpreter and they would talk too long about the different points that I could not keep in touch with it at all.

I suggested that we have printed a quarterly report blank for the pastors to fill out, something like the following:

> Name of pastor
> Church served
> SS service held during quarter
> Average attendance at SS
> Preaching services held
> Average attendance at preaching services
> Open-air service held
> Other special meetings
> Number of sermons preached
> Number of pastoral calls
> Number dealt with personally
> Number of inquirers
> Number of conversions
> Number baptized
> Number additions to the church
> Total SS offerings
> Total church offerings
> Total paid on pastor's salary by the church

They have been having semiannual meetings, but thought a quarterly meeting would be helpful if the expenses of hotel keep could be met by the mission. I reminded them that I was compelled to pay both hotel bills and traveling expenses to conferences when I was pastor. Their travel expense is now paid for their work to and from their appointments.

Matsukawa said meetings were formerly held quarterly but the expense upon the pastors was too great. Said they could not pay the hotel bills, even though the mission did pay travel expenses. All felt that such a meeting would be profitable and suggested that if the mission would pay half of the hotel bills, it could be done. Mr. Sakurai expressed appreciation that the mission board has done so much for the Japanese pastors but expressed the opinion that they could not live on their salaries. I suggested that I was gathering data from all denominations on the salary question and that I would present this to the board at Dayton and hoped they would pay an average salary, neither the highest nor the lowest. This seemed to be satisfactory.

At ten o'clock, we started to pay a visit to the mayor but found he was not in, so we went on to the Tsukidate Middle School where I was to speak at 11:00. The principal is Mr. Taira. We were a little early, so the physical director had the boys do some *jiujitsu* for us. They are being systematically trained to defend themselves, and they are apt pupils.

We then went to the office and had tea, after which the entire corps of teachers conducted us to the assembly room where the boys had assembled at the sound of the gong. At the voice of the director, in strict military precision, the 200 boys between 14 and 18 years of age stood and bowed to us as we took our seats. The principal introduced us, and I spoke for 30 minutes to as interested and interesting audience as I ever saw. Mr. Abe interpreted, and Dr. Woodworth followed with a few remarks. The principal thanked us for coming, the boys bowed, and we departed, bowing as we started.

We were again conducted to the office where tea and cake were set before us. As we were about to sit down, the physical director invited us out to see the boys play ball. I had used several ball illustrations, and they wanted to see me perform. The nine came out in their uniforms, and some tennis players invited me to play. They had great fun watching me, and I enjoyed it immensely. I then took a picture of the school. The baseball boys were not satisfied and wanted me to get out and play baseball, but I excused myself by saying I had not played for 15 years, which was very true. We had a good time, and the boys seemed especially well pleased.

After dinner, I took a picture of the pastors of the northern or Sendai field. Then we entered into another conference. I asked the pastors what line of enlarged work they thought we should attempt—schools, dormitories, kindergartens, evangelistic. Matsukawa says it is a defect in our church that we have no schools in Japan. He compares us to the Disciples, who started on the same basis as we did but are far ahead of us now because they started with schools. Sakurai says we must have a middle school for both boys and girls, but at present the first need is a theological school. I asked him if there were prospects for students. If a good school is established, good students will come, he thinks. Mr. Ogata thinks such a school should be at Sendai. Mr. Sakurai does not know where but thinks in some city.

Mr. Kitano prefers a middle school, but [if] we cannot have that, wants a dormitory near a college or university. He refers to the YMCA, which has a successful dormitory in Sendai near both the college and university. Mr. Naruse thinks the theological school must be first as we need more preachers. He thinks it would be located at Tokyo under ordinary circumstances, but for the Christian church, the North would be better, as these churches are better feeders to such a school. Mrs. Watanabe thinks dormitory should be first, and Sendai appeals to her. Mr. Sumita says the central part of our church is Tokyo. Feels Utsunomiya should be center instead of Tokyo. He feels that we should attempt to conduct girls' school there. He thinks we should build another dormitory there at the girls' school. Thinks we should change the center of our work to Utsunomiya. Mr. Abe says a boys' and girls' middle school would be welcome, but if not, we should try to take the girls' school off Mrs. Fry's hands if she so desires. A dormitory would be next in order, and prefers Sendai. He thinks we can send ministerial students to other theological schools.

I asked for estimates as to cost of boys' middle school to buy land and erect building and operate for a year. Matsukawa says Y100,000 would be necessary for buying land, putting up building, and furnishing equipment for a school of 300. (I learned later that the government prefers a school of 800.) Matsukawa says it would require two or three foreign teachers and 12 Japanese teachers. They all prefer that the principal be foreign and the assistant Japanese. The cost to run the school would be about Y15,000 for the 12 Japanese salaries. This number of teachers should gradually be increased to 20. The salary of the three foreign missionaries would be extra. They think the salaries of the Japanese teachers should be Y125 a month. The teachers in government school average about Y131, and in the Azabu Middle Schook Y90, but they say the teachers in the latter school have the privilege of supplementing their income by outside teaching.

I asked next if we had to decide between a boys' or girls' school, which it should be. Matsukawa says a boys' school, which should be located at Ishinomaki.

At 3:30, Mayor Ozitumi of Tsukidate, Dr. Oikawa, and some 40 citizens came to the parsonage to extend to me an official welcome from the town. This was considered a very important and august affair, and it really was. There were 50 or 60 men gathered, and they included practically all the town officials. The Rev. Naruse opened the meeting. The Rev. Kitano delivered the address of welcome for the pastors of the northern field. He said he had met Dr. Bishop and Dr. Morrill on their visits to Japan and had looked forward for the past year to meeting me and was glad I had come. He told of the efforts in this northern field and expressed their appreciation of the help of American friends. He said he hoped the American friends would continue to help. The mayor, Mr. Ozitumi, was then introduced. He is a banker and was formerly mayor of a neighboring town, Furikowa, and also formerly a member of the House of Peers, an office held only by large taxpayers. He is an elderly man of medium height and somewhat thin. He read his well-prepared speech. I secured it and am having it translated.

I responded to the mayor's speech in a message of 35 or 40 minutes, conveying the greetings of Dr. Bishop and Dr. Morrill to them, expressing my appreciation of their welcome, and telling them of my purpose in coming to Japan and what I hoped to do here. I spoke of the beauty of Japan and America, of which we are both proud, and then at their request I spoke of the California-Japanese problem. It is the most persistent request I have had. Everywhere I go, the citizens seem to know all about the trouble and want to know what America is going to do about it. I refused to state any solution except Christ. There is no other. Both America and Japan must become Christian. They listened most attentively.

After my speech, tea and cakes were served. As the guest of honor, I was shown to the seat of honor (on the floor by the *tokunoma*, or sacred place), and there were set before me a package of the finest of cakes (different from those the others received). The town photographer then took our pictures, and I had him take one with my camera. The doctor, Oikawa, was detained and came late, but he spoke with great feeling of my visit. He and his family of three girls and wife are all Christians and most splendid people. He said my visit had done much good, for which I am glad. After the picture was taken, the officials with many thanks and much bowing took their departure. It was considered a great day, and it certainly was for me.

Dr. Woodworth and I took a walk for a few minutes' rest.

I secured one of the advertising posters concerning our conference here and also had it translated.

The pastors of the northern field, in honor of my visit to this field and especially to the conference at Tsukidate, presented me with a very beautiful tea set, consisting of a teapot, six cups, and a hot-water pitcher. It is in a rich design. The Rev. Naruse kindly agreed to pack it and ship it parcel post to America.

Mr. Koneda, a Buddhist priest, attended the evening meeting. He is a nice-looking fellow and richly dressed. He tells me there are 70,000 Buddhist temples in Japan, 150,000 priests, and 50,000,000 followers. There are also 3,000,000 *tenknai* followers (nearly the same). He says people may be Shintoists, Buddhists, and Confucianists all at the same time. Several district Buddhist officers were with the priest. The latter is smooth-shorn, as is the district officer. The other gentleman has an Abrahamic black beard. Koneda was well loaded with drink, as I happened to discover by sitting next to him.

The Rev. Sumita conducted the evening service and did it very well. The Rev. Matsukawa spoke first, touching on the Japanese-Korean question and the California question. He said Japan should treat Korea better. The Koreans receive only one-third the wages Japanese do. His audience was half asleep before he finished his long address.

Dr. Woodworth followed with a short gospel message. It began to rain, and someone suggested we might continue the meeting until it stopped. I thought we were in for an all-night session. The priest, Koneda, took advantage of the opportunity and without invitation began to speak. He spoke at great length, but Dr. Woodworth was unable to understand him. I learned later that he said the Christians had once listened to a Buddhist priest, so he had come tonight to listen to the Christians. The balance of his speech I did not get.

Mr. Nikaido of Kannari spoke next, giving his testimony in a very helpful way. The Rev. Sumita, in an unassuming way, gave a most effective testimony. After tea, we broke up into little groups to talk. Dr. Oikawa was very concerned about our proposed trip to Iwagasaki on the morrow, saying there was an epidemic of typhoid fever there and all public meetings were forbidden. The doctor of the town had died from the disease. Retired at a late hour.

Thursday, September 23   ⸻   ◆   ⸻

Continued the conference with the pastors this morning. I asked what the cost of a dormitory would be. They replied Y40,000 for land and buildings, that it would cost not more than Y750 a year to keep up, and the boys would pay Y2 a month room rent, so that the plant would be practically self-supporting. Mr. Kitano thinks Japanese friends would contribute Y1,000.

I asked what they thought would be the cost of building and land and equipment for a theological school. It develops that all, including Dr. Woodworth, feel that a theological school is out of the question unless we have a boys' middle school. Mr. Abe says the theological school must be at Tokyo.

I suggested that this view upsets all their talk of yesterday urging a middle school at various places. If the theological school must be at Tokyo (and they seem to think that is the place), the middle school would have to be there too. And according to their present reasoning, there is no use to consider a theological school at all unless we have the middle school first. They feel that a simple Bible school for boys graduating from the middle school would be wrong because the boys at 18 would not have sufficient general knowledge to know how to study the Bible.

Dr. Woodworth thinks a special Bible school course after middle school graduation, followed by college and further theological training, is the proper way.

I asked about the evangelistic work, which had not been mentioned. Matsukawa
thinks a single woman missionary should be located in the North to work among
the women. A Bible woman should work with her. Mr. Kitano says personal work is
the most important, that it should be done by pastors, and that members should be
taught to do personal work.

Mr. Naruse says personal work also. Thinks two pastors should work together in
special meetings. Dr. Woodworth says if the students learn to do personal work in
the Bible school first, they can keep on at it during the years of further study. Mr.
Sakurai says churches should work together. He believes in pastor's going together to
hold special evangelistic meetings. Mrs. Watanabe says a single missionary is needed.
Mr. Sumita says he has not thought about it, as he has so recently entered the
work. Mr. Abe says a new family should be located in Ichinoseki for evangelistic
work.

I asked each one how many converts they have had since last September. Mr.
Naruse says two at Tsukidate, one of whom has left the town, and one at
Wakayanagi. Matsukawa says four at Ishinomaki. Sakurai, four at Wakuya, one of
whom has moved. Mrs. Watanabe says four at Iinogawa. Sumita says two at
Narugo. Kitano has had 30 at Sendai, among the students mostly. Abe has had
seven at Ichinoseki.

I asked for any further suggestions they might have. Mr. Abe is getting into the
schoolwork excellently at Ichinoseki. Matsukawa says he wants a single woman missionary at Ishinomaki. Says she could, among other things, do kindergarten work.

Dr. Woodworth suggested that I ask them how much Bible study they put in
each day, including sermon preparation, list of inquirers, visiting, prayer lists, etc.

Matsukawa says he studies at various times during the day but says he can't
afford to hire help, so has to help at home. I suggested that I was gone from home
all day and that my wife had to do all her own work. Matsukawa says he studies
about two hours a day. He has 15 on his prayer list.

Sumita says he reads six chapters of the Bible a day. Kitano says he spends two
hours on the Bible, two hours on magazines and papers, two hours on other books.
He visits in the afternoons. Has some kind of a meeting nearly every night. Has 20
inquirers on his list. Abe says he spends three hours in Bible study. He teaches
English in the middle school in the mornings of Monday, Tuesday and Thursday.
Prepares for prayer meeting and Sunday services on Wednesday and Saturday. Has
seven inquirers. Naruse does not study regularly, has five or six inquirers. Sakurai
has three inquirers, studies some, but not regularly. Mrs. Watanabe reads one
chapter a day, about a half hour, has three inquirers.

I delivered a closing message, thanking them for their suggestions and pledging
them that I would help all I could. I urged them to plan their day's work to be more
efficient, by personal Bible study, by Bible study for sermons and prayer meetings, a
deeper prayer life, a list of inquirers on their prayer list, and definite personal work.
I also urged the teaching of the great truths of the Bible such as faith, prayer,
stewardship, etc. After this conference, we closed the session with a session of
prayer. Mrs. Oikawa, the doctor's wife, presented me with a beautiful Japanese

picture. Mr. Naruse charged us the modest sum of a few yen each for the two full days and one extra meal.

Received a telegram from Kitano, who had gone ahead to Iwagasaki, that a meeting there was impossible, when a telephone message came from the same place saying a meeting would be held at the school. We loaded our bicycles and at 2:00 P.M. were on our way after expressing our very deep appreciation of the splendid meals and entertainment.

As we left the town, we came upon a group of Japanese building a bridge. They had constructed a wooden derrick and had rigged up a pile driver composed of a very heavy block of wood some six or eight feet long and more than a foot thick. This was governed by a rope passing through a pulley overhead, and to this rope were fastened a score of other long ropes with a man or woman at the end of each, all standing in a circle about the pile driver. One of the women was acting as director. She would sing a little tune, the other workers would respond, and at a certain place in the tune, they would give a strong pull together, sending the pile driver halfway to the top. She would sing again, and they would respond with another song and another pull, sending the block to the top. Then another song, and another response released the block, which fell hard upon the pile being driven. It was a most unusual sight.

We had to be ferried across the river, which was done by means of a boat and a wire cable. The charge was not great. We had a pleasant ride for seven miles to Sawabe just a half mile from Kannari. Left my typewriter here, and we went on to Iwagasaki, seven and a half miles farther. This part of the road was very rough, having been freshly graveled, but in just 1 hour and 25 minutes from the time we left Tsukidate, we pulled up at the schoolhouse at Iwagasaki.

Instead of finding a meeting of church people as I had been told, we found the children of the primary school. There are 750 of them. Our audience was about 250, as it was after school hours. As we rode through the town, two boys ran after us all the way to the school, their wooden shoes clattering like horses' hoves as they went along. I spoke about 25 minutes.

We then visited a Mr. Kato, an old man past 80 who has been a Christian for 43 years. He is very well fixed but has never given much to the Lord. He said he wanted to give something and offered a piece of land for a church. The piece he offered is a corner near the outskirts of the town, but not as far out as the three Buddhist temples. He said he would give 200 or 300 *tsubo*, whichever we desired. We said 300 would be acceptable and asked when the papers would be made out. He said he had given the land to his daughter and would have to consult her first. He likely intends to give her another piece in place of it, but she is not a Christian and is bitterly opposed to Christianity, so trouble may be brewing. I talked with him about God's goodness to him and told him I was glad he intended giving back to God some of what God had given him. He seemed pleased.

After praying with him in the middle of the road, we started for Kannari. It was late, and when we reached Sawabe, it was quite dark. Secured my typewriter and started for Kannari a half mile farther. When I called for my typewriter, I handed the boy 10 sen for keeping it, but he was not expecting anything and misunderstood my meaning, so he brought me a glass of *sake*. No thanks. Then he insisted on returning my money as he wanted nothing for caring for my machine. We made him keep it.

We bought a Japanese lantern here, as the police require bicycle riders to carry one at night. As we left the town, we saw a manpower train on a narrow-gauge track. They push the flatcars by hand, and when they reach a decline, the men jump on and ride. It is called a *jinsha*. This road is 17.5 miles long, extending from Iwagasaki to Ishikoshi station.

After a more or less hazardous ride, ringing our bells constantly to avoid speeding bicycles, slow-moving carts, and weary laborers returning from their day's labor in the dark, we reached Kannari, our destination for the night. The Japanese are supposed to turn out to the left, but I find they turn any way or no way as they feel inclined, so I have learned to dodge.

We stopped at the Kannari Hotel. Pastor Kitano, of the Sendai church, was with us as this is one of his outposts. The hotel keeper was delighted to see us, explaining that they had no guests that night. This hotel has the same barnlike appearance in front as most of them. Stepping inside on the bare ground, we left our shoes, stepped up on a well-polished floor, and greeted a half dozen or more girls and older folks, all bowing their heads to the floor.

The first room is the kitchen, the guest room being in the rear. They were cooking supper in the open fire built on the ground in a bare spot, with floor surrounding it. The smoke goes out a hole in the roof. There is also a sort of oven in this hotel, and they conserve fuel by feeding straw to the flames. Going to our room, we were given bathrobes, and being hot and dirty from our ride, we proceeded to take a bath.

The bath in this hotel is next to the kitchen, with walls on three sides but the fourth side open to the gaze of guests or servants going to and fro from the rooms of the hotel. I believe missionaries are likely to become callous and to yield too much to the customs of the natives in these things. I suggested to Dr. Woodworth that by a little patience they might be able to teach the natives the difference between heathen and Christian customs in these things. But the easier way is to take it for granted that it makes no difference to them and do as they do. He says they note the differences in the fact that missionaries do not use the maids for immoral purposes, as do the ordinary guests. When one learns that the average wage of these hotel girls is about Y1.50 a month plus board and that they are expected to cater to every wish of the guests, one can readily see how easy a prey they become to ill-meaning men.

The maid brings in the *hibachi* (fire nest) made of metal or clay in which are ashes surrounding a charcoal fire. The water kettle is set on, and tea, together with grapes, apples and little white cakes, is soon set before us. The fruit is most pleasing after the hot ride. There was great bustling in the kitchen preparing the evening meal for the guests. It was composed of rice, two kinds of raw fish, sliced pickles and some sort of unpalatable stew.

As we ate, our two Abrahamic friends, Nikaido and Ogata, whom we met at Tsukidate, came in. Nikaido lives here; Ogata lives at Shinden. Nikaido is the man who gave to the Kannari church a quarter acre of ground (garden land) and Y2,200 in money. Ogata is an old fellow who preaches some but is lazy and dirty. His

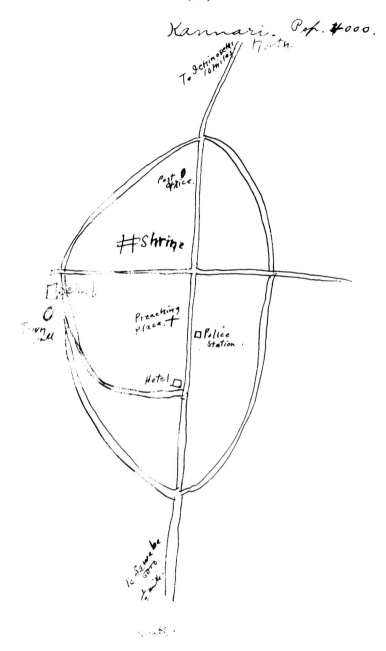

Kannari. Pop. 4000.

To Ichinoseki 10 miles   North.

Post Office.

#Shrine

Preaching place. †

Police Station.

Town

Hotel

To Sawabe Sapporo Yamki

Map of Kannari (by the author).

daughter makes the living as a midwife. He talks incessantly and says nothing. We will hear more of him later as we are to visit his town. I offered him my raw fish, and he accepted with sparkling eyes. Before he finished, he had cleaned up most of my supper and the raw parts left by Dr. Woodworth.

We have on hand some Y1,400 for a building here, and the men present said they believe they would secure a lot this year. There were present two other prominent men of the town.

Friday, September 24 ———— ◆ ————

It rained some in the night but was clear and warm today. I got a picture of the hotel with a Japanese horse and wagon passing. Worked my typewriter several hours while Dr. Woodworth and Kitano went calling. A number came in to watch the strange machine.

At noon, the mayor sent a copy of the invitation he had sent to 50 prominent citizens to give me a welcome at the church tonight. It read as follows:

> Dr. Minton has come to Japan to attend the World's Sunday School Convention, and today he has called on our village. So we wish to see him and to hear several things about religion, education, and politics, etc. and we will show him our hearts to welcome him. So please come at six o'clock to the Christian church. Admission 20 sen.
> Sugawara Kojiro,
> Mayor of Kannari

The admission price was to pay for the refreshments, as I afterward learned.

At one o'clock, we went to the primary school where I was scheduled to speak. Japanese-style, they had not had their dinner, and we drank tea and waited until nearly two o'clock. The children were then assembled, and I spoke. After the speech, we had more tea. Then Dr. Woodworth took a picture of the teachers with myself, Kitano and Nikaido in the center.

From here, we went to Nikaido's house, at his request. On the way, he showed me a stone erected to the memory of his wife, who suffered 26 years in bed. The citizens of this town, of which he was formerly mayor, put up the stone. He then showed me one erected to his daughter, who so faithfully nursed his wife. At his home, he presented me with a memorial read at the funeral of his daughter and also five teacups with an inscription to his daughter and her mother. It reads: *Nikaido Katsui* (daughter) *Nikaido Fumi* (Nikaido's mother) *Faithful daughter memorial.*

IWAGASAKI

Population 3,000. No church organization. No church building. Ten Christians. Services held in hotel. Kitano goes here once a month. This is the town where Mr. Kato is to give land for building. SS once a month, with attendance of 50. Church service attendance six or seven. Hotel room costs Y1, paid by mission. They pay nothing on the salary. Need a man to stay here. Members would help pay if there was a man on the field. Work began here 30 years ago by Bro. Jones.

KANNARI

Population 4,000. Began work here 30 years ago. Kitano comes here once a month. SS once a week. Mr. Okina teaches Bible class every Sunday. Attendance at church service monthly 20. No organization, no church building. Meet in rented house. Mission pays rent Y2.50. They pay nothing on salary. Pay 90 sen

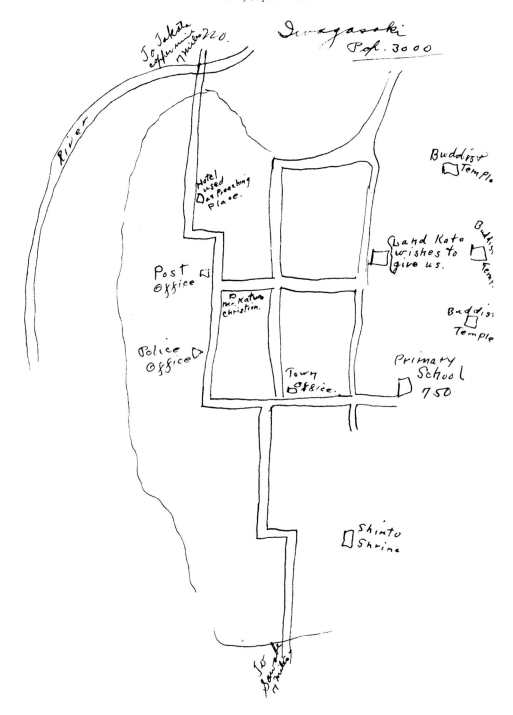

Map of Iwagasaki (by the author).

month to the home missionary fund of the Japan Conf. This is the church having a quarter acre of ground and Y2,200. They expect to buy a lot this fall and build. Forty-five miles north of Sendai. People are indifferent, as is true of practically all these towns.

HIROBUCHI

Kitano preaches here once a month. Shinden is about a half mile from here. Combined population of the two towns 2,000. Ogata, the old man who preaches some as a home missionary of the Japan Conference, lives here. No other preaching here. No SS, no church organization, no building. Services held in a member's house, taking turns. Fifteen Christians. No rent for houses used. They pay nothing on the salary.

TAKATA

Kitano visits Takata, 1,000 population. Also Hanabuchi, 2,000; Kowaguchi, 2,500; Hanayama, 2,000, a time or two each year.

Takata is seven miles north of Iwagasaki. Hanayama is five miles west of Takata, Hanabuchi seven miles south of Kawaguchi, Kawaguchi 12 miles south of Takata, Iwagasaki 50 miles north of Sendai.

At 7:45, a committee called at the hotel for us and conducted us to the preaching place where assembled the dignitaries of the town. The room, like most preaching places, was back from the street. It was nicely decorated with beautiful pictures of Bible scenes. One of the noticeable things is the fact that when these people become Christians, they make an effort to live cleaner, and the very expression of their faces is changed. It was raining as we started, and we were furnished Japanese umbrellas, while the young man led the way with a Japanese lantern. At the entrance, a large Japanese lantern was hung.

The room was full of people, and many stood outside. The mayor, Sugawara Kojiro, introduced to me with many bowings. He is a fat good-natured-looking fellow about 55 or 60.

Mr. Kitano announced the hymn, and the meeting (as I thought) began. He then spoke for 20 minutes about my coming to Japan and also touched on the California and Korea questions. He then announced another song, and I was informed the meeting was just then formally begun. The mayor read his speech, which Kitano interpreted for me.

I responded with a 30-minute speech, touching on the matters the mayor had mentioned and then launching into a description of the power of Satan and of Christ on a man's life, applying it throughout to these citizens. It was based on the story of the madman at Gadare, though I made no attempt to tell the story, as I felt it would be unnecessary and take too long to explain to them since I surmised they had never heard it. Dr. Woodworth interpreted. The interest was excellent, but he criticized the speech, saying they did not know the story. I responded that I left it out intentionally as unnecessary.

Nikaido arose and delivered a message following along what I had said. I noticed a number of men talking earnestly, and finally one of them who is a Christian held a long conference with Kitano. I realized that something was wrong but could not discover the difficulty. Kitano finally told me that they wanted me to speak longer and wanted him to interpret. They said they liked the way I spoke but Dr. Woodworth could not interpret it right. I was embarrassed to know what to do.

But when Nikaido finished, Dr. Woodworth jumped to his feet and spoke at considerable length, telling a joke or two. I think he sensed the situation. The man kept insisting that I should speak further. When Dr. Woodworth finished, Kitano spoke briefly and suggested that I extend my thanks for the reception. I did so, with Kitano interpreting, by a little joke on Dr. Woodworth. I smoothed over the difficulty and then, with the most attentive audience I have yet had, I poured in a heart-to-heart talk that I believe was prompted of God and that I hope will do much good. After my first speech, refreshments had been served, consisting of fancy cakes and tea. Three very fine boxes of cakes were set before Kitano, Dr. Woodworth, and me. On the fancy wrapper were the words *yayo onkashis*, meaning Japanese and Foreign honorable cakes. We departed at a late hour.

Saturday, September 25 ———— ◆ ————————————————

Paid our bill, amounting to Y3.70 each for from supper September 23 to after breakfast today, plus Y1 each tea money. The first night at supper, Dr. Woodworth asked for a spoon, and they brought us one each. They were so quaint, I wanted one, and the hotel proprietor gave it to me this morning. Packed our grips on our wheels and had a native take our picture, and were off for Wakayanagi seven and a half miles from Kannari. The road was terrible. It had rained in the night, and it was slippery. For a long way it led along the manpower railroad and was quite high. Some times we had nothing but a very narrow path to ride on, so that a turn of the wheel a little too much to the right would have sent us down a 30-foot embankment. Hundreds of men and women (mostly the latter) were carrying gravel up the steep bank for the road and railroad. They were utterly indifferent to our passing and persisted in slowing up right in our path. More than once, I struck their poles as I passed. Two women carry a pole over their shoulders, with a rope-net affair between them in which the gravel is carried. Arrived at Wakayanagi at 9:30 A.M.

The Rev. Naruse, the pastor, met us, having come over from Tsukidate. He showed us the picture of the Tsukidate town welcome. It was very good. We stopped at the home of Mr. Okuyama, an inquirer. He is a druggist and says he will have to quit serving sake to the doctors if he becomes a Christian.

WAKAYANAGI

Population 8,000. We have been working here 30 years. No church, no church organization. Meet in a home. Only one Christian. The Rev. Naruse comes here once or twice a month. SS attendance 15, church attendance three or four. Pay

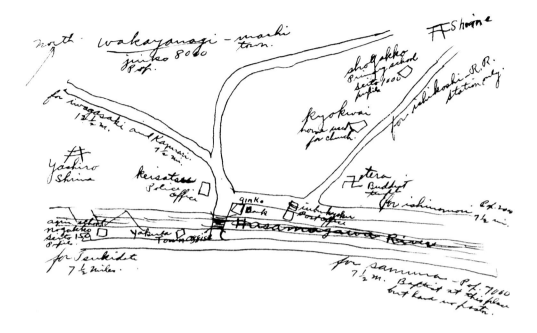

Map of Wakayanagi (by the author).

nothing on salary. We have been working here for years. The Disciples and Presbyterians used to work here but gave it up. There is one Disciple Christian, one
Presbyterian, and one of our faith in the town. They all attend our meetings. Pastor
Naruse does not speak English and gave me the map with names spelled in Japanese
with English letters. I reproduce it here with the English equivalents added.

MASAKA

Naruse goes here once a month. Population 1,200. Five miles west of Tsukidate.
Have been there but a short time. No church building. No organization. Meets in
hotel. No Christians. SS once a month, attendance 60 or 70. Preaching service attendance two or three. Failed to get a map.

We went from Wakayanagi to a Dosojin temple—a place of ancestral god worship. This particular temple is the place of worship of the sex organs. A goddess is
worshipped, and the offerings are images of the male organ of sex. There were scores
of images of the male organ of sex, of all sizes. It is thought that conception is more
certain if the act of coalition is performed here, and a mat before the goddess provides for this. It is also thought that worship of this goddess insures health and
crops. The offerings are of stone and wood.

The temple is located two and a half miles from Wakayanagi, and we rode our
wheels over the most difficult road yet. Dr. Woodworth said he felt sure that few if
any tourists to Japan had ever seen such a temple. The road was not much more
than a path and was slippery from the night's rain. One had to be extremely careful

to keep from slipping into the slimy mud of the rice fields on every side of the path. We climbed a steep ascent to the temple, set in a clump of trees. I took a picture. From here we rode our wheels back on the treacherous road with all our baggage aboard to the Ishikoshi station where we took the train for a 14-mile ride to Ichinoseki.

The Rev. Abe, the pastor, met us at the station with several of the boys of his church, who as usual carried our baggage. We were escorted to the Abe home, which is a parsonage next to the church. The ground upon which the church and parsonage is located comprises 500 *tsubo* near the center of town. There is a very fine large garden. This land was bought by us at a cost of Y3 a *tsubo* and is now worth Y12 a *tsubo*. The church and parsonage are in good condition.

Immediately upon arrival, we left our baggage and struck out to get pictures of the Reformed Presbyterian and the Greek churches, the only other religious organizations in the town. We found the Greek church too far to reach that afternoon but called on the native Reformed Presby. pastor at his home next door to the church. I secured a picture of the church, with the pastor and Dr. Woodworth standing before it. It was not a good location for a picture but may suffice to show that the building is not at all equal to our building, having the Japanese thatched roof, very dangerous for fire, and in many other respects inferior to ours. The pastor told me he has a membership of 26, with an average attendance of ten. Sunday school, 118. His salary all told is Y60, plus house and travel expense to outstations. The church pays Y3 of this amount. He is a graduate of the Tohoko Gakuin, Reformed Presby. theol. school at Sendai. He preaches at four other places. Holds only SS and only twice a month at the other four places. None of these places give him any support. They are located 7.5, 5, 5, and 4.5 miles, respectively, from Ichinoseki. Several of the boys were still with us, so we took them around, and Dr. Woodworth and I together treated them to apples and chocolate, which they seemed to appreciate.

THE REV. ABE

Returning to the Abe home, I secured the following information: The Rev. Kiyoshi Abe is 35 years old and has a wife and four children—a girl, 7; a girl, 4; a boy, 2½; and a baby girl, 2 weeks.

He became a Christian at 18 at Watanoha under a native Reformed Presby. pastor and was baptized by him at Ishinomaki. He graduated from the fishery school at Watanoha, then worked as a clerk in his father's store a year or two. Entered telegraph school at Sendai at 17. Stayed there eight months, then returned to Watanoha to enter the telegraph army, after returning from which he entered the Theological Bible School of Dr. Woodworth and Miss Penrod for three years. Graduated there and became pastor at Moka. Ordained at Moka 1912 where he served five years. Came from there to Ichinoseki.

ICHINOSEKI

Population 10,000; 55 miles north of Sendai. Has an indepenent Greek church in a suburb across the river. Reformed Presby. church with pastor in the field who visits four outstations. Church is weak at present.

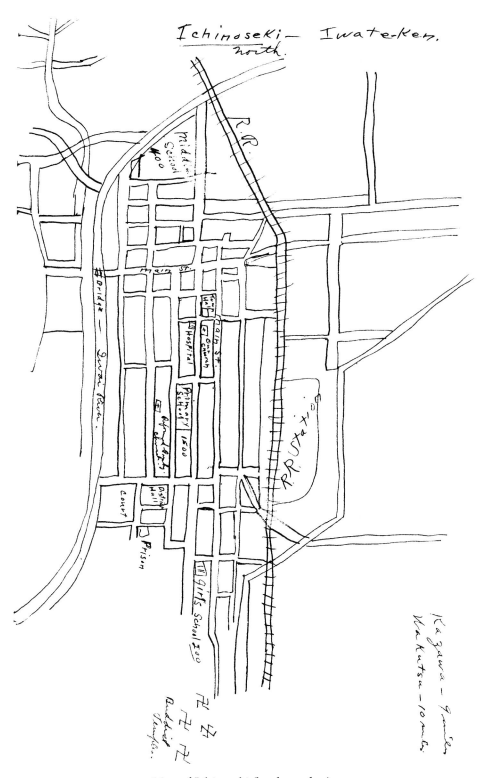

Map of Ichinoseki (by the author).

Christian church has a good building, a church organization with 23 resident members. Services every Sunday. Average attendance 15. SS every Sunday, 60. Prayer meeting attendance 7 or 8. Work started here 30 years ago. Parsonage next to church. Church pays Y3 a month on pastor's salary. The Rev. Abe teaches three days a week in the middle school. Town indifferent but no opposition.

The church members include such persons as a Mr. Abe, sec. to the RR station-master; three school teachers; middle school boys; bank clerk. There is one middle school with 400 pupils, one girls' school with 200 pupils, one primary school with 1,050 pupils, and four Buddhist temples. A farming community.

KAZAWA

Population 1,000. The Rev. Abe preaches here once a month. It is nine miles from Ichinoseki. There is no other preaching. Has SS of 50. No church organization. Holds meeting in rented farmer's house in the town. Rental is 30 sen a month. No Christians.

Worked my typewriter for a while before supper. Mrs. Abe served an elegant Japanese supper.

At 6:30, eight boys came together, and Dr. Woodworth taught them an English Christian song. I assisted in the singing. The boys took hold of it with vim. They are anxious for the English, but Dr. Woodworth sees to it that they are taught the sentiment of the song. He says that in the wintertime they sit on *tatami* (mats) around the *kotatsu* (a framework with a small charcoal fire underneath and a quilt stretched over the top) with their feet stretched beneath to keep warm. Here they sing the songs and learn the great truths of the Bible. From what experience I have already had, I can bear out the truth of Dr. Woodworth's statement that to sit thus for several hours at a time is excruciating in the extreme. I have done nothing else for the past week, and my knees are stiff and sore.

At 7:30, I spoke on "The New Birth" to about 30. Abe interpreted. This was followed with another reception. S. Abe, the RR man, and Mr. Akasuka ("red deer") are the most prominent members of the church. While pastor Abe is in America, these two men will likely look after the church. They do some preaching now. Mr. Abe gave a very fine welcome address. Pastor Abe believes the right way to do the work is to train a small group instead of handling a large number. He seems to be doing fair work. Three of the most promising boys are Tokawo Takahashi, Tatsuo Suzuki and Makoto Suzuki. Pastor Abe just tells me that he desires to have Sumita take his work while he is away. The two brethren mentioned above feel that they can do it.

Pastor Abe feels that a missionary family should be located at Ichinoseki. He says it is too much for one missionary to attempt this work from Sendai. At the welcome meeting, S. Abe gave the welcome address, to which I responded.

Before the evening service, I had Dr. Woodworth ask how many were Christians, explaining that I wanted to make an appeal. Only two or three boys responded to his question. Pastor Abe said there were about half who were not Christians. I made a strong appeal, and then at the reception Dr. Woodworth thought the interest was such that some of the boys would decide. He had one of the Christian boys do personal work, with the results that he secured ten names to the simple statement "I decide to accept Jesus Christ as my Savior and to give my life to Him." He showed the list to Pastor Abe and asked him if these were all new decisions. He said no, but that most of these had not been baptized. It then developed that of the 26 present, all had already decided for Christ.

This goes to show the various shades of meaning Orientals attach to the word *Christian*. One can explain all about a thing and get what seems to be a very plausible and satisfactory answer, only to find a little later that they didn't mean that at all. It takes Oriental minds a long, long time to understand some things, while in other things they are quick to learn. You ask them a question, and they take a long time to discuss it together before they will give an answer. Their slow, monotonous way of doing things is very trying. And the time they waste in perfunctory bowing and tea drinking is a shame. They seem to have all the time necessary for these things but not for definite Christian work. They do not know the very simplest fundamentals of the Christian life, as I see it, though some have been Christians for years.

It looks to me as though the pastors were not training their people in the things I mentioned in my closing message to the pastors of this field. And the reason they do not is that they have not learned them themselves. For example, Abe's church pays Y3 a month on his salary. His salary is Y59 a month plus house and garden, a tithe of which is at least Y5. If all his members should do as well, the income of the church would be considerable. The three teachers receive an average of not less than Y100 a month, and the RR man not less than Y100.

Sunday, September 26 ◆

Left for Ishinomaki at 9:17. As we boarded the train, I noticed three little girls sitting across the aisle in the third-class coach. They were singing, and as I listened, I noticed that song after song was a Christian song with Japanese words. One of the favorites was "Jesus Loves Me." And they sang them well. Dr. Woodworth finally asked them where they were from and found that they were from Iinogowa where Mrs. Watanabe works and they had learned these songs of her. It was a real living testimony to the power of the gospel and made me proud of the fact that we have a mission in Japan.

We had left our wheels at Ishigoshi where we boarded the train yesterday and had left instructions to have them put on the train as we came through. This was done without any difficulty, and at 1:20 we pulled into the Ishinomaki station. Pastor Matsukawa, Mayor Takayama and Mr. Takahashi, who is greatly interested in education, were there to welcome us. We were informed that the greeting was set for 3:30 and that they desired to show us the mountain containing the city park, with a view of the ocean.

We walked up a high hill and on the way passed the home in which Dr. Jones lived while a missionary to Japan. I took a picture. The former home of Miss True is

Tetsudobasha (railway horsecar) in northern Japan. W.P. Minton is the passenger leaning out of the car.

next door to this. A very beautiful place. A long walk finally brought us to the park overlooking the Pacific Ocean. It was my first view of the ocean since I left the boat at Yokohama, and it filled my breast with conflicting emotions. I thought of the long ride home and the long weeks before that ride begins and of the loved ones over there, and I wondered what they were doing. When I arrived at Matsukawa's a little later, a letter from my wife was handed me, having been forwarded from Tokyo. Nothing has ever done me quite so much good.

As I stood on the mountainside, we could look down upon the islands of famous Matsushima, one of the three most celebrated beauty spots of Japan. Looking farther to the left across the bay, there was Kinkozan, the sacred island, where up to a few years ago no woman was allowed to set her foot. That has been changed, however, and women are now free to ascend the heights. Here are settled a large number of sacred deer and monkeys and other animals.

We were taken into a very fine teahouse and served tea, grapes and apples of the very finest variety.

The population of Ishinomaki is 20,000. The mayor is interested in a middle school here as there is at present none in the town. He says the *ken* will not build one because they have built so many in nearby towns. There are four primary schools now, and another is already contemplated. The government is careful to increase the primary schools in order to make it possible for all Japanese children to learn to read and write, but with an increase of 700,000 in her population every year (soon it will be 1,000,000), she is utterly incapable to handle the middle school problem. There is also a commercial school started, though as yet they have no building. This school already has 150 pupils and seven teachers. They estimate the cost

Home of the Rev. D.F. Jones, in Ishinomaki where the Christian Church Mission work began in 1887.

of a building for the commercial school to accommodate 200 pupils to be Y50,000. They estimate a building and equipment of a middle school for 400 boys to be Y70,000. It would take 500 *tsubo* of land at an additional cost of Y25,000. The mayor says if the mission would build the school, the town would help by securing the land for us at Y1,000, thus affording a saving of Y24,000. The contemplated land was formerly a prison site and hence *ken* land. It now belongs to the city. It is out somewhat but not too far for a school, as many are built that way.

There are in the four primary schools, 5,000 pupils. There is a girls' school of 200 pupils with eight teachers. A boys' school of 400 would require 20 teachers.

The principal of the commercial school gets Y105 a month.

I asked the mayor if the giving of the land by the *ken* or the town would obligate the mission in any way to conduct the school along any lines they might desire. He said he thought no strings would be tied to it. Other land in a convenient place would cost Y10 to Y20 a *tsubo* near the outskirts of the city.

The nearest middle school to Ishinomaki now is 20 miles. Boys from here usually go to Sendai, 43 miles SW. They live in dormitories and boardinghouses.

Three counties here have no schools and would send their boys to Ishinomaki. The population of the three counties is 140,000. The value of the sea products for this *ken* (Miyami) is Y15,000,000 a year. This is the principal business. The site of this park was the home of a famous lord 300 years ago.

At 3:30 we were escorted to the city hall. I was told we were to have a meeting at the church with a few present. Imagine my surprise when I stepped into a room full of 250 of the most prominent citizens of the city. They wanted to know about the California question. The mayor introduced Pastor Matsukawa, who spoke

The city of Ishinomaki by the Sea where the Kitakami River flows into the Pacific. The Christian Church began its mission work here in 1887.

of the twofold purpose of my trip and introduced me to speak. It was the most diffi-cult situation I have yet faced.

With fear and trembling but with trust in God to guide me, I faced that au-dience and for 50 minutes told the gospel story the best I could. I said my purpose in coming was first of all to seek to understand the needs of Japan so that I could urge American Christians to help her more; second, that I was to attend the World SS Convention at Tokyo. I spoke of the Christian businessmen who were to come, of the fact that Count Okuma had invited it and the emperor had given Y50,000 toward it, that they must have considered it worthwhile to do so, that the SS stood for the teaching of the Bible, that the Bible taught about God, about sin, about for-giveness through Christ who died to save men, that when men came to God through Christ, He gave them new hearts, new aims, new love for God and for each other.

I said the California question could not be solved by political methods; it could not be solved by commercial methods; nor could it be solved by social methods; that we were not prepared to face the question until both America and Japan became Christians. I said I regretted that there were so many both in America and Japan who did not know God and I hoped that the day would soon come when both nations would know God, that then, and not until then, could they solve their problems on the basis of Christianity, and that there was absolutely no other sure way of solving them.

Following my message, which received rapt attention, we were escorted to the mayor's office for tea, but Mr. Takahashi, the educator, remained and spoke to the men. I learned afterward that he took exception to my speech and said that for the last six years America had been trying to bleed every nation and that this was

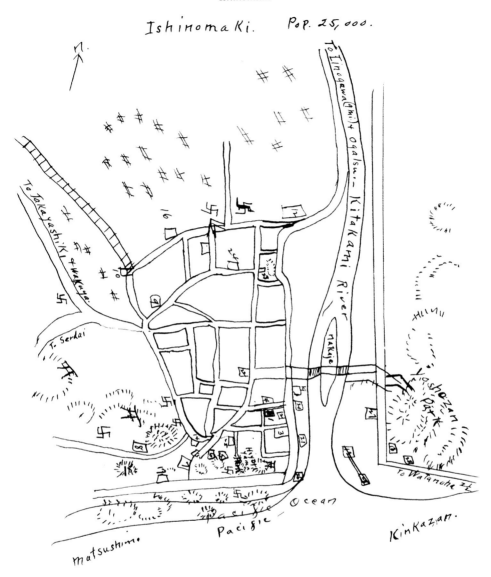

1. Christian church
2. Post office
3. Hospital
4. Tax office
5. Commerce School
6. Geinyakusho
7. Primary school
8. Girls' school
9. Court of Justice
10. Station
11. Nihon Kurisuto Kyukai
12. Primary school
13. Primary school
14. Public office

15. Library
16. Dento Kaisha
17. Primary school
18. Meteorological station
19. Police office
20. Shimbun Sho
21, 22, 23. Banks
24. Reformed Church
25. Forestry office
26, 27. Dept. of Home Affairs Eng. Work
28. Greek church
    Buddist temple
    Shinto shrine
    Rice field

Map of Ishinomaki (by the author).

not the time to talk Christianity to Japan. He ignored altogether my statement that America was not Christian and that both America and Japan must become Christian before they can settle their problems. He refused to come in for tea but dismissed the crowd and went home, seemingly in a great huff.

At any rate, the officials extended me a formal invitation to a dinner in my honor on Tuesday night, which we decided to accept.

Came to Pastor Matsukawa's home for supper, where the good news from my wife awaited me. Had a fine supper.

PASTOR MATSUKAWA

He is 50 years old, has a wife and four children: girl, 14; boy, 11; girl, 6; boy, 1 month. Became a Christian through Bro. Jones in 1885. Mr. Toshio Ota of this place was the first convert of our mission in Japan and Pastor Matsukawa the second. Both became preachers, Mr. Ota having died some 13 years ago.

Pastor Matsukawa secured his education under The Revs. Jones and Rhodes, under the former for two years and the latter for three more. He was ordained in 1897. At Wakayanagi he preached five years; at Tsukidate, seven years; at Wakayanagi again, four years; at Ichinoseki, six years; at Ishinomaki, four years, where he continues his work.

ISHINOMAKI

Church building and parsonage on 60 *tsubo* of land. There is a church organization with 30 members. We have worked here since 1885. Ishinomaki is financially prosperous but morally rotten. The church is in a prosperous section near the wharf and therefore in the worst section possible morally. Ishinomaki lies at the mouth of the Kitakami River, at the Pacific Ocean. Among the members is one public official, one electrician, merchants and farmers. They have service twice a Sunday. The average attendance in the morning is small. In the evening the attendance is about 15. Prayer meeting attendance 4; SS attendance is 40. The church pays Y1 on the salary.

The parsonage is two-story. The land when originally purchased cost Y200, the church Y250, and the parsonage Y70. The land is now worth about Y20 a *tsubo*, or Y1,200. The church building is now worth about Y2,000, and the parsonage Y1,000.

The Presbyterian church here has a membership of 40, with a resident pastor. His salary, including children's allowance, is Y60.

The Greek church is at present in bad condition, as are most Greek churches due to the Russian situation. This Greek church is on the island that is part of the city and is independent.

TAKAYASHIKI

Pastor Matsukawa goes here once a week. Population 1,500. Two miles north of Ishinomaki. No other preaching. No building, no organization. Four Christians. SS attendance 60. Meets in farmer's house. Rent 80 sen a month.

Pastor Matsukawa also goes to Ogatsu once a month. It is 20 miles east of

Ishinomaki. Population 1,500. He holds children's meeting only, with an attendance of 50. Meets in hotel; two or three Christians.

Maps of Ishinomaki, Takayashiki and Ogatsu are to be furnished me by Pastor Matsukawa next month.

WATANOHA

Pastor Matsukawa holds service here once a month. It is 2.5 miles south of Ishinomaki. Services are held in the home of one of the members. The member is a Japanese clogmaker (Japanese shoe). He is quite prosperous and says he has been more so since he became a Christian. He gives more generously than anyone else. Twice a year he gives Matsukawa a present of shoes and clothing. Attendance at services here averages ten. There is no room for SS. There are no other Christians but this husband and wife (Mr. and Mrs. Kozo Abe). There is a Presbyterian service here once a month with about ten Christians.

Matsukawa also goes to Iinogowa to conduct Bible study once a month. Attendance six women. Seven and a half miles NE from Ishinomaki. Mrs. Watanabe, our Bible woman, is here.

At the Sunday evening service at Ishinomaki, there are about 50 present. I spoke on "The Seeking Saviour." Mr. Matsukawa is supported by the Huntington church. His daughter, Ohidi, is also supported $50 a year by the Huntington church. She is head girl in the second year of the Baptist Bible School in Sendai. She expects to do Christian work.

They gave me her picture to take to the Huntington church. Also gave me the picture of Toshio Ota, the first convert of our mission in Japan.

Monday, September 27 ——————— ◆ ———————

I took a picture of the Matsukawa family, but the little girl refused to come into the picture. Mr. Uwano, a friend of the church and city official but no Christian, was present and stood with the group. Just as I was about to snap the picture, an old fellow and a couple of girls stepped in and refused to budge, so I snapped them all.

Took some films to the photographer and packed light baggage for a day-and-night trip on our wheels. As we rode out of town, I snapped two types of beasts of burden. One was a horse carrying a load of hay on its back. The other was a man and a horse-powered vehicle with a colt running along beside. At first, the two men thought I wanted just the colt, and the man riding jumped off and stood the colt out by itself. I explained I wanted him on the horse, and he got on. Then the man drawing the cart thought I didn't want him and proceeded to unhitch himself and back away. I finally got him hitched up and took the picture, with Dr. Woodworth rubbing the colt's nose to keep him quiet. Next took a rice field with the rice being cut and hung to dry. The yield is 50 bushels to the acre.

Rode seven and a half miles to Hirobuchi and a mile farther to Shinden.

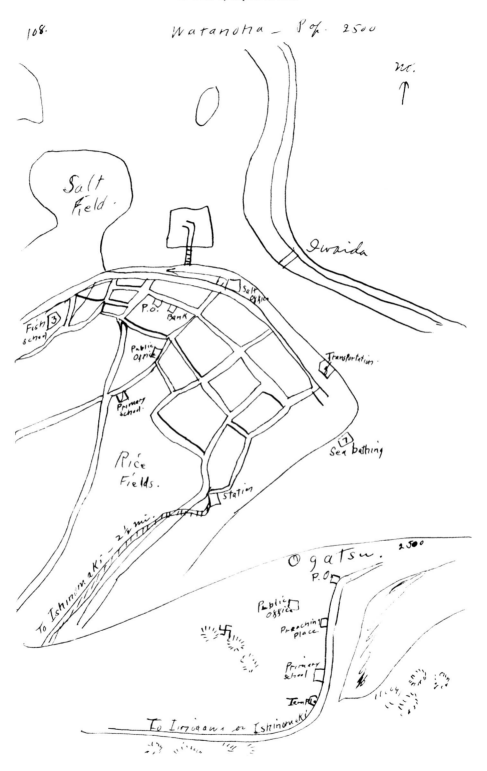

Map of Watanoha (by the author).

Road scene with a man riding a horse and pulling a cart. Another man behind him is guiding the cart. Dr. Woodworth is standing by the pony.

Met the home mission worker of our Japan mission here. His name is Kyozo Ogata. He lives in a miserable hovel and is 70 years old. He has been a Christian 27 years, being converted by the Rev. Nakajima, pastor of the present Baptist Tabernacle at Tokyo. Came to this field through McCord's influence and was baptized by him about 12 years ago. Picked up most of his training himself. He goes to Tokyo every year to brush up. He goes to the Holiness Bible School and whatever theological school entertains him best and listens for all he is worth. Stays about a month. The Japanese mission pays him 8 yen a month, and he secures the balance of his living off his daughter, who is a midwife.

One daughter is the wife of Imaide, the Bible teacher at Kannari. Ogata belongs at Ishinomaki. Another daughter lives in Tokyo and is married. Has become a Salvation Army believer.

He talks whenever he can get an audience at Hirobuchi, pop. 2,000, seven and a half miles north of Ishinomaki; Shinden, pop. 1,500, half mile west from Hirobuchi; Oshio, pop. 1,500, adjoining Shinden on the SW: Kitarura, suburb of Shinden on the east; Fui, another village of 2,000, two miles east of Shinden; Akainuno, pop. 3,000, one mile south of Shinden; Takaki, pop. 6,000, six and a half miles SW of Shinden; Maeyaji, pop. 5,000, six miles north of Shinden; Nago, pop. 4,000, five miles west of Shinden; Oyaji, pop. 4,500, six miles east of Shinden. He goes to these places as the spirit moves.

There are two Christians at Oyaji, one at Nago, three at Takaki, three at Okaimura, two at Oshio, three at Kitamura, two at Fui, 11 at Hirobuchi and Shinden together, and one at Maeyaji.

No other preaching in any of these places. They give him nothing. Meets in the homes. The people are too busy for SS. Mostly farmers.

Another method of transporting loads. These ponies usually snapped viciously if one got too near to them.

After taking Ogata's picture, we went on three miles east to the fine country home of Mr. Yamoto, a member of Parliament. He was baptized by Kitano. This is the finest Japanese home I have ever seen. It is approached by beautiful hedges on either side of a spacious entrance. A large building stands at the entrance, with the gates in the center. This building is a sort of a storehouse and servants' quarters. There are many smaller houses about, but the main dwelling is a large building, old, but very well built. The rooms are very large and numerous. The woodwork is of the very finest.

A large square *hibachi* stands in the center of the living room. The mats and *zabatons* (mats for sitting) are of the finest quality. The ornaments and woodwork are of different kinds of material in each room. A magnificent garden fronts the house in which one sees not only all kinds of plants, but trees, a miniature river and mounds of beautiful green. The Japanese have a gift at fixing up the smallest bits of space as a miniature landscape. In the sitting room there is a small Shinto shrine. The family is Christian, but the grandmother still worships the old ancestors. Before the image were cake, cookies and other delicacies—offerings to the ancestor.

Tea, Japanese pears and cookies were set before us in beautiful lacquer trays. I secured a picture of this fine home with Mrs. Yamoto, the grandmother, and Dr. Woodworth standing before it. It was housecleaning day, and the mats and bedding were out in the sunshine. The contrast between this home and Ogata's in Shinden was most vivid. His is the dirtiest and most unsightly, while this is the prettiest I have seen. A number of men working on Mr. Yamoto's farm. They receive a regular wage of 60 sen a day and board. During the rice harvest, they receive 80 sen and board. The women (many of whom work in the rice fields) receive 50 sen and board.

Home of Mr. Yamoto, Christian member of House of Peers.

From Mr. Yamoto's we rode 13 miles to Wayuka where I wanted to retake some pictures as the former were taken on a dark day. Arrived at 12:30. We had brought along some cookies, called *monaka*, a famous product of Ishinomaki. Mrs. Sakurai added tea, persimmons, grapes and sweet potatoes, so we made out in good shape.

Dr. Woodworth slept until two o'clock when we planned to leave by wheel for Iinogawa, but at two o'clock Mrs. Sakurai brought in a big dinner consisting of the special Japanese dish made of scrambled egg and spaghetti. There was also a regular American fried egg, rice and onions. It was extremely difficult to get away with even a reasonable part of this splendid dinner, but it was necessary to do so under the circumstances.

Dr. Woodworth announced that we would change our plans and take the train partway, which we did, to Kanamata, 12 miles. From here we rode three miles to Iinogawa. This was a most beautiful ride along the river, which is one of the large rivers in Japan. Small boats of all sorts ply up and down this river. There is some passenger traffic for short distances. We had to ferry across the river, and I took a picture of the ferryboat—a long scow with the ancient Japanese oarsman at the rear and another man with a smaller oar at the prow. The water was very rough, and as they came across, it looked as though the heavy load they carried (including three heavy carts) would capsize the craft. We paid 7 sen each for the ride, then mounted our wheels and rode along the mountainside with the river, the valley and another mountain range extending along the other. With the white sails of the fishing craft extended to full capacity standing out against the dark green of the nearby range, we feasted our eyes on another of Japan's numberless enchanting scenes. We reached Iinogawa at about 4:45, and I attempted to secure a picture of Mrs. Watanabe in front of her preaching place. The rooms are off the street back of the barber shop.

She lives there and holds service regularly, with children and women mostly. Her report follows:

MRS. WATANABE

Mrs. Toki Watanabe – age 50. Converted at 11 years of age at a woman's meeting in Tokyo. Has been connected with us 36 years. Husband was a pastor of our church 22 years. He died 14 years ago, and she has been a Bible woman ever since. Studied with a Miss West, a Presby. in Tokyo, six years. Worked at Ishinomaki first, then Ichinoseki, Akabani, Iinogawa.

IINOGAWA

Population 4,600, 42 miles NE of Ishinomaki. No church organization. No building. Rented preaching place Y6 a month. SS and prayer meeting weekly. Sunday School attendance 53. There are 20 Christians here. Prayer meeting attendance weekly, three.

At Mrs. Watanabe's we met Mr. Kato, who though not a Christian has taken an interest in the church to such an extent as to see that it is properly registered in the county, a very difficult procedure, it seems. A young man had made a large number of flags, which were arranged around the room. There were several young people present. I was feeling quite bad with an upset stomach, so we soon went to the hotel and rested for an hour. Took a bath and lay down until seven when a boy came breathlessly in and asked us to come to the church. Here we found Mrs. Watanabe in the throes of convulsions caused by overwork and anxiety in regard to the meeting. We had to leave her and go on to the hall alone.

Upon our arrival at five o'clock, I had been informed that I would have an audience that night of from 600 to 700. Dr. Woodworth had told me yesterday that I would have none but children, though today he admitted he was not quite sure. I objected to the haphazard way of arranging meetings. In nearly every place I have been, I have been misinformed as to the type of meeting and also as to the type of people present. At the meeting tonight, we found instead of our audience of 600 a handful of 20 sleepy men, to which was added later five or six girls. Mr. Kato explained that next door on one side was a moving-picture show and on the other a magic-lantern lecture.

I decided to give the same address I had given so successfully at Ishinomaki, but Dr. Woodworth began to interject a number of things in his interpretation, which, when I hesitated, he said were fuller explanations. I remembered that those explanations had not been necessary the day before when I held my audience for 50 minutes. I labored under the real difficulty of feeling that my message was not being accurately interpreted and failed to deliver it as it should have been. Dr. Woodworth went on speaking after I had closed. I know now why the foreign mission secretary of the Reformed church on a recent visit to Japan refused to speak, saying he had a horror of interpreters.

We went to the magic-lantern lecture afterward and to my surprise found the

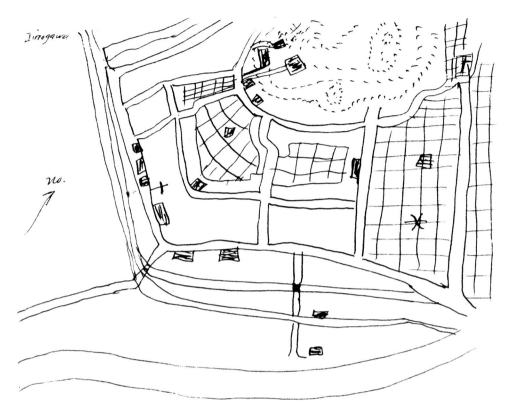

Map of Iinogawa (by the author).

lecturer to be Mr. Takahashi, of educational prestige in Ishinomaki, who had met us there Sunday and had taken the floor after my speech to register some objections to it. The room was dark, and he did not know we were present. He was showing pictures of the world with its various countries. He showed the empire of Japan, explaining that she had increased her possessions through Manchuria, Formosa and Korea. He said Japan was little but mighty. She had conquered the giant Russia, and if the giant America were not careful, she might look for trouble too. It was an out-and-out military speech, and Mr. Takahashi is a typical military propagandist. He has an imposing personality and is a commanding speaker. He next showed a number of pictures of war scenes and Japanese soldiers, and stirred his audience to fighting fervor. We did not stay until the close, but I wondered what he would have thought had he known we were present. We will likely meet him at the dinner at Ishinomaki tomorrow. Retired, expecting to ride back to Ishinomaki before breakfast.

Tuesday, September 28 ———— ◆ ————

At 5:30, we were ready to start on the nine miles back to Ishinomaki. Our hotel bill was 2 yen each for supper and night's lodging. This is considered very high. We had a delightful morning ride. At the ferry, we were charged only five sen each, the old man explaining that he charged seven sen last night because the river was rough.

Arrived at Ishinomaki in just an hour from our starting time. Cleaned up and had breakfast, after which I got a haircut and egg shampoo. The charge all told was 50 sen (25¢). I gave the barber 60 sen (30¢). He did a good job too. We then took our wheels and made a four-mile ride into the country to see the mother of our first convert and first preacher, Toshio Ota. We found she was in Sendai, so I'll get her picture there. Came back and found we did not have time to accept an invitation at the girls' school.

At the Rev. Matsukawa's, we met Keisuke Baba of a nearby town. He is a farmer but wants to be an evangelist. Dr. Woodworth told me yesterday we would not have a meeting at Watanoha, but today he informs me that I am to preach there at 2:30. Climbed the hill and took a bird's-eye view of Ishinomaki, and at 1:45 started on our wheels for Watanoha, three miles away.

We held the meeting at the home of Kozo Abe, a *geta* maker (shoemaker) who became a Christian under Bro. McCord 17 years ago. His wife became a Christian very recently under Dr. Woodworth. Mr. Abe says his business is much better since he became a Christian. A little group of children gathered as I attempted to get a picture of the shoe shop, in the rear of which the services are held. Dr. Woodworth sang a little song, and as they gathered around him, I snapped the crowd and had a picture of a typical street meeting. We went into Mr. Abe's home and were served delicious watermelon and tea and wafers. About a dozen gathered together for the meeting. The Japanese have oceans of time. They will stop their work anytime and for most anything. I had to go to the second barber shop this morning before I secured a haircut because one barber didn't want to open his shop. The other fellow had to be coaxed, though there is no legal holiday.

After the meeting at Watanoha, we rode back to Ishinomaki in time for the dinner with the town officials at five o'clock.

Secured my pictures that I had left to have developed and was stunned to find the bill Y5.00. There were only three rolls of six each and 16 prints, so the bill was outrageous, but we had not bargained beforehand and were stuck for the bill. I vowed then I would bargain beforehand after this.

I was feeling quite bad and getting worse, the result of eating some boiled cabbage. The mayor and another city official called, and we had to go over with them the prospects of a boys' middle school they want us to start there. I have already compiled some figures as to cost of land and buildings, etc. I secured today the figures concerning the present girls' school at Ishinomaki. The annual budget for running expenses of this school of 200 girls is Y15,000. The average of the teachers' salaries is Y50 a month. The principal, who is a man, receives Y90. The estimated value of the plant, including land, building and equipment, is Y38,000. There are no dormitories. Dormitories will cost Y90,000 additional.

The Y105,000 estimated for boys' Sunday school would not include dormitories but does include gymnasium.

We discussed the school question at some length and finally went to the best hotel in town for the dinner. Here we met by three other officials: I. Hoshi, princ. of primary school; G. Indo, another primary princ.; and V. Okayaki. We were escorted to a very fine room upstairs and supper served.

I was so very sick that I could not bear the sight of supper of any kind, and especially a Japanese supper. When you know that the average seasoned missionary does not attempt more than four days at one time on Japanese food and we had been out twice that long, and my first experience, you will not wonder that I was sick, though I had been feeling excellent until I ate the boiled cabbage. At any rate, the meal was served in all its oriental style, and as Dr. Woodworth said afterward, "It was the most unpalatable stuff I have seen in many a day." I managed to eat a few pieces of sea ear and a little rice, but beyond that I could not eat.

My comforting thought was that I could eat very slowly and these men would eat rapidly, as all Orientals do, and the ordeal would soon be over. But to my dismay, they seemed to realize that the courteous thing to do was to eat slowly, and they took great pains to do so. The pains were much more mine than theirs, though, I am sure.

Following the meal there were long discussions on various subjects. They were anxious to know about our school systems, our machinery, and many other subjects, which I enjoyed telling about in spite of my terrible sickness. I felt sometimes that I could simply not stay until we were through. Finally apples were brought and then good black coffee, American-style. This was a relief. The meeting finally adjourned, and we started home, our hosts following us and every little while stopping for the parting words. I thought we would never reach home. And when we did, I went right to my mat on the floor upstairs. I put in a sleepless night with the worst case of old-fashioned *colorea morbus* I have ever had.

Wednesday, September 29 ——————— ◆ ————————————

I was unable to get up in the morning, and we had to call off our trip to Kinkozan and Takayama lake. It proved a good thing that we did as it set in to rain in the afternoon and lasted all night. We decided to attempt the noon train for Sendai. I shall never forget the solicitation of the Japanese household of Matsukawa. They were so anxious to help and did everything they could for me. I seemed to get a little better, but very little.

Yet I thought I could risk the three-hour trip as Dr. Woodworth said we would make direct connections at Kogota. So at 11:45 we went to the depot and were soon on our way. We decided before we left the house that we had better buy second-class tickets instead of third class as the latter have no sanitation arrangements on the trains to Kogota. But Dr. Woodworth bought the tickets and of course bought third class as usual. I was scarcely able to stand and started for the second-class coach when he directed me to a third-class car. I reminded him that we were to go second class, and he did not know what to say. I could feel I was getting worse, so I had to insist that he go back and exchange the tickets. The events of that ride proved the wisdom of my choice, for I could scarcely make it home.

At 3:30, we arrived at Sendai and went straight to the Woodworth home. I was unable to eat a mouthful of even a good old American-style supper. Went to bed early.

Thursday, September 30 ———————— ◆ ———————————————————————

Spent a miserable night. The trouble seems very little improved. There was a
reception today in honor of Dr. Lampe of the Reformed church to which we were
invited, but I was too sick to go. Woodworths went, and I managed to get in a little
work on my typewriter, though it was extremely difficult to do so.

Friday, October 1 ———————— ◆ ———————————————————————

Felt some better today, and this morning we rode out to the Sendai Orphanage
of which I have read so much in the past few years. It was a real delight to see this
practical bit of Christian work in operation. It is not so small, either. The land com-
promises some six acres, part of which makes a fine garden. There is a large main
building; the supt.'s home; the home of the business manager; four boys' and four
girls' cottages, only two of each being used now, the other four being rented; a
house for small children; a hospital; and another house being rented to an outsider.
The last-named house together with that of the supt. are without the grounds proper,
as is that of the business manager. The main building, which is used for office purposes, school purposes and dining rooms, faces the entrance, being set back in a
clump of beautiful trees with a fine lawn of shrubs in front. Extending back from the
main building and forming a large hollow square for a playground are the eight cottages, four on each side, with the somewhat larger building at the rear for the
smaller children. Off to the left as one walks back through this hollow square is the
hospital building.
    April 1, 1920, the balance sheet of this institution was as follows:

Cash on hand 4/1/1919	Y 1,625.48	
Income 1919–1920	10,714.44	
Borrowed from endowment	542.97	
Expenditures		Y12,860.67
Cash on hand 3/31/1920		22.22
	Y12,882.89	Y12,882,89
Total current indebtedness	Y2,542.97	

There is a total endowment fund of Y35,425.25.

The institution was formerly a M.E. undertaking, but they let it go so that now
it is supported by voluntary gifts from some six or seven different denominations
and other institutions. The supt., Miss Louisa Imhof, is still paid by the M.E.
Woman's Board the sum of $700 and house rent, and this salary is to be raised this
next year. The other two salaried officers are Mrs. Kata Oka, asst. to the supt., who
was connected with Japanese work in Los Angeles for five years, and Mr. Kesaburo
Onuma, business manager. A glance at the personnel and the place in general would
lead one to believe that it might be more ably managed, though those in charge are
doing their best under the circumstances. Miss Imhof is quite old.
    For educating, clothing, light, food, etc., it costs about $90 a year to care for
each child. They usually ask $30 from churches supporting an orphan, this to cover

Another scene from one of the pageants of the World Sunday School Convention, Tokyo, 1920.

tuition only. Our church supports 16 through various church organizations in America. I secured a corrected list of the names of these children and those who support them. Later I took a picture of Miss Imhof and 15 of these.

There are 66 in the orphanage between the ages of 3 and 18. I secured a photograph of the playground with the surrounding cottages.

After dinner we rode way out to the Baptist compound, a long way from the center of the city, on a beautiful site and with most commanding buildings.

Met Mrs. Ross, wife of the Rev. Ross, who has charge of the evangelistic work for the Baptists in the Sendai and Muraoka fields. They have a beautiful home within the compound, other missionaries no doubt living with them.

Mr. Ross was absent, but she informed me that he visits ten preaching points, all but one or two of which have native pastors in charge. One or two of the churches are one-half self-supporting. With the exception of Shiogama, one of the half-self-supporting churches, all these other churches are north of all our preaching places. One independent church is located in Sendai and is not under the charge of the Rev. Ross. The pastor of this church receives about Y50 a month, not as much as the pastors of churches receiving help, but he prefers this work because it is independent. This is almost universally true of independent pastors.

Mr. Ross does some preaching but specializes in organization. His aim is to make the churches self-supporting. Students in seminaries are fewer than formerly due to ability to secure more money in other work and also due to shortage of evangelistic missionaries. Some of the Baptists have recently died, and some have left for other work.

The Baptists have three girls' schools and one boys' school, one business school, a woman's dormitory in Tokyo, kindergarten training school, boys' seminary, dormitory at Waseda University, one evangelistic worker at Sendai and one at Tokyo. Mrs. Ross says the work is going down because two-thirds of it is educational and the other third, evangelistic, is not able to supply students to the schools. Hard to get missionaries from America. This would indicate to me that there is something wrong with the system that allows one end, which is the feeding end (evangelistic), to go down. She thinks the work with students is the best work for permanent work. Mr. Ross has an English Bible class (in several places), of great value.

We visited the girls' school located here, under the guidance of Miss Smith; we had the privilege of seeing the entire institution. There are 150 girls, 60 of whom live in the one dormitory and the balance coming in for the day. They are taught domestic science and many other branches, including music and considerable college work.

There are 19 Japanese teachers and five foreign teachers. The dean, who is a Japanese man, receives Y150 a month, and the head teacher, also a man, receives Y120. The lady music teacher, Japanese, receives Y55 a month, the English teacher Y48, the matron of the dormitory Y36, the kindergarten teachers Y36. The janitor receives Y30. All have to furnish their own board. Annual budget of girls' school is Y40,000.

The girls pay Y2 a month for tuition, Y2 a month for light and room, and Y10 a month for board.

The three single foreign teachers, all women, receive $69 a month, which together with a special bonus this year ran up to nearly $1,000 each for the year. Their outfit allowance was $250. They are allowed medical bills. They have a furlough of eight months off the field every five years. Single men receive $100 a month.

There are the following buildings in the compound; main building, dormitory for 60 girls, janitor's house, evangelists' house, house for foreign teachers. The main building is scientifically arranged for school purposes, with rooms for various kinds of work, such as sewing, domestic science, laboratory, music room and practice rooms, a fine chapel looking exactly like a church, etc.

There are 2,000 *tsubo* in the compound, worth now about Y15 a *tsubo*. The main building would cost Y150,000 to build now, or three times the original cost. The dormitory would cost Y15,000. The foreign house would now cost Y20,000 to build. It is a very fine house.

We came home just at dark, feeling we had seen a really great institution. After dinner, I was so exhausted that I could do nothing but listen to some phonograph music played by Dr. Woodworth.

This attractive young woman takes a break from her work at the beach.

Left: Young Japanese girl in a flower garden.

Below: The Japanese are great lovers of all kinds of beauty from the flower kingdom.

Right: A schoolboy in native dress.

Below: The silk industry ranks among the most important in Japan. In addition to the large silk enterprises many private homes cultivate their own silk worms and sell the cocoons to the large corporations. The young lady is feeding mulberry leaves to the worms.

Above: Doing the family ironing. It seems that the garments are taken apart and washed and ironed in sections, a smooth board being both ironing board and iron with the aid of the sun. Opposite page, top: Four women in work costume pick tea on one of the many tea hedges. Opposite, bottom: People working in a rice paddy.

Above: Interior of the Ieyasu Temple, Nikko. Right: In Nikko, steps in the midst of the Cryptomeria trees leading to the tomb of the former Emperor Ieyasu.

Opposite page, top: Entrance to one of Japan's countless temples. This one is the Yomeimon Temple in Nikko. Bottom: A group of people putting thatch on the roof of a one-story house.

Top: A young girl displays her dolls. Bottom: A social tea in Japan.

Top: Close application to fancy work such as this in stuffy and ill-lighted rooms is not conducive to the best of health. Bottom: Winding the silk from the cocoons by means of rapidly rotating spindles. Thousands of little girls are employed in this exacting task.

Above: Primitive methods are still used in threshing rice, also in polishing it. Left: Irrigation was a prime requisite of cultivating rice in Japan. As late as 1920, the water was carried from one field to another by such a primitive footpower method as is shown here. Opposite page, top: In a sea loving country like Japan, there's always a great demand for toy boats, but the toll on the girls who paint them is tremendous. Bottom: A mother in the home sorting the silk cocoons.

Above: A toy vendor in Tokyo. Below: A religious festival in Japan. The men are carrying an ark containing the spirit of a departed ancestor. Opposite page, top: A cake vendor in Tokyo. Much of the cake is made from the bean curd of the soybean. Opposite page, bottom: A vendor of pottery.

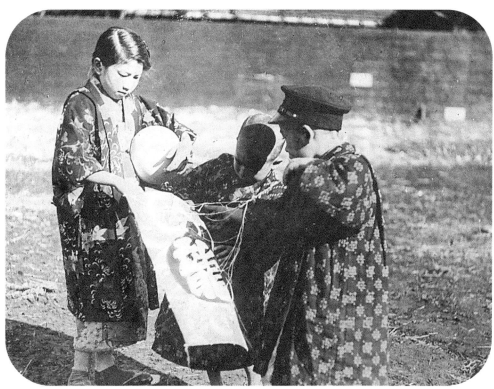

Above: Flower vendor with flower cart and two small children. Right: Elderly Japanese man in costume with a young girl in costume in front of a small statue of a dragon-like figure.

Opposite page, top: Potential circus performers. Bottom: Children kite flying.

A boat with two fishermen on the lake. Mt. Fujiyama is in the background. (Probably a commercially produced photograph purchased by the author.)

III. The Eighth World Sunday School Convention

Saturday, October 2 ———— ◆ ————————

Spent another bad night, but not so bad as the two previous ones. This morning we called on Dr. David B. Schneder, president of Tohoku Gakuin, the school of the Reformed Church in America, which is located in Sendai. They have here a theological, a higher school and a middle school. In another part of the city they also have a girls' school. This is the headquarters for the work of this denomination in Japan.

The school is North Japan College. The theological school has 12 students, who come from the six northern provinces, or *kens*: Miyagi, Nagano, Hokkaido, Yamagata, Iwate and Fukushima. The tuition is Y2.75 a month, 11 months in the year. The boys board themselves, usually in clubs with a monitor from the teachers in charge. They hire a cook. Theological boys live in the dormitory.

Two courses are offered, the A course of three years following the graduation from the higher school, which is virtually a college, and the B course of four years following the graduation from the middle school. This latter is the shorter course, and Dr. Schneder said they would gladly drop it if they could, but they must keep it to supply preachers for the church and to keep up the theological school. At present only four boys are in the A course and eight in the B course.

Students from other churches are admitted on equal terms. There are three Americans and six Japanese on the faculty of the theological school. New graduates from the theol. school receive as pastors—single men, of B course training—Y45 plus a bonus a/c H.C.L. this year of Y5 each. Single men from the A course receive Y50 regularly. When he marries he receives Y60, and Y5 for each child. About half the boys stick to the Reformed church pastorates after a few years.

MIDDLE SCHOOL

The middle school of the North Japan College has 500 boys. The present dormitory accommodates about 70. Others stay in private homes or boarding houses, though the latter is discouraged by the faculty. Their tuition is Y2.75 a month. They board themselves in clubs with a teacher in charge, hiring a cook. Teachers are in charge of districts of the city, and they visit the lodging places of the boys at certain

A group of young Japanese with Dr. Woodworth (back row, center) and Angie Crews (sitting, first woman on the left).

times. About one-seventh or one-eighth of the boys remain beyond middle for the higher school or college.

There are 25 teachers in the middle school, 23 of whom are Japanese. The salary of the highest-paid Japanese is Y80 plus 60 percent special allowance for this year. The estimate for replacing of the building, which was destroyed by fire, without equipment is $100,000 (Y200,000) to accommodate 540 students. To do this, the foundations of the old building will be used. The old building cost about $56,000.

There are about 5,000 *tsubo* (4 acres) in the middle school grounds, worth now Y30 a *tsubo*. It was bought originally as follows: ¼ at Y1.50, ¼ at Y3.00, and ¼ at Y7.00. The equipment, including steam heating and scientific equipment, will cost $20,000 (Y40,000). To restore the dormitory will cost Y48,000. It will accommodate 100.

Dr. Schneder says any school would be glad to accept a teacher from another denomination. He thinks small churches should unite in a middle school project and suggests the island of Shikato where there are no schools, or between Kobe and Nagasaki on the west coast at Nigata. He also says Utsunomiya is a fine place. About half of the boys go out as baptized Christians. He thinks others are baptized later. The total budget for the running expense of the middle school is Y43,869.25 a year.

The budget for the whole plant, including theological college and middle schools, is about as follows:

Estimated Receipts

Gifts	Y60,700
Tuition	17,500
Exam. fees	250
Entrance fees	250
Room rent	300
Sundries sold	400
Lab. fees	200
Textbooks sold	200
	Y79,800

Expenses

Beneficiary aid	Y 3,800
Industrial home	1,500
Travel	700
Allowances	700
Honorariums	700
Wages of servants	3,000
Reference books	1,500
Textbooks	300
Paper, etc.	350
Printing	400
Equipment	1,000
Furnishings	1,100
Supplies	650
Fuel	2,200
Light	250
Postage	400
Advertising	400
Repairs	1,200
Taxes	500
Sundries	5,000
Clerk	2,100
Assistants	850
Salaries	52,400
	Y81,000

New missionary families coming out under the Reformed church receive a salary of $1,300 and from $50 up in children's allowance, depending upon the age of the child. There is a graduated scale, so that after 20 years of service the missionary receives $1,600. Medical bills and rent are provided by the board. Outfit allowance is $600. Term of service is seven years. The single women receive salary of $800.

We were unable to find Mr. Iglehart of the Methodist church or Mr. Ross of the Baptist at home.

Went to the Rev. Kitano's and took the picture of the church, and also of the Rev. Kitano and wife. On the way, took several snapshots of interesting bits of life in a Japanese city.

Spent the evening packing for the trip back to Tokyo on the morrow. I very much dislike to make this trip on Sunday. I find the missionaries very, very careless about the proper observance of Sunday, and I believe they miss many opportunities for impressing the Japanese people with the sacredness of the day by missing it themselves. The program outlined called for spending this Sunday at Sendai.

Dr. Woodworth planned the trip and wrote the brethren at Tokyo to postpone the proposed *bukwai* (pastor's meeting) until after the SS convention, though it was officially scheduled to take place Monday, October 4. Our planning was done on the basis that they would make the change, though I warned Dr. Woodworth that I doubted if we should ask the change and if they would make it even if we did. He felt sure they would, but a card from Tokyo gave me the information that Dr. Woodworth had carried the card asking them to change the date three or four days in his pocket, so they could not make the change, even had they decided to do so, without much inconvenience. They did not feel that they should do so anyway, so we were compelled to change our plans again, a thing we have done constantly because of not looking ahead.

I believe the Lord helps us out of hard places when we get into them unavoidably, but I do not think it is fair to use poor judgment and carelessness and then expect the Lord to come to our rescue. I suggested the same to Dr. Woodworth.

Sunday, October 3 ——————— ◆ ———————————

Left Sendai for Tokyo at 8:25 on the express train. We took third class, expecting to change if my condition was such as to demand it. But I stood the trip much better than I expected. The third-class fare, including the extra fare for this express train, was Y4.79. This also carries us over several electric lines in Tokyo to the Shibuya station, where it was possible to send our baggage out to the house yet tonight.

As we traveled, we passed hundreds and hundreds of soldiers on the march. Japan is literally alive with the idea that Japan is to grow by warfare. The old German idea in which they had placed so much hope is still alive in spite of the German defeat.

We passed a funeral procession out in the country. The mourners were strung out for a long distance ahead of the casket. The latter was in a fancy-looking, ark-appearing, templelike little house in fancy colors and was carried on the shoulders of four men, and a man accompanying them carried some kind of a banner with an inscription on it.

Reached Fukushima at 10:25 — 46 miles from Sendai — 23 miles an hour on an express train.

The man who sat next to me in the little stuffy third-class seat spoke very good English, and I discovered that he had spent 28 years in America. He is part owner in a high-class restaurant business in Chicago, located at Wilson Ave. and Sheridan Road, one of the very best places in the North Side of Chicago. He says his daily income is about $250, and on Saturday and Sunday about $500 and $650, respectively. It takes 22 employees to conduct the business, with four additional on Saturday and Sunday. It takes $400 a month for rent. The head chef receives $175 a month and board; the second chef $150. He caters to a good class of people.

He says the California question troubles no one in Chicago. This man is in Japan on a visit to his aged parents and other relatives. He says some of his old friends here want him to settle down in Tokyo. He is on the way there to meet a man who wants him to go into partnership with him in a new European restaurant there. But he says he wants to go back to Chicago. He says he has many more friends there, and then he would not be bothered with a host of relatives such as he has here.

I mention this as one type of Oriental. This man is 45 years old and not married. He has taken on Occidental life so that his former Japanese life does not appeal to him at all.

A little later, a large number of boys boarded the train, and we learned that they were from the Imperial Government Railroad Training School in Tokyo. Mr. Kazamatsu, the manager of the school, saw that the boys all had seats and finally sat down beside me. He proved to be a most congenial gentleman and spoke very good English. He gave me some very interesting information. He said he was returning with these boys from a tour of the railroads covering about 1,000 miles. This is done semiannually. There are about 750 boys in the Tokyo school and there are six such schools in the empire. Recently they advertised for 50 new boys and received 3,000 applications. They gave them a series of stiff examinations in reading, mathematics and physical tests, thus eliminating all but 80 of the boys. He said that during the war they found it very hard to secure suitable boys for training but that it was much easier since the war.

The boys range from 16 years old up to 48 and train for various branches of the service, such as guards, ticket agents, freight agents and clerks, conductors, firemen and engineers. The training is from six months to a year, depending upon the branch of service. An engineer, however, must have practical service as well as theoretical and technical training, and requires about five years training before he is given full control of an engine.

The best-paid engineers receive Y150 a month; the poorest, about Y90. A ticket agent receives about Y100 a month. Every branch of the service is covered in this school. While studying, the boys receive Y30 to Y45 a month, depending upon the line of service followed. They are given their uniforms and a room in the dormitory but must pay Y15 a month for board. English is taught in the school.

A railroad man receives an annual pass over all lines. The highest paid receive second-class transportation and the lower third-class. Their families receive one pass a year to any point. It is interesting to note here that the Japanese government receives from 80 to 90 percent of its income in passenger traffic from the third-class passengers and gives them by far the worst treatment.

It takes a large number of men to run the RR. From Sendai to Tokyo (220 miles), about 5,000 men are employed on this one line. Many of the ticket agents work 24 hours and are off 24 hours, but in some branches such as freight and baggage there are eight-hour shifts now. This requires more men. For example, at Utsunomiya 600 men are employed in three shifts of eight hours each.

I have noticed that it requires a very large number of men in Japan to do a small business. For example, I went into a bank in Sendai to get some money. The bank is not large and does not have a very great amount of capital. The room is not large, but there must have been 50 or 60 bank clerks there. A bank of the same size in America would easily be run by a dozen men. I placed my check, signed it properly, and handed it to a clerk; he did something to it and handed it to another, and I think six or seven different clerks at least handled that check before it finally came back to another window. When I turned in the check, I was handed a metal number and told to sit down until the number was called. After a considerable wait, the number was called at a different window, and I received my money. The same thing is true of the post office.

Mr. Kazamatsu has traveled a year in America and believes Japan should adopt a wide-gauge road, though to do so would cost an initial outlay of Y400,000,000. The fare is low (about 2.25 sen third class and doubled each time for the better classes). He says it must be low to enable the Japanese to ride at all. A Japanese can ride only 100 miles third class on a day's wage, where an American can ride in America 200 or 300 miles on a day's wage. Mr. Kazamatsu says he was well treated in America. He spoke highly of the American YMCA.

He is not Christian, but his family is. He says he loves to read the Bible, but he is sorry he can't find God. Dr. Woodworth talked with him some time. He seemed deeply interested.

After a long ride, we arrived at the station in Tokyo where we were to change to the electric lines. Mr. Kazamatsu instructed the boys to look after our baggage, which they did in fine fashion. The electric cars were crowded. We made several changes and finally entrusted our baggage to a *kuruma* at the Shibuya station, who trotted on ahead to Kasumi cho while we followed, mostly afoot. At about 6:00 P.M. we arrived at 26 Kasumi cho, glad to get back. Mr. Grant, who takes lunch and dinner here, and Mr. Hirzel, who lodges here, were here, and I also met Miss Stacy for the first time. She appears to me as a woman of real missionary spirit. It was a real rest to spend a quiet evening with these friends. Retired at nine o'clock.

Monday, October 4 ──────── ◆ ────────

Arose at five and enjoyed the luxury of cleaning out my favorite traveling bags and rearranging things a bit after carrying them for three weeks with a constantly increasing accumulation of souvenirs, gifts, etc.

At 7:30, we started for Oji where a meeting (*bukwai*) of pastors of the Tokyo and Utsunomiya fields was scheduled. We stopped downtown, and I secured a supply of 130A films. To play safe, I bought nine rolls at a cost of Y1.10 a roll. I consider this reasonable as they are 45¢ each in the states. This dealer said he would develop a roll for 25 sen (12.5¢) and print for 10 sen (5¢) each. This is very much less than the Ishinomaki man charged.

At Oji, we met Pastors Takahashi of Oji; Kimura of Utsunomiya; Ogata of Shinden; Irokawa of Moka; Muraoka of Yaita; Tsujimura of Otawara; Matsuno of Azabu, Tokyo; Ishigaki of Naka Shibuya, Tokyo, and also Mrs. Ito, Bible woman of Azabu, Tokyo.

The morning session was opened with a long and I believe helpful prayer service. I was then introduced and spoke for most of an hour on "The New Testament

One of the principal railroad stations in Tokyo.

Church." The Rev. K. Matsuno interpreted for me beautifully. The attention was very good. After the morning session, I had Dr. Woodworth take a picture of the group.

A great festal *dumberi* was served at noon, consisting of unpalatable fish, vegetables and rice in large separate bowls. Fortunately, Dr. Woodworth can't eat it much better than I can, so we enjoyed the remains of our lunch from Sunday.

The afternoon session opened with a welcome meeting for me. The Rev. Ishigaki, of Naka Shibuya, spoke first. He stated that there was a very great crisis in Japan. First, pastors were lacking in power. Second, the board in America had not been able to supply the necessary money for advance work. Lack of advance was a time of great danger to the church. If this continues as it has been, the church in Japan can never attain self-support. The number of missionaries has been neither increased nor decreased for years. Perhaps a new plan must be adopted. There can be no success, he said, unless the missionaries, the mission board and the native church work together.

Mr. Tajima, for years treasurer of the Azabu church, spoke next. He said 30 years ago the Rev. Jones started work at Azabu. We had in those early days only three preachers.

He is anxious because the church does not advance. In some respects Japan has advanced at full speed. He referred as an illustration to the increase from Dr. Woodworth's first bicycle in Tokyo to the present large number of bicycles and automobiles. But he said that Japan was slow to advance in religion. The Azabu church gives Y600 or Y700 a year to all purposes. This is our most advanced church, which is about half self-supporting.

Following these welcome addresses, I responded, thanking them for the

Group of Ohio delegates to the World Sunday School Convention.

courtesies extended me and taking up the points mentioned in their addresses. I emphasized the need of power on the part of pastors and urged them to claim that
power, which God promised to his servants.

The more I see of our pastors, the more I feel that they are lacking in this
spiritual power and that the admission on the part of the Rev. Ishigaki that they
lacked power, it seems to me, is well timed. I laid great stress on this as I did at the
northern meeting. I encouraged them in the face of the present obstacles by the
thought that all things are possible with God and that perhaps they were facing a
challenge to their faith at the present time.

Following this, tea and cakes were served, and then we had a long conference
considering the future work of the church here. I asked them to express themselves
freely as to just what they felt the great needs to be.

Mr. Irokawa, of Moka said the greatest need was the increase in salaries of
workers. He said he could not educate his children on his present salary. He says if
the board would start a middle school and grant special privileges to pastors' children, it would help.

I replied that I was investigating the salary question. I suggested that the logical
way for a salary increase to come was through the local church.

The Rev. Ishigaki replied, but evaded my last suggestion. He said it would take
half his salary to educate one of his children. Feels that his church cannot do more.
He says we need a school. We should have had one at the beginning. Members of
our church in the country come to the city and go to churches of other and larger

denominations because these denominations have schools. We have to send our theological students to other schools, where they usually stay because they see how much larger the denominations are and how much greater their work is.

I called attention again to my suggestion that the increase come from the churches.

Mr. Tajima said that whole families must be evangelized. Most of the Christians in our churches now are women and children, but these have no power over the money and hence cannot give much.

I outlined my plan for securing reports covering the work done during the quarter. I then asked for further opinions as to just what the Christian church should attempt to do in Japan as an enlarged program.

Mr. Muraoka says the people in his own field know Christianity but doubt the missionary or pastor has come to stay. So he feels we must build churches first. Says Buddhist priests put up temples first thing.

Pastor Takahashi speaks from his own standpoint. He feels the need of a theological school completely equipped to teach along lines of social service. We need trained leaders. He says his training was not complete enough so that he can meet the problems of the social life of Oji, which is a great industrial center.

The Rev. Tsujimura says he needs a church building in his field. Also needs a kindergarten. He has needed it since he went there ten years ago. The officials of the city say if he does not start one, the city will and it will not be a Christian kindergarten if they start it. The Rev. Takahashi speaks again and adds that we must increase the native workers and missionaries. He says we should have a missionary family in every field.

The Rev. Kimura pleads for an adequate Japan Christian paper to represent the interests of the Japan Christian church. Says we need one large enough to give notes of the work of the pastors. The *Shimei*, edited by the Rev. Kitano, is too small.

The Rev. Matsuno says the school would be a good thing but is so expensive to build and equip. He says we must increase our evangelical work, or our churches will die and the ministry will suffer from lack of men. He says the dormitory idea is good but feels it too would be too expensive. He feels keenly the need of larger salaries for our pastors. Thinks they should receive nearer 200 yen than 100 a month.

I explained that I hope to be able to speak at least once at each of their places and asked that they prepare the maps of their towns with location of the church, schools, temples, etc.

Miss Stacy came at noon, and after the afternoon service, we went back to Kasumi cho where we enjoyed a very excellent dinner, prepared in honor of Miss Stacy's birthday. After dinner, Bro. and Sister McKnight and I took a walk through Juban. Juban is the principal trading street of this section, and at night it is a veritable beehive of activity. It seems that everybody for miles around comes out on the street. And to accommodate the trade, the merchants bring their goods out of the stores and spread them out right on the street. It is curious to watch the people squat down around a pile of bolts of cloth and pick out what they want. We stopped to buy some cloth and as usual soon became the center of a curious group. I also secured a box of chocolates for Miss Stacy. To make sure it would be fresh, I

The temporary building erected in Tokyo for the World Sunday School Convention 1920 with statue of Christ in the foreground.

had him make up the box right there, and it was quite a novel sight to see the way he went at it. He managed, however, to make up a very commendable box, though I could not vouch for the freshness of the candy.

Tuesday, October 5 ◆

The Sunday school convention opens tonight at seven o'clock, and delegates are coming in constantly. There will be perhaps 600 foreign delegates, which is not so large as they had hoped for. Only a few are coming from Korea and none from China, because of race feeling.

Spent all morning writing up my notes and got a lot of work done. Had several callers, among them the Rev. Irokawa of Moka, who said my message of yesterday had resolved him to try some new plans in his work based on the New Testament church. Took a little walk after lunch and mailed some cards. Wrapped some pictures of Mr. McCord for gifts to the missionaries and native pastors. At four o'clock, Mr. Garman came, having landed from the *Empress of Russia* this morning. He said he read in the *Herald* that my wife's mother had died. It was the first news I had received of it, and I can hardly believe it. I shall look anxiously for a letter today. One does not realize how helpless he really is until such things happen.

At about four o'clock, the fire bell rang, and a few minutes later we heard that the new SS Convention Hall, to be used for the first time tonight, had burned to the ground. It seems unbelievable. Garman and I took wheels and rode to the center of the city, and our fears were confirmed as there was nothing left but a mass of twisted steel. The chorus was practicing when the electricians attempted to light up the great electric sign "The Light of the World." Defective wiring caused the great curtain to catch fire, and in 20 minutes the large but flimsy papier-mâché building was down. Had the convention been in session, many lives would have been lost. As it was, reports claim no lives were lost.

We had some close calls on our wheels, as it was getting dark when we returned and we rode rapidly. Garman had two collisions.

The convention was to convene anyway tonight in the YMCA, but we were not able to get back.

Wednesday, October 6 ──────── ◆ ─────────────────────

Garman, McKnight, Dr. Woodworth, Miss Stacy and I went to the convention this morning. The place was crowded, but it was announced that on Thursday the Imperial Theatre would be used. Today the Salvation Army Hall is being used as an overflow meeting place.

The first address was given by Marion Lawrence, the veteran SS man. His theme was "The Worldwide Progress of the SS Movement." [See Appendix, entry 1.]

There are 30,000,000 in the SS enrollment of the world today, with an average attendance of 100 or more for each school. The total enrollment of the SS is about 35,000,000; 85 percent of all churches in America were in the SS first; 80 percent to 85 percent of church members come from the SS; 40 percent of the SS are below 13 years of age; 71 percent of conversions occur before the age of 25; and this is the SS period.

Mr. W.G. Landes, statistician, said that in July 1913 the enrollment of the SS was 30,000,000 and in 1920, 30,439,574. The reason for no larger increase, he said, was the war.

In the afternoon the entire convention was invited to a reception at one of the imperial gardens, Shijiku Imperial Garden. No caps are to be allowed, and dress suits are suggested, though a sack-coated individual will be admitted, provided he has the SS credentials. Many Japanese have never been in this garden. Mr. Garman and I went and found it a very fine garden. It covered several acres of ground, in fact a large number, and was full of beautiful flowers. We were piloted through the entire grounds and finally brought to a large tent. Here tea and cake were served. I had the pleasant experience of having a lady turn round quickly and knock a cup of hot tea out of my hand in such a way as to baptize me with its contents. I pitied her more than I did myself as I was unhurt except for a wet collar and coat. We were told the mother of the present emperor used this as her favorite garden.

In the evening, at the YMCA, Prof. H. Augustine Smith, the musical director, led in a very effective song service emphasizing the life of Christ. Slides were used, and the singing was in both English and Japanese. Prof. Smith does not care for

The temporary World Sunday School Convention building in flames just before the opening session was scheduled to begin in 1920.

the ragtime music so often used in SS today but believes in the old hymns of the church, and he uses them very effectively.

Following the song service, the evening was given over to messages from many fields as to the work of the SS in each.

Mr. Erdman, of Hawaii, said there are 10,000 Christians in Hawaii. The island was formerly all Christian, but now there are so many Orientals there that it is necessary to rechristianize the land. There are many barriers of language and religion. Of the 10,000 young people in Hawaii, seven out of ten know absolutely nothing of Jesus Christ.

The Rev. Wartlaw, of Denmark, said there are 935 SS with 10,000 members in that land.

Miss Kearns, of New Zealand, gave a message from that land.

The Rev. Bower, of Java, Borneo and Sumatra, said there were 60,000,000 people there with 25 different languages; 35,000,000 of these live in Java; 59,000,000 of those people are Mohammedan.

Dr. Poole, the successor of Dr. F.B. Meyer of London, led in prayer.

A resolution expressing appreciation of our Japanese hosts was read and adopted by a rising vote.

This was followed by the reading of messages of sympathy from Americans and Japanese alike.

The Imperial Theater, Tokyo, which was immediately placed at the disposal of the World Sunday School Convention, after the destruction by fire of the temporary convention hall.

Mr. Darling, of Australia, followed with a word from that land.

Mr. Swinehart, of Korea, said the regular attendance in the SS of Korea was 186,000. He introduced a Korean pastor who in spite of the Korean difficulty at this time, which prevented the delegates from that land coming and in spite of the opposition of his friends, came at his own expense to the convention. He was dressed in pure white with a white flowing robe and a long beard. The Japanese permitted him to speak, and he gave a stirring message that would no doubt have been more stirring had the interpreter felt free to interpret it literally and had he not exceeded his time limit. He said there were 400,000 Christians in Korea. The Koreans have already sent four missionaries to China.

He made a heart-searching appeal for help for the persecuted Koreans. He said more delegates would be present from Korea, but 1,000 were in jail, and many had recently been killed in the churches. The old man spoke with great feeling, and the interpreter had to guard his interpretation. The time limit was reached at the critical moment in his speech, and he had to stop.

Thursday, October 7 ⸻ ◆ ⸻

We attended the fellowship meeting conducted by Dr. W.E. Beiderwolf every morning from 8:30 to 9:00. This was followed by the presentation in song of the life of Christ, with Prof. Smith leading.

Japanese garden.

Mr. Marion Lawrence was made chairman of the day. The first speaker was Bishop George H. Bickley, of Singapore, who spoke on "The Necessity of a World Savior." [See Appendix, entry 2.]

Duet by Prof. and Mrs. Smith, "Watchman Tell Us of the Night."

Announcement that the *Monteagle*, with 115 delegates on board, will arrive Saturday. A wireless was received saying that they had begun the convention on board on schedule.

Mr. Trumbull then spoke on "The Living Christ as the Life of the Individual." [See Appendix, entry 3.]

Announcement was made that George W.L. Foster, of Toronto, is painting the portraits of the emperor and empress and that they will be unveiled Saturday. Bishop Welch closed the session with another stirring message on "The Power of the Cross," John 12:20–33.

Professor H.R. Augustine Smith, conducting a choir of 800 voices singing the "Hallelujah Chorus" at the World Sunday School Convention held in the Imperial Theater.

Thursday evening, Prof. Smith illustrated the songs again with pictures from the life of Christ. There was also a chorus of 500.

The theme of Thursday was "Jesus Christ, the World's Redeemer."

The Rev. M. Uimura spoke on "The Sufficiency of Christ for the New Day, for the Orient," continued by Pres. D. Webster Kurtz, of McPherson College, Kansas. [See Appendix, entry 4.]

McKnight, Miss Stacy and I attended this meeting together, and after the service it was suggested that we patronize the only drugstore in town that serves real American sodas. We went and found that they had sold out of ice cream, so we had to be content with the soda flavored.

Friday, October 8   ◆

Had my first view of Fuji this morning. It is an inspiring mountain.

The first song at nine o'clock was "Come Thou Almighty King." Prof. Smith emphasized the fact that this was written during the Reformation and was written to point back to the Holy Bible. He noted that it taught the Trinity. He also mentioned that all these old hymns were written in 3/4 time, to represent the Trinity. Common time was introduced from another source. The 3/4 time was represented by the

Sunset behind Mt. Fujiyama with farmers' fields in the foreground.

circle, the most perfect symbol. When common time was introduced, the circle was broken, hence the C for common time.

Friday's theme was "The Bible, God's Revelation to the World."

Mr. P.B. Selden, of Erie, Pennsylvania, a leading layman, presided at this meeting.

Bishop S.S. Waltz spoke on "The Bible as a Record of God's Revelation of Himself." [See Appendix, entry 5.] Prof. Watanabe of the Disciple church gave the translation.

During the announcements, Prince Tokugawa, pres. of the House of Peers, was introduced. He presented to the presiding officer, Mr. McLaren, a new gavel, making his short speech in English, which was interpreted. The gavel is made of cashi wood. Mr. McLaren accepted the gavel in a neat speech.

Took my films to the photographer for developing and find that I can get slides made at 60 sen each for plain and 70 sen each for colored.

In the afternoon we went to the YMCA where I placed an order for a lot of Korean cloth, made by the boys of the Shondo School. It is very durable cloth and will make good shirts. I ordered four colors of three and one-half yards and two other colors of eight yards for dresses for wife and girlies.

We then went to Hibiya Park where the city of Tokyo gave a royal welcome to the convention. The park is beautiful naturally, and this was enhanced by a massive evergreen arch at the entrance with the word *welcome* on each side in gold. We were given souvenirs of beautiful silk bows for the pin and a beautiful silk doily with the flag of Japan and the SS flag worked on it. There was also an artistic program showing the orders of the day. After taking a picture of the arch, we went in and had tea and watched the fireworks until we were told to go to the refreshment tent where a most appetizing foreign supper, with some Japanese dishes additional, was served. During the supper, Mayor Tajiri of Tokyo gave a welcome address to which Dr. Brown responded. This was followed by three *banzai* for Tokyo and for the foreign delegates.

In the evening a pageant was given, entitled "The SS from Bethlehem to Tokyo." It was a very well rendered pageant. [See Appendix, entry 6.]

Mr. W.H. Goodwin, of Montreal, a businessman, spoke on "The Bible in Individual Life." It was an excellent address.

Telegrams were read from Bergden, Norway; Dr. J.H. Jowett of London; and Pres. Woodrow Wilson.

Prof. Henry E. Dosker, of Louisville, then spoke on "The Bible as a Social Force." [See Appendix, entry 7.]

During the evening I sat on the front row, and I was interested in a Japanese shorthand writer. He was quite rapid.

Saturday, October 9   ━━━━ ◆ ━━━━━━━

Theme for the day: "The Christian Heritage of Childhood."

Dr. H. Kosaki spoke on "Childhood in the Orient." [See Appendix, entry 8.]

Announcement was made at 9:45 that the *Monteagle* had arrived and the 115 delegates were on Japanese soil. Mr. Arthur Black, who just came from the *Monteagle*, was introduced as the chairman of the day. Mr. Landes relinquished the place for him. Mr. Black stated that nine sessions of the convention had been held on board. He brought greetings from the SS union of Great Britain.

The Rev. Alvaro Dos Reis, of Brazil, was introduced to speak on "Childhood in Latin America." [See Appendix, entry 9.] He invited the next convention to Brazil.

The Rev. J.W. Butcher followed with a message on "Childhood in War-torn Europe." [See Appendix, entry 10.]

Bishop Welch closed the morning session with a strong message on "The Bible's Crowning Fact." [See Appendix, entry 11.]

Remained at Kasumi cho this afternoon and wrote up my notes and some letters.

The Saturday evening program opened with another song service under the direction of Prof. Smith. This was followed by the second of the series of pageants. The title of the second pageant was "The Rights of the Child." [See Appendix, entry 12.]

Mrs. J.W. Barnes attempted to deliver a message but suffered an attack of heart trouble and had difficulty in getting through with it.

Bro. McKnight and I did a little shopping and came home. I bought three pairs of black socks for Y2.10 and a bag of apples for Y.40.

Group of delegates to the World Sunday School Convention in front of the Imperial Theatre.

Sunday, October 10 ————————◆————————

Went to the Azabu Christian Church this morning. Took a picture of the Sunday school and also of the church people. I preached the morning sermon, the Rev. Matsuno, the pastor, interpreting.

In the afternoon we went to the World SS Convention Demonstration. It was one of the most remarkable displays I have ever seen. The crowd that gathered at Hibiya Park where the speaking was held and the parade formed was estimated at from 15,000 to 20,000. There were literally thousands of Japanese children in line, coming from the SS of all Tokyo and vicinity. This was a practical demonstration of the future opportunity of missionary forces to make Japan a Christian nation. With their many-colored dresses and suits, together with the flags designating the various schools and the beautiful colored SS banner each child and adult carried, the color effect was simply indescribable. Besides the children, there were missionaries and delegates from many lands and a host of Japanese citizens. I noticed besides the banners of the various Sunday schools and other Tokyo organizations, banners of Japan, Korea, China, Siam, Brazil, Holland, Sweden, Scotland, Canada, America, Argentina, Philippines, Java, India and New Zealand. I took several pictures of the group. Never before in the history of Japan, and perhaps of the Far East, has there been such a gathering of Sunday school forces.

After the program of songs and speeches and many *banzais*, the parade formed with the representatives of various nations leading in alphabetical order. The line of march was over to the Ginza (Tokyo's principal business thoroughfare) and down the Ginza and over to the gate to the Imperial Palace. As the great host marched along, multitudes lined the sides of the streets watching. Bands played, and one

Top: A group of Japanese Christians with the Azabu Tokyo Christian Church in the background, the author and the Rev. Matsuno seated in front, Dr. Woodworth, Miss Stacy and Mr. Garmon at the rear. Bottom: The Azabu Tokyo Christian Sunday School in front of the rebuilt church following the 1923 earthquake. This photo was sent to the author after he returned home possibly to reassure him of their well-being.

Christian song after another was caught up by the marching bands and wafted to many ears that perhaps had never before heard them. Certainly such a procession would make a deep impression upon these people, to say the least.

It was a long march of perhaps a mile and a half to two miles, to the entrance of the palace. When our section arrived, there were thousands already there, but we stood on the high approach to the gates for fully an hour watching the long column coming up to meet us. The bright colors and the shining faces of the thousands of young people and children of this great non–Christian city made an indelible impression on my mind that shall never be effaced. As the sun went down in the west, the great column was finally swallowed up in the mass of humanity about the palace entrance, and with many *banzais* the crowd dispersed and hurried to their homes or to the Imperial Theatre for the evening meeting. At the park where the parade first formed, a large sheet of paper was tacked up containing the words of the principal song of the afternoon, written, I presume, especially for the occasion. [See Appendix, entry 13.]

At the evening meeting, the Rev. Dr. Jordan, pastor of Bethany Church, Philadelphia, presided. He came as the personal representative of John Wanamaker, and he spoke of Dr. Pentecost, pastor of Bethany Church, who was to have spoken tonight but who died suddenly August 1.

Scripture lesson by Bishop H.J. Hamilton, of Seoul. The Scripture was read in Japanese by Hon. Sho Nemoto, member of Parliament, and a prominent temperance worker.

The first address was given by Pres. D.W. Kurtz, of McPherson College, Kansas, on "Winning the World Through Its Childhood." [See Appendix, entry 14.] This address was followed by a short film depicting the modern Good Samaritan.

Address by Dr. W.C. Poole, pastor of Christ Church, London, England–"Healing and Helping a Wounded World." [See Appendix, entry 15.]

At the parade in the afternoon, I had a long talk with Dr. S.H. Wainwright, manager of the Christian Literature Society of Japan. This organization I have described in earlier notes. I visited it while Dr. Peeke was acting as manager during the absence of Dr. Wainwright. The purpose of the society is to disseminate Christian literature in the Japanese tongue. Several papers are published and sent to the young people of the schools. A large number of tracts are published also, and a great deal of good is done. The organization is supported by the sales of literature and by gifts from the various denominational boards. Dr. Wainwright congratulated me on the fact that I had actually gotten out of the beaten paths and gone into the real mission work. He said most secretaries never really see the field. He also said that he knew of no man who was more effective with students than Dr. Woodworth.

Monday, October 11 ———— ◆ ————

Dr. Woodworth went back to Sendai today. I secured my laundry and found the bill amounted to Y1.60 for three shirts, four collars, four kerchiefs, one union suit, one pair heavy pajamas and one towel. Went to the Imperial Theatre as usual.

The Ohio delegation had a picture taken. The theme of today was "The SS and Education."

At the morning session, pictures of their majesties the emperor and empress of Japan were unveiled. These pictures were painted by a SS convention delegate, Mr. John W.L. Forster, Toronto, Canada, and presented to the royal family by the association. Mr. Forster was given an advantageous place at the depot where the emperor and empress left their train upon returning from Nikko recently, and though he could not be seen by them, he was permitted to look at them as they passed to their carriage. Then the clothes they wore were later brought to his room, and with the help of these and pictures of them, the portraits were painted. Japanese artists also helped him with suggestions. The unveiling was a very solemn affair. Mr. Brown and a Japanese official stood before the lowered curtain, the rostrum of which was covered with potted flowers. There was perfect silence in the theatre as the curtain was raised, bringing into view two massive frames holding the portraits. The frames stood upright and were surrounded with flowers and the flag of Japan. The entire audience was standing, and as the curtain reached its height, we were instructed to bow to the pictures, after which the national anthem was sung and the curtain again lowered.

There is a very grave question in my mind as to whether or not the SS convention is doing the right thing by making so much over the high dignitaries of Japan who are not Christian and who make no profession of being such. Baron Shibusawa, who has had such an active interest in the convention, is not a Christian but an avowed Confucianist. He says he is interested in Christianity because it has so much in common with Confucianism. Some years ago, he told that to John Wanamaker, and Mr. Wanamaker replied that the two religions might have many things in common but that there was one great difference: "Buddha is dead, but Christ is alive."

The Rev. J.C. Robertson, of Toronto, was chairman for the evening. The first address was given by the Rev. John T. Faris, D.D., on "Possible Cooperation Between Secular and Religious Education Agencies." [See Appendix, entry 16.]

Bishop Welch spoke on Matt. 20:20, 28. [See Appendix, entry 17.]

Miss Stacy, Mr. Garman, and I lunched downtown and started for Kamakura at 12:25 on a special train as guests of the town. The ride was a beautiful one through Yokohama, a distance of some 35 miles from Tokyo on the seacoast. It is a historic town, and it was quite interesting to see the townsfolk turn out to greet us. There were seven groups of us, designated by different-colored ribbons.

We were met at the station by a great throng of citizens, and after the entire group had gathered, we started for a three-mile walk through the town to the famous Buddhist image Daibutsu. It is 50 feet high and stands out in the open among the trees of a beautiful grove. Although the town is in the "strategic zone," we were given special permission to take pictures of the image.

The image is hollow, and we entered by a low door and climbed up into the head. It is quite large. There were altars and a small shrine inside. I secured a small model of the image.

Our party of 50 was then escorted to the home of Mr. Abasuki, a wealthy resident of the town. Here we found neatly decorated tables standing in the garden

The famous bronze Daibutsu in Kamakura.

where a fine lunch was served. The lunch was foreign-style and very, very good, consisting of orange soda, several kinds of sandwiches, fruit gelatin, cakes and tea. A souvenir lunch in a pretty box was given to each guest to take home, and another souvenir consisting of a specially prepared medal was presented by the Welcome Committee of the town. As we left, we were given a beautiful dahlia, with which the tables were decorated.

After lunch, we were escorted to the beach and had a fine view of the Pacific Ocean.

Returning to the station, we joined in many hearty *banzais* and with the bands playing finally pulled out of the station on our return trip.

On the train we had a pleasant chat with Dr. W.E. Biederwolf. We also met the future husband of Ohara, the cook at Kasumi cho. His name is Mr. Takagi, and his home is in California.

The evening session at the Imperial Theatre opened with a song service. The first address was given by the Rev. W.E. Chalmers, D.D., educational secretary of the American Baptist Publication Society. His subject was "The SS Program for Religious Education." [See Appendix, entry 18.]

Address, Miss Magaret Slattery: "The Full Achievement of Personality, the True Aim of Education." [See Appendix, entry 19.]

Tuesday, October 12 ———— ♦ ————————

Met Miss Hird, of the Canadian M.E. church, whose work is evangelism at Ueda, a city of 30,000 north of Karuizawa. The pastor is a young man, not married, a graduate of a college and theological graduate from Aoyama School in Tokyo. He receives Y35 a month and a house to live in. The church pays Y14 of this amount. The membership is about 50, but the supporting members include only about ten. The average evening attendance is about 20. The members are farmers, one doctor, etc. The doctor is the principal supporter. In the forward movement of the Can. M.E., this church was given a quota of Y3,500, which they raised.

Miss Hird says there is something wrong with their pastors, as they do not teach the fundamentals. She says it may be that the theological seminaries do not teach them. The Y14 a month includes about Y4 a month that the two lady missionaries themselves contribute.

Bishop Welch spoke at the morning session on "The Love of Righteousness." [See Appendix, entry 20.]

Following this address, Prof. Smith led us in "Stand Up for Jesus." He said that the song originated in Philadelphia in 1885. During a revival there, a dying minister said to his fellow ministers, "Stand up, stand up for Jesus." Mr. Duffield, who is in this audience, caught this up and wrote the song.

Address, the Rev. Rufus Miller, SS secretary, Reformed church: "The Community School as a Social Force." [See Appendix, entry 21.]

Address, "World Program for All Lands," by Frank L. Brown proved to be a statement of the budget of the SS Association and an appeal for funds to handle it. Mr. Marion Lawrence made a brief appeal in which he said that the true elixir of life is enthusiasm for God. This, the eighth convention, is the greatest of all. We are here to put religious teaching into all the world. We are here to talk about continents, not backyards.

Mr. Brown presented a budget for the next four years; $40,000 was raised toward a budget of $100,000.

Took lunch with the Rev. Abe and discussed the proposed year's study in America. We decided that inasmuch as the government requires that a Japanese shall have a signed statement from some responsible person agreeing to care for the finances of him in America and inasmuch as that has not been agreed to by the mission board, and furthermore, inasmuch as the spring would be a better time to enter the Moody Bible Institute for a course in SS methods, he shall wait until that time.

In the meantime I am to seek the backing of the board as to his care while in the states but with the understanding that the Rev. Abe is to make every possible effort to work his way through. He is to save what he can while here this year, and I am to seek to secure some means of employment for him while he is in school.

Tuesday evening, the pageant "The City Beautiful," was given. [See Appendix, entry 22.]

Wednesday, October 13   ◆

The first address of the morning was given by Rev. J. Williams Butcher, of London, on "The SS, as a Builder of True Citizenship." [See Appendix, entry 23.] The theme of the day was "SS and National Life."

Address, the Rev. F.W. Langford, "The SS as a Teacher of True Patriotism." [See Appendix, entry 24.]

Address, Bishop Herbert Welch, "The Basis of Fellowship." [See Appendix, entry 25.]

Following this address, the Rev. Alvaro Dos Reis, of Brazil, presented the Japan Committee with a Brazilian Bible wrapped in a Brazilian flag.

The following is a diagram of the flag and a description of the meaning of the colors of the flag:

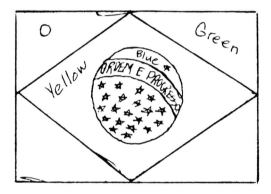

    The green stands for the beautiful flowers of Brazil.
    The yellow for the gold in her hills.
    The blue for her wonderful sky.
    The twenty-one stars for the states of Brazil.
    The one star above the girdle for the capital city, Rio de Janeiro.
    The motto of the girdle, *Ordem E. Progresso* (Order and Progress).

The Bible and flag were received by Dr. Kozaki, and while a little boy from Brazil, a relative of the Rev. Alvaro Dos Reis, played the Japanese and Brazilian anthems on the piano, the two flags were intertwined.

At four o'clock this afternoon, the delegates were the guests of the Patrons' Association of the World's Eighth SS Convention. This organization is the organization of Japanese that has supported the Tokyo convention. The great Imperial Band played a number of selections, after which Viscount Shibusawa, who has been very actively interested in the convention had his speech of welcome read. Owing to illness, he was unable to be present personally. He said he had often been asked why he, a follower of Confucius, should be interested in the SS convention. He said he had talked with Mr. Wanamaker when in America, and he had told him that he was interested because the SS stood for international peace. Second, because of the SS's spiritual significance. The SS gives spiritual life to those who follow its teachings. He expressed an appreciation of the messages delivered on religious education for childhood and the divine musical pageants. Two other speeches were made by Japanese. Justice McLaren, the conv. chairman, made the first response, followed by a response by Dr. Brown. He said, "The speeches we have listened to this afternoon are so in line with the theme of the convention program for the day, 'The SS and National Life,' that we shall print them in the convention records."

I digress again here to say that my fear is growing that the convention will lose its beneficent effect upon Japan as the sponsor of Christianity if it continues to interweave the speeches of avowed non–Christians with those of the Christian faith. The tendency to look up to and to favor the high officials of Japan, regardless of their religious faith, is apt to break down the strong position that Christianity should hold as the true religion of the true God. While these other religions may have many things in common with Christianity so far as moral and ethical teachings are concerned, there is one great outstanding difference that must constantly separate them—that is that the head of Christianity still lives, while the heads of these other dead religions are themselves dead. And to become a Christian means more than merely to accept the ethical teachings of the Bible. It means to recognize oneself as a sinner and Jesus Christ as the only Savior from sin by his shed blood on the cross as a sacrifice for sin. I very much fear the convention is treading on dangerous ground.

Count Uchida, the minister of foreign affairs, made a speech in which he said, "This convention marks an epoch in the history of the Japanese nation. In this new era of reconstruction upon which we are entering, your counsel and advice is desired in the solution of social and ethical problems. You are missionaries of international goodwill and ambassadors of international peace."

Mrs. K. Yanagi sang two very high-class solos. Miss S. Ogura played two classical piano solos.

I did not get notes on the evening program.

Thursday, October 14 ———— ◆ ——————————

I had scarcely gotten seated for the morning session when Dr. Brown announced my name as one of a group who were to meet at once in front of the theatre to attend a very special function that had been arranged and to which he felt we must go. It proved to be an invitation from some 30 members of the House of Peers, the highest legislative body of the Japanese government, to about 100 officers and speakers of the WSS to take dinner with them at the Peers Club. We were taken to the club in autos at 10:30. At the clubhouse we were shown every attention. We were introduced to Prince Tokugawa, president of the House of Peers. He is a very interesting character as he is the last of the long line of *shoguns*, who ruled Japan with a military hand. His full name is Iesato Tokugawa, and he is the fifteenth decendant of the Tokugawa Shogunate, which remained in power for about 250 years and secured for the strife-torn nation a surprisingly long period of peace after centuries of civil war. Ieyasu Tokugawa was the first of this line of *shoguns*. The beginning of the epoch (extending from 1600 to the restoration of the mikadoate in 1868) also saw the most complete development of the feudal system, the eradication of Christianity, the intercourse with foreigners confined to the Chinese and to the Dutch at Nagasaki, and the closing of the country, making of it a hermit nation.

In spite of this fact, it was in this period, 1853, that Commodore Perry came to Japan and succeeded in delivering Pres. Filmore's famous letter to the ruling *shogun* that eventually opened Japan to the world.

The fall of the Tokugawa Shogunate occurred Oct. 14, 1867, a date that is considered the great turning point in Japan's history if not a signal event in the history of the world. The shogunate of Tokugawa had held power for nearly three centuries, holding a court of Yedo that lacked no attribute of stately magnificance or autocratic strength. On the day mentioned, Prince Iesato Tokugawa, whom I shook hands with at this reception, consented to lay aside his power in favor of the emperor. It is possible that in doing so he saved himself from the fate of many of his predecessors, and there is no doubt that he has now more power than he could have had otherwise. Quoting Terry: "This date marked the overthrow of the dual system of government, the practical extinction of feudalism; the putting aside of conservatism; and the emerging of Japan on the road 'which since has led her to one of the highest places among the progressive nations of the world.' The Meiji, or 'Era of Enlighted Government' (245th since the Taikwas Era of A.D. 645–50), was inaugurated with the downfall of the Shogunate and the Imperial Restoration. Mutsuhito, the 123rd Emperor, was crowned at Kyoto, Nov. 12, 1868."

We were also introduced to Baron Oku, president of the House of Representatives. He also shook hands American fashion. There were a number of other peers and barons present.

After an informal social hour in the spacious and beautiful rooms of the club, we were escorted to the dining room where an elegant dinner was served. At the theatre I had met a Mr. Holsted, who is an electrician in Tokyo. He is a Christian and has given much of his time to the convention. When the building burned, Mr. Holsted got three good photographs of the burning structure, which were shown in slides last night. At our table there was Mr. Cole, of Salem, Massachusetts; Dr. Takeshi Ukai, pastor of Ginza M.E. Church, Tokyo; Mr. John D. Haskill, Wakefield, Nebraska; and Mr. Sho Nemoto, member of Parliament, 15 Shiba Shikoku, the man who every year for a long time has vainly entered a temperance bill for the protection of minors. He told me he was also the sponsor of the free-education bill, though I did not have time to find out the content of the bill.

Among others I met personally were Baron C. Shiba, "Membre de la Chambre des Paris de Japan" (thus his card reads), and Baron N. Kuroda, member of House of Peers.

After the dinner a speech of welcome was read from Baron Shibusawa, who was unable to be present on account of sickness. Prince Tokugawa read a speech also, as

Placing a stone at the base of an idol, an act of sincere devotion and worship.

did Baron Oku. I quote in full one of the speeches, which I think was the one sent by Mr. Shibusawa. [See Appendix, entry 26.] This comes from a man who does not profess to be a Christian but an avowed Confucianist.

Justice McLaren and Dr. Brown responded, after which Baron Sakatani read a speech and on motion of Dr. Brown, he was made member of the World SS Association. He does not profess to be a Christian, and there is considerable criticism on the part of both foreigners and Japanese that Dr. Brown had exceeded his authority.

It was stated by Dr. Brown that this dinner given in the rooms of the members of the House of Peers was the first of its kind in history where SS representatives were thus recognized by such an assembly.

After dinner, we were taken in autos back to the theatre, and a few minutes later, Miss Stacy, Mr. Garman and I as official delegates were on our way to Tokyo station to take the 12:55 train to Yokohama where we were to be the guests of that city for the afternoon. The party was divided into three groups, represented by white, pink and red flowers. The wearers of the white, our group, were taken to the 12:55 train. We missed it by one minute but took the 1:16 train with the pinks.

Arriving at Yokohama, we were taken in autos to the Yokohama Park. As we entered, we were given a souvenir pin and books illustrating the city, also an official program of the afternoon. At the park we were given seats in the open before a juggler's stand and a bandstand. The first juggler used three sticks and a ball. The second was a girl who juggled tops on a stick, a sword edge and a fan, opening the fan with the top spinning on its paper edge. The third stood on his head on a small standard and turned completely around. He then lighted a cigarette. Again on his head, he drank a glass of water, and finally he went through dancing motions, still on his head.

During the entire program, fireworks were set off, releasing flags of many nations, national emblems, etc., which floated gracefully to the ground.

Following this, the band played a number of selections. At 3:30, the following program was carried out:

1. March by the SS children
2. Hymn
3. Address of welcome by the mayor of Yokohama and president of the Welcoming Committee
4. Address by the president of the convention
5. Hymn by the SS children
6. Doxology
7. Benediction

On the train returning to Tokyo, we witnessed the most beautiful sunset I have seen since coming to Japan. It was a sunset on the water, with Fujiyama in the foreground. It cannot be described. The various tints of the sky changed constantly, and with a small wreath of clouds floating around the majestic mountain in the changing rays of the sun, one was entranced by the sight.

We went at once to the theatre for the closing program of the Convention. The pageant "The Court of Christianity" was first presented. [See Appendix, entry 27.]

Before the pageant, the great choir of perhaps 800 voices was led by Prof. Smith. This choir was about three-fourths Japanese and one-fourth American. Prof. Smith has done a really great thing by coming over here and in the space of a few months gathering together such a large group of Japanese and teaching them to sing effectively in English such master productions as they sang. The kind of music he stood for throughout the convention was of the worshipful type of the old hymns. His vivid word pictures and descriptions of the origin of the hymns were most helpful features.

Following the pageant, a number of different people were introduced who had done special work during the convention or in preparation for it. Among others, four boys were brought to the platform and introduced as the four who rescued one of the pianos from the burning building. Many *banzais* were given for different persons.

Miss Magaret Slattery gave the closing address of the convention on "The Ever Present Christ, the Hope of the New World." Miss Slattery did not really devote herself to this theme but spoke on the present crisis in China and made an appeal for funds for the China sufferers. After the convention, an offering for this relief work was taken at the doors.

As we went out, we were given souvenir artist reproductions by the Patrons' Committee, a box of candy by the Marinaga Candy Co., and numerous other leaflets and souvenirs, among them a little tube of digestion tablets from a local druggist.

At the Eighth World SS Convention, there were 996 registered foreign and Japanese missionary delegates divided among the following lands: Siam, 1; India, 5; Holland, 3; Formosa, 1; Africa, 1; Netherland Indies, 1; Scotland, 4; England, 5;

Australia, 7; South America, 4; Hawaii, 8; Philippine Islands, 23; China, 17; Korea, 43; Japanese missionaries, 307; Canada, 70; U.S.A., 480; Doubtful, 16.

Friday, October 15 ———————— ◆ ————————————————

Remained at the house all day trying to get caught up on some letters and other writings. Found that I was pretty well fagged out after the long grind of the past few weeks.

IV. Sightseeing and Exploring

Saturday, October 16 ——————— ◆ ———————————

We had a Japanese wedding here this afternoon. Miss Hara, our cook, was married to a Mr. Takagi of California, who came here as a delegate to the SS convention but with the intention of getting married while here. The couple had never met until last Sunday afternoon, six days before the wedding. The wedding had been arranged by the Rev. and Mrs. Matsuno, pastor of our Azabu Church, and was arranged in true Japanese-style. The young man was an old acquaintance of the Rev. Matsuno who after inquiring as to the characteristics of the girl, decided that he would be the proper person for her and by correspondence with him in America arranged the match. They had exchanged pictures and corresponded, though they had never met. The original plan was for her to go to America with the last boatload of picture brides, before this was stopped by the California agitation. But she failed to get off. She was then asked if she wanted to give up the match and choose a husband here, but she said she was betrothed to this man and would not let the delay interfere with it. So it was arranged that he should come for her.

We decorated the house as nicely as we could and went together in having made for her a very nice American dress.

At two o'clock, the guests began to assemble, and at about three, to the strains of *Lohengrin*'s "Wedding March," played by a young Japanese girl, the bridal party descended the stairs, Mr. and Mrs. McKnight acting as best man and bridesmaid. The Rev. Matsuno performed the ceremony, which was Christian throughout, the single-ring service being used.

Following the ceremony, tea and cake were served. I then had the privilege of taking the picture of the bridal party.

Later on, a magnificent Japanese dinner was served on lacquer trays, but at a table. The dinner closed with the cutting of the bride's cake and the boxing-up of the leftover dinner for the guests to take home, true Japanese-style. At the wedding I met the Rev. Kunio Kodaira, pastor of the largest Congregational church in Tokyo. The church has a membership of 250. The pastor receives a total salary of Y120 a month and parsonage, the church paying Y20 a month of this salary. The church also pays Y28 a month to benevolences and the parsonage rent. The total amount raised by the church each month is Y90. A new building is contemplated, the American board to assist. The Rev. Kodaira has spent a number of years in America, several of his children being born there. He says they declare they are going back to America when they get big.

147

About nine o'clock, the bridal couple left. He left alone first, to secure a *kuruma* for her to ride to the station. As he went out the door, we showered him with rice, true American-style. Later on, the *kuruma* came, and the bride went away alone, the pastor following on the streetcar. They took the eleven o'clock train for his home, some 40 hours ride to the south. They will leave for America in November.

Sunday, October 17 ━━━━━━━ ◆ ━━━━━━━━━━━━━━━

Went to the Naka Shibuya church this morning in the rain and preached there at 10:30. The Rev. Ishigaki is pastor. There were about 20 present. A description of this church will be given later.

I noticed in the church little pieces of wood painted black and looking very much like color samples of paint used in the U.S.A. Upon these were written the names of the church members in white. The blocks were hung in family groups.

This afternoon we attended the Tokyo Union Church, an organization of foreigners in Tokyo that worships in the Ginza M.E. Church. The Rev. J. Williams Butcher of London preached.

Came home in a heavy rain and spent the evening at home.

Monday, October 18 ━━━━━━━ ◆ ━━━━━━━━━━━━━━━

Wrote some letters and received a letter from my wife dated September 21. It seemed good to hear from home, even though the letter was a month old.

This evening Mr. Garman and I went to the home of Mr. Taizumi in Shibuya for supper. This is the father of Y. Taizumi in Defiance College. We met the father and mother and two sisters. Another sister attends school, and another brother is in Manchuria. They treated us with the utmost hospitality and served a very fine Japanese and American meal combined. The meals for guests are usually ordered from a caterer and brought in. We spent a pleasant evening together talking about the son and his work. They seemed very appreciative of what little I had attempted to do for the boy. The family is well-to-do, but the father is not in sympathy with Christianity.

Tuesday, October 19 ━━━━━━━ ◆ ━━━━━━━━━━━━━━━

Spent the morning writing up my notes for 10 or 12 days past. After dinner, Mr. Garman and I went to the photographer to see about getting a lot of SS, Japanese and some of my original Kodak pictures made into slides. We found that this man, Kinjko Shokwai, has so many orders ahead that he cannot mail these to me before the middle of January. I have a very good set of pictures, which he said would make good slides. I think I shall have to risk having them made here as the cost is about one-third what it is in the States and the work seems quite satisfactory.

Remained at home and read tonight.

Wednesday, October 20 ——————— ◆ ————————————————

On our way to Yokohama today, Mr. Garman and I went to order some slides of the SS convention and also some from the films I had made. The name of the firm that is to do the work is Kinjo Shokwai, 4, Takekawacho, Kyobashiku, Tokyo, Tel. 835 Ginza. I ordered some 50 or more slides, mostly from my own negatives, and later on I am to order some of the SS slides. At present the firm is so rushed with orders that it cannot keep up, and it is impossible to secure them for some months, so I will have them sent to America after I return. Was glad to learn that every negative I desired a slide from was sufficiently good to be used.

We spent the day in Yokohama in a driving rain. I ordered four shirts made with an extra pair of cuffs to each at a cost of Y1.85 each. The Korean cloth from which they are to be made cost Y1.08 a yard, or Y3.78 for the three and a half yards necessary for each shirt. Thus each shirt will cost me Y5.63, or $2.82. In America a shirt of similar material would cost at least twice as much, and it is doubtful that such material could be secured there at all.

I also secured my ticket for the return trip to America on the *Shinyo*, which is scheduled to sail December 4. Did considerable shopping, buying *kimonos* for each of the family, including a cheap one for myself and also some Christmas gifts and material for a missionary exhibition.

We took dinner at a Russian restaurant, Y1.50.

Thursday, October 21 ——————— ◆ ————————————————

Left the house at 5:45 A.M. in a downpour with Brother Garman for Mashiko, an outpost of Moka, one of our preaching places in the Utsunomiya field. Bought a *unagi dumburii* for breakfast. It consisted of an earthen bowl holding more than a pint of boiled rice covered with a layer of *unagi* (eel) well cooked. There was also a small box holding two pieces of *daikon* (a sort of Japanese radish) and two slices of pickles. The price of the whole breakfast was 60 sen (30¢) each.

Saw a trainload of soldiers at one station. At Ueno station where we took the train, we met Mrs. Watanabe, our Bible woman of Iinogawa. She has been in Tokyo since the opening of the SS convention. She explained that she had been sick. Her two sons were with her. Her daughter is attending school in Tokyo.

Arrived at Moka at 10:30, and the Rev. Irokawa met us on the train. We went five miles farther north to Mashiko, his outpost station.

MASHIKO

A town of several thousand people, with a total of 7,000 people within a radius of one mile from its center. It is 78 miles northwest of Tokyo and 10 miles southeast of Utsunomiya across country. To reach Utsunomiya, one must go round about by rail.

The Rev. Irokawa has been preaching at Mashiko until lately but at present can rent no preaching place. There is a young girl who is in school in Tokyo but who

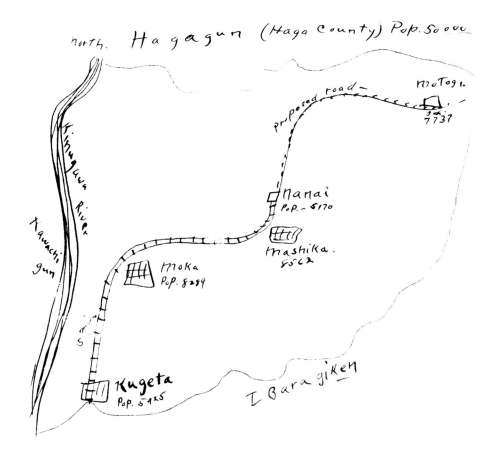

Map of Hagagun (by the author).

lives here, and she is the only Christian in the town. Within a radius of one mile from the town, there are the usual number of Shinto shrines found about such towns. We visited several of them and also a large Buddhist temple. In fact, the temple and several of the shrines are built on the same plot of ground, strengthening the statement made by the Buddhist priest at Tsukidate that people could be both Buddhists and Shintoists without conflict. We visited one very tiny shrine set up off the ground which was dedicated to the strengthening of the feet. We found a large number of sandals hanging on nearby trees. They were of all sizes, and many or all of them were new, having been offered to the god in the hope that the offerer would receive strength in his feet thereby.

We returned to Moka at 12:22. The Rev. Matsuno, who is to interpret for me on this trip, did not come as we expected. We went to the hotel and rested until two o'clock when we went to the primary school where the town officials had arranged a reception for me. The mayor, Mr. Konda, met us. He has been a citizen here 30 years. Also met Mr. Shintuo Mishimoto, the principal of the school where the meeting was held.

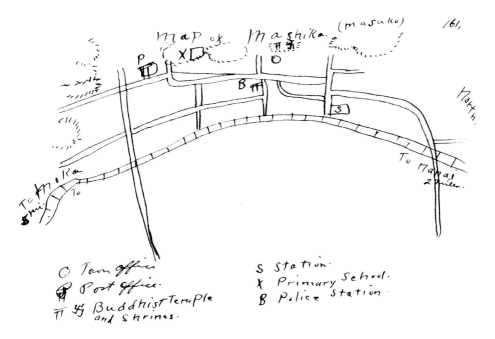

Map of Mashika (by the author).

Mr. Matsuno came on the 2:40 train. We went into a large room filled with about 150 citizens, and I spoke for 50 minutes on "The Principles of World Citizenship." A few minutes after I began to speak, a man near the front began to talk loudly and started for the platform. Several men grabbed him and after a hard tussle succeeded in dragging him out of the room. He was a drunken *kuruma* man. The attention was scarcely diverted for a moment, and even those next to the man paid little attention to him. In America, I fancy that it would have been difficult to hold the attention. Secured the following information from the Rev. Irokawa:

THE REV. Y. IROKAWA

Lives at Moka Machi, Tochigi ken. Became a Christian in 1893 through the Rev. Jones and Mr. Ota (our first convert) at Ishinomaki. Studied Christianity three years before he accepted it. Met the Rev. Watanabe (husband of our present Bible woman) and the Rev. Nakazama. While the latter was pastor at Ishinomaki, Miss Penrod baptized Mr. Irokawa.

He has a wife and seven children. The oldest son died while a theological student. The ages of the living children are as follows: girl, 21; girl, 19; boy, 17; boy, 14; girl, 12; girl, 3; boy, 2.

The Rev. Irokawa had eight years of elementary-school education at Ishinomaki. At 16 he entered the private school of English language at Ishinomaki where he studied two years. At 32 he entered the theological school of Dr. Woodworth and Miss Penrod at Tokyo. Before this, however, for some 16 years he farmed.

He has been preaching for 15 years. Began preaching at Utsunomiya where he remained eight years. Then spent five years in the pastorate at Ishinomaki and has been at Moka two years.

MOKA, TOCHIGI KEN

Population 8,000. Located 68 miles northeast of Tokyo and 11 miles east across country from Utsunomiya, but 50 miles by train.

We have had preaching here about 15 years. The Rev. Irokawa and Brother Fry started the work. Then Mr. Sano (now in New York City) came and held daily Bible school for two summers. Then O. Takahashi (now in Hololulu) came one summer, and the Rev. Abe and the Rev. Irokawa's son held the school together one summer.

After graduation from the theological school, the Rev. Abe took this field as his first resident pastorate. He was here five years.

The work is supported by the woman's board of the Erie Conference.

Preaching and kindergarten are held in the pastor's home, which the mission rents at Y13 a month.

There are 11 resident church members. Preaching is held weekly morning and evening. The average church attendance is five in the morning and ten at night. The average attendance at SS is 35; at weekly prayer meeting, five or six; in the kindergarten (recently started in May), 45. When Mr. Fry visits the fields and speaks, the students attend the services, and the attendance is about 20. He comes monthly and gives a magic-lantern lecture on Saturday evening to about 100, mostly children. He preaches Sunday and speaks at the middle school on Monday before returning to Utsunomiya.

The Rev. Irokawa holds street meetings in the summer and distributes many tracts. He feels that the people are becoming interested. There are now seven inquirers.

Two of the members are businessmen, one an official in the court, one a teacher in the primary school. The church pays Y1.50 a month on the salary.

In this town there is a middle school of 500, a primary school of 1,000, a girls' school of 200, and an agricultural school of 150.

The kindergarten was started in the spring of this year, with Mrs. Irokawa (a trained kindergartener) and her daughter in charge. The average attendance is 43 daily. The kindergarten is now self-supporting. Mrs. Irokawa and daughter receive Y36 a month together.

The greatest need here, the pastor thinks, is land for a church. They are gathering money for it now and have on hand Y12, having just begun to raise the fund. Land here would not cost a great deal a *tsubo* as most of it is owned by three men who have cornered it. It will not become cheaper.

Had supper at the hotel, which proved to be considerably American in style, with fried pork and cutlets. With a slice of bread and jam that we had brought along, we got along nicely.

In the evening we went to the Rev. Irokawa's where about 22 people, including eight schoolboys, had gathered. I spoke on "The Friendship of Jesus." I urged an

Portrait of the Rev. G. Sano, an early convert of Dr. Woodworth and now one of the most faithful pastors in Japan.

immediate decision after the service. On the way from Moka to Mashiko in the morning, the engineer of the train left his engine in charge of the assistant and came back to ride with us.

He was a fine-looking young man, and the pastor stated that he was not yet a Christian but was an earnest seeker. He was very attentive to us. I took his picture in his engine cab. At the close of the evening service, he tarried after the others had gone and asked to be baptized. The decision to become a Christian had been made. I went to the hotel full of joy.

After the town reception in the afternoon, the town officials hurried away to the hotel to give a reception to a judge who was leaving the town. The reception was in progress right next to our room when we came back for supper, and following their supper they had the *geisha* (dancing women of ill repute) come in and give an entertainment. Their weird music and strange dialogues were anything but pleasing to us, but the guests assembled were laughing loudly and long when we left for the evening meeting. We were thankful upon our return to find that the banquet was over.

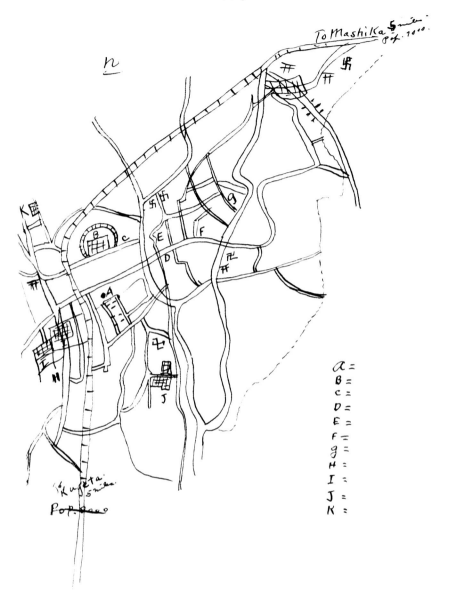

Unfinished map of Moka (by the author, who never filled in the legend key).

Saturday, October 23 ──────── ◆ ──────────────

    Had fried eggs for breakfast in the Moka Hotel. Fine. Also some Japanese food. Some pickled plums were served, and the Rev. Matsuno said it was the belief of the people of Japan that if one would eat one of these plums in the morning, good luck would follow all day.

    After breakfast we paid our bill, amounting to Y2.50 each plus 50 sen tea money and went to the middle school where I spoke. We then went to the pastor's home to see the kindergarten and attend a mothers' meeting.

While waiting at the school, Mr. Matsuno stated that Premier Hara had really offered the Parliament buildings to the SS convention but that they were not suitable to be used. He also stated that Dr. Brown and Justice McLaren had been given an audience with their majesties, the emperor and empress. He further stated that literature attacking Japanese policy in China had been received from China but that it was not allowed to be distributed. At the middle school I spoke to nearly 500 fine-looking boys. It was an inspiration. As I entered, they stood at attention and bowed as only Japanese boys can.

Hurried from here to the Rev. Irokawa's where the kindergarten of 45 little tots was in progress. Mrs. Irokawa and daughter Ei certainly are doing a fine work with the songs, exercises and hand work. The children pay 1 yen a month and come two and a half hours (9:00 to 11:30) each day six days a week. And on every other day they bring their *bentos* (lunches) and stay from 9:00 to 1:00. I took their pictures and also one of the group of 50 men and women who came for the mother's meeting to follow. The town seems to be back of the kindergarten, and the opportunity is great.

Left at 12:30 for Utsunomiya. We had some bread and jam with us and ate lunch at one of the transfer points. At Oyama, the last transfer point, we found nothing but an express train going within two hours, so we paid 65 sen extra and took it to Utsunomiya, arriving at 3:30. A number of girls from Mrs. Fry's school were there to meet us, and they piloted us to the hotel where Mr. Matsuno had preceded us with the baggage in a *kuruma*.

The Rev. Kimura soon came, and I secured the following information:

THE REV. KINNOSUKE KIMURA

Address, Yojo Machi, Utsunomiya. Age 36. Has wife and three children. The children are a girl, Yoko, meaning "sun" (name of wife's grandfather), aged 5 years; a boy, Tadamichi, meaning "faithful to the word," aged 3; a girl, Nobuko, meaning "faith," aged 1.

The Rev. Kimura's mother attended Episcopal church at Tokyo and took him with her. At 8 he was baptized. Went to primary school, then to St. Paul's Episcopal Middle School at Tokyo, and then to college at the same place. Later he attended the divinity school connected with St. Paul College.

The Rev. Kimura preached first at the Episcopal church in Utsunomiya, where he remained about six years. He was dropped by them because they had to retrench and was then taken up by our mission and given the Christian church at Utsunomiya, where he has been for two years.

UTSUNOMIYA

Tochigi ken capital. Utsunomiya is about 66 miles northeast of Tokyo. The population is 60,000. The population of Tochigi ken, of which Utsunomiya is the capital, is a million souls.

Following are the churches in the city: M.E., resident pastor, membership 45. Pastor's salary Y60 of which the church pays about Y8. Pastor had no children

1. Girls' school – 20
2. G. church
3. M.E. Church – 300
4. Roman Catholic
5. Girls' school – 40
6. City office
7. Presby. Church
8. Primary schools
9. Sal. Army
10. Holiness
11. Greek(?) Church
12. Sunday school – 300
13. Com. School – 300
14. Episc. Church
15. Fry's home
• S.S. conducted by girls' school

Map of Utsunomiya (by the author).

but had he children, he would receive Y6 for each a month. They have no church building, but meet in pastor's home, which is rented. The Japan Forward Movement of the M.E. is attempting to raise Y600,000 in three years, of which Y13,000 is to be put into land and church and parsonage here. They have about half of it raised.

Episcopal church. Membership 40. Resident pastor. Salary Y90, of which the church pays Y12. There is no children's allowance paid. Children may attend the mission schools free. They have a church building and parsonage. Parsonage was

The Rev. Kimura and family, for a number of years pastor of the Christian Church, Utsunomiya, Japan.

built by a missionary but is being bought by the Japan mission of the Episc. church as rent—seven years to pay. The average attendance of SS is 50. They also have a kindergarten.

Presbyterian church. Membership 40. Resident pastor. Salary about Y60 or 70, of which the church pays Y4 or Y5. The Rev. Kimura is not sure as to their children's allowances. The SS attendance is about 40, but the pastor is the only teacher. They have a Japanese church building and parsonage owned by the mission. They are in bad location, so building a new plant has been postponed.

Holiness church. Membership 20. Resident pastor who receives Y50, the church paying Y3 or Y4 a month. SS attendance 30. No church building but rent a parsonage where meetings are held. They plan to build.

Salvation Army. Membership 15 or 20, but very changeable. Two ladies in charge who live here. Salaries Y30 and Y25, respectively. A house is rented for services. The church pays Y4 or Y5 on salaries. The SS attendance is 40.

There is also a Roman Catholic and a Greek Catholic church, but the pastor knows nothing of either of them.

Christian church. Membership 60. Salary of pastor, including children's allowances, is Y57, of which the church pays Y4. The church building and parsonage are rented from Mrs. Fry at a low rental. The SS attendance averages 60.

Union prayer meetings are held once a month, the M.E., the Holiness and Christian churches uniting. The attendance is 50 or 60. The girls' school of Mrs. Fry has its own prayer meeting.

Our church has started a YMCA, an organization of young men, and they have their own prayer meeting once a month with an attendance of 15. This organization came through the influence of the lending library, of which Mr. Garman is in charge. A student saw the advertisement of the library in a paper and started to read the literature. He then started to the Utsunomiya church, bringing boys with him, and thus the organization started.

Our kindergarten attendance is 35. Each pays Y1 a month. Miss Natsue Furu-yama is the teacher. Mrs. Fry controls the kindergarten and pays the salary.

There are the following schools in Utsunomiya: Utsunomiya Middle School, where Mrs. Fry teaches English, 600 students; Shimotsuke Middle School, 500; Tochigi Commercial School, 500; Utsunomiya Commercial School, 300; Tochigi Agricultural School, 300; primary schools numbering five, with a total enrollment of 6,000; Tochigi Girls' School, 700. They pay Y4 tuition a month, while Mrs. Fry's girls pay only Y1 a month. The teachers in this school receive an average of Y80, while Mrs. Fry's teachers receive an average of less than Y30. The school has 40 teachers. Mrs. Fry's school of 30 girls has 3 teachers beside herself.

Utsunomiya also has the following: School of Art and Industry, 300; Kyowa Sewing School, 400, tuition Y3; Asachi Girls' School, 40; normal school for men, 300; normal school for women, 200; 15 Buddhist temples; 15 Shinto shrines (there are many different sects).

The Rev. Kimura feels the need of a Bible woman because most of his members are women.

At seven o'clock, we went to the church for a welcome meeting. Met Miss Sato, Mrs. Fry, Mrs. Awana and others, among them Mr. Taketa, a teacher in the middle school and a fine Christian. He speaks English well and gave his address in both Japanese and English. A schoolboy also gave a welcome address on behalf of the YMCA.

During the social hour, I had a good talk with Mrs. Awana and also met Mr. Kawakura, who was chosen chief engineer of the emperor's train between Utsunomiya and Nikko. During the refreshments, the boys sang us a song, and the girls followed with another. Miss Sato and Mrs. Awana also sang. Miss Sato had a number of girls blacken their faces and act out in pantomime "Old Black Joe" while she sang the song. Mrs. Fry had gone home early. I wondered if she knew what they were doing and what she would think of it.

After the Benediction, I suggested that they shake hands American-style. They did so with vim. Miss Sato then led the girls in the song "Good Night, Mr. Minton, Mr. Garman, Mr. Matsuno." We responded with "Good Night, Ladies."

Before supper tonight, we took a bath. We were each brought a large bathrobe, which we donned, and proceeded to the bathroom downstairs. It was simply the washroom with a bathroom attached. The tub was about three feet across and heated from the side. We squatted on the floor and soaped ourselves good, then sponged off while we waited for the two men occupying the tub to get out. When they finally got out, we crawled in, two at a time, and steamed in the hot water. A cold sponge followed, and we were ready for supper.

Sunday, October 24 ───────── ◆ ─────────

At nine o'clock we went to SS at our church. There were 82 present at SS. Mrs. Awana and Miss Sato both teach classes of girls. Mrs. Fry teaches the young men.

Classroom scene.

I was introduced to Hiroshi Sekine, a soldier in the Engineering Department of the army. He is a member of the Sendai church and a very earnest fellow. He said the regular soldier in the army receives Y18 a month, board and clothes. An engineer receives Y120 because of his special work. A regiment is composed of 600 men.

The SS was very interesting. I spoke at the close and asked them to sing "Jesus Loves Me." They did it in Japanese and then to my surprise in English.

Following SS, I took a picture.

At the morning service, Mr. Garman read a sermon in Japanese on "God's Desire for Friendship." Following this, the Rev. Matsuno spoke on the meaning of baptism, as several girls were to be baptized. One girl's parents refused to let her come this morning because she wished to be baptized. She slipped away and came and was baptized. There were eight girls in all, and this service saw the last one of Mrs. Fry's school baptized, one having made the decision this morning. One of the girls baptized was the first graduate of our kindergarten here. The girls were taken into the baptistry and sprinkled standing in the water.

After dinner, we visited Imaizumi Nichiyo Gakko. This is one of Mrs. Fry's 11 SS's, conducted by girls from her school. She sent the girls to conduct us to the school. It was a long walk through town and down beside the railroad at the edge of town. The SS was held in a home rented by the mission in a very poor section. The girls did well. I spoke and sang and had them sing. Then took a picture; 85 present. While the house was a very poor house, I was impressed by the sight of a miniature

Group of small to pre-teen children. These children differ markedly from the children in other pictures in that they are all barefooted and all are dressed in what appear to be hand-me-down American clothes.

garden about 90 inches long by 50 inches wide just outside the back door. By placing a barrel full of water outside the fence, they had succeeded in creating a small fountain that emptied into a tiny lake full of goldfish. There was a little island, and on the mainland several miniature trees with grass and flowers growing about. Although in so small a space, the scene was really beautiful and demonstrates again the fact that the Japanese are lovers of the beautiful.

The Rev. Matsuno told me that the Japanese have a superstition that twice a year they must make offerings to the moon. This occurs on August 15 and September 13, according to the lunar calendar, the latter being the same as our October 24, which is tonight. We saw a number of offerings to the moon in the home where the SS was held and also in various other places. At this home, we saw cooked sweet potatoes, radishes, large moon-shaped balls of rice paste, boiled rice, daikon, chestnuts and wine.

After the afternoon SS, Mr. Taketa and the Rev. Kimura called on us. I asked the price of land here and find it was Y80 a *tsubo* on the main street, but that a good location could likely be secured near our church for Y8 a *tsubo*. It would seem that there are enough boys' schools here.

The opposition to Christianity is great. At the evening service, we found a very large attendance. As a rule, they have no evening service. There were perhaps 125 present. The Rev. Matsuno spoke on the SS convention. I followed with a message on "The Lamp of Light," using a Japanese lantern and an oil lamp as illustrations.

Mr. Taketa interpreted well. Good interest. I enjoyed the day immensely and made many new friends.

Monday, October 25 ———— ◆ ————————

In the middle of the night, several drunken soldiers came into the room next to ours and called for some *geisha* (evil women) and some *sake*. The proprietor said it was too late. They argued loudly for a little bit, then in anger got up and left.

Took pictures of the Frys' home. Mrs. Fry has 30 girls in her school. Ten of these are day pupils living in Utsunomiya. They all pay Y1 a month. The girls who live in the dormitory pay Y1 a month tuition and Y7 a month for board. The three teachers receive about Y75 a month, or Y25 each. Mrs. Awana receives Y23, Mrs. Taketa Y25 and Miss Sato's salary has not yet been determined. Third Church, Norfolk, is to pay it. Her expenses coming back were all paid by Mrs. Fry. School runs ten months a year.

If ten scholarships were to be paid by friends in America, the school would be self-supporting. Mrs. Fry expects to bring Miss Fumi Sato back as soon as she can get the money. Just now, she is hard-pressed by high prices.

The school has a curriculum embracing high school studies and music. Fifty sen a month is charged extra for music.

Went to the school and took a picture of the girls, also two interior rooms and the building. The building is three-story and has recitation rooms, dormitory and other rooms. There is a small museum, science apparatus (though not extensive), etc. The girls seem to enjoy themselves very well.

The Rev. Kimura has a SS once a month at Shirasawa six miles from Utsunomiya. The attendance is 15 or 20.

This morning the police called on the Rev. Kimura and apologized for not having a guard for me at the meeting last night. But he told him he felt I was safe since it was a Christian meeting. He said he would send word to Yaita, where we went today, to have the police protect me there. The Rev. Kimura told him I was perfectly safe.

At 12:15, we started for Yaita. Some of the girls and the Rev. Kimura saw us off. Third class was so crowded that we took second and ate our lunch on the train. It consisted of buns and jam, fruit and chocolate. The second-class fare was Y1.04.

The Rev. Muraoka met us at the station, and we went at once to the hotel across the street from the station. In five minutes we were on our way to speak at a girls' school at 2:00 P.M., being informed that at four o'clock the town would welcome me. On our way, we paid our respects to the police office, the town office, the tax office, the bank, the county office and the agricultural school, finally ending up at the girls' school. There are really two or three schools combined, there being about 80 girls and about 900 primary boys and girls. The ground covers two acres.

The girls were quite interested and sent their greetings to the girls of America.

At four o'clock, a town reception was held. There were about 60 present. The president of the agricultural school gave the address of welcome. He spoke with great eloquence on the contribution of America to agricultural work in Japan and stressed the fact that the good relations between Japan and America should be continued. I followed with a short response, explaining the purpose of the SS convention and that it aimed at right international relations. During tea, Mr. Garman gave a very interesting temperance address by simply contrasting the difference between America now and what it was the last time he was home. There was a newspaper representative from a Utsunomiya paper.

THE REV. A. MURAOKA

Age 39. Married and has six children: a girl, Aika ("love"), age 12; girl, Nobuko ("faith"), age 11; girl, Motsuko ("hope"), age 9; girl, Eiko ("glory"), age 7; boy, Hiromichi ("propogating the way"), age 5; girl, Mitsuko ("light"), age 2.

He was converted in 1904 at Wakuya under the Rev. Kitano. Studied agriculture at the school in Wakuya two years, then at the agriculture school at Sendai two years, then at Dr. Woodworth's Bible school in Tokyo two years. Then he took a special course of the theological department at Tohoku Gakuin at Sendai for three years. Postgraduate work of one year at the Tokyo Theological School at Tokyo, of which the Rev. Uimuri is pres. He was here one year.

Began preaching in 1906 at Wakayanagi where he remained five years. Came to Yaita in January 1911. While at Wakayanagi, he also worked at Kannari and Iwagasaki.

He says he studies at night now, reading magazines and books. Calls some in daytime but cannot study because of the noise of the children. Studies the Bible an hour a day with a commentary.

YAITA

Population, including surrounding territory, is 12,800. We have had work here about 14 years. It is located 20 miles north of Utsunomiya and about 85 miles north of Tokyo. We have no church building, but services are held in the pastor's home rented for the purpose. The rental is Y7 a month but will be increased if the house is properly arranged for services, as at present, there is a carpenter's shop at one end.

The present resident membership is six. One a merchant, one a schoolteacher recently converted, two farmers and one a private teacher of sewing. One is a city official.

Pastor's salary is Y60, including children's allowance. The church pays 25 sen a month on this. Raise about 1 yen a month for other things.

The average church attendance (evening only) is eight or nine. Average SS attendance ten. No prayer meeting.

The town respects the church but is indifferent. The Rev. Muraoka holds some street meetings and has good audiences. Has a home department of those unable to come. He teaches in seven different homes. Also has cradle roll.

There are at present 12 inquirers. The pastor feels that the greatest need at present is a permanent church building. The people need to feel that the work is to be permanent. There are the following schools here: primary school, 1,000; girls' school, 80; agriculture and forestry school, 130.

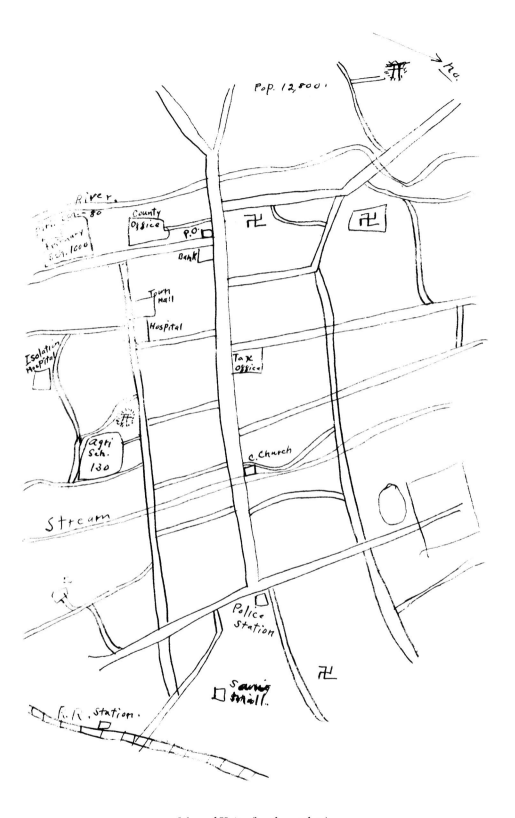

Map of Yaita (by the author).

The Rev. Muraoka has a lending library, established since last January for adults and children, especially the latter. About 400 loans have already been made.

At the evening service, we found 78 teachers, town officials, schoolboys and girls gathered. This is quite unusual as the average attendance is 8 or 9. I spoke on "The Glorious Gospel," and the Rev. Matsuno followed with a story of his father and mother and God's answer to his prayers. The attendance of school boys and girls was remarkable in view of the fact that just a few doors away a minstrel of some kind was holding forth on the street. A teacher, Mr. Kato, was recently converted and seems to be a very fine man.

Following the regular meeting, about 25 remained for tea and cake, during which time Mr. Fujita, the merchant, spoke a word of welcome expressing appreciation of our visit and telling of the great need for a church, which he hoped the mission board would help to build. I replied, telling of our interest and our desire to help, that there were many needy places and we were trying to help all. I suggested three things they could do for themselves: (1) tithe; (2) win others by personal work; (3) pray. Mr. Garman spoke a few minutes, and at 10:30 the meeting closed with a very good spirit. But before we closed, I gave to the girls present some of the pennies sent to girls of Japan by the girls' class at Madrid, Iowa. I was surprised when the girls gave me a dozen Japanese pennies to return to their American girlfriends. I had given about 60 of the pennies to the girls at Utsunomiya.

Tuesday, October 26 ———————— ◆ ————————

The Rev. Muraoka called at eight o'clock and stated that my visit had been a very great help to him in his work. He said the principal of the girls' school was so pleased that he wrote him a letter of appreciation for my speech. The teachers also stated that they had attended the town reception and were well pleased with the message.

The Rev. Muraoka stated that the visit had given him a grip on the town and a new spirit for work. He then stated that the salary question was bothering him a great deal. He has six children, named to represent Bible life, such as Faith, Hope, Love, Glory, Light. These are all girls. The boy he has called Hiromichi ("propagating the way"), after Dr. Kozaki, a great preacher in Tokyo. He wants the boy to be a preacher, but on his present salary it is not possible to give him training, nor would the boy desire to attempt to support himself at the present salary.

I responded, again stating our desire to help, etc. At nine o'clock, we went to the agriculture and forestry school where I spoke to 180 boys on American agriculture and forestry. They were an interesting lot of boys.

Following this message, we hurried to the hotel, then to the station. Hotel bill, including tea money, was Y3.00 for supper, night's lodging and breakfast. The food and other service was very good too.

Went from Yaita to Nishinosuno by train, about eight miles. Here we took a couple of tiny horsecars on a tiny track and went two miles to Otawara. The car is called *tetsudobasha*, meaning "railway horsecar." Garman took my picture as I got aboard. The fare was 15 sen each, and 10 sen extra for our baggage. On the way, we passed a Shinto shrine with at least 150 *torii* before the shrine. Two approaches to the shrine had been completely filled with *torii* jammed together side by side, so that as one approached the temple, he walked through a solid arch of *torii*, some new and painted bright red, others old and rotten.

Arrived at Otawara at 11:00 A.M. and went to the Rev. Tsujimura's where we remained for dinner. Mrs. Tsujimura formerly cooked for Woodworths, and she set a fine meal (mostly American) before us. Besides the stew and rice, there was bread and delicious grape jelly.

After dinner, we went to the middle school of 400 boys. The hours from one to three were reserved for us, but the school is some distance out, and we did not reach there until nearly 1:30. We were taken into the principal's room for tea as usual. Mr. Ishii, the English teacher, talks very good English. After tea, we were escorted into the large assembly hall full of boys between 14 and 18. As we entered, the physical director as usual called the boys to attention. They stood perfectly motionless until we reached our seats, then at his signal bowed and sat down. Mr. Garman spoke first, giving his message of yesterday but somewhat more elaborated, speaking 35 minutes. Mr. Matsuno interpreted for him and then, to rest the boys, spoke briefly in Japanese directly of the SS convention. At 2:30, I began and spoke for 30 minutes. It was a most satisfactory meeting in every way. Before I began, I gave the boys a breathing spell by asking the physical director to have them stand at attention. He did so and gave them some breathing exercises. They enjoyed it immensely.

After the meeting, Mr. Ishii and the principal showed us the buildings. There are four buildings on a plot of over 10,000 *tsubo*. Mr. Ishii said they had 250 applicants for the new class this year but could receive only 100. These were chosen through tests in geography, arithmetic and reading.

The middle schools of Japan are composed of five grades. The primary school is composed of six classes, ages 8, 9, 10, 11, 12, 13; the middle school, ages 14, 15, 16, 17, 18.

As we went around the buildings, we saw the boys out on the drill grounds with their guns (supplied by the government) getting ready for a two-day sham battle.

The boys pay Y3 a month tuition and Y1 a month extra for athletics and equipment.

From the school we returned to the Rev. Tsujimura's, took a picture of the house, which we rent and will soon be hemmed in by other houses, the landlord building all around it. Then went to the depot to see about trains for Nikko and took a walk through the town.

After supper at the hotel, we went to the pastor's home for the evening meeting. There were several entertainments nearby, but it was impossible for us to accommodate all who came to the meeting. There were about 70 in the house and 20 or 30 standing outside. I spoke on "The Great Invitation," and the interest was excellent. The great part of those present were not Christian, and I made a strong plea for them to decide tonight. The Rev. Matsuno followed and stressed what I had said. Following this meeting, about 30 remained for the reception. A young man named Shichiro Hanyuda gave the welcome address, first in Japanese and then, to my surprise and delight, in excellent English. I responded in an effort to instruct the

Christians and to stir the unsaved to become Christians. I urged them to decide to-night to become Christians and to tell the pastor of their decision following the service. After tea and cake, we departed.

A young man went along with us and began to speak in broken English. He said, "Mr. Minton, I thank you for your kind and long address." I hardly knew how to take the latter part of it, but Mr. Matsuno explained afterwards that he meant for my well-prepared and painstaking address. The young man seemed to be very much interested, and before we reached the hotel, he said, "I have decided tonight to accept God, but I had no opportunity to tell Pastor Tsujimura." I gave him such words of help as I could before he left us at the hotel. He is a teacher in the primary school. His name is Mr. Ando.

At the evening service, the Rev. Takuni of the M.E. church at Nishinoshuno (several miles from here) and several of his members were present. He is an elderly man and has been there only a short time. It seems the pastors change there often. He has 30 members and receives a salary of Y60, the church paying Y12.5 of this amount.

Wednesday, October 27 ━━━━ ◆ ━━━━━━━━━━

The Rev. Tsujimura came at eight and gave me the following information:

THE REV. K. TSUJIMURA

Age 40. Has a wife and an adopted son, Nobuyuki ("going in faith"), age 7.

The Rev. Tsujimura was converted in 1891 at the SS of Dr. Kozaki's Congregational church at Tokyo. He attended primary school at Tokyo and later went to night school at the Ginza M.E. church for a year. Then for five years he worked in the Okasaka Hospital at Tokyo as a clerk and office help. This hospital is financed by one family in England, belonging to the Friends church.

The Rev. Tsujimura studied Bible at night school during this time under Dr. Whitney, the supt. of the hospital. He then studied under Dr. Woodworth at Kasumi cho, from 1905 to 1909, and during two years of that time, he acted as supply for Oji and Akabane ("red wing") where we then had work but has been discontinued since.

Dr. Whitney recommended that he attend Dr. Woodworth's school. While at Dr. Woodworth's school, he attended an English school at Kanda. From Dr. Woodworth's school he came to Otawara where has been for most of the time since. During two years of that time, he went back to Tokyo as assistant pastor of the Rev. Matsuno's church at Azabu.

He says he studies about two or three hours each morning, Bible and magazines. Then calls and does other pastoral work. He has 28 inquirers. This was formerly a very discouraging work, but now it looks much brighter.

OTAWARA

Located 33 miles north from Utsunomiya. Population is 13,000, and including the surrounding territory, the population is 35,000. No other work is done here. The

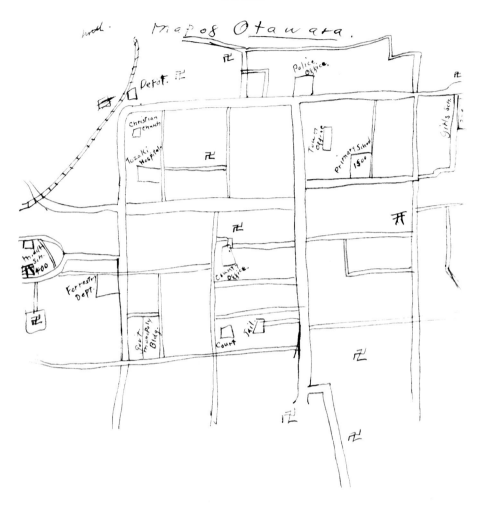

Map of Otawara (by the author).

town is low morally. There are 70 *geisha*, four licensed houses with 14 girls, and about twice as many unlicensed girls as there are *geisha*. There are also 200 concubines.

Our church has been unfortunate in having a pastor some years ago who went wrong. It is the Takahashi who is now in Honolulu. We have no church building, but the pastor lives in a rented house where services are held. Rent Y7 a month. There are six members, including the pastor and his wife.

His salary, including allowance for the child, is Y48, the church paying none of it. The church raises about Y2.50 toward church expenses.

The average church attendance is seven or eight morning and evening. SS attendance 35. Prayer meeting four.

The four members are occupied as follows: one primary teacher, one a wife of a member of Parliament (she was formerly a geisha, now an earnest Christian and blind), one railroad employee (Mr. Hanyuda) in the government monopoly office, handling tobacco and salt.

Sewing class at Otawara with the wife of the Rev. Tsujimura seated in the center.

There are two Buddhist temples and eight Shinto shrines in the town. We have been at Otawara since 1904. Mrs. Tsujimara is doing very good work teaching sewing to a dozen girls.

KUROBANE

Seven miles north of Otawara. Population, 6,000. There are really two towns in one, separated by a river. No church organization and no Christians there. The Rev. Tsujimura holds service three times a month in the hotel. Attendance at SS 70 to 100. Mr. Fry shows pictures there once a month, and the Rev. Tsujimura speaks. We have been here since 1912 at times, steadily since 1917.

We took the 9:02 train for Kurobane, planning to return and go on to Nikko in an hour. At the station, I took a picture of the Rev. Tsujimura, wife and son. Mr. Hanyuda presented me with a beautiful Japanese lady's purse, the gift of the church.

We walked through Kurobane, and I took a picture of the town. There are three shrines and three temples here. We missed the train and put in the time checking some maps.

As we came to the station, we noticed a little machine pounding rice by water-power. The rice lay in a bowl under cover, and a heavy block of wood was suspended above it on a long horizontal pole at the end of which was a long trough just under

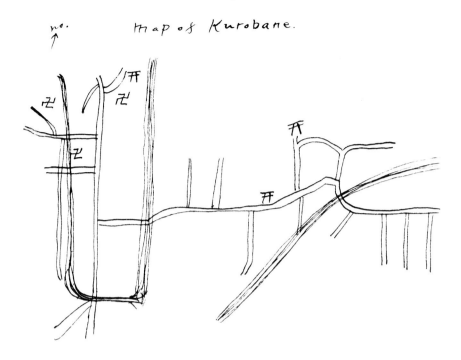

Map of Kurobana (by the author).

the fall of an irrigation ditch. The water from the ditch would fill the trough, and when it was full, the weight of the water would lower it, thus raising the wooden block suspended over the rice. As the trough emptied itself, it would rise suddenly, allowing the block of wood to fall heavily upon the rice. By this method, the rice was hulled.

The Rev. Tsujimura told me that another young person had decided to become a Christian last night. When we stopped at Otawara on our way back, Mrs. Tsujimura met us at the station and told us that another young man had called this morning and said he was determined to attend services more regularly.

We came on to Nishinosuno and found an express train leaving in a few minutes, when we had expected to have to wait two hours. We decided to take it, as it would get us to Nikko more than two hours earlier and get Mr. Matsuno home much earlier.

Arrived at Nikko in a heavy rain at 4:10 P.M. In spite of the rain, the scenery as we climbed the mountain was beautiful. For most of the way from Utsunomiya to Nikko, the road is lined on both sides with great cryptomeria trees planted very closely together and more than 100 years old. At the station, we found foreign hotels, Y10 a day. Walked a mile up the winding street and past the sacred bridge, used only by the emperor (painted red). We investigated several hotels and finally located a Japanese room without meals at Y2 each. This was a small room and not in a regular hotel. We decided to take it and went back for our baggage, which we had left near the station. On the way, we struck another hotel at Y4 for room and two meals, with the privilege of having one of the meals foreign-style at no additional cost. The location was so much better, we decided to take it. Got our baggage and notified the other man of our change. He seemed very grateful that we had notified him. Mr. Garman says that when a Japanese looks at a room and then says he will come back later, that is just the polite way of saying he doesn't want it, and he never does return.

Got some fruit and buns, and went to our room to rest. I feel like taking it easy for a day or so after averaging about four speeches a day for four days.

Thursday, October 28 ─────── ◆ ──────────────

Although it was raining when we retired, the sun was shining brightly this morning, and its glory was enhanced as it shone upon the beautiful maple trees and cedars covering the mountains in this beautiful spot—one of the most beautiful in Japan and especially famous at this time of the year for its maple leaves in color. We soon knew why the Japanese say, "*Nikko mirumade, Kekko to iu na!*" (Until you have seen Nikko, do not say splendid!") *Nikko* means "sunny splendor." It is a town of 8,000 in the NW part of the Shimotsuke Province. Thousands of people, Japanese and foreign, come to Nikko every year. The best time of the year is in October when the maple leaves are in color.

Our Japanese hotel keeper had a regular foreign breakfast of fried eggs and pork cutlets brought in from the outside.

The day was beautiful, and immediately after breakfast, we started out for a trip to Chuzenji Lake and the Kegon Falls—famous all over Japan. While waiting for a car, we visited some shops full of curios. The car was crowded to the limit, but we squeezed in and rode five miles up the mountainside between some of the most gorgeously colored mountains I have ever seen. The trees are not as large as our maple trees, and the leaves are different shape, some having seven and some nine points. As we rode, it looked as though these maple, cedar, birch and other trees were lying flat against the mountains, different colors predominating at different places. The only comparison I can think of is the most beautiful Turkish rug of Oriental design lying in great uneven folds over numerous peaks, with sometimes red, sometimes brown, sometimes purple or yellow predominating.

On the way up, we passed two beautiful falls, called Hannya and Hodo falls. A little farther on, we passed a large black rock called Magnetic Rock. We applied our knives but found no magnetism.

As we went on and on, up and up the five-mile winding road to the lake, we were constantly stopping to view the ever-changing color and schemes of the cedar- and maple-covered mountains, new peaks and new streams and falls making their appearance at almost every turn.

The road itself is worthy of note. It is a well-built road wide enough for one automobile to pass over without difficulty. On the mountainside of the road, a great wall of solid stone blocks is built that supports the next tier of road higher up as it winds back and forth up the steep ascent. *Kurumas* carry many people to the summit, two men being necessary to each one in order to negotiate the climb. We walked the entire distance and enjoyed it immensely.

Truss bridge over mountain stream.

As we went up, Mount Nantai, capped with clouds, stood towering at our right. A shrine is built on its summit to the memory of Kobo Daishi, a scholar who years ago traveled over these mountains establishing Shinto shrines.

At intervals on commanding promontories, little teahouses are located, and the owners do a thriving business, I fancy, setting tea and cake before the toiling climbers who stop a few moments to rest and enjoy the beautiful views. The climb is not nearly so exacting as that of Asama or Fuji owing to the more gradual ascent and the fine road to the summit.

We noticed a great cable extending over the high mountain range and little hanging cars running at regular intervals in each direction. We learned later that they were carrying gravel and cement over the mountain for the construction of another large power station. The tremendous waterpower in these mountains is being converted into electric current to supply power and light to Tokyo and intervening towns.

The Ashio Copper Mines are located in these mountains where there is a sufficient intake from Kegon Falls to develop 10,000 horsepower. This is the largest copper mine in Japan, 7,000 men.

Reaching the summit of this mountain, we began to descend by a winding-stairlike path to the foot of Kegon Falls. We first came upon the Shirakumo Falls (White Cloud Falls), and it is true to its name as it spreads itself out in a wide turbulent expanse of white water falling and tumbling over a fairly steep precipice and then rushing on in a mad current to the intake of the copper mine mentioned before. This walk took us right into the spray of the falls, and I succeeded in washing my hands in an eddy near the foot and also picked up some stones at the same spot.

A full view of Kegon Falls, Nikko.

Going on some distance farther, we came to an outlook almost on a level with the pool at the foot of the Kegon Falls. It was a thrilling sight to view the great white bridal veil stretch of water as it left the level of the stream above and dashed 250 feet in a great white sheet against a green background to the pool below where it dashed its spray high into the sunlight with an indescribable sparkle, then hesitating a moment or two, as if to catch its breath, dashed on down the mountainside in one wild, raging stream, fed by countless little rivulets from tiny falls spurting out of the rocks all the way around the barrel-shaped rock cliff of which Kegon Falls forms the center. The rocks, wet with the spray of the great falls and many smaller ones, are of beautiful color as they catch glimpses of the sunlight penetrating far into the depths of the barrel.

Part of Kegon Falls in northern Japan. Note Foreign Mission Secretary Minton in the foreground.

This falls has been the scene of numerous suicides by leaping from its summit. It might be called the popular or even official suicide resort of the empire. People come from all over the country, write their names and some parting message on the rocks or trees at the top, and then leap into the roaring waters as they fall to the level below. So many have suicided here that police have to be constantly on guard to prevent high-strung people from doing so. A great barbed-wire fence is stretched around it.

Mr. Garman took my picture standing near the falls. In fact, I nearly got a soaking by attempting to get too near. I took Mr. Garman's picture on the bridge at the foot of Shirakumo Falls.

The coloring of the mountains cannot be described. Some have red predominating, with a great variety of other colors—purple, brown, yellow, orange. In some, the purple predominates, again the brown or the yellow. In the sunlight, it is the most gorgeous sight I have ever seen. There are maple trees, cedar trees, birch, cherry (famous for their June blossom but not for fruit), fir, pine, beech and the towering cryptomeria.

For the foot of Kegon Falls, we turned back past Shirakumo Falls and climbed to the head of Kegon. Here one can see the stream that feeds the falls and can get a view of the distant stream as it leaves the pool at the foot, but the sight is not nearly so thrilling as the one from the foot from which we had just come. We also went partway down the mountain here and secured a good view from about the middle of the falls.

Returning to the summit, we went on farther up to Chuzenji Lake, which is the source of this mountain stream, Daiya-gawa, feeding the falls. It lies in the midst of the mountains, many feet above sea level, and feeds not only the falls but the neighboring mountains and the valley far below. It is a picturesque spot, with the quaint Japanese houses of the village skirting the lake and hugging the mountain.

On the other side of the lake are a couple of foreign hotels, which rather mar the beauty of the place. We went to a foreign hotel, the Lakeside, and found that tiffin would cost Y3.50 each, so we left and went to a Japanese restaurant where we got beef and eggs American-style with a touch of pork and potatoes. To this we added some buns and strawberry jam and cakes, the whole outlay costing Y4.40 for both—a little more than the cost of one at the hotel. It was a very good meal, to which we did ample justice after the long climb. As we looked into the water of the lake, we could see a beautiful reflection of the colors from the surrounding trees on the mountainside. We were about 4,200 feet high at the lake.

Coming down, we gathered a few leaves of different colors. I had also gathered some stones at the two falls and at the foot of Mount Nantai.

The descent was much quicker than the ascent. Many times we cut it short by going straight down from one road ledge to another along paths others (usually natives) had made.

We came in at 5:45 and took a good Japanese hot bath, then had supper. The Japanese supper at this hotel is about as poor as any I have yet struck, but with a foreign breakfast and dinner, we were willing to take it as it was.

Friday, October 29   ───────   ◆   ───────

We visited the famous Nikko temples this morning. We passed by the Sacred Red Bridge. It is 83 feet long and 18 feet wide, and rests upon two *torii*-fashioned pillars of gray granite. The bridge is one sweeping arch across the wild rushing river and is heavily lacquered in red above and black below. The clamps are of brass and other gilded metals. It is used only by the emperor or in extreme cases by others when the wooden bridge is out of commission. The raging torrents formed in the mountains by excessive rains often cause great washouts and destroy many bridges and roads. General Grant was once invited to walk over this sacred bridge but declined, saying it was too sacred to be defiled by him. This act made his fame even greater in the eyes of the Japanese people.

A legend says that when Shodo-Shonin was searching for Mt. Nantai, he came to the Daiya-gawa and found no bridge to cross. As he meditated and prayed, a dragon came and asked his trouble, and upon learning that he wanted to cross the stream, secured a red and a black dragon, and ordered them to make a bridge, which they did by stretching their wings out across the river, upon which immediately there grew a long stretch of green grass over which the famous Shonin crossed in ease.

The temples at Nikko are divided into two groups, the Ieyasu and the Iemitsu, the former to the right and the latter to the left as you enter. The shrines were built by Hidetada, the son of Ieyasu, of the Tokugawa Shogunate. The latter commanded his son to select a site and erect the mausoleum to receive his ashes. When the father died in 1616, the son carried out his father's orders at Nikko. Tokugawa Iemitsu, eldest son of Hidetada, followed his father's example and emulated his grandfather's order by building several adjuncts to the main shrine where his own body was laid as a final resting place.

Purchasing a ticket for 90 sen each, we went through many of the temples and saw the wonderful carvings. There was the Hall of Three Buddhas, the great bronze bell, the pagoda, with its richly decorated five stories rising 105 feet and a 42-foot base.

Shoes had to be removed, and hats and overcoats, when we entered the shrines where priests were telling visitors of the carvings or selling postcards and charms to all who would buy.

The treasure house of Ieyasu Shrine was a most interesting place with its many fine relics of the *shogun* period well preserved. The famous carving of the three monkeys is on the stable that housed the horse, recently deceased, that carried Prince Kitashirakawa in the Formosa campaign of 1895. The carving is called Koshin and represents the day of the monkey in the Japanese calendar. The native conception is that these monkeys (*saru*) will neither see, hear nor speak any evil, whence they are called blind (*mi*), deaf (*ika*) and dumb (*iwa*). We visited the tomb of Ieyasu, standing at the summit of the hill upon which the temples are built.

We got into a group of commercial school boys, and as usual, two of them who wanted to learn more English attached themselves to us. We were not unwilling as they were able to tell us something of what their Japanese guide was saying.

The crest of the Tokugawa Shogunate is in evidence everywhere, even the rafters on the temples being studded with brass ends upon which the crest has been hammered out.

After our visit to the temples, we visited several shops, and paying our hotel bill, took the 11:30 train for Tokyo. We were at the hotel two nights and took supper and breakfast there each day, the breakfast being a foreign meal brought in. Our bill was Y4.00 a day, plus Y.75 a day tea money, or a total of Y9.50 each for the two days—very reasonable for Nikko.

Arrived at Tokyo at 3:45 and were at Kasumi cho soon after 5:00. Found letters from my wife, mother, sister and also from the office.

Saturday, October 30 —————— ◆ ——————————————

Went downtown this morning to get some money and to look after my slides. Am securing a large number from my own Kodak and also some of the SS convention and of child life in Japan.

Spent the afternoon writing postcards and a letter to my wife. So tired and sleepy tonight, I got very little done.

Sunday, October 31 —————— ◆ ——————————————

Yesterday, October 30, is set apart annually to celebrate the birthday of the emperor. The city is trimmed gorgeously for the occasion and for the three-day celebration in connection with the dedication of the shrines built to the former emperor Meiji.

We planned to visit a number of Japanese churches and SS today but found that the children of all Japan were called upon to go to their respective school buildings today to sing the national anthem, see the unveiling of the emperor's picture, and hear the reading of the *Imperial Rescript*. [See Appendix, entry 28.] This *Rescript*, on education, is regarded with peculiar veneration by the Japanese people, who consider it the statement par excellence of their duties as subjects and citizens.

We visited the Azabu Evangelical Association church, also the Azabu Methodist Protestant church. They have a nice building, near Kasumi cho. There are 13 *tsubo* of land in this plot.

We next went to Dr. H. Kozaki's church, the Reinanzaki Congregational Church, on a street by the same name. Dr. Kozaki is president of the Japan National SS Assn. and a leader in Japanese Christian life. He is a very fine gentleman. We met him in the church, and he very kindly showed us over his plant. The Rev. Matsuno, our Azabu pastor, was formerly his assistant and teacher in his theological school, which since had been discontinued.

The Rev. Iwamura (Dr. Kozaki's son-in-law) is now his assistant. He also met us. He was the interpreter for Prof. Smith, leader of the SS conv. music.

Dr. Kozaki had the distinction of having his picture unveiled by the SS convention while he sat on the platform.

The church and parsonage of this plant are side by side on a corner lot of 300 *tsubo*, bought 30 years ago for Y700. The large brick church building was built four years ago at a cost of Y60,000, of which $10,000 (Y20,000) was contributed by Arthur Curtis James, a millionaire businessman of New York and a friend of Dr. Kozaki. The balance of the money was raised by the Japanese.

There are 28 classes in the SS, one of which is an English Bible class of university students taught by Mrs. Coleman when she is able to come. (Mrs. Coleman is wife of the SS secr. of Japan.)

The church auditorium seats 500, including gallery. There is a small pipe organ, imported from France and said to be the best in Japan. The English Bible class meets in the large library where a fine collection of books is contained. Dr. Kozaki and the Rev. Iwamura both have fine study rooms in the building. Dr. Kozaki has written a book on Christian doctrines, which has been translated into English but not yet printed.

The average SS attendance is 300, and average church attendance is 200. The church has a kindergarten.

Recently they bought land and buildings adjoining them, containing 400 *tsubo* at Y70,000, upon which they expect to build a brick primary school to accommodate 200 students. It will cost Y100,000, most of which will be contributed by Japanese. The church is independent financially, though a part of the Japan Congregational church. Dr. Kozaki plans to make his primary school a strictly Christian school.

From here we went to the Kudan M.E. church. On the way, we passed the finest of the imperial palaces. It is in full view. The emperor cannot live in it because it is too damp. As we rode, we saw the emperor's carriage of red and gold entering the present residence grounds of their majesties, accompanied by a large mounted escort and a number of carriages of other officials. We were too far away to see if the people in the carriage were the emperor and empress, but it is likely they were. Later, I found that it was the crown prince, who was out reviewing 10,000 troops on the parade grounds.

The Kudan M.E. church is one of the most prominent in Tokyo. Took a picture here, as I did at Dr. Kozaki's church.

Went next to Dr. Uemura's church, the Nihon-Cirisuto Kyoki (the Japanese Christian Church, Presbyterian and Reformed combined). On the way, we passed Dr. Uemura's Bible school, where our Mr. Taizumi attended.

Dr. Uemura is much interested in Japanese independent work. He has a church of 1,000 members. The building seats 700 but not so well arranged for SS work. There is an assistant pastor.

Met Dr. Uemura just as he was leaving the church after the morning service. The average attendance is 200 and the SS attendance 400. They have six evangelistic workers and Bible women. They are partially supported by the church. The church has many lawyers, judges, members of Parliament, and such in its membership, and is the strongest church financially in Tokyo. It does more than any other church to establish new churches. Four members of the House of Commons are members, also some seven or eight professors of the universities.

There is an educational department, including 70 or 80 teachers of primary, middle schools and the universities. The church is on only 150 *tsubo* of land, the building covering 100 of it. They plan to rebuild at a cost of Y250,000. They have been assured that if they raise Y100,000, they can secure the balance or at least that much more from America, but the pastor wants them to raise the whole amount here. The present building cost Y22,000, all raised by Japanese.

Pastor receives Y4,000, assistant pastor Y800. The six workers receive a total of Y2,000, and give only halftime to the work, doing other work for the remainder of their support.

The annual budget, covering what goes through the treasury, is Y12,000. There are some outside gifts. Envelopes for monthly contributions are distributed once a year. Pledges are made annually at the church for so much a month. No great appeal is made for the pledges, the pastor feeling that if a member is a real Christian, the giving will come. When a new member is baptized, he is told that giving is part of his duty and he is expected to give. Very few do not give. The lowest is 20 sen a month, and the highest is Y20 to Y30 a month. Then, on special occasions, special gifts of gratitude for prosperity are made to the church. Sometimes a member gives many thousand yen for school or other purposes.

Regularly the church gives Y500 to the denominational end of the work of the church. Gifts for calls in addition are made at the regular services as occasion demands. The Y500 or Y600 is paid to the denominational work out of the budget of Y12,000 paid in by monthly contributions. The pastor emphasizes the spiritual life and does not urge giving directly. He believes that if the spiritual life is right, the money will come. This information comes from Mr. Yamamoto, supt. of SS and elder in the church.

After dinner, we went to the Ginza M.E. church for the Union church service. The Rev. Reischauer preached. He suited his message to the holiday being observed by Japan in honor of the deceased Emperor Meiji, whose shrine was to be dedicated tomorrow and Tuesday and Wednesday. The Rev. Reischauer believes that the desire of the Japanese to worship the emperor's spirit is a patriotic attitude that may be diverted to Christianity when it is thoroughly understood that Christianity makes for true patriotism.

After the service, the Rev. Dr. Wainwright, supt. of the Christian Literature Society, took Bro. Garman and me home with him for supper. We had a most delightful time. This society published as many as 40,000,000 pages of literature a year before the paper shortage came on. Now their work is somewhat curtailed, but it is still a great work. The *Morning Star* is a fine religious sheet published by them, and they also publish many other tracts.

Monday, November 1 —————— ◆ ——————————————

This day marks the beginning of the three-day celebration at the dedication of the new shrine for the former emperor Meiji. This is called the festival of Chinzasai or the festival of the installation of the spirit of God. The shrine occupies a plot of ground of 200,000 *tsubo*, or 100 acres. It has taken six years to build it, and the total cost, including land, buildings, etc., is about Y20,000,000. The approach to the shrine has been rebuilt, as has the road leading from it at the other side. A great many *torii* adorn the roadway, some given by the city and the prefecture. The entire city is to be given over to this celebration, and the three days are declared national holidays. The streets present a remarkable appearance with their many flags and lanterns before every house and every place of business.

The usual number of 1,050 streetcars has been increased temporarily to 1,160 to take care of the crowds expected; 300,000 talismans and charms have been made to sell at the rate of 10 and 5 sen each.

The purpose of all this is shown in the following article which appeared in a Tokyo newspaper:

Receiving the emblematic representation of the spirit of the emperor Meiji from the hands of the personal representative of His Imperial Majesty, the emperor, Prince Ichijo, chief priest, will place the emblem in the most holy spot of the newly built shrine to the accompaniment of sacred Shinto music and in the presence of empire, prefecture and church officials and dignitaries tomorrow morning (Monday), thus performing the rite of Chinzasai, or installation of the apotheocized emperor.

The emblem representing the spirit of the emperor Meiji will be carried on a plain white wooden casket. After it has been deposited in the most holy place, the chief priest will read the Chinzasai ritual. The entire service will last from eight o'clock in the morning to eleven o'clock. At one o'clock the shrine will be thrown open to the general public. No amusements other than fireworks will take place at the shrine the first day, these being given Tuesday and Wednesday, when the priests will also confer blessings on the visitors.

Although the festival is primarily religious, it is probable that the actual celebration will dominate the three days. All sorts of amusements will be conducted. The emperor Meiji reigned with great power, and throughout his reign, great progress in peace and prosperity were made. Viewed in this light, the three-days festivity for the Meiji Shrine at Yoyogi will have an added significance, as it will once more impress upon the people how good the emperor Meiji was and remind them of their duty to pay reverence to his spirit with renewed sense of gratefulness.

All the wards of the city have had smaller shrines built and deposited at prominent places, and there are numberless small shrines of individuals everywhere. This morning we were aroused from our work by the slow, monotonous, but regular beating of a large drum, which seemed to be drawing nearer. It finally came into sight in front of our house, carried by several men and beaten by another. A short distance behind, a great crowd of men were carrying the shrine of this ward. It is a good-size affair and richly built and decorated. It was resting on a large platform of crossbeams, which in turn rested on the shoulders of the men. This shrine is supposed to contain the spirit of some ancestor and is moved not in a straight course, but in zigzag fashion about the streets, making visits to other shrines and other spirits. As the men sway back and forth along the streets, they chant unceasingly and with some rapidity one word, "*Yassha, yassha,*" which so far as I could learn has no particular meaning. All day long, these shrines bearing ancestral spirits have been moving up and down the streets all over the city.

I remained at the house most of the day, writing.

Tuesday, November 2

Did some writing this morning, and after an early lunch, we all started out to see the shrine of Meiji, feeling it would be worthwhile to see firsthand this Oriental celebration in an effort to learn just how much of it is religious and how much custom and how much true patriotism.

The cars were not running our way, so we walked about a mile and a half to the entrance of the shrine grounds. All the way there were great numbers of people, and when we reached the entrance, we found it entirely blocked and great numbers of policemen trying to control the crowd. It is estimated that there are 250,000 visitors in the city. After a long wait, a whistle blew, and we went forward toward the first green *torii* of monster size across the street. From then on, we would walk a few feet, then pause and wait until the police gave the signal to advance again. As we neared the second *torii*, we were halted for a very long period, and the sun was shining hotly. There were a large number of babies and children in the crowd, and they suffered terribly, either from the sun as it beat upon them hanging to their parents' backs or from the crush of the crowd.

The signal was finally given, and we went forward a short distance. Another wait and another short advance. As we went under the second arch, it seemed certain that many people must be injured. The crowd surged from side to side as it sought to pass beneath the arch. *Geta* were tramped upon and torn from the feet, many being left behind. Hats were knocked off and lost, and it was extremely difficult to keep one's feet. Even if you did keep them, they were sure to be trampled upon by countless *geta*.

As we paused, I looked back and caught sight of the long endless line of men, women and children surging up the road toward the shrine. I raised my Kodak over my head and took a chance at snapping a picture or two without focusing. We passed through a number of *torii*. As we neared the shrine, the police held ropes across the street, and we were permitted to proceed from one to the other only on their order.

It was amusing to see the hats of the policemen flying in every direction as they attempted to lift the rope to let the surging crowd pass on. Yesterday there were between 130 and 140 accidents in the crowd, several of which proved fatal. We finally reached the shrine, with the crowd at a dead run. As the shrine was reached, great numbers of the people produced coins, usually one-sen pieces, and threw them toward the great offering box always found suggestively before the entrance to a shrine. As they threw the coins, many of them stopped short, clapped their hands and bowed their heads in an attitude of worship. Many did not thus stop, but a sufficient number did to impress one with the utter hopelessness of that to which and for which they prayed. I could not help but wonder to just what they did pray, and I left the shrine saddened beyond words at this sight of blind leading blind, for such it all is. What need for the light of Christianity!

This evening I took Mr. and Mrs. McKnight downtown for dinner in order that we might have time to talk over quietly some of the work of the field. We had an opportunity not afforded at the house where so many are usually present. Following supper, we visited a number of shops along the Ginza and then had some ice cream at Hoshi's Pharmacy, called the center of Tokyo by foreigners because the ice cream is so much like American.

I was glad to learn of Brother McKnight's desire to enter the evangelistic field and feel he will do good work. He is also in sympathy with many plans that seem to me to be wise for our work. It was a very helpful evening spent together, and I think worth the Y10 it cost. I plan to have Miss Stacy go with me some night soon for the same purpose.

Wednesday, November 3 ——————— ◆ ———————————

Went downtown this morning to secure some developed films. Also did a little shopping, getting some chests and tea sets to be used in demonstrating Japanese life

On the way to the dedication of the Great Meiji Shrine in Tokyo.

to our people in America. As I returned home, I found the people still moving the spirits of ancestors about from place to place. It is estimated that on yesterday afternoon between one and three o'clock, 600,000 visited the shrine. We were in this crowd. At a speech delivered yesterday during the city celebrations in connection with the dedication of the shrine, Mayor Viscount Tajiri said this among other things: "While in life, his late majesty was looked up to by the multitude of his subjects as the sun is, and now his august spirit is to rest within the shrine to look after the empire forever."

Last night we saw a number of streetcars most beautifully decorated with chrysanthemums and maple leaves. They were run over the city lines. A great display of electrical decorations was shown before the entrance to the Imperial Palace.

Spent the afternoon working at the house, and after dinner tonight, Brothers Garman and McKnight and I visited the great vice section of Tokyo. Dr. Woodworth and I had ridden through this section in *kuruma*s in the daytime, but we felt we should see it at night in order to understand the problem aright. We did not start until nearly nine o'clock and reached the district sometime after ten. As the cars approached the section, we could notice a distinct change in the crowd. There were large numbers of men, old and young, and some were hilarious from the use of *sake*, while others were going in separation from any companionship, bent on their fiendish errand.

Leaving the car, we started to walk through the great section of the city set apart under license for the purpose of ruining the bodies and souls of thousands of girls. The district is called Yoshiwara. As we approached, we noticed many fine automobiles lined up along the streets, the owners or renters being within the houses. The entire section of seven acres is brilliantly lighted at night, and the houses have a fine-looking appearance. Some are built of brick and others of costly wood. They may not be strongly built, but they are certainly made to look as attractive as possible. The keepers of these houses pay a government license and are thus under government protection.

The pictures of the girls are displayed, in fine clothes and much paint and powder, in expensive frames set in a row in the long corridor before each of the houses. The men walk along this corridor and view the pictures. If they see a face that appeals to them, they apply to the secretary who sits in a box near the entrance, and he makes the arrangements for the man to visit the girl's room. In the larger houses there are two entrances, with a secretary at each end of the corridor. As we walked along outside the corridor in the street, these secretaries kept calling to us in an effort to entice us in.

There are 3,500 girls in this seven-acre district, and some of them receive as many as 20 guests in a single night. Many of the girls are sold into this life by their parents to help meet the cost of living. It is not considered such a serious thing in Japan for a father and mother thus to sell a girl, for the girl is not considered to be worth much anyhow. In looking at a pretty young daughter, neighbors sometimes congratulate the parents on the fact that she is good-looking and will bring a good price from the den keepers. Think of such a life for a pure girl!

But she does not remain pure very long. All sorts of men visit the place, with all sorts of diseases. One contact with these men may start a life of utmost misery, and it is almost impossible for a girl to live such a life very long without becoming contaminated. The girls are subject to physical examination every so often, and the government and keepers make much of the fact that by this procedure the patrons are protected from contracting disease. They have not realized that a girl might be perfectly free from disease when one man enters and vilely polluted when he leaves, so that the next man is subjected to the utmost danger of disease. Since many girls are forced into this life, the men who act as secretaries in the evening act as guards in the daytime to prevent them from escaping.

As we walked through street after street, we found men in front of practically every building. Among them were many young men who by their actions showed that they were there for their first time. Many were trying to joke with each other to cover their embarrassment; others were at the point of losing control of themselves completely; still others were closing the agreement and were being ushered into the hotel-like houses and up to the rooms. As the flimsy door hangings opened back for them, we caught glimpses of the beautiful flowers and other draperies that adorned the lobbies. From above came the sound of *geisha* music or the hoarse unnatural laughter of the men and girls in the various rooms.

Many men came to the buildings and in a very businesslike way, as though accustomed to it, made their arrangements, and walked in. I was impressed too with the sight of a number of very old men whose very faces showed what lives they had lived. Once in a while, a girl who was not busy would peep out from behind the curtain or even stand in the doorway, seeking to attract customers. Again, some man would ask to see the girl he had picked out before he entered, and she would be brought to the door where she would do her best to entice him in. She usually

A Japanese child makes a purchase from this vendor of sweetmeats.

succeeded. I noticed at one place a beautifully gowned and very young-looking girl standing out on a balcony over the street with a man by her side who seemed to be the secretary. She was seeking to draw someone in.

I tried to study the faces of these girls as I caught fleeting glimpses of them. Some, no doubt, have been drawn into the life without any resistance on their part. They, at least, pretend with some success to enjoy it. They try to appear vivacious and attractive, and some of them no doubt are. But their charms soon fade as a year or two at such business is bound to work its vengeance. Three to five years is the usual length of their lives. Others seemed to be performing their part simply for the sake of an existence. As they looked out upon the passing men, they had the appearance of starving eagles looking for their prey. The pictures of the girls in the beautiful frames certainly did not honestly represent most of the faces we saw. Others of the girls seemed to me to have the look of haunting fear and the dread of the next ordeal. It is altogether likely that in the course of a few weeks of such a life, the finer characteristics would be lost, but I am confident that to some of these girls the life is a living death.

We noticed the prices and found them ranging from 30 sen up to a yen or two for each patron. In some places it was so much an hour. At one place, we noticed that the price was 30 sen (15¢) an hour. Think of offering to the brutal passions of a so-called man the very life and soul of a very girl of 14 to 25 years of age!

We walked up and down the streets for most of an hour. At one place, we noticed the priests or representatives of priests gathering money, presumably for some shrine, perhaps the Meiji. The resort keepers usually threw out a small piece of money in a businesslike and yet somewhat contemptuous way.

There are usually from 3 to 25 or 30 girls in a house, depending of course upon the size of the house.

As we left the place, we noticed other houses not so brilliantly lighted and with no keeper at the door. Instead, the girls themselves were at the front, chatting with any who might stop and seeking to make their own arrangements to sell themselves for an hour at a time to the will of whoever might pay the price—and little do they realize how great that price is destined to be. A few paltry sen may look cheap for an hour's so-called pleasure, but in the days of reckoning, both here and hereafter, what will the cost be?

At several streets, I noticed a number of children running about. I do not know where they belong but suppose that they are the children of some of the girls or perhaps of nearby poor people who are compelled to live near these infested districts. Yet there are no signs of poverty in the higher-class section of this district. Quite the contrary, there are all the indications of wealth and luxury and ease. The deception, if it be deception, is well maintained.

We returned to Kasumi cho shortly after midnight with dejected spirits and aching hearts for these poor slaves of ignorance and brutish passion and wrong conceptions of filial relations, and the age-long false sense of the rights of a girl in a Japanese home.

Thursday, November 4 ———————— ◆ ————————————————

This morning we visited the Rev. P.S. Mayer and wife, missionaries for the Evangelical Association, whose headquarters are at Cleveland in the States and Tokyo in Japan. They also have a mission in China. Mr. Mayer is treasurer of the Japan Mission of this church and gave me very valuable and accurate information, which follows.

The membership of the Evangelical Association in America and Canada is 125,000, thus being about the same size as our church's. They also have work in Germany and Poland, with a membership of about 25,000, but the two bodies are more or less separate.

In Japan this church does evangelistic work in Tokyo and north to within a short distance of Sendai and west to Kobe. The evangelistic work predominates, though they have perhaps as many kindergartens as any mission in Japan, there being 11 EA kindergartens in different sections of Japan. They also do some educational work, such as a Bible training school for women and an English night school here at Tokyo.

The night school reaches clerks and some students who desire to get a command of English. The course covers four years—one a preparatory year and the other three covering the main course. The aim of the school is evangelistic, the workers seeking to reach the students for Christ through offering them the course in English. Mr. Mayer thinks that they are not doing good work along this line, that most of the boys get nothing but English. He attributes the failure to the fact that the Japanese principal of the school and some of the teachers are not evangelistic themselves.

A church building is used for the school, which meets five nights a week. It is self-supporting, in the sense that the salaries of the teachers are paid from the tuition funds. The two missionaries who teach in the school are paid their regular salaries as missionaries and give part of their time to this work. The salary of the Japanese principal is also paid by the home board.

Besides the two foreign teachers, there are five native preachers, all of whom are active pastors of churches in a nearby territory who give two or more nights a week to the school. One man who gives two nights a week to this work receives for it Y8 a month, which supplements his salary of Y40 a month as pastor of one of the churches. He is a single man.

Mr. Mayer has a Bible class on Wednesday night, with an attendance of 80 percent of the boys. He believes there are great possibilities in the night school but feels that it must be conducted on a different basis. Not only is the principal of the school not evangelistic, but the pastor of the church where the school is held is not evangelistic.

The boys pay Y1.50 to Y1.70, depending upon which class they enter. There is also Y1 entrance fee.

The curriculum consists of reading, writing, grammar, composition, translation and conversation.

In the ten years of the school's existence, they have had 1,000 students, about 50 of whom have stayed for the full course and graduated. There have been some conversions from year to year, but last year there were none. There have been in the past as many as ten in a year. Two young men have come up through this school to the seminary and have been studying for the ministry.

There are nine Evangelical Association churches in Tokyo and its suburbs. Seven of these organizations have church buildings.

The principal of the school is the native presiding elder of the church and receives Y125 a month, his work including the oversight of the church as well as principal of the school. He has no children's allowances, but the mission pays Y30 a month for his parsonage.

A preacher in the Ev. Assoc. Mission starts his work at Y40 a month for a period of two years, which is a probationary period. This is the salary, whether married or single. For the second two-year period as a deacon, he receives Y45, then for three years Y50, and then a Y5 increase each year, up to Y70 a month. A single man does not receive higher than Y45 a month.

Children's allowances for a native pastor are Y2 a month from birth to 12. Then, if a child goes to middle school, the amount is raised to Y5 a month from the ages of 13 to 18.

Mr. Mayer says the board at home passes upon all salaries, for native workers as well as the missionaries, and they have been considering giving the native pastors a raise of one third. He does not know what action has been taken concerning it.

Preachers for the Ev. Assoc. train in the Aoyama Gaguin, the M.E. school here. The Ev. Assoc. has the privilege of putting one teacher in this school and paying his salary. He teaches either in the college department or the theological department, but

Large group of people on athletic field with barrack-appearing buildings in the background.

in the former case he teaches a theological subject. The Ev. Assoc. contributes voluntarily to the Aoyama Gaguin Y1,500 a year, besides providing the board and so forth for each student they send to this school. This amounts to Y21 a month, the boys handling the amount and paying their tuition etc. out of it. A boy sent to this school must sign a paper, together with several other guarantors, declaring that he will work a certain number of years for the Ev. Assoc. in return for the support they give him while in school.

If the boy has the right preparation, he enters the regular five-year seminary course, which includes certain college studies. If he has not had sufficient preparation or is an older man, he takes a three-year Bible course instead. The former are called *honkwa* men and the latter *bekkwa* men. The Ev. Assoc. has five boys studying in the school at present, two of whom are *honkwa* men and two *bekkwa* men, the fifth being more nearly *honkwa* than *bekkwa*, but not fully up to them. They have not had any ministerial candidates to enter this school for two years.

Mr. Mayer believes in sending choice young men to America and that all the mission should do is to secure a scholarship from the college they wish to attend, leaving the young men to provide for their own keep while in America. Mr. Mayer admits that it has often been found that when a young man comes to America, he very often does not want to come back to Japan to stay permanently.

Their Bible Women's Training School has 50 students. There is a five-year course. There are two foreign missionary women who teach and seven Japanese teachers, some men. The salaries of the women teachers are from Y30 to Y40, while some of the men who teach are pastors giving only part of their time to this work at

A missionary home on the campus of Aoyama Gakuin in Tokyo.

a corresponding salary. The students live in the dormitory and are supported by the women's board of the Ev. Assoc., which pays them Y15 a month while in school, and from this they must support themselves, paying board, etc. The Ev. Assoc. has about 26 Bible women at work at present. Their salaries range from Y25 to Y30.

Mr. Mayer says the Bible women present a real problem. Some churches are about to discontinue them. It is a question whether it is a good policy to have them. They often cannot work well with a pastor, and the tendency is more and more to put the work here on the same basis as that in the States. Note: I am wondering if the place of the Bible woman should not correspond to that of the assistant pastor or pastor's secretary in the States.

The salaries of the kindergarten teachers run about Y25 to Y35. The prospective teachers are sent to the Tokyo kindergarten training school for six months' training. The best workers are in Kobe where they are trained in Miss Howell's training school, which seems to be more thorough.

The average attendance in the Ev. Assoc. kindergartens is about 50 each. They are about half self-supporting. Two teachers are in charge of each.

The Ev. Assoc. has a rule that the board at home pays no more than 80 percent of the total salary budget for native pastors. The Japanese Conference decides what proportion of the salaries of a local pastor shall be made up by the local church, and they are expected to raise it.

There are two classes—conference churches and mission churches. The conference churches pay all their incidental expenses and at least Y8 a month on the

Students and faculty of Aoyama Gakuin (Dr. Woodworth is in the insert). This photo was sent to the author around 1926.

pastor's salary. The mission churches are under missionary supervision, while the conference churches are under the supervision of the Japanese presiding elder. The conference churches are organized, and the others are not. The conference churches have assumed 25 percent of the salary budget, so that the mission churches have it easier.

One church is self-supporting, paying Y70 and rent amounting to Y30 a month to the pastor and all incidental expenses. On the 25 percent basis assumed by the conference churches, each has really to pay at present at least Y12 a month instead of Y8. The highest amount paid on a pastor's salary outside of the independent church is Y30.

The Japan Mission of the Ev. Church has an aid society for aged native pastors. The Mission will pay Y2,500 if the native church will raise Y2,500. This is to be put into a permanent fund and only the interest used in case of the death or retirement of a native pastor.

The Evangelical Association has 16 missionaries (including wives of missionaries and single women) in Japan and the same number in China, their two mission fields.

The annual budget for the Japan field last year was $46,000. Of this amount, the woman's board assumes $24,000. All of the budget is administered through the general board at home, upon which the woman's board has representation.

Children leaving one of our Sunday schools in Japan.

SALARIES OF MISSIONARIES

New missionaries receive $1,300 for the first four years if married, $1,400 for the next four years, and $1,500 for the balance of their time of service. If the missionary has served as a pastor at home, his years in the pastorate entitle him to the higher salary in proportion to the years he has served as either pastor or missionary.

The board plans to increase these salaries by about one-third according to rumor. It has not been settled yet, but Mr. Mayer has been ordered to pay each missionary an allowance equal to one month's salary pending the action of the board. The action will be retroactive to January 1, 1920.

Single ladies receive $700, with a $50 increase each four years, up to $800.

The board pays income tax, language school fees and rent. They pay medical bills above $20 upon recommendation of a committee in the field. They pay no drug bills, even on a doctor's prescription. They do not pay for a nurse, though Mr. Mayer thinks they should, as usually the nurse is more valuable than a doctor. Children's allowances are from 1 to 11 years, $100; from 12 to 18, $125.

Term of service is seven years, with a year off the field to follow. The board pays rent at home not to exceed $35 as yet. No rule on this. Furlough salary is the same as in the field.

An evangelistic missionary in this church has charge of a district. Mr. Mayer has five preachers under him with a number of outstations. He acts in the capacity of a presiding elder. He visits the farther fields at least once in three months but reaches the nearer fields more often. He usually has a meeting with the officers of the church where the church is organized, followed by a preaching service. During the day, he visits inquirers with the pastor. He is also taking tracts, Bibles, hymnbooks, etc., to sell and finds it worthwhile. He sends religious papers to inquirers through the mails. Has 60 on his mailing list. He also assists in short evangelistic efforts at the churches when it is possible. The mission makes an allowance of Y20 a year for evangelistic meetings in each field. The meetings are for two or three days, as this is the common practice in Japan. The longer meetings do not do so much good.

The mission outlines courses of study for the young pastors to follow and examines them at stated times. Sometimes a pastor fails to pass the examination. The plan ensures study.

The Evangelical Association in Japan had 145 conversions last year.

Mr. Mayer's home is one of two very nice mission homes built on a plot of land two and a half acres, originally bought with the idea of erecting a seminary adjoining. Since they have gone in with Aoyama, they do not need a seminary and have decided to build a kindergarten instead.

These two mission homes were built at a cost of Y7,000 each in 1914, but it would cost at least Y20,000 each, Mr. Mayer thinks, to build them now. The land is worth now about Y40 to Y50 a *tsubo*. They have just built a kindergarten and church combined in another section of Tokyo on a rented piece of land of 100 *tsubo*. The cost of this building in which the two single missionary women make their home was Y12,00 ($6,000). My Mayer thinks it is not well built and will soon need repair. The 170 *tsubo* upon which this house was built cost Y11,900, or Y70 a *tsubo*.

Mr. and Mrs. Mayer insisted that we remain for luncheon, and we had a most enjoyable time with a very good lunch, more like a dinner.

From here we went downtown where I did some shopping and then went to the photographer's where I ordered some 30 slides or more (35) on industrial, social and child life in Japan. These, in addition to a few scenes and the slides I am having made from my own films, run up to about 135 at present. I plan for about 150.

Came home just in time for dinner and found a letter from my wife, my brother Roy, W.H. Martin in Puerto Rico, and also some Western states timetables. Wrote six long letters before I retired at midnight.

Friday, November 5 ──────── ◆ ────────────────

My birthday, but I'm keeping it all to myself. Fearful of being hammered.

Got a haircut at 25 sen and spent the balance of the morning catching up on my notes.

After dinner, Mr. Garman and I made a trip through Naka Shibuya where we have a church. *Naka* means "middle," there being three sections called Shibuya, of which our church lies in the middle section. The section lies about four or five miles southwest from the Ginza, Tokyo's main business street.

We rode bicycles and went first to the Aoyama Gakuin, the Christian school established and carried on by the Methodist Episcopal church. There are 1,200 students in the several departments, which include a boys' middle school, a girls' school (soon to be moved to a new location as a separate enterprise), the college proper and the theological department. The professors we hoped to interview were not in, so we had to postpone our investigation here until some other time.

From here we rode northwest to one of the great military parade grounds. This is located near the famous Meiji Shrine just dedicated, and many booths and concession tents were being removed from the grounds. An army airplane hovered overhead, making one feel more keenly than ever what a varied life the Japanese people live. These parade grounds cover a large area owned by the government. As we entered the parade grounds, we passed the military prison, Mr. Garman explaining that they could have bought land here for a home at a reasonable price but that the prison was an objection because of the earthy noises sometimes emanating from within. This is about a mile to a mile and a half from our church.

From the parade grounds we rode west to the agricultural department of the Imperial University, which is located scarcely a mile west of our church in a fine community. There are many students here, and the opportunity for dormitory work seems to be great. The idea has seized me that if we could build a dormitory here on a fair-size plot of ground with a missionary residence nearby, we could do a fine piece of work among students and perhaps start a work that would open the way for the establishing of a middle school later on, and in the same spot. With a dormitory might also be run a night school where there is also a great field among young people.

As I write out these notes, I have paused to talk with Tokutaro Oishi, the young man who assists Mr. Garman. He has two and a half years yet in the Waseda University and is above the average as a student. Just last week or so he took an examination for a license to teach in the middle school. Three hundred took the examination, and he was one of the 14 who passed it. He is a fine Christian boy, and I have been wanting to find out just what his ambitions for a life work are. I asked him what he wanted to do, and he replied that he felt he would like to give his life as a social worker among people of the lower class. He stated very frankly that he had come from the lower class and that he wanted to help them to a better life.

But he said a financial difficulty stood in the way. As a social worker, he would want to be a minister, but the salaries of ministers are so small that he could not properly take care of his parents, who are dependent upon him. He said his parents are old and that they had gotten into financial difficulties so that they now owed a debt of Y1,000, which he felt it was his duty to pay off. He has many brothers, but they have no education and earn such small wages that they cannot pay it.

He has been asked by Waseda University to be prepared to accept a position with them as a teacher of English literature or economics when he graduates in two and a half years. They will give him about Y150 a month. He feels he will have to do this kind of work until the debt is paid off. He told me that if it were not for the debt, he would be happiest in the other work. He said frankly that he feared his faith was not large enough to expect God to take care of the debt on the salary that our ministers receive here in Japan. He said that if the salary were large enough to make it possible for him to take care of the debt, he would rather go right into social service work when he graduates.

A large group of Japanese. Nearly all of them are in uniforms with military style hats. It appears that this may be a picture of a military school with its baseball team.

I suggested to him that it might be possible for us to establish a dormitory near some of these large schools and put him in charge for several years, and by that time we may have social service work developed at Oji of such a nature that he could be put in charge of that work. He seemed impressed with the idea. The opportunity for this type of work at Oji is very great.

This dormitory plan grows upon me as a field of work that we might profitably enter with the hope of its leading us to the school work. Even if it did not lead us to the school work, it would be worthwhile work of itself, and the night school might easily be added to it. Of course, in all this work the evangelistic side must be kept in mind, as the other without it fails of reaching the goal of winning these boys to Christ. Here it depends upon the man in charge. He must be thoroughly imbued with a passion to win others to Christ and must use these agencies mentioned as the means to that great end.

I believe we could safely entrust such work to Oishi-san. He would also prove to be a valuable man as principal of a middle school if we should launch into that work.

Waseda University, with more than 5,000 students (largest in numbers in Japan), is only three miles north of our Azabu church and only four miles east of Naka Shibuya church past Aoyama Gakuin, which is about a mile east of our Shibuya church. Somewhere in this locality would be a fine place for a dormitory, I believe, and also an opportunity for a middle school as there are no middle schools in that particular location other than that at the Aoyama, and there are not nearly enough middle schools to meet the demand.

Since the agricultural department of the Imperial University is only another mile west of Naka Shibuya, a dormitory in this section would attract students of several schools, as they often live in dormitories across the city from the school they attend.

From the agricultural department of the Imp. Univ. we rode south to a lot we once had a chance to buy at a reasonable figure. It is only a little way from the school and less than a mile from our Shibuya church. Mr. Garman explained that we did not buy it because it was so much wider than it is deep and they feared a large house might be put up at the rear and cut off the afternoon sun. The lot has about 300 *tsubo* in it, and I told him I felt he had made a mistake not to buy it, that such a thing as a large house next door could happen anywhere, either in Japan or America, and that the shape of the lot was not at all against it for residence purposes. It is a fine location with some fine Japanese homes going up all around it, and it no doubt is worth much more right now than we could have bought it for a year or so ago.

He did not know whether it was still for sale. He then raised a third objective, that it was situated between our church and a big vice section. But even this does not appeal to me as a good reason for not buying it, for we may find it necessary to change the location of our church anyway because of the vice district, and in that case the location of this lot would be ideal, as we would likely want to move out that way. I was much impressed with this lot. About Y60 a *tsubo* was asked for it when it was for sale. Mr. Garman states that you cannot count on prices, though, until you actually prepare to close the deal, as sometimes a large price is asked that is shaved down when the deal seems in sight, and again a small price is asked as a bait that is increased as you show interest in the purchase.

From here we rode through the vice district that has recently sprung up between this lot and our church. The buildings are somewhat new, and the little squatty house-shaped streetlights indicate which of them are used for vice. They are licensed, but there are likely many more nearby that are not licensed. This district lies a little northwest of our church, perhaps less than a ten-minute walk. Our pastor's rented house lies between this section and our church, it being about five minutes' walk from his home to the church. A main business street for this section separates the vice district from the block in which our church is located.

We next went over to see a lot just a block west of our church, which contains about 230 *tsubo*. The location is quite good, but the lot is low and would hardly do for a foreign residence. It might, however, be worth considering to make this the lot for our permanent church and either sell the present location or use it for a foreign residence, though the latter does not appeal to me, for a reason soon to be disclosed. This lot is worth considering if we intend to stay in this territory, and Pastor Ishigaki thinks there is a great work to be done here in spite of the vice sections, which the church as such can hardly expect to touch.

We went from here over past our church to a lot some three or four blocks southeast near a primary school and a short distance from a Presbyterian church of 100 members. This lot contains 500 *tsubo* and is on a high place from which the territory slopes down to the north and east, thus forming a sort of natural dividing line. Mr. Garman has objected to the shape of all three of the lots mentioned, but to me this has not been a serious consideration in any case.

In the case of the last two lots mentioned, the most serious consideration to me has been the fact that so many houses of vice are in such close proximity. Not that we would turn our backs upon such work, but the type of work we are fitted to do is different than the type needed here. Such work requires specially trained workers and special equipment, neither of which we have. Our work is along church lines, with a kindergarten and perhaps later a night school. Parents who send their children to our kindergarten are asking whether we receive children from these houses of vice. The two cannot be mixed. Yet there is such a house almost across the street from our present location, and another is being remodeled right by our side. It is a serious question whether we ought to attempt to stay in this location. Mr. Garman thinks the vice section will tend to become segregated in the district recently built and through which we rode before reaching the business street separating it from our present location. If this is done, he thinks these near us may gradually drop out. To me it looks quite doubtful.

Now, as to our lot itself. We have a fine lot of 390 *tsubo*, which we bought together with the Japanese house still on it in June 1918 for Y16,000. In this house Miss Watanabe, head kindergarten teacher, her mother and Miss Nakai, the other teacher, live. Church services are held here, and the kindergarten is conducted in this building. It is a very fine lot, and the house is in good condition. We have been working in this community for ten years.

The location is difficult to describe. On one side is the vice section already spoken of. On the other side is a good residence section. It is near the main thoroughfare already mentioned, which connects it with the suburbs and also with lines to the city, the Ginza being four or five miles southwest. The church is about a 20 minute walk east from the agricultural school. There are three primary schools within 15 minutes' walk to the southeast and north.

There is also a Buddhist middle school of 600 pupils about 40 minutes' walk west of our school. A new government commercial school has been started recently about 15 or 20 minutes south of us. There are already 500 students enrolled, and it will become larger. There is a Presbyterian church 15 minutes' walk south of us, with a membership of 100, and another Presbyterian church north of us with a membership of about 30. This latter is an independent church in that an independent Japanese worker rents a place and conducts services for his little group of followers. He is partly supported by Dr. Uimura's church; his wife acts as a midwife, and he also works at Dr. Axling's Baptist Tabernacle, the social institution already described. The other Presbyterian church already mentioned has a pastor living in Tokyo, but not in his immediate field. They have a rented building also. Our church is really in the best location, it seems to me.

Our average church attendance is 16 or 18. We have no evening service. The average SS attendance is 70. Average prayer meeting attendance, four or five. Prayer meeting is held on Wednesday night, and a cottage prayer meeting has been begun on Thursday nights at different homes, with an average attendance of 11.

The women have a monthly meeting, with attendance of 15. Some of the leading members are a wholesale and retail dealer in seeds, a retired colonel of the Pharmacy Department of the army, an active lieutenant colonel in the same department, a retired major who is now disciplinarian at the M.E. Aoyama Gaguin, a paint manufacturer, an agent for the manufacturing of pillows and comforters, a student at Waseda University (Mr. Oishi, of whom I just wrote), and Mr. Zendo Takahashi and wife (servants in 26 Kasumi cho, the former in a theological school).

The pastor, the Rev. Ishigaki, receives a salary of Y61.87, of which the church pays Y11. This includes children's allowances. The church pays its own expenses and Y3.50 a month to the conference fund. This conference fund is for home mission work, printing the little church paper of which the Rev. Kitano of Sendai is the editor; the Japan Forward movement; etc. The church raises some benevolences at Christmas and in June to send to the hospital on Flower Day.

The kindergarten was organized five years ago, and it now has about 40 to 45 average attendance. The tuition is Y2 a month each. Miss F. Watanabe and Miss Taki Nakai are the teachers. The former's salary is to be raised from Y25 to Y35 a month at once. She can secure Y45 in the Baptist training school as a teacher of teachers. The other salary will likely be raised in proportion. This kindergarten is not fully self-supporting. It runs from 9:00 to 2:00, five days a week. The children bring thier *bentos*.

Miss Stacy conducts a music class on Wednesday afternoon from 1:30 to 2:00 for the kindergarteners just before they go home. There is then a play hour, during which the older children from the primary school come, and Miss Stacy teaches them from 3:00 to 4:00. They pay 20 sen a month for this advanced teaching. She now has about 15 of these older children. We secured this information from the pastor, the Rev. Ishigaki, who said he started a daily vacation Bible school for girls of about 14 to 16 years of age. This was conducted in the summer an hour each morning. Four girls attended. He was not sure that it was very successful.

He would like to have a church building, separate from the kindergarten, thus having the social service work carried on in a building to itself. He feels that if we could move a few streets away from the vice district, it would be better, but rather than move too far away, he feels we had better stay where we are. This is a strategic point in the middle of a great fan-shaped district that needs strong religious activities.

THE REV. SHOSABARO ISHIGAKI

Age 30. Has wife and four children: boy, Nohikatsu, meaning "faith is the victory," age 12; boy, Masamichi, meaning "straight is the way" or "the just way," age 8; boy, Yoshimichi, meaning "the right way," age 6; girl, Keiko, meaning "grace girl" (*ko*=girl), age 3.

He was converted at Sendai in Mrs. Fry's Bible class. Baptized by Mr. Fry in 1903. Graduated from the primary school, then entered a lawyer's office as a helper for two years. Then he came to Dr. Woodworth's Bible school at Tokyo for three and a half years. Then he preached at Yaita and Otawara three years. Came back to Tokyo and entered our theological school for two years. Was ordained after graduating from this theological school in 1911.

Went to Utsunomiya, where he stayed seven years. Has been at Shibuya two years. He studies Greek NT and pastoral theology in the morning for two and a half hours. Prepares his sermon on Friday and Saturday, based upon his study of the week. Plans to make about two calls a day besides other matters that come up each day in connection with his work.

My birthday passed safely, unobserved. Good joke. Remained at home this evening writing a few cards.

Saturday, November 6 ⸻ ◆ ⸻

At ten o'clock this morning, the three pastors of the Tokyo field and their wives, together with the Bible woman, Mrs. Ito, met with the missionaries in their usual monthly get-together meeting. The service opened with singing and prayer, after which I gave a talk on "The Reinforced Life." Dinner was served at twelve o'clock, and after a social hour, the pastors departed.

This is a very helpful meeting, and I think it should be encouraged. I believe the other two fields could profit by such a meeting. They usually spend some time discussing their work together. Before they left, I secured the following information from the Rev. Takahashi and wife: The Rev. Fusataro Takahashi is 60. Has one adopted son, Yoshio ("straight" or "righteous" man), age 23. He is freight clerk on the *Korea Maru*, upon which I came to Japan.

The Rev. Takahashi was converted in 1883 at Tokyo under Dr. Kozaki. He was educated during the period of the feudal system before the present educational system was started and studied mainly under tutors. There was usually a tutor for each study.

He took some Bible work from the Rev. H.J. Rhodes while he was here and secured a diploma by the rather irregular way of simply securing a blank diploma from the Baptist Theological School and having one of the Baptist professors and Mr. Rhodes sign it.

He began his work as pastor at Ichinoseki, 1891. Was ordained 1895 by Dr. Woodworth.

He was at Ichinoseki four years, then went to Oji for a year and a half. From here he went to Sendai in 1897 for two years, then to Azabu for seven years. Then back to Ichinoseki for eight years and then to Oji again where he has been about nine years.

OJI

Oji is a suburb of Tokyo on the north side, with a population of about 40,000. Ours is the only church in this section. The Disciples and other denominations formerly had work here but gave it up because it is such a hard field.

It is a manufacturing section. There are three large paper mills here, one manufacturing government paper, another stock for newspaper, and the third Japanese stationery.

The biggest concern here is the government arsenal of three huge plants. One makes big guns, another cannon and another small guns and carriages for the large guns; 7,000 are employed in the cannon plant.

There is also a factory for weaving cotton cloth. And still another making patent medicine.

The Japanese stationery factory employs 300. The newspaper-stock factory employs 1,500, and the government paper factory 1,500 in day and night shifts. A thread-weaving factory has a dormitory housing 2,000 of the women employed. More are employed in this factory, coming from surrounding communities.

Our church is on the west side of this section, among some of the factories and perhaps a mile from some of the larger factories. We own the church and the parsonage here.

The church membership is about 30. Among them are seven who own their own homes and are merchants; one family belongs, the head of which is a government official; 15 are laborers in factories and working in their own small manufacturing plants, the work being done by hand; six are students. We began work here 32 years ago under the Rev. Jones.

We have services morning and evening. Average morning attendance 15, and the evening the same. Average SS 70. Weekly attendance at prayer meeting four. Mr. M. Kitazawa, who is membership and social secr. of the Tokyo International YMCA (Japan, China and Korea) has about 20 boys in the Oji church who are members of the YMCA. They meet twice a month for Bible study, and the Rev. Takahashi teaches them. Mr. Kitazawa was born and raised in Oji and belongs to our church.

There is also a women's meeting once a month for Bible study, with an attendance of five or six.

The Rev. Takahashi receives a salary of Y68.50 a month, of which the church pays Y5.50. The church pays its own expenses and a conference assessment of Y3.25 a month. Nothing else regularly.

We have a kindergarten here. The tuition is Y1.50 a month plus some extra for heat in winter. It meets from 9:00 to 2:00 five days week. Some come to play much earlier, possibly because both parents are at work. The school is not self-supporting.

The Rev. Takahashi wants to reach the laboring man. Would like to get into the dormitories of the women workers and give direct Christian teaching, but as yet the owners will not permit it. He would like to conduct dormitories and also day nurseries for children. He would also like to conduct consolation meetings, meetings to get the minds of the workers off their work and give them diversion after work hours. Thinks entertainment might be given of the right sort.

He feels that the day nursery is one of the most important but one of the hardest to conduct because it means taking the children before daylight and keeping them until after dark. Many come to the kindergarten to leave their babies, thinking it is a day nursery. A day nursery would give access to the people better than any other phase of our work.

Some have been conducted by a man privately, but all but one have been discontinued because he took other work and his wife and daughter could not handle so many. They received government help in the day nurseries they conducted.

The Rev. Takahashi has five or six inquirers. He spends his morning reading and writing, including Bible study and sermon preparation. Afternoons he plans various activities, sometimes calling, sometimes regular meetings, sometimes reading.

Took a short walk before supper tonight and went to bed rather early—about ten o'clock.

Sunday, November 7 ——————— ◆ ———————————————

Brother Garman and I walked to Naka Shibuya this morning where I preached on "Ye are the salt of the earth." Took a picture of the SS after the session. After the morning service, two young women were baptized. One of them is the new servant at Kasumi cho, the other the single sister of Mrs. Zendo Takahashi, who works at Kasumi cho as cook.

I met Miss F. Watanabe at Naka Shibuya. She is the fiancée of Y. Taizumi, of Defiance. She wants me to take a gift to him. A very bright girl and head teacher of our Shibuya kindergarten. She is one of the nicest-looking Japanese girls I have yet seen.

From here we hurried to Azabu church, where a combination welcome meeting for me and silver-wedding-anniversary celebration for the Rev. and Mrs. Matsuno was held. The real anniversary was last April 3, but owing to the sickness of the daughter, it had to be postponed. We had a very enjoyable time, taking lunch together. Among many other speakers, I gave a short talk.

From here we went to the Ginza M.E. church for a Union church service for English-speaking. The Rev. Benninghoff, who has just accepted the acting pastorate of the church, preached on "A Great Adventure."

From here Miss Stacy, Mr. Garman and I walked through Hibiya Park where the great chrysanthemum show is on for this month. I saw the most wonderful flowers I have ever seen. They are set in pots, sometimes one, sometimes two or three or four in a pot, and so arranged in the booths as to show a large variety of colors and styles together. There is sort of a threefold objective in view, it seems, in raising each plant—first to secure the largest and most perfect blossom of a certain variety, in which effort each plant is permitted to bear only one blossom; second, to secure the most delicate and varied color possible in each one; third, to secure as many blossoms on a single plant as possible. There are many different varieties of chrysanthemums, and I presume there may be a fourth objective in trying to secure new varieties never yet grown.

They are wonderful plants. It was impossible to count the varieties and colors. Some are like great fluffy snowballs eight inches across or even more. Some are of the curled-petal variety, and still others have petals that string out from the center in every direction. Then there are single plants bearing as many as a hundred or more blossoms four to eight inches in diameter each. There are others bearing a very small variety of blossom with perhaps five or six hundred or more on each single stem. In order to secure the right effect, these flowers in growing are trained to drop over the side of the jar gracefully so that all the blossoms may be displayed to advantage.

I noticed one flower that had been trained to grow right down through the bottom of the jar, or else after it had reached its growth, the inverted jar had been set upright. At any rate, the jar hung from the ceiling of a tent, and the flower swung below it loaded with blossoms. In the park, many beautiful scenic effects have been worked out with flowers of all descriptions. There is also one section devoted to a study of pests attacking flowers and fruit, and another section devoted to the proper scenic or garden effects along the line of landscaping gardening.

After our visit to the park, Miss Stacy left us, and we went to the restaurant for a bite of supper before starting for Oji, an hour-and-a-half's ride. At the restaurant we met a Mr. Fesperman, of the Reformed church, who stated that he was teaching a Bible class at one of the downtown churches on Sunday evening. He formerly studied at the Reformed Theological Seminary in Dayton.

Mr. Matsuno met us on the same car, and we went together to Oji where he interpreted while I spoke on "The Seeking Savior" to a very attentive audience. Before the service I met Mr. Kitazawa, the secr. of membership and social life of the YMCA of whom I just wrote. He told me he had been called to take a similar work on Honolulu and was to sail on the same boat I take December 4 (*Shinyo Maru*).

During the service he sang a solo in Japanese. It was a beautiful song, he has a beautiful voice, and above all, he sang it with genuine effectiveness. I was so impressed that I complimented him publicly on the effort.

After the service, a number of YMCA boys brought their Bibles and Testaments, and had me write my name and address in them. I fancy I shall receive an avalanche of letters when I return to Dayton.

After the service, Takahashis served us tea, apples and candy. During the evening, I told what I had done at Shibuya and Azabu during the day, gave a penny to each one present. (In the former instances, just to the young ladies. Here, to all.)

One of the men was especially interested, and it developed that he was a collector of old coins as a business. He slipped home and came back with a most interesting collection of coins for Mr. Garman and me. He gave me a set for myself and one for Mrs. Minton. It consisted of one large oval-shaped coin used some 50 years ago for a sen. It states on it *Tempo sen* and was supposed to be equal to 100 mon, or 10 *rin*, which equals 1 sen. It was made in the reign of Tempo, but it was found that instead of containing the required amount of copper for 100 mon, or 1 sen, it contained only 80 mon, or 8 rin. From this coin it became the habit to speak of people who were not quite properly poised mentally as *Tempo sens*.

There is in this collection an *ichimon*, one mon, or one-tenth of a rin; a piece worth a rin and a half; another worth two rin; also a rin piece. It is a most interesting collection, and I will make good use of it. Returned home at a late hour.

Monday, November 8   ⸻ ◆ ⸻

The *Tenyo Maru* sails for San Francisco today, and Mr. Garman and Miss Stacy went to Yokohama to see Miss Hara, their former cook, now Mrs. Tageta, off for her new home in America. I spent the morning catching up on my notes, and it was a long, arduous morning's work.

Continued my work in the afternoon, succeeding in getting off an article to Dr. Morrill, "Covering the Sendai." Continued this type of work in the evening until a fairly late hour.

Tuesday, November 9 —————— ◆ ————————————————

Wrote to Dr. Morrill concerning the CM for February. Want to get it under way now.

Mr. Garman and I called on the Rev. Matsuno to get some information on his life and work and also of the Azabu church. But he was out of town for a few days.

We then called on the Rev. W.H. Hayes, of the United Brethren Mission. He is in charge of the evangelistic work and is at present the only UB missionary in Tokyo. They have two mission homes here and one of their churches in the same compound. The houses are well built, and there is ample space around them. On the way to Mr. Hayes' we stopped a moment and saw one of their kindergartens in progress. This church has a wing built off of it for kindergarten purposes. The government regulation states that a kindergarten must not be held in a room used for religious purposes. This plan meets the demand.

At Mr. Hayes' we met Mr. Brubaker of Dayton, Ohio, who is the general SS secretary of the UB church in America. He came to the SS convention and has remained over to do some work among the SS here. Has been here five weeks. Returns Thursday on the *Kashima*. It seemed quite nice to meet a man from Dayton and to learn of the work he is doing.

Mr. Hayes gave us the following information: The UB church has a membership of 354,000 in the United States and mission fields. About 1,500 compose the Japan membership. There are ordinarily three missionary families here in Japan. There are two centers, one at Tokyo and the other at Kyoto. The 1,500 members are in about 20 local organizations, with some nine or ten church buildings in the Japan field. The UB church has about 400,000 people allotted to them here, according to the allotment of the Board of Federated Missions.

The organization of the UB Japan church or conf. is worth noting as it is different from any other here. The Japan conf. handles its own finances. The budget for the Japan churches is made out by a joint conference of missionaries and local churches. The mission treas., Mr. Hayes, pays over to the treas. of the Japan conf. the money designated in the budget for their work, and this treasurer handles the funds on the order of the Japanese pres. of the Japan conf. There is an ad-interim comm. composed of three missionaries and six Japanese brethren who look after the affairs between the annual conference sessions, but the Japan conference is allowed great freedom in carrying on its work. This partially accounts for the small number of missionaries required to handle the work here.

Native pastors are obtained by picking up young men in the churches, who are sent to the Congregational Seminary, Doshisha Gakuin, at Kyoto where the UB have an arrangement by which they support a missionary as professor of religious education in the seminary, paying his salary and choosing the man themselves. Then they also pay $600 a year toward the support of a Japanese professor whom the school heads at Doshisha select.

The UB supports the students sent to his seminary to the extent of Y25 per month and tuition extra. But they have a plan by which they get these men to earn practically all of the Y25 by doing practical work among the churches as assistants to the missionaries and pastors. By this plan, they do not give outright near all of the Y25 allotted to each.

They have ten men in the seminary now, and Mr. Hayes says that their salary plan and the plan of the native church organization is appealing to Japanese pastors from other denominations, so that they could draw many of them into their work if they so desired, but he says they do not need them as they are well supplied.

In order to enter the seminary, the young man must have a middle school diploma and take an examination before he can enter Doshisha, where they now have a course covering five years, embracing the college work and the seminary in that period.

When a man graduates from Doshisha, he must act as pastor for four years before he is ordained. During his first year after graduation, he receives Y60 a month as the minimum salary. He receives in addition to this one-half of whatever part of it is raised by the local church. For example, if a man is starting in after graduation, his minimumn salary is Y60. If the church raises Y20 of his salary, the board rule is that he shall have half of that added to his Y60. In other words, the board would in reality pay Y50 of his salary, and he would receive the Y20 paid by the church, making his salary Y70. By this plan, the pastor is encouraged to get his church to give more, and as he does so, he is benefited financially, and the board has the burden of its financial obligation to that church lightened.

The basic salary the second year is Y62; the third year, Y64; the fourth year, Y66; and after the fourth year when he is ordained, it continues at Y70 indefinitely. That is to say, the board will not pay more than Y70, but the maximum salary allowed a native pastor is Y100. That is to say, if a man serves until his basic salary is Y70 (after four years) and then his church raises Y30 toward his support, the mission would decrease the amount of their support to him from Y70 to Y65, and by the addition of the Y30 raised by the church, his salary would be Y85. If his church should raise Y60 toward his support, the board would decrease their support from Y70 to Y40, and by the addition of the Y60 raised by the church he would receive a salary of Y100. But if his church should increase their support to more than Y60, his salary would remain at Y100, while the board would decrease the amount of their support in proportion as the church increased. By this plan, each church gradually becomes self-supporting. Each church is expected to increase its support every year.

The 20 congregations of the UB Japan church raised last year for self-support outside of what they raised for their running expenses Y3,708. Next year they are expected to raise Y4,646.

These churches raised last year a special evangelistic fund for use in promoting evangelism in their churches—Y800. Next year they are to raise Y900. Three years ago, they raised Y500 for this, and four years ago, Y300.

They also have what they call a self-denial week, in which they raised last year Y300, and next year they are to raise Y400. This fund is used in the Japan conference for SS and other special work. They also have what is called Otterbein Day, in which they raise about Y200 each year. Last year, the increase in the Japanese churches' gifts was about Y1,000, and next year they expect it to be Y1,228.

(Mr. Garman says their churches are located in better districts financially than ours, but five of them are right here in Tokyo, and three of them just beyond our

Oji work or at least between there and Utsunomiya. I am wondering if we have not failed to follow a definite system with our churches here that would have brought them to larger self-support.)

At Christmastime, the UB Japan churches raise about Y60 apiece. On all new church buildings put up by the board, the local Japan church must raise one-tenth of the cost.

One of their missionaries (at Kyoto, I think) recently built a home at a cost of Y25,000 plus Y9,000 for the lot. This was last year, and Mr. Hayes states that it could be done for much less now as prices of building materials have dropped.

They have done no buying of land lately, but Mr. Knipp, one of the two men at Kyoto, recently bought from his own private means a building at Kyoto to be used for the YMCA purposes. He secured this money, I learned from Mr. Brubaker, through the sale of his residence property in Dayton to Dr. W.H. Denison.

Mr. Hayes has three pastors under his direction, together with one Bible woman and one native assistant who goes with him in his work a great deal of the time. His work is in the country outside of Tokyo in Chiba ken. There are also five UB churches in Tokyo where he occasionally helps, but they are really not under his charge. The UB Japan mission has five kindergartens along with its other work.

MISSIONARY SALARIES IN JAPAN UB

The basic salary of the UB missionary to Japan has recently been raised from $1,200 to $1,700 a year, and applies to all the missionaries regardless of their term of service in the field. Rent, medical allowances, income tax, etc. is also allowed. The medical bills are allowed up to $50. Above that amount, a statement must be sent to the board at home for approval. As yet, no such bills have been refused. They have run close to Y500 once or twice. Children's allowances are $200 up to 10 years and $300 from 10 to about 20 years of age. They are also given a summer allowance of $50 a family to apply on travel to the summer home, etc. Mr. Hayes says it is not adequate but that the attention of the board has not been called to it, and consequently it remains the same as before the raise in salaries. The outfit allowance is $300, though the missionary asked that it be made $400.

Mr. Hayes says the three missionary families here have petitioned their board to raise their salaries to $2,500 each. He says they hardly expect to get it, but they feel it should be higher than even the $1,700 recently decided upon.

YMCA workers receive $3,000 plus the regular allowances, and say they can live fairly well on it.

The Federated Missions Council of Japan recently recommended an increase in missionary salaries of 100 percent.

Returned to the house for lunch. This afternoon we called on Dr. A.K. Reischauer, professor in the theological and college department of Meiji Gakuin (the school of the Pres. and Dutch Reformed church combined). Dr. Reischauer is also executive secretary of the Woman's Christian College of Japan, a new school being opened in Tokyo for higher education of women, with six boards already cooperating and three more expected to do so. The present cooperating boards are the Baptist North, Canadian Methodist, Disciple, Methodist Episcopal North, Presbyterian

North, Reformed Church in America (this is the official name of the Dutch Reformed). The three boards expected to unite are Reformed Church in America, Methodist Episcopal South, and Congregational.

The basis of cooperation is as follows: The expenses of the institution are divided into two classes of units. One is composed of the permanent property units of $5,000 each, and the other the current expense units of $1,700 each at present, but which will be increased somewhat each year as the full work is undertaken. Any board that desired to cooperate can do so by agreeing to provide one or more of the above units. To do so entitles them to representation on the Cooperating Committee in America and the board of trustees here, the latter consisting of 15 members, five of whom are prominent Japanese educators, the other missionaries representing the cooperating boards.

The Cooperating Comm. in America representing the cooperating boards has Dr. Frank Mason North as chairman, Miss Alice M. Davison sec. and Mrs. DeWitt Knoas treasurer. Other members are Dr. R.E. Speer, Mrs. Henry Peabody, Miss Rose Beatty, Miss Charlotte H. Conant, Mr. R.A. Doan, Mrs. Wm. Bancroft-Hill, Miss Grace Lindley, Mrs. W.A. Montgomery, Miss Florence L. Nichols and Dr. T.H.P. Sailer.

There is also a supporters' league in Japan, consisting of such men as Viscount K. Kaneko, Viscount Shibusawa, Baron Nakajima, Hon. S. Ebara, H. Nagao, etc. Some of these men are Christians, and all are interested in higher education for men and women because it will bring about better understanding between the people of Japan and the West.

The pres. of the college is Dr. I. Nitobe, and the dean is Miss T. Yasui. The student body comes from all parts of the empire. At the opening of this, the third year of the school in its temporary quarters at 100 Tsunohadzu, Yodobashi, Tokyo, 187 new students applied for admission, and the enrollment stood at 194. About half of them come from Christian schools and half from govt. and private schools; 65 percent are Christians.

The five courses offered, with others to follow, are liberal arts, Japanese language and literature, English language and literature, social service, and business. Science, household science, education, journalism and music are to be added as soon as possible.

A campus of nearly 24 acres has been purchased, at a cost of about $150,000, situated on a fast-car line west of the city within 45 minutes of the Central Tokyo Station. This land cost about Y10 per acre. It was bought without the full amount in hand in order to avoid the constantly rising prices. It is hoped that the full amount may soon be met by the boards in America together with private gifts. And it is expected that the amount will later be raised by the Japanese friends, so that the original $150,000 given by Americans for land may be returned to be used in putting up the buildings, thus becoming part of the permanent invested funds. The Japanese members of the board of trustees expect to do this later when the effect of the heavy giving recently made to the SS convention has worn away.

The cost of the first buildings, consisting of administration-classroom bldg., dormitories for about 250 students, and three faculty residences, is estimated at about $175,000. The entire set of buildings will cost about $500,000.

The girls pay at present Y55 tuition each year of 11 months. Those living in the inadequate dormitory pay Y15 a month for board.

The budget for the third year is $32,000. About one-seventh of this is met by tuition and fees, the balance from board appropriations and other gifts.

The need for such a school is apparent when one learns that Japan has over 50,000 young men in her colleges and universities and less than 2,000 young women in institutions above the high school grades, though 20,000 girls graduate from the high schools every year. The only government institutions above high school grades are two normal schools intended to supply teachers for the lower schools. Of some 30 new colleges the government is now establishing at the cost of millions of yen, not one of them and not a sen of the money is to benefit young women. There is no question that this is a worthy undertaking that ought to be properly supported.

The Meiji Gakuin in which Dr. Reischauer is a professor has a middle school, a college and a seminary department. A commercial course has recently been added, which has become so popular that there is danger of the institution becoming top-heavy in this direction.

There are 660 in the middle school, though the limit should be 600. The Japanese who are at the head of it are apt to allow such crowding, Dr. Reischauer says. Yet it seems that the policy of allowing more power to the Japanese is growing in favor.

There are no dormitories connected with the middle school, Dr. Reischauer stating that he thought it was not so necessary for that school but a fine thing in connection with colleges and seminaries.

They are contemplating such dormitories now. There is a dormitory now for theological students, of whom I think he said there are about 25 distributed between the two cooperating boards, the Presbyterian and Dutch Reformed (Ref. in America).

The tuition in the middle school is Y5.00 a month, and the teachers receive from Y1,000 to Y1,500 a year salary.

There are about 19 students in the regular theological course and eight in the special course. It is planned to eliminate the special course (for students short of preparatory work) and make such students special students, allowing them to take what they are able to.

Meiji Gakuin is planning to change the course of study somewhat. The middle school course in Japan is a five-year course through which students may enter college. The present arrangement is for a five-year course covering two years' college work and three years' college and seminary combined. They plan to make the college work three years to admit students from the fourth year of the middle school.

The two cooperating boards are to give Y25,000 each year toward the budget of Meiji Gakuin.

Dr. Reischauer thinks it would be folly for a small church to attempt a middle school because of the high cost initially and the continuing cost of administration, and also because of the difficulty of getting suitable teachers. He says it is much better to cooperate in a college enterprise with some other board. He also feels that a dormitory for middle school boys is impractical but says a dormitory for college and seminary men is a fine thing as it brings the missionary into contact with a fine class of men who are destined to be leaders. The initial cost of building a dormitory is the big outlay, after which the institution becomes nearly if not quite self-supporting.

Such men as Reischauer and Benninghoff are men of large vision, and they are attempting large things, and their work certainly deserves large support.

This evening I took Miss Stacy downtown for dinner at the Central Station Restaurant. We had time to talk over quietly some of the plans for future work. She is desirous of making the kindergarten work her lifework here, and it seems to me it is a great opportunity for her to serve the Kingdom. After five years of service here, she hopes to use her furlough for Bible study in some Bible school, after which she will be ready to come back here and continue her work. My thought is that she should be put in charge of organizing and conducting the kindergartens throughout our mission field.

Wednesday, November 10 ——————— ◆ ————————————————

This morning, Mr. Garman and I called on Mr. Phelps, YMCA secretary for Japan. He stated in response to my question concerning increasing the force that it was not their intention to bring any more general secretaries from America but rather to train the Japanese to do this work. He said that they would likely bring out a few specialists such as a boys' work specialist, etc., but that even these would come to train Japanese workers to become specialists along the same line.

Mr. Phelps stated that they are giving the Japanese members of their committee the right virtually to dictate the policy of their work, the foreign members accepting their judgment in practically everything.

At his invitation, we are to take lunch at his home, November 24, meeting him at the YMCA at twelve o'clock of that day.

From here we went to see the Rev. McKenzie of the Canadian Methodist Mission, but finding him away, we called on his colleague, Dr. Armstrong, Ph.D., who has recently come to Tokyo from another section of their work. He has written a book on Shintoism in Japan and proved to be a very interesting conversationalist. The Canadian Methodists have a church located right in the midst of a number of dormitories connected with several large universities and commercial schools. The CM do not own the dormitories, but the boys come from them to the church where a student organization has been formed. There are about 20,000 students in this district attending Imperial Univ., a higher commercial school, and other colleges.

The CM church here has a Japanese pastor in charge of the church, and Dr. Armstrong is beginning to organize the boys. The church work and the work among the students must be carried on in the same building, and it has raised the question what adjustments should be made so each man can do a full man's work and yet not interfere with what the other is doing. They have decided that if the Japanese put up half of the money and the mission the other half, the work could be carried on together. They do not know as yet how it will work. There is an English Bible class in the church Sunday morning. Then on each Sunday evening at 6:30 a purely English service is held, followed by the Japanese service at 7:30 conducted by the pastor.

Dr. Armstrong feels that it is rather late to attempt to organize a student asso-ciation under purely foreign auspices. This raises the same question Mr. Phelps raised about giving the Japanese more freedom in planning and conducting the work. Of course, in the YMCA you have an international organization to work with, which no doubt makes it different from the church at home. If Mr. Phelps is correct in his views, and if they should hold good in relation to the church, it would be a ques-tion whether to send any more missionaries to Japan.

Dr. Armstrong thinks Mr. Phelps is an extremist, and there is ground for such belief. The former mentions a little Canadian Methodist church nearby that is en-tirely under Japanese control. The building is run-down. The Japanese pastor ex-pressed the hope that money might be forthcoming, but it does not come. Dr. Arm-strong therefore questions whether the time has come to give the work over to the Japanese. My own feeling in this is that the Japanese church should increase her giv-ing until the bulk of the money comes from them instead of America before control of the work is delegated to them. It is, however, desirable, I think, that the effort should always be placed on drawing out the powers of the Japanese with the thought of gradually decreasing the control of the missionaries and increasing the control of the native workers just as rapidly as they show their ability to raise funds and handle the work.

Dr. Armstrong says that about ten years ago, the question of Japanese control was strongly urged but that the wave receded and the missionaries became more ser-viceable than ever, and he feels that this wave will pass off the same way, though not so easily. He thinks there is a great chance here still for men from America to come out for a lifework. He says that even if a man comes out for only ten years (a thing he believes could happen now), he will be even more fully prepared for a message at home because of his experiences here. He believes there is a field for a generation of missionaries here yet. He thinks there will be a religious wave sweeping the country soon that will demand the services of every missionary available.

The M.E. Japan church has launched a great forward movement to raise Y600,000. The M.E. South, M.E. North, and Can. Meth. are united in Japan as the Japan Methodist Church. These are self-supporting churches, and a Japan mis-sionary society supporting half-self-supporting churches.

The three mission boards subsidize this Independent Japan Conference with a certain budget each year, which the Japanese conference handles themselves. This budget is to be decreased every year and is practically wiped out now. The Japanese Forward movement composed of these independent churches is raising the Y600,000. As weaker churches of either of these three missions become half self-supporting, they are handed over to the Japan mission to be controlled by them from that time on.

The Canadian Methodists have 19 families and 30 or 40 single women in Japan, and need more. They are connected with the M.E. school at Kobe, in which school they have five men. They are also doing social service work here in Tokyo and aim at evangelistic work. They run a dormitory near one of the middle schools. Some ministerial students have been found through the dormitory, depending largely upon the personality of the missionary in charge. The students pay a trifle for room rent and handle their board on the club plan with a missionary acting as adviser.

Mr. Garman and one of our Christian Japanese pastors near a torii – the entrance to a Shinto shrine.

The Can. M.E. do a great kindergarten work. Wives of missionaries find it a great means of securing entrance to homes.

They also have a home for poor children. The supt. at one time sent out rice bags with Scripture texts upon them. He asked that a handful of rice be put in the bag daily if possible. Half of the rice necessary for the children's meals was thus obtained. They conduct day nurseries also and find them a great help in securing access to the homes.

Dr. Armstrong does not know the scale of salaries for native pastors. Last year, the missionaries received a bonus of $300 each family. This year, the salaries were raised from $1,200 to $1,600 as a basic salary. From 1 to 7 years of service, the salary is $1,600. From 8 to 15, it is $1,900. From 16 up, it is $2,100. Children's allowances are 1–6, $100; 7–12, $150; 13–18, $200. The board pays rent, income tax and medical bills of any great size. The missionary is to pay medical bills up to $50. Above $50, the bills are paid by the home board. All medical bills must be sent to the board for approval.

Previously the mission agreed not to pay its helpers more than the Japanese pastors of the independent churches received.

From here we went to the Rev. Rollin McCoy's for dinner. Mr. McCoy is connected with the Disciples' boys' school, and we went over the work of the school thoroughly. There is a plot of ground here of about four and a half acres. The girls' school is adjoining. There is also a theological school. The theological course offers a two-year arts course to those having diplomas from the middle school, and those not having such diploma must take an entrance examination covering all the middle school courses. This is followed by a three-year theological course open to graduates

School children directed by their teacher entering a Japanese Shinto Shrine.

of the Bible school, two-year art course, or its equivalent in some other school or college doing work of *koto* (higher) grade.

The middle school has 200 students, which is their present capacity. There are 13 Japanese teachers and two Japanese administrative officers; one missionary teaches English. The board of directors has five missionaries and four Japanese members. The tuition is Y4.50 a month. Only a few of the boys live in the dormitory. This school is called a *chugakko* since it is controlled by government regulations, and according to these rules, no religious services are permitted in the rooms used for school purposes. In this case, however, the authorities know that they conduct Bible classes and preaching services in the schoolrooms after school hours. A *gakuin* is not recognized in the same way by the government, and its standing is not considered quite so good.

Mr. McCoy admitted that none of the boys from the middle school has yet been drawn into the theological course with a view to becoming a minister. The board has recently sent a young man to do evangelistic work among the boys in the hope that it will lead some of them into Christian lives and the ministry. About 50 of the 200 boys are Christians.

The mission gives Y125 a month toward the middle school, the balance being cared for by tuition. The principal of the school, however, is paid outside this amount given by the mission. The mission pays his salary separately, amounting to Y150 a month and rent. This year the government granted Y770 to increase the salaries of the teachers. The average salary of the teachers is about Y85, none of them receiving as much as Y100 except the principal. The teachers usually teach other places to supplement their salaries.

The theological school has only six students at present. They have but one course of three years above the two-year arts course. The mission gives scholarships of Y19 a month from which the boys support themselves.

There are two full-time teachers in the theological department, both graduates of American colleges. One receives Y150 a month, including rent, the other Y130. The principal of the girls' school also teaches part-time in the theological school, and there is another part-time professor.

The Disciples have seven missionary families, one single man and 11 single women in Japan. They have three church buildings in Tokyo. The majority of their missionaries are evangelistic.

At Osaka there is an English Institute with girls enrolled in the day courses and boys at night. One family and one single lady are connected with this. They do not plan to enlarge their educational work but want better equipment. There are about 30 graduates from the middle school each year. The government would permit them to add two years beyond the middle school and admit graduates from this to the universities.

The Japan churches of the Disciple mission are about 25 in number. None of them are fully self-supporting. Some are partially so. They will not locate a man in a field unless the local church will pay at least Y5 on the salary. A church without a regular pastor is known as a preaching place.

The present salary scale is as follows for a single man:

Church	Mission
Y 5	Y50
10	55
15	60
20	65
25	70
30	65
35	60
45	50
55	40
65	30
75	20
85	10

For a married man add 10 yen to the amount paid by the mission each time. Ordinarily they expect these amounts to change for the church every two years. The preaching places get preaching services through the missionaries and the settled pastors when they can come.

There is an evangelistic committee of five missionaries and five Japanese who worked out this schedule. They have full powers to control the work, merely report to the mission, subject to the appeal of the mission. Any action passed must be favored by at least three missionaries and three Japanese on the committee.

The Japan churches are divided into four groups: (1) preaching places, or *konisho*; (2) mission churches paying Y5 or more on a pastor's salary plus current expenses, excepting big repairs and rent; (3) self-governing church, *gigikiokai*, paying at least Y15 a month on the salary and all expenses except as above; (4) independent churches, paying all of the pastor's salary, etc.

There are about 1,400 members in Disciple churches in Japan (25 in number). Roll was revised three years ago, cutting it down. They now have a campaign working up to the fortieth anniversary of the beginning of the Disciple work in Japan, 1923. Nine churches are aiming at independence by that time. The membership aimed at is 400, budget of Y30,000 while it is now only Y7,000. SS increase, of course. Posters are used to advertise this: "Each one win one"; "Read a chapter in the Bible daily"; "Contribute something to the work each Sunday"; "Pray for it daily"; "Attend church regularly"; "Lead one to Christ every year."

The budget for the Disciple Mission for this year is $30,000, which has been increased about $3,000. Next year they are asking for $41,250, plus $9,000 specials.

There has been a stiff fight in the Disciple church between the liberals and the conservatives on the question of baptism, and the withdrawal of the conservatives, which has been threatened, would injure work here.

The budget is divided as follows:

Evangelistic	$19,500
Educational	16,800
Gen. misc.	5,000
Specials	9,000

The Disciple church has recently effected a union of all their boards, moving their headquarters from Cincinnati and uniting all the boards under one general board.

MISSIONARY SALARIES

The new basis for salaries in the Disciple church places the married man at $1,500 a year and a single man at $850. Single women same. Children's allowance $100 from 1–6; $150 from 7–10; $200 from 11–16; $250 from 17–18; $250 from 19–21 if in school.

All medical bills must be submitted to the board at home, but they are always paid. No dental bills are paid. Outfit allowance is $200 for family and $100 for single person. A special bonus of $100 per person was given the missionaries the past two years, and this is being continued at their request while prices are so high. Term of service is seven winters for the first term and eight winters the second term. Furlough off the field 14 months.

The Rev. McCoy expressed the hope that our two churches might get together, at least over here, and establish a larger school somewhere around Oji. A social settlement could be established and a larger middle school and seminary started. He suggested selling the present plant and going into a plant in a more desirable location a little farther out. His idea, and mine too, would be to go half-and-half, with a board of control composed of equal representation from both churches. It bears consideration.

The Thunder God.

Left: A two story Japanese building
with a peaked tile roof.

Below: The Rev. C.P. Garman on the
bridge overlooking Shirokuma Falls.

Right: A Japanese building overlooking a mountain valley.

Below: Sacred bridge of the Emperor of Japan at Mako. One of the three most beautiful spots in the country.

Above: This sewing class for Japanese girls was one of the methods used in the efforts used to evolve the Christian home life. Below: The children imitate their elders on the great religious holidays in transporting the spirits of departed ancestors.

Above: Men with long hooks are pulling refuse, rags, etc. out of this canal in the Honjo ward of Kobe. Sewage runs into the canal from the houses, in some cases.

Below: With seven-eighths of the country mountainous and only one-twelfth of Japan tillable soil, the problem of raising enough food is stupendous. Terraced rice fields up the mountainside like these are a common sight.

A typical fishing smack.

Crossing the Kitakami River in northern Japan.

A river through the slum section of Kobe. This shows a panoramic view of the city skyline. For many years it was the seat of Kagawa's efforts.

Japanese fishing smacks in the harbor at Kobe.

Wherever one goes in Japan, one finds the inevitable Japanese garden. Whether it be on a scale to compare with the royal gardens or the tiniest spot in the humblest quarters, the Japanese garden is always beautiful. (Probably a commercially produced photograph purchased by the author.)

V. Touring South of Tokyo

Wrote all morning, cleaning up my notes and writing duplicate articles for the *Herald* and the *Sun* on "The Program of the Eighth World's Sunday School Convention," and "Side Lights from the Sunday School Convention."

Went downtown after lunch and got some money and did a little shopping.

Garman and I took the 9:00 P.M. train for Nagoya. We engaged a second-class sleeper berth, and all we could get were uppers. The seats in the sleepers are wide, and some run lengthwise, while several in the middle of the car run as do those in our sleepers. In either case, they make only single beds. Partitions are placed as in our sleepers, with curtains in front. The toilet and lavatory are each just large enough for one individual at a time. The upper berth has no light except what filters through from the car lights. There is one improvement in this upper berth, though, over that of those in America—namely, there are two small windows on the side that enable one to see out by drawing back the curtains. There is also a sort of ventilating system in each berth, controlled by pushing open a little sliding disk. The size of these berths proves that they were made for Japanese. The attendants are very courteous, and we got along all right. It was great sport trying to dress and undress in such close quarters.

Friday, November 12 ──────── ◆ ────────────────────

Arrived at Nagoya on time at 6:30 A.M. after a ride of 235 miles from Tokyo. Second-class fare was Y10.53, including Y1.30 extra fare. Upper berth, second class, was Y3.00. Checked our grips and had breakfast at a nearby restaurant. It consisted of two fried eggs, fried potatoes, and bread, butter and coffee, and cost us 85 sen each or 43¢.

After breakfast, we went to the home of the Rev. Leigh Layman, of the Methodist Protestant Middle School. We arrived just in time for chapel at eight, and I was called upon to speak without a moment's notice. Spoke to 650 boys, and they gave me fine attention. The English teacher interpreted and proved to be one of the best in this part of the country. After I had finished, he told the boys in Japanese that they had just heard a fine speech.

The MP Middle School is a *chugakko* middle school. This means that it is under government supervision, and consequently it is against the law to teach religion in the school, but Mr. Layman told me to say anything I wanted to. He said the inspectors, whose duties are to inspect the schools at unappointed times, were usually quite lenient in this regard if the other work was up to standard.

Mr. Layman says that three-fourths of the boys attend Bible classes outside of school hours voluntarily. One-tenth of the boys are baptized every year. He says they get ministerial students from the middle school. One was secured through this channel last year.

This is the only Christian middle school among 15,000,000 people. They have 4,000 *tsubo* of land, which is now worth Y30 a *tsubo*.

The MP church is planning a community center in another section of the city, with 1,000 *tsubo* of land. This, with two missionary residences, a church, a night school, and kindergarten, is to cost Y125,000, including cost of land. (Note: Either this is an underestimate, or other estimates I have heard are over estimated, or the price of land and material here is less. I am quite sure the price of land is less, as this is a rather out-of-the-way town so far as big business is concerned.)

The MP Middle School has at present a small dormitory and five other buildings. Plan is to rearrange the location of these buildings. The mission home is at present right next to the school, and the church, I think, is on rented land. The present buildings and land, not including the mission home, are worth about Y200,000. Mr. Layman thinks 10,000 *tsubo* of land is necessary for their enlarged plans and says it could be bought much cheaper outside and that it would be just as good as to location, for the students will come to it.

Mr. Layman is enthusiastic for a school as a means of reaching the boys. He thinks the school needs a live young missionary to reach the boys, and this suggests the conviction that I have long since reached—that the spiritual results obtained through the indirect methods of schools, dormitories, etc. is dependent upon the personality of the man in charge.

This school costs the board Y743 a month ($372) outside the salary of Mr. Layman, the one missionary in charge. The head of the school is a native. Mr. Layman is treasurer of the MP Mission in Japan.

The tuition is Y4 a month. There are 50 boys in the dormitory who pay Y13 a month board. There are 20 teachers. The principal receives Y150 a month and pays his own rent. The head of the English department receives Y130 a month; mathematics teacher, Y120. The average of the other teachers is about Y70 for those teaching full-time. Still others teach only part-time, at Y40 or Y50 a month.

The MP has no salary scale for native pastors. They ask the church to pay all it can, on a salary decided in each case on the merits of the case in question. The mission pays what the church cannot. The two missionaries determine practically what the salaries shall be, although the churches are supposed to help decide theoretically. Mr. Layman wants a scale adopted giving all the native pastors the same scale of salary for 12 years, irrespective of individual ability and then, after the 12 years, allow the best men to push ahead as much as they can.

The salaries of MP pastors are approximately Y40 for first three years, Y43 for the next three years, Y46 for four years, Y50 for five years, Y55 for next five, and then Y60 for the balance of service. The children's allowances are from 3 to 6 years, Y2; from 7 years to middle school age (13), Y3.00. While in middle school (13–18), Y5 plus tuition.

The home membership of the Methodist Protestant church is 200,000. They have missions in China and India just started. Mr. Layman thinks they should have concentrated on Japan. There are only two missionary families, and at present one is on furlough.

The MP has 18 organized churches and 40 preaching places in Japan, extending from Tokyo southwest to Yokamichi, 40 miles west of Nagoya. In the MP church, an organized church is one belonging to the Japan conference and must have 30 members, 20 of whom are 21 years of age. The organized church must pay all its current expenses and Y10 on the pastor's salary. They cannot organize for two years and up to that time are absolutely under mission control.

There is a question whether the financial basis should be required for conference membership. The Japanese conference of the MP church has full control of its own work, but under supervision of the board. This has to do only with the spiritual development, the missionaries handling the financial end of it entirely.

The Japanese church does not bother any questions of policy, laws, finances or property. When they become strong enough to own property, they are to have control.

The 18 organized churches have only eight church buildings, the balance being rented houses. There are 22 native ordained men, 15 unordained. They are ordained after a three-year correspondence course of study or the equivalent in some seminary.

Two of the churches are fully independent and pay their pastors Y75 a month each. One church in Tokyo is giving Y30 a month on salary. One at Yokohama giving Y45, another Y12, another Y15, another Y27, etc. at various places.

The total membership of the 18 churches is 1,500; of the 40 preaching places, 700.

The MP church has a girls' school at Yokohama with 250 students. The woman's board controls this. They have four single-women missionaries in Japan. Two of these are at Yokohama. Two are doing evangelistic and kindergarten work.

They have a night school at Yokohama with 300 enrolled. This is handled by the board, but there is no missionary there at present, Mr. Layman having been shifted to Nagoya while the other missionary is on furlough. The Yokohama night school is conducted by a businessman. Tuition is Y1.50 a month, and the board pays Y90 ($45) a month toward the running of the school. There are four teachers giving part of their time to this work at Y25 a month, five nights a week. They average 10 or 12 baptisms a year from this work. Church is held in the night school building, and there is a chapel service every night.

The MP also has a school for the blind in Tokyo, with a Japanese superintendent and 50 students. It is recognized by the government. The superintendent handles the school, giving full-time to it, and in addition he gives some attention to the church of the MP in Azabu. He receives Y85 as supt. of the blind school and Y10 as pastor of the church. He provides his own house. The blind school teaches the ordinary branches and massaging, and other such work of the hands as the blind can do. The school is held in rented property. Want the government to give land for Y15,000 building they want to erect. Tuition is free. Four teachers give full-time to the blind school, at an average salary of Y40. The budget of the school is

Y760 ($380) per month, including the salary of a Japanese solicitor who is soliciting money for the new land and building at a salary of Y75 per month. They expect to receive Y5,000 from the Japanese and Y10,000 from the board for this work.

The MP also has five kindergartens under the woman's board, with an average enrollment of 75 to 100. Tuition is charged, but I did not get the amount.

The budget of the MP board for Japan work, not including missionary salaries, is Y44,000 ($22,000). The assets from evangelistic work given by the Japanese is Y4,200, as against Y3,500 last year. Tuition from the middle school last year was Y28,000. The mission asks for Y29,000 ($14,500) from the home board for evangelistic work and Y10,000 ($5,000) to aid the blind school, night school and middle school.

MP MISSIONARIES' SALARIES

After 15 years of service, the two families now in the service receive $1,500 each. The children's allowance is $100 for children from 6 to 20 years old. There has been no new missionary family for 15 years. No medical allowances are made, but the board pays the income tax and furnishes homes for the missionaries. The term of service is six or seven years.

(Note: the fact that in spite of having no new missionaries for 15 years, the MP has 18 organized churches and 40 preaching places, a night school and a middle school, also a blind school, shows that some efforts must have been made and the board must have concentrated its efforts on these outstanding features years ago. It would lead one to feel that we have somehow failed to concentrate our efforts of the past 25 years in such a way as to show any very large definite work. These three institutions stand out in the achievements of the MP church, as do similar institutions in other churches. It must have taken money and energy to start such enterprises. Yet the MP church is not so much larger in proportion than our church for the work the two missions are doing. And the missionary force of the MP church is much smaller than our own. It argues for a concentration of talent and money on one thing until it is well on toward success before undertaking anything else.)

We next called on Dr. McAlpine, of the Southern Presbyterian church. This church has a membership in America of 370,000 and mission work in Japan, Korea, China, Brazil, Mexico, Cuba and Africa. They have 15 married men and about 30 single women in Japan.

At Nagoya they have a finely equipped girls' school called the Kinjo Jo Gakko (Golden Castle Girls' School) in honor of the great castle (Tenshu Kaku, or Oshiro) built here in 1611.

The SP has a theological school at Kobe and a rescue school for girls who would otherwise be sold by their parents.

The girls' school at Nagoya has 250 students and turns away 75 every year for lack of room. The tuition is Y3 at present but will soon be raised to Y4. There are 14 full-time teachers and 11 part-time teachers. In addition to these, others give special lectures from time to time.

The budget of the school is Y20,000 the So. board paying Y10,000, the balance coming from tuition and other sources. There is one dormitory accommodating 70 girls and in charge of one matron. Board and room is Y9 per month but must be raised to Y10 or Y11.

The average salary of the full-time teachers is Y80. The principal, who is an unusually fine man, receives Y200, the head teacher Y125, three men teachers Y120. There are six women teachers, of whom one is an American. The salary of the native women teachers is about Y60. There are five full days of school each week. They have chapel daily and a Bible course for every class. There is also a Sunday school normal class.

Last year, 23 were baptized, and 47 had already been baptized. The balance were not Christians. In the dormitory, 34 of the girls are baptized out of the 70. The dormitory life is better for this than that of the day pupils, who come in from the city for instruction in the classroom. Some go out after graduation and go to Yokohama to enter the Bible training school there. There are three there now and four at the mission kindergarten training school at Nagoya under the supervision of Miss Young. Two others go to the kindergarten training school at Kobe. All the full-time teachers but two are baptized. About half of the special teachers are Christians. They have a Backers' Society of prominent Japanese businessmen who contribute to the school. They have given Y40,000. Want Y400,000, of which Y200,000 will be used for buildings and Y200,000 for current expenses and equipment. They have the land, which cost Y20,000. The information about the school was furnished by the Japanese principal, Prof. Yoishi Ishiwara.

Dr. McAlpine said the native pastors in the SP church receive about Y50 per month, plus Y4 for each child until they get into boarding school when it is increased to Y8.

The independent SP churches are under the Japan Nihon Christio Kiokai, a Japanese organization of independent churches coming from the Southern Presbyterian, the Northern Presbyterian, the German Reformed and the Dutch Reformed churches and also from the work of the Union Woman's Christian Missionary Society. This is a strong organization composed of a number of very strong churches that the various missions mentioned turn over to the Japan organization as soon as they are self-supporting.

All preaching places and churches alike belong to this, but the SP board administers the funds of those not yet independent.

Dr. McAlpine could not give much information as to missionaries' salaries due to the fact that he has just returned from America. He said, however, that the new salary schedule just revised by his board gave the basic salary for married men at $1,625 and for single women $900. Children's allowances are extra, but he did not know how much.

NAGOYA

Sixth largest city of Japan. Prosperous manufacturing city. On north shore of Atsuta Bay and right bank of the Shonai River. Capital of Owari province, with 450,000 people. A busy yet easygoing, comfortable place we found it. It is noted for the production of cloisonne, porcelain, clocks, fans, lacquered wares, embroidery, and for its many cotton, spinning and silk-threading mills. The most famous thing about it is the well-preserved castle built supposedly by underlords voluntarily for Tokugawa Ieyasu, but in reality built by them under pressure from him as the ruling *shogun*. It was begun in 1611 and completed in two years. A family by the name of Nagoya resided there in the fourteenth century.

We took lunch at Nagoya with the Rev. and Mrs. Layman. After lunch, we visited the Nihontoki porcelain factory where the famous *noritoke*ware is made. Baron Morimura established this work, and a brother of his is still connected with it. The founder is dead. Mr. Murai is now at the head of the factory, and the best ware is exported to the Morimura firm in New York City. Only the transferred de-signs are sold in Japan because the Japanese do not want to pay for the best.

Mr. Murai, to whom we had a card of introduction from Prof. Yoichi Ichimura, princ. of the Kinjo Jo Gakko (SP girls' school), was out of the city, so his assistant took us through the factory. (Baron Morimura, when alive, gave Y10,000 toward the girls' school.)

The office building of the Nihontoki Company is a large building with many clerks. We presented our card, and after considerable questioning to establish our identity, we went into another office or reception room where we left our coats, Kodak and umbrella.

As we walked through the plant, we were told that they employ 5,000 men. They work 10 hours a day with a 15-minute rest at ten and three and a 30-minute rest at noon.

We went first to where the different kinds of rocks used in making the porcelain are stored. This kind of ware is made of kaolin, gray-white felspar, of granite, blue-white quartz, etc., all of which are secured near here, with the exception of the kaolin, which is shipped in large kegs from Carlsbad. This kaolin makes the porcelain better in some manner. I do not know the different kinds of rocks, but the first we saw was in large flintlike lumps of an agate color. The next were about the size of an egg-shaped baseball (if there is such a thing) and looked like gray heads, very smooth. Then, besides the kaolin in barrels, there were several kinds of clay.

We next passed the huge grinding machines where these materials are ground to pieces and mixed together. Huge stone rollers running round on a table then mash the materials into powder. During the process, water is mixed with it in some way, and when we saw it next, it had been thoroughly mixed and rolled by large stone rollers into a tough clay. This wet clay is then cut into blocks and sent to the various molding rooms where it is molded by hand into many different kinds of vessels.

I could not take notes as I went, so have to write all of this from memory. I can recall seeing them molding cups and saucers, plates, tea sets, salt-and-pepper sets, doll heads, doll tea sets, vases, jardinieres, gravy bowls, soup bowls, platters, pitchers, fruit plates, fruit dishes, and various other dishes necessary to full dinner sets.

The clay is laid out on a revolving circular table about a foot across, and many of the smaller pieces are deftly molded by hand inside and out. The skill and rapidity with which they were turned out was marvelous. The larger pieces and the more difficult smaller ones are shaped in molds made of gypsum, and in these molds they are hollowed out by hand on the revolving tables. The gypsum molds prevent the clay from sticking. These molds are made by the same company right here, and the gypsum is secured in the neighboring mountains.

For the larger pieces, the molds are in sections. Some of the very finest ware is thus made, and one wonders how the workers ever learn to fashion them to so thin and yet so even a surface, and all by hand. The men who do the heavy work, and also these molders, receive about Y1.50 (75¢) a day. It is very exacting work. The company provides but few homes for the men, most of whom are married.

A few women, comparatively, were doing molding, and those who were receive from a yen to Y1.20 a day.

As the pieces are fashioned, they are carried off on long trays and placed in the hands of other deft workers who smooth them down and put on the finishing touches preparatory to burning them.

This factory has 28 large kilns where the porcelain is burned for 40 hours at a temperature of 1300 degrees, according to our guide, who did not know whether it was Fahrenheit or Centigrade. It is probably neither.

After being burned, the porcelain pieces are taken to one of the many departments where they are given the patterns. Girls and boys were placing a specially prepared colored paper on the different pieces, forming various patterns. This is the transferred ware, the porcelain being burned again for three hours in another special kiln, during which the paper vanishes and the imprint of the design is burned on the dish. The porcelain is burned in a series of trays, with burnt clay standards separating each piece to prevent cracking. These stacks of porcelain are placed in a steel container and sent into the furnace for three hours at a certain temperature, and come out on the other side finished so far as the burning process is concerned. The transferred porcelain is cheaper and is not exported. The more expensive hand-painted ware is sent to New York. The paper used in making these transferred designs was bought in Germany before the war, but since then, it has been made by the firm here in Japan.

There are many departments where the handpainting is done by boys as young as 12 years of age. Most of them do not look more than 16. They have a model before them, and by the use of a brush and certain paints, some of which are imported from France, they print the simplest or most elaborate designs with a delicate but accurate touch. The work is very exacting and the light not especially good. These boys and the boys and girls putting on the transfer paper receive 60 sen a day (30¢) for nine hours' work.

The handpainted ware is subjected to three hours in the furnace, just like the transferred ware.

I saw some of the most delicately tinted work and some of the most elaborately colored work being done by these boys, in all sorts of designs and on all kinds of porcelain, from saltshakers to large jardinieres more than three feet in height.

After the porcelain is burned to fix the designs, the still-warm product is taken to the inspection room where women tap them to determine by the sound whether they are cracked. This requires keenness in hearing.

They are further inspected to insure perfection of design and then sent to the packing room where they are polished thoroughly and then wrapped in paper for shipping. From this stage they are packed in cartons with excelsior and placed in snug wooden boxes. Large storehouses contain many thousands of pieces ready for shipment.

As we left the factory, we noted that the workers were taking their 15-minute afternoon rest. The boys of the handpainting department were playing ball. As we reached the entrance, we saw a number of the women workers nursing their babies. Several old women and little girls, caretakers of the babies while their mothers worked, were standing about waiting to take back their precious burdens when the others go back to work.

We returned to the depot and found a fast train leaving at 4:18 that would get us to Kyoto at 7:30. We decided to pay the Y2.50 extra to go second class (only first and second class on this train) because it would get us to Kyoto, a strange place, two hours and 20 minutes earlier than the slow train. As we left the town, we saw the famous castle Tenshu Kaku, or Oshiro, described above.

I purchased a small model of the two fishes and the castle they adorn as crests.

The famous potteries of Seto are located in a town by the same name, some 12 miles from Nagoya. We did not have time to go out. The ware made here is known as *setomono* (Seto goods or things). Although the first crude pottery made in Japan was made in the North, Gyogi, coming from Korea in the middle of the eighth century, is regarded as the founder of the art in Japan. In 1223, Kato Shirozaemon (or Kagemasa), a native potter, studied in China and after six years came back to Seto where he settled and developed the art in this town, in Owari Province. He is called the father of pottery. *Setomono* became the generic term for all ceramic manufactures in Japan.

Five thousand men are now employed at Seto, which is really a suburb of Nagoya. There is a school of ceramics here and a pottery museum. The ware is made of kaolin, gray-white felspar, granite, blue-white quartz, etc.

Before dark, we saw some very beautiful scenery as we rode along. I wrote up all the notes about the ceramics works on the train, practically all but the history of it from memory.

This second-class car has numbered seats, to which our tickets assigned us, that are quite comfortable. We ate in the diner (my first experience), and it cost us Y1.80 (90¢) for a very good meal.

While on the diner we met a Mr. Sims, formerly a missionary, but now in business at Kobe. He told us of a new plan being considered to enable missionaries to get supplies cheaper. He said there are 1,000 missionaries in Japan, of which 700 are in the field at any one time. It costs about Y100 a month for each, or a total of Y70,000 a month each, for their keep. The average expenditure for goods from America is 40 percent of the income. Allowing a wide margin, he stated that by a cooperative effort at least 15 percent could be saved to each missionary. The capital required for the enterprise is Y100,000 in 400 shares at Y25 each, Y10 of the share to be made payable on completion of the organization and the balance on call. One party agrees to take 1,000 shares. There would be a board of directors and an active manager. The store management would be under an experienced foreign merchant. These stores would sell to the general public as well as missionaries. The budget would be about Y18,000 a month. This is worth considering.

Arrived at Kyoto at 7:31 and took streetcar to the Rev. E.S. Cobbs, a Congregational missionary who keeps a sort of hotel for transient missionaries. Found a nice big room awaiting us, and after writing some postals, I took a hot bath and turned in for the night.

Saturday, November 13 —————— ◆ ————————————————

Visited Mr. Shively of the UB Mission, who is teaching in the Doshisha school (Cong.). He is pastor of the Union church, along with the Japanese pastor, the Rev. Hatanaka, and asked me to preach Sunday afternoon at the service for foreigners. No way to get out of it. (Has new home, cost Y25,000.)

We next went to the Kato cloisonne works. The work is all done by hand. The foundation is copper, upon which brass wire is cemented in all sorts of fancy designs, and then this is baked. Sometimes silver and gold are used in creating something of a color effect in the design.

After the wire design is baked on, the molds made by the wire are filled with enamel made of rocks from the mountains nearby. This first layer of enamel is then baked, and then another is put on, and it is baked again. Then the top coat is put on and baked again. After this, it is polished with 20 different kinds of stones. The enamels are of several colors, depending upon the kind of stone used. This concern employs 30 men. I bought a pin and had a couple pieces of the rock thrown in. I saw a pair of large urns sold to a Frenchman recently for Y4,000. They required four years to make.

We next went to a damascene shop and saw them making the real damascene. This is made on a steel foundation. First thing done is to chisel very fine and close lines all over the surface in four different ways. This is done to make it possible to inlay designs of various kinds. The gold or silver wire used in inlaying the designs is made from gold or silver leaf cut into strips and then rolled into wire by hand. This wire is hammered into the crossed and recrossed chiseled lines on the surface of the steel in any designs desired. It is thoroughly pounded in with a mallet, then in some way treated with nitric acid. It is then oxidized by being laid above water for several days and allowed to rust. It is then washed in salt water and heated. This process continues eight times a day for eight days and is done to prevent rusting. After oxidizing, it is burned in a strong fire many times, from 70 to 100. The metal is air-cooled, then the gold and silver only is polished.

Apprentices get their food and Y15 a month. Experts get Y300 a month working piecework. The work is so exacting that they work hard for a while and then must take off weeks at a time to rest. It takes three years to learn to mark the steel with the lines. Each man seems to confine himself to one part of the whole process.

While walking across a stream, we saw men setting dyes by washing them in the stream, and I got a good picture.

Kyoto is the ancient capital of Japan and at present about the fourth largest city, with a population of about 440,000. There are about 85,000 houses. It is the most beautiful city I have seen in Japan. Situated among the mountains on a beautiful plain, it enjoys a delightful climate. The fact that it was the ancient capital accounts

An unusually fine street in the ancient capital city of Kyoto, considered one of the most beautiful cities in the entire country.

for its wide streets, beautiful parks and magnificent temples. No city that I have seen here has a better appearance than Kyoto. It ranks first too in the manufacture of metalwork ceramics, fans, dolls, silks, etc.

We visited the famous Chionin ("chee-wo-neen") temple and found it of pure Buddhist architecture set in a splendid grove of lofty cryptomeria and pines. There are plenty of maples in the hills behind, which flame with color in November. The temple is reached by a long flight, or rather successive flights, of stone steps.

We saw here the Big Bell, second largest in Japan, weighing 74 tons and 10 feet 10 inches thick. It was cast in 1633.

We next went to Maruyama Park, full of its cherry and maple trees. At the entrance is a cherry tree more than 200 years old and so tottery that it is bolstered up all around with props. I took a picture. It is called *gion-no-yo-zakura*, or "night-blooming cherry," because of the local custom of decorating it with lanterns during the cherry-blossom season.

A walk of a few minutes to the south brought us to a long flight of steps leading to the Yasaka Pagoda, a five-story structure built in 1618 from whose base one can secure a wonderful panoramic view of the surrounding country.

Next we went to the Kiyomizu dera (pure-water temple). The main temple is 53 feet high, 88 deep and 190 long. Here we saw the Obinzuru god who has been so persistently rubbed by those having bodily ailments, who believe that this would heal them, that the face was entirely rubbed away and a new one was glued on. This one is also partly rubbed away. Buddha is supposed to have empowered him.

Nearby is a rickety old shedlike house in which are hundreds of monkeylike stone images of the benevolent Jizo, where mothers with sick babies pray fervently for them and other mothers, believing he has healed their babies, bring bibs and tie

An old cherry tree (much revered) at Kyoto, the ancient capital of Japan. Missionary C.P. Garman in the foreground.

them around the stone images. We saw a woman doing this very thing as we stood at the entrance. I shall never forget the expression on her face.

We went through Teapot Lane, a long winding lanelike street, practically every store of which is given over to the selling of earthenware of many descriptions.

Took lunch at the Café Palista, famous for its Brazilian coffee. We were shown many courtesies by the proprietor, who took us upstairs to a semiprivate room. We ordered several things and finally were served coffee, for which the waiter apologized, saying the coffee urn had gotten out of order. The coffee was cold. He finally took it back and warmed it. We gave a short order, and the waiter brought us soup, which we did not order. We told him we had not ordered it, and he said he brought it because he thought we would like it. We thought this was one of the ways the newly opened restaurant was seeking to draw trade, so took the soup. But when we paid our bill, the soup was charged for at the regular rate. Stung!

After lunch, we visited the Kinkozan pottery, where the famous *satsuma*ware is made. We saw a molder molding a large urn by hand on a revolving table. The clay (for only *satsuma* clay is used in the best makes, though stone is used in the other grades) is ground up and mixed in great steel revolving grinders. It is then mixed with water to a certain consistency and placed on large round tables where a system of rollers in two pairs for each table work the clay on both sides and the top until it reaches the proper consistency for molding. It is then sent to the various molding rooms where it is molded into all sorts of vessels from miniature urns to the very largest and finest. The man we watched was making the cheaper ware, but it was hand work. These large urns are made in two pieces. First the top is deftly shaped on the revolving table. Then the larger part is made. These two parts are then fitted together and worked with the hands to become one piece. One man can make about 40 urns of this size a day and works by piecework on the cheaper wares. But he is paid by the day on the more delicate work.

After being molded, the green product is sent to one of the 77 kilns and burned for 10 hours. It is then taken out, glazed, and sent back to the kiln for 60 hours. The first coat of covering paint is put on after the first burning. Then the more delicate designs are painted by hand and the burning continued. In all, this ware is burned three times — the first time 10 hours, the second time 10 and after the glazing 60.

After watching the men paint the difficult designs on some of the vases, we went into the stockroom and examined the different kinds of ware. I bought two very tiny pieces. It is very expensive.

From here we went to the great Higashi Hongwanji, or eastern temple of the Hongwanji branch of the Monto sect of Buddhists. It is a new structure 230 feet long, 195 deep, and 126 high, and was built in 1879 to 1895 at a cost of Y7,000,000. It is one of the largest in Japan. Ninety-six huge *keyaki* (pillars) support the great roof of tile. When the call went out for donations to build this temple, the Buddhists responded in genuine Japanese fashion. Those who had no money gave wood and stone, to the value of 1,000,000 yen. Many gave of their time. Hundreds of peasants made some personal sacrifice toward the building of the temple. The women, in their usual spirit of devotion, cut off their long black hair and made of it 29 immense hawsers (called *kezuna*, human-hair ropes). With these the great pillars were pulled into place. One of these, perhaps the longest one, is still there. We saw it in the portico of the temple, and it is said to measure 226 feet long and 13 inches in circumference. I do not doubt this statement in the least as I studied the great rope thoroughly. This is one more testimonial to the devotion of hundreds to Buddhism, but it is also a testimony to the devotion of womanhood to religion, whatever kind it may happen to be. One can see here just how greatly Christianity will influence the future of Japan if the womanhood of this great country is brought to Christ.

From here we visited the Nishi Hongwanji temple (west temple) nearby. In going through these temples, it is interesting to watch the devotees as they come for worship. Here comes an old woman, carried on the back of a *kuruma* man who is paid to bring her. She is not long for this world and comes once again or perhaps for the first time in her life to see the temple — a thing she has set her heart on for years. Perhaps she comes from a distant upcountry village from which she has gone out into the fields these many years to plant rice seed, then transplant it spear by spear in long rows, then go out into the fields every week or two during the growing season to puddle the plants by stirring the muddy water, standing ankle-deep in it the while in the broiling sun or the downpouring rain, puddling it to keep out the weeds. Then she helped to harvest the crop in the fall, and all the time she has been thinking of the great temple and hoping she might someday go there to worship. Her opportunity has come at last, and she sees it with aged dimmed eyes. One cannot fathom her emotions as she gazes upon this object of her lifelong thought.

Then here comes an old man bent upon the same quest. Or a middle-aged man comes, as I saw one, and after throwing his offering into the great box, as they all do first of all, he kneels and chants a long prayer in the same monotonous way,

Entrance to Kinkozan Pottery Company, famous for their product throughout Japan.

then gets up and goes to another nearby shrine where the same process is repeated. Or here comes a younger businessman. He is in a hurry, but he feels a sense of duty in coming. He fumbles in his pocketbook, a few coins jingle in the box (by the jingle, you guess they are 1- or 2-sen pieces, or 10 sen at the most), he claps his hands a time or two, and without kneeling, bows his head a few times in quick succession, repeating a prayer as he does so. Replaces his pocketbook and looking around in a half-shamed way, slips out as quickly as he came while the more devoted stay for long seasons. Or here comes a young bride. She has tasted but recently the bitterness of becoming a slave to her new husband and especially to his parents, and in the first sorrow of her young life, she appeals to the temple for help. Or here is a mother who has lost or is fast losing a much-loved little one. Can she not get help from the temple altar and its great gods of wood and stone and brass? But most interesting of all are the schoolpeople who come. The primary children make annual pilgrimages to these famous temples. They do not know their meaning, and there is no worship in their coming, but they are in this fashion coupling up with their studies, learning the old religion. But when the boy of the middle school or the commercial school or the university school comes, it is different. He has been reading of other nations and of other religions perchance. He has begun to look askance at the close-shaven priest and to doubt the sincerity of his seemingly august demeanor. He comes into the sacred structure and gazes about with minutest care at the wonderful carvings. But when it comes time to worship—no, not he. He throws no coin, he makes no prayer. He doesn't believe in this old religion. The pity of it all is that in most cases he doesn't believe in *any* religion. He has reached the age of skepticism, and unless he is caught and won now, he will bring in a new Japan that will be materialistic to the extreme and carry danger and trouble with her throughout the civilized world.

Toward evening, we called on Mr. H.H. Grafton, YMCA sec. at Kyoto. A friend, Mr. H.L. Seamans, of Columbus, Ohio, had given me a card of introduction to him. Mr. Seamans is state student sec. of Ohio. We spent a pleasant hour with Mr. Grafton. Supper with Shively.

Sunday, November 14 ━━━━ ◆ ━━━━━━━━━━

In the morning we visited several native churches. The first was the Rokuyo Cong. church. *Rokuyo* means "south capital." This church has an average SS attendance of 60, but it varies much, as we found by going over the records with the young man in charge of the office. The Rev. Enomoto is the pastor. The church is independent, and they have a fine building. There are nine classes in the Sunday school.

We went next to the Heian Cong. church. The Rev. Yamaguchi is the pastor. The church membership is 250, not counting the absent members. It is independent. The pastor's salary is Y110 a month, including rent. A new building was built in 1918, at a cost of Y40,000 at that time. This was all raised by native church. The superintendent of the SS, Mr. Fukui, is also assistant pastor, giving full-time to this work. He is a graduate of Doshisha University. The church supports him and a Bible woman and a caretaker, also the secretary—all on full-time salary. The church raises Y3,000 a year.

The SS attendance today was 93. There are 17 classes, each in a separate classroom. The church has been independent from the beginning, 40 years ago. We stepped into the auditorium as church began and found about 70 present, of which half were students. Someone kindly handed us two sets of postcards showing various views of the church.

We went next to the church of which the Rev. H. Hatanaka, the man who did the best work as interpreter at the SS convention, is pastor. His church is an independent one belonging to the Japan Congregational Conference, called the Kumai Christio Kiokai. It has a resident membership of 450, with some 300 nonresident. The budget of the church raised each year is Y4,000. The pastor has a Bible-woman assistant. The SS averages about 120.

The Rev. Hatanaka is a graduate of Oberlin and spent a year or two as a YMCA worker in Pittsburgh.

The morning service, which was in Japanese, I thoroughly enjoyed, from the very expression of Hatanaka's face as he spoke and because Mr. Grafton, who sat next to me, gave me a brief outline of his thought. After the service, I took a picture of Mr. Garman, Mr. Hatanaka and Mr. Grafton.

We took dinner at Cobb's, and after dinner we all went down to the afternoon English service. There was a very good attendance, including some Japanese. Mr. Shively and the Rev. Hatanaka had charge of the service as joint pastors. I preached on "The Enthusiasm of Christian Service." There was good interest, and many spoke words of appreciation after the service, but how genuine they were no one can tell.

We stopped a few moments with the Rev. Burgaw on the way home. He is in evangelistic work for the Presbyterian Church North. He says they have one independent church in Tokyo, which pays their pastor Y50 a month. There are about 50 active members. A joint committee is formed in each presbytery, composed of all missionaries, and an equal number of Japanese elected by Japanese presbytery. This committee has charge of all the work of the presbytery, fixing salaries, opening or closing points, etc. The salary is decided on the merits of the local case, as are the children's allowances.

The missionary in charge of evangelistic work in each district handles all money from America, paying all salaries, etc. A district has a joint committee like the presbytery joint committee. Mr. Burgaw has seven pastors with one point each. Three church buildings are owned, and four are rented places. The policy of the secretary of the Presbyterian Church North is to get the church to build the buildings as its own. Mr. Burgaw thinks it does not work in Japan, though it does in China and Korea.

The missionaries in Japan want a building-and-loan fund to advance to churches for building. Then let them pay for the building as rent. This is a good suggestion, and I think it is worth trying.

They have a pension scheme for the older pastors; Y12 a month is to be used for the wife of a deceased worker. When a man retires, he gets one-third of his average salary during the time of active service. They encourage pastors to start savings accounts, and the mission gives four percent interest.

Missionaries' salaries in the Presbyterian Church North are to be $2,200 under the new plan, with medical bills, including doctor's fees and doctor's prescriptions but no bills for any other treatment or any other medicine. They pay one-half of the dental bills. Children's allowances are $200 from 1 to 10, $300 from 11 to 15, $400 from 16 to 22 if the child is in school.

We spent the evening at Cobb's. Mr. Downs, who teaches in the Doshisha, lives here. A very fine young fellow. Gave me a booklet of statistics on Doshisha.

Mr. Cobb gave the following information on the salaries of Congregational missionaries. Under the new ruling, those who have served less than 15 years are receiving $1,625 and an allowance of $400 this year. Those who have served over 15 years are receiving $1,700 and an allowance of $400. Children's allowances are from 1 to 7, 10 percent of the salary; from 8 to 12, 15 percent of the salary; from 13 to 20, 20 percent of the salary. Single women receive $850 and an allowance of $100 for household. They have asked for a new salary schedule of $2,500 minimum for families and $1,300 for single missionaries. They have not yet heard what their board will do.

Monday, November 15 ◆

We went through the grounds of Doshisha University before going to the train. I have already described the work of this famous school. On our way to the station, we passed through the former palace grounds, which is now a famous park. We had walked through the park several times on Sunday and enjoyed its wide roads, its well-kept lawns, and the fine old trees that are to be seen everywhere. It is one of the most restful spots I have yet seen. I shall not soon forget the pleasant days at Kyoto.

We left for Osaka at 9:00 A.M. after having paid our bill at Cobb's, which amounted to Y7.50 each, which is very reasonable indeed. Mrs. Cobb only asked five yen each, but according to other prices, we knew that was too low.

While at Cobb's, we met a Miss Bell who says she expects to sail on the *Shinyo* for Honolulu December 4, so I know at least one of my fellow passengers.

We went to Osaka second class at a cost of Y1.39. In the second compartment there were 16 Japanese at one time when I took notice of the number, and all men, presumably businessmen. Of the 16, 7 were dressed in foreign clothes, which is to me a sign of the times.

The country through which we traveled was a wide plain with beautiful mountains on the right nearby and on the left in the distance. The plain is covered with rice fields, and the farmers are quite busy cutting the rice and hanging it up in the fields or stacking it, preparatory to threshing a little later.

It seemed warmer as we approached Osaka. Kyoto was surprisingly cool, accounted for by the fact that it lies in a sort of basin surrounded with mountain ridges on three sides. We were told that Kobe was warmer. After an hour's ride through this beautiful plain, the numberless factory stacks of Osaka came into view, and at 10:07 we pulled into the Umeda Station at this great industrial center, with the harbor on our left as we entered. Osaka comes from *o*, meaning "bay," and *zaka*, meaning "hill." It is a great manufacturing city and second largest in Japan, with nearly 1,500,000 inhabitants and 266,494 houses. The Yodo River runs through the city and is a dirty-looking stream, utterly out of place among the very nice business houses lining at least part of its bank. The more than 800 bridges spanning the many streams in and around Osaka have given it the title of "the Venice of Japan." I called it the Pittsburgh of Japan when I saw its factories' stacks. There are more than 6,000 industrial establishments in the city; 60,000,000 yen of cotton yarn is produced by some 27 cotton spinning mills.

We were met at the station by Mr. Mura, Mr. Miyake and Mr. Converse, all of the YMCA. They took us by auto to the Osaka Hotel where we met the Rev. Mr. Ellis, SS secr. of Montana for the Presbyterian church, and his son-in-law, Mr. Dosker, who is a Presbyterian missionary. Here we learned that the afternoon program we were expecting to take part in had been changed to night and Mr. Ellis and I were to speak. The committee told us that machines would be at our disposal and that they would be glad to show us whatever we wanted to see.

We were taken to the Baikwa ("plum blossom") girls' school, which is run entirely under Japanese authority. There are two Congregational missionary teachers. There are 550 girls, and the budget to run the school, exclusive of the missionaries' salaries, is Y30,000 a year. The principal told me that two-thirds of the teachers are Christians. I took a picture of the girls while they were having their exercises in the playground. We visited a number of the different rooms and found a most enthusiastic lot of students and teachers.

The committee entertained us with a fine luncheon at a very up-to-date restaurant. Mr. Keodzumi, a Christian businessman whom we met at the Yokohama reception, or rather on the train going to the reception, sent word that he was sorry he could not attend the luncheon. He is a member of the World SS Association.

After luncheon, we motored to the Ohara Institute of Social Research, one of

Rice hung up until time for threshing.

the most interesting and unique institutions I have visited. It has been established by Mr. Ohara, a wealthy businessman, for the study of social questions. We met Mr. Takata, who is the head of it, acting as secretary. There is a great library full of social service books of all kinds. The whole plant is given over to research work along social lines. Two laboratories for map work, etc., are in the building. Leading educators from all over Japan come here for research.

We also met Mr. Obayashi, who is just completing a survey of recreation features of Osaka. There is a magazine reference room, where I noticed such papers as the *London Times*, the *New York Times*, *Economic Review*, the *Survey*, etc. There is also a library office.

We next visited the stackroom of this famous institution and found 6,000 volumes. Two men are on their way to Europe now to collect books for this library to keep it up-to-date. I noticed books on the labor question in America, Europe, England, etc. There are two lecture rooms. They are holding two classes a week, studying social problems, these on Wednesday and Friday nights.

The institute was established February 9, 1919, and the splendid new building was opened on May 3, 1920. It cost Y150,000 and the 1000 *tsubo* of land cost another Y100,000.

There are 19 workers on the staff of the institute. The purpose of this institute is to survey social problems and publish the best work of investigators, to give lecture courses and to publish periodicals on social service. Two volumes have already been published—one on social hygiene and one a labor yearbook. There are 21 rooms in the building.

From there we went to the Municipal Welfare Department headquarters. We found the city doing welfare work for its 107,000 or more workmen on a great scale.

School boys and girls in Japan are given a rigid course in calisthenics.

They have a Labor Bureau with 12 branch employment bureaus, three dormitories for men without homes, and six restaurants. In the one we visited, we found an employment bureau, a restaurant and a dormitory. The young man who guided us stated that they had 30 applicants for work a day and were able to secure work for about 20. There are 86 rooms in the dormitory, accommodating four to six in a room. Costs 10 sen a night for share of the room and a good hot bath. The meals are served at 12 sen a meal. The dormitory is always full, and they have to turn away a dozen every day. The city handles the dormitories to help solve the housing problem.

Five men are needed to manage each of these buildings. About 600 meals are given in the plant we visited, 200 at breakfast, 250 at night and some fewer at noon. From June to December last year, a six-month period, it cost Y38,000 to run the three dormitories. The income from the 10 sen a night is Y28,000 so the city pays out Y10,000 in six months. The expense of the six restaurants is Y50,000 which barely covers the cost of the buildings and equipment. The meals are given at 12 sen a meal, and any deficit is made up by leading businessmen of the city.

Three assistants keep the rooms in order, cleaning and brushing them daily. A washwoman keeps the bedding clean. Except on rainy days, the rooms are closed from 7:00 A.M. to 5:00 P.M. daily. There is a lobby upstairs for lectures. Some men stay for a long time. They leave their possessions with the authorities, but not in the room.

Some of the rooms are made especially homelike, and the men who save their money and show special homelike traits are given the preference of these rooms without extra charge. One condition of this is that they have money in the savings bank. One section is reserved for students who are working their way through school. I noticed a shrine and a *torii* in the middle of the group of buildings. There is a barber shop and a bath open from 4:00 P.M. on. Haircut 20 sen. The city has 100 dwellings and is building more to rent at nominal rent to workingmen with families.

There is a Child Welfare Department in connection with the dormitory we visited. They give medical and education consultation for the parents of the children. Household and domestic problems concerning children are taken up and discussed. The children are also given a physical examination. Later on, vocational advice is added. There are meetings for parents. There are two kindergartens—one for those whose bodies are not especially strong and one for weak-minded children. They expect to secure apparatus for investigation by tests into child psychology. Feebleminded children are brought for examination.

We visited the lecture hall for the Parents' Association. Saw some of the boys undergoing mental tests. The teacher would give out a list of words while the boys sat with their hands folded. Then he would give the word, and they would write as many of the words in regular order as they could while he timed them. There are also an educational consulting room and a medical examination room. Two doctors are hired full-time by the city, also two nurses. There is a library.

The kindergarten rooms were very interesting. Besides the regular kindergarten room, there is a special room for the feebleminded kindergarteners. Among the playthings I noticed a sort of boat or cradle arrangement made so that a child could sit one in each end of it and rock back and forth like the rocking of a boat.

From this institution we went to the Mitsukoshi department store. There are several of these department stores in Japan run by the same company, and they are called the "Wanamaker's of Japan." We took one of the four elevators, of which there are eight, to the top floor, and from here we walked to the roof garden. Here we had a fine view overlooking the city. I took several time exposures but do not know how successful they will be. The roof garden is especially arranged for the delight of customers and is a splendid example of the Japanese ideal of beauty in nature. There were all sorts of growing plants and miniature lakes and rivers artistically arranged. And in the midst of all this there stood the inevitable Shinto shrine, to which our attention was directed by the ever-present *torii*.

Our guide then directed the auto driver to take us back to the hotel, where we sought to get a few minutes' rest before the evening meeting.

But we had scarcely gotten settled when the Rev. Peter Jusaku Fujimoto, pastor of the Jonan Christ Church of Osaka, came in and introduced himself as my interpreter for the evening. He wanted to get some idea of my speech. We went over it together, and I found him very intelligent, with a fine knowledge of English and a keen regard for details. He told me he had taken the name Peter at the time of his conversion. *Jusaku* means "good harvest," and *Fujimoto*, "under the wisteria tree," *fuji* meaning "wisteria" and *moto* "under." *Jonan* means "south of the castle," and Christ Church means the Church of England. His membership is 200. The yearly budget of the church is Y1,500. The SS attendance, 50 to 80.

A group of some 12 leading pastors and laymen of Osaka gave us a dinner at

6:00 P.M. here in the hotel, The Osaka. Mr. Ozassa, secretary to the mayor of Osaka, represented the mayor, and the Rev. K. Morita, president of the Osaka SS Union, was introduced as chairman of the evening meeting. The Rev. Arakawa, another pastor, proved to be the best English conversationalist I have heard in Japan. We had a delightful time at dinner. The secretary to the mayor gave a brief address of welcome, to which we responded informally. We then took the machines for the Osaka Congregational Church where the evening meeting was to be held. There was a select group of middle and primary school and Sunday school teachers present as this was a special meeting designed especially to encourage teachers to begin Bible study. There were about 150 present.

I spoke first on "The SS System of America." The Rev. Ellis followed on "The Social Influence of the SS." Between our speeches, the two speakers of the evening and the two interpreters and the chairman stood on the platform while a flashphoto was taken of the assembly. Following the service, we were taken back to the hotel in *jinrikishas*—my second experience in them. It was a great day.

Tuesday, November 16 ━━━━━ ◆ ━━━━━━━━━━━

There are 19 self-supporting and 27 aided churches in Osaka, of about a dozen different denominations. The total membership is 7,076, and the total SS enrollment is 4,891, of which 166 are men and 173 women. There are 14 kindergartens, with an enrollment of 660; four girls' schools, with an enrollment of 1,025; 9 boys' schools, with an enrollment of 3,732; 3 theological and Bible-training schools, with an enrollment of 43. Five institutions carry on social service work. There are also five institutions for rescue work, including two orphanages.

There are 49 SS in all, with 339 teachers and 4,891 pupils. This includes branch SS of the 12 cooperating denominations; 44 missionaries make this their headquarters.

Wrote some cards this morning and left at 11:00 A.M. in auto for the cotton spinning mills of Kanega Fuchi. This is one of their branch factories. Talk about auto riding in a big city—this one took the cake. We had more hairbreadth experiences in 20 minutes than I have ever had in a similar length of time in my life. The streets, with no sidewalks, are of course full of people—walking, pulling carts, riding bicycles, driving oxen or horses, children running hither and thither, women shopping—all on streets scarcely wide enough for two autos to pass, even in low gear. We wound in and out among this intricate maize of humanity mingled with dumb brutes and crude vehicles, the driver of our car sounding the horn almost incessantly. He had an assistant on the seat with him, and we were glad many times that he had, for he proved to be a splendid help in watching the narrow and most dangerous places.

An auto driver in any big city of Japan has to know his job. This helper had to get out several times to clear the way for us. This reminds me that I have seen teams of fine horses once in a while in Tokyo and Kyoto driven to a fashionable carriage in which ride some august personages, and before these horses a runner always goes, shouting to the people to get out of the way. It reminds one of the Bible story of the "forerunner."

Many women of Japan are still doing the hardest kind of manual labor such as is represented in this scene. The boy goes along because there is no one else to care for him.

But to come back to my story—on one or two streets, the driver's assistant had
to get out and get permission of the police before we were allowed to enter. Time
and again I held my breath as I felt sure some poor unfortunate native was about to
be run down. We finally turned off on a street that led right along the high bank of
a river, and it looked several times as though we would slide into its dirty depths,
but we finally drew up in safety before the gate of the cotton spinning factory.

After receiving our cards, the manager took us through the mill. We entered
one room where 850 looms run by electric power were loudly proclaiming themselves
as they drove the shuttles back and forth making the cotton cloth. The manager
said they had two other factories the same size as this one. Girls attend these looms,
working ten full hours a day. There are 2,500 girls and 400 men in this factory alone.
They have five holidays a month. In one of the buildings there is a large recreation
room with a stage. At certain times, theatricals and other entertainments are given
for the benefit of the workers. There is also a large dining room where meals are furnished free to those living in the dormitories, who are paid by the month. Others
pay a small amount for each meal. There is also a hospital with five doctors employed by the company.

Another feature of this plant worth noticing is the school, which is run for the
benefit of the younger workers who have not lived up to the law in completing the
primary school course. This is compulsory, and the company gets around this difficulty by supplying a school right in the plant and making it possible for the younger
boys and girls in the factory to go to school three hours a day, just enough to meet
the law's requirement in completing the compulsory-education standard.

The company also runs a store where the employees can purchase what they
need at reasonable prices.

One of the modern silk or cotton mills now increasing in numbers in Japan. Many of them, however, still need better regulations of the hours for working women and children.

The great dormitory where 1,600 of the 2,500 girls are housed has five wings. There are 16 girls assigned to each 24-mat room. A mat is three by six feet. In the corridors, mottoes are hung. One of them was interpreted for me as "Love your inferiors."

There is a vast toilet room for the girls. In this room, besides the washbasins in large numbers, there are 300 mirrors before which the girls take turns in making their morning toilet. The bathroom has two large baths in it.

Upstairs there is a large social room used for night classes in sewing. A Buddhist priest holds services at times. There is an altar at one end. Sometimes stereopticon pictures are shown. We learned later that the former manager, who is now in America, invited Mr. and Mrs. Converse of the YMCA to come and do religious work among the girls, and they have been doing splendid work until the manager left; this new one will not allow them to come in.

The girls receive 50 sen a day at the start and are increased monthly as they gain experience; Y1.50 is the highest they receive.

Mr. Miyake, who piloted us around all morning, went to lunch with us at the hotel and then took us to Nara in the afternoon.

Nara is about 60 miles from Osaka and is a long climb into the mountains. As we went riding up the mountains, Osaka gradually dropped out of sight and then reappeared time and again, constantly growing smaller as we went. We passed many rice fields, some large and some quite small, and terraced up the mountainside until they looked as if they would fall off. Thus the Japanese conserve the land and increase the food supply. I snapped a picture from the moving train. We passed through four tunnels on the way up, one of which was more than a mile long and took us eight minutes to climb through. We came down through the same tunnel tonight in about five minutes.

Nara is a beautiful little city, with about 33,000 population and nearly 7,000 houses. It is thoroughly Japanese. It was founded in A.D. 710 as the capital of Japan, continuing as such till 1784 with the exception of two years. One of the first things we noticed as we climbed the hill into the town was the famous Nara Deer Park, and we were soon in the midst of the tame animals, which eat out of your hand. I bought some little oranges and fed them while Garman took my picture. Many signs throughout the park warn visitors not to become too familiar with the sacred deer "for fear of danger."

We saw the Kasuga no Miya Shrine, founded in A.D. 710. As one approaches this shrine, one notices hundreds of metal lanterns hung on both sides of the road. At the right is the tiny Shira, fuji-no-taki (White Wisteria Falls), which is little more than a stream of water dropping from what looked like a spout some 20 feet from the ground on the slope of the hill. A large red *torii* guards the entrance to the park.

Near this shrine we saw the famous grafted tree, upon which we saw growing wisteria, nandine, camelia, elder, cherry and maple branches. The tree is called a banyan tree.

We took rickshas to save time and had our pictures taken in them. Saw Wakakusa Yama, a grassy slope, as the name suggests, 1,126 feet high. Saw San-gwatsu-do (Third Moon Temple) and Ni-gwatsu-do (Second Moon Temple).

We also saw and rang the big bell, 9 feet 2 inches in diameter, 13⅓ feet high, and 10 inches thick. It weighs 48 tons and was cast in 732. This is the third-largest bell in Japan. It cost us a sen each to ring it. This was done by grasping the heavy rope suspended from a large suspended log and swinging it to strike the bell with the blunt end of the log. We had heard the bell booming quite often during the afternoon, and I fancy the man in charge takes in a good many sen in the course of a year.

The Nara-no-Daibutsu is a great bronze image housed in a fairly good building. It is the god of light and sits on a lotus bloom. This image contains 500 pounds of gold, 16,827 of tin, 1,954 of mercury, 986,180 of copper, and a large amount of lead. It weighs 500 tons. It is the largest of its kind in Japan, 53½ feet high, 18 feet across the breast, with a face of 16 by 9½ feet, mouth and nose each 3 feet wide, eye 3 feet 11 inches, etc. The head was so badly damaged by fire that a new one was put on in 1183.

We visited one or two other temples and shrines, also the Nara Products Company, and then returned to Osaka in time for dinner at 6:00 P.M.

After dinner we walked to the YMCA night school. Mr. T. Yamagata, the head of the school, met us and showed us over the large plant. There are 1,000 in the night school studying English in nine different classes; 500 in the night school are studying the middle school course. There are 500 more in the day school studying the three-year commercial course. The English course is five years, and the middle school course is three years. Of these 2,000 students, perhaps the majority are apprentices in the shops. In many cases, their employers make them come for a period of time to learn English or some phase of commercial work.

The school runs five nights a week. The tuition averages Y3 a month. There are

Dr. Woodworth is visiting a fruit grower in northern Japan.

two periods of an hour each, from seven to eight and from eight to nine. Once a week there are three periods, one of which is a Bible class. Five pastors give one night a week for this Bible class teaching; 25 teachers in the English department besides the five pastors.

A spiritual lecture is given every Wednesday night before the regular class periods. The aim is constantly to keep the Christian message before the students.

It costs about Y15,000 to run the school. The income is Y50,000 so the YMCA is supported by the surplus income from this school. It is a paying proposition financially.

New applicants are coming in daily. They have to wait their turn and enter by passing an examination. The actual number of graduates at the end of the five years is very few. Last year there were 16. The reason for the small number is that most of the students come for one, two or three years to get certain phases of English, and then they drop out. But 1,800 come and go each year.

The head teacher teaches eight hours a day and four nights a week. Many government teachers give a night a week or more to the work. The head teacher says the classes are too large for the best work and wants to work out a system of smaller classes. The largest class now has 350. There are at present 15 classes.

These students work 48 hours a week and get about Y20 a month and board and lodging as apprentices. Outside working hours, they must sweep the houses of the employers and run errands, etc. The employers usually pay the tuition of the boys.

The 500 in the day school are compelled to come by their parents because they have failed to pass the entrance examinations in the government middle school. Mr. Yamagata says they are hard to keep interested and disciplined properly. There is little difficulty along this line with the night school students.

Bell at Nara.

As we talked with the principal, a group of boys gathered about us, and finally Mr. Garman stepped into a vacant room and began to teach some of them. A number of them stayed with me, and one who could speak English quite well explained that they were to have had a class but that the teacher could not come, so they were not to have it. They begged me to go to their room on the third floor and give them a lesson in English. Not knowing just how far one should go in a matter of this kind, I declined to go up but did agree to give them a lesson right there. So I sailed in and had the most interesting and the most interested class I have ever seen. I used the conversational style, correcting their mistakes as we went. Some of the boys were a little shy, but others forgot their shyness in their desire to learn, and we had a fine time for a little while, until Mr. Garman came out and announced that his class was through. By this time, the entire corridor was jammed with boys eager to hear what I had to say.

This is just one example of what can be done on a greater or smaller scale most anywhere in Japan. I had difficulty in tearing myself away. I did so by teaching them to say "good-bye." They wanted to say "good-a-bye," but at least some of them got it right. I created a good laugh by replying to their last good-bye with the Japanese "*sayonara*."

Took a good bath at the hotel and turned in at 10:30.

Wednesday, November 17 ———————— ◆ ——————————————————

All day yesterday, Mr. Miyake accompanied us and gave us helpful information. Our bill at the hotel is cared for by the Osaka SS Union, and it will be large as it is a fine hotel with excellent meals and good service, European-style. We had a large double room, finely furnished, and the service was excellent. In the middle of the hollow square that the building forms, there is a miniature garden with a fountain, trees, hills, fish, etc.

We left Osaka at 8:55 for Kobe. We stopped at a suburban stop and visited the Kwansei Gakuin, a very large institution conducted jointly by the Canadian Methodists and the ME South and the Japan Methodist church, the latter coming into organic administrative control but the former two jointly owning and managing the same. The three bodies have each an equal representation on the board of directors. Final control is vested in a joint educational commission resident in the U.S.A. and Canada. There are three from each board on the board of control in America. The grounds now embrace 22 acres. There are 1,675 students in all the departments. The courses offered are the academy, or middle school, corresponding to our high school and the college department, with subdepartments in commerce and finance, literature and philosophy, and Bible and theology.

The teaching staff of the whole school, including ten missionaries, is 64. Student enrollment is 1,675. Value of grounds and buildings at present, $660,000. Income from tuition and entrance fees, $30,000. Income from mission boards and other sources, $55,000. Total income, $85,000. It has government recognition. A university expansion scheme is being worked out, with the hope of having a university in operation by 1923. For this, $300,000 is needed for buildings and equipment, $300,000 to be invested under government approval and $1,000,000 for endowment.

The administration of Kwansei Gakuin is in the hands of a board of directors of twelve men, four from each of the three cooperating bodies, Japan Methodist, ME South, and the Methodist Church of Canada. Final authority is exercised by a joint commission, representing the Canadian and American churches, in all matters of general policy and appointments to important offices.

Each of the two mission boards gave $25,000 last year toward this work, the balance being raised by tuition, etc.

The theological department offers three courses: (1) the regular course of five years above the middle school graduation, two years of preparatory work, and three of specialized Bible and theological training; (2) special evangelists' training course of three years, in the vernacular, to train for Christian work and other than the ordained ministry; (3) special SS teachers course of one year.

There are at present only 27 students in the theological department and the number, according to the president, Dr. Bates, is decreasing for various reasons. They get a few ministerial students from the middle school they conduct, but Dr. Bates thinks not nearly as many as they should, though they have a chaplain in charge of the religious life of the school.

The college department offers two courses, the literary and commercial. There is a dormitory for the college men, and they pay Y17 a month for board.

The middle school at Kwansei is what is called a *chugakubu*, not a *chugakko*. The *chugakko* conforms to all government regulations, which means that religious instruction in the school is not permitted. The *chugakubu* conforms to government regulation in everything except that it has religious instruction in the school. They have to report regularly to the government.

Boys in the *chugakko* are given the privilege of postponing compulsory military training during the period they are in school. They are also admitted to higher schools without difficulty. The middle school course covers five years, from which graduates can go to the colleges or universities.

The whole student body meets every morning for a short chapel service. One hour each week is devoted to direct Bible study in the classroom. There is also a YMCA and a religious work committee.

In the middle school department there are 18 classes with 855 students. Of 800 applicants last year, only 200 could be received in the new class. The total number of the alumni is 640. The teaching staff consists of 35 teachers, including two foreigners. Fifty boys live in the dormitory, paying about Y17 a month board. The tuition of the middle school is Y44 a year, in addition to Y1.50 examination fees and Y1.50 for registration.

The budget of the middle school is Y50,000. Of this, Y14,000 was a special bonus, which since has become a part of the regular salary budget. The income from tuition and fees is about Y34,000. The two missions make an annual grant of Y8,000 each toward the middle school. The joint commission in America, consisting of three from each board, takes up all matters of policy and refers them to the boards of each church with recommendations.

The new building recently put up for the middle school cost Y200,000. It is of concrete and accommodates 800. There is no chapel building for the middle school boys.

Dr. Bates is president of the entire institution. Then there is a dean of each of the three departments. These men are Japanese. The principal of the middle school receives Y2,550 and house. The head teacher, Y1,950. Two other teachers receive Y1,500 each; two others, Y1,440 each. The lowest-paid regular teacher gets Y1,080. All but the principal pay their own rent. Sixteen of the middle school teachers, including their principal, are Christians.

Dr. Bates thinks about 600 *tsubo* of land should be taken for a middle school this size, which should include homes for the missionaries and native teachers.

This institution is located on the outskirts of Kobe beyond the city limits. It is a 30-minute ride from the center of the city. The land is now worth Y75 a *tsubo* right here. Some want Y120 a *tsubo*. The school paid Y5.5 for the first land they bought here ten years ago.

Dr. Bates thinks, like Dr. Kozaki of Tokyo, that denominations should establish primary schools as well as middle schools. Also thinks technical schools should be established. He says further that he believes boys' and girls' schools should be located in the same city, as it will tend to bring the right kind of young people together and ensure better home life when they marry, as they will have more things in common. When a girl or a boy with middle school or college training marries one without, there are bound to be differences of living standards.

The membership of the Methodist Church in Canada is 400,000. They have two mission fields, Japan and China, and appropriated this last year $700,000 for the two fields. They have 70 missionaries in Japan and 200 in China. This church has three girls' schools in Japan.

MISSIONARIES' SALARIES, CAN. METHODIST CHURCH

Salary of married men, $1,600 from 1 to 6 years, $1,900 from 7 to 15 years, $2,100 from 6–16 years on up. Children's allowances: $100 from 1 to 6 years, $150 from 7 to 12 years, $200 from 13 to 21 years, but this allowance for the last three years is conditional upon the child being in school.

This mission found that in comparison to the 1913 scale, the cost of commodities here had increased 325 percent in 1920. They asked for salaries running from $1,600 to $2,200, with children's allowances of $100 to $300. The above new schedule shows that they received almost what they asked. This is a 50 percent increase over 1913.

The furlough allowance is $50. The board does not agree to pay medical bills and pays no such bills of less than Y100. Bills of more than Y100 are presented to the board and passed upon by them. Does not know salary of single women as the woman's board sends all single women out.

We went from here on into Kobe and established ourselves at a rather forlorn-looking hotel called the Central Hotel, at Y7.00 a day, including meals.

Kobe is a busy foreignlike city of great commercial importance at the head of Osaka Bay, in Settsu Province, Hyogo ken. It is fifth in size in the empire, with a population of 450,000, with 100,000 houses. It covers 14 square miles and is growing rapidly as its trade with the West is increasing in a great way. It lies in a half-moon piece of ground along the shore of the bay with the mountains crowding in close behind the full length of the city, so that its growth must be along the shore in each direction. It has a fine harbor, and many ships from all parts of the world make this one of their chief stopping places. It looks more like a foreign city perhaps than any other city I have seen.

After tiffin at the hotel, we went to the YMCA where we met the secretary, Mr. Swan. The Y is at present in temporary quarters, their fine building having been torn down in order that the street might be widened. But they are already working on the new building, which will be a splendid center for the young of that city.

From here we went to the Palmore Institute, an institution run by the Methodist Church South. Mr. Oxford, a layman, is in charge of the school. It enrolls 1,200 a year, but only 600 at one time. There is a day department for shorthand and typewriting. There are 100 men and 50 women in the day department each month; Y2 an hour is charged for the use of the machines and time and a half for more than an hour. For irregular students, the charge is more. All classes come to the day department, from those barely able to read up to college graduates. Even businessmen of all nationalities come. They are given instruction to start them, then all it takes is practice.

In the night school the tuition is Y2 a month for the first two years, Y2.25 for the third year, and Y2.50 for the fourth year. They enroll 1,200 each year and turn away 2,500. Ordinarily they have a waiting list of 600. Only 600 can be accommodated at one time. Desk capacity is 300, but they crowd things by using chairs. The building is very ordinary and not particularly adapted to the work, I should say. About 20 percent of the 600 are absent each night, which eases things a bit.

There are all classes in the night school—chief of police of the foreign section, supt. of the public schools of Kobe, the son of a baron who was waiting for a commission, a retired military officer who was on duty in the Russian War, ricksha men, sons of ricksha men, factory men and clerks are among those received. They have chapel every night, and though not exactly compulsory, it is well attended.

There are 17 on the faculty, some teaching only one night a week. Three are on duty all day, and assistants to the number of 7 are on duty all the time at night.

The total expenses of the night school are Y10,000 annually, of which Y5,000 is paid to teachers, not including the two missionaries, who salaries are paid extra to this budget by the board at home. The school at present could be self-supporting even to paying the salaries of the two missionaries.

The Southern Methodists own the property in which the work is held. The work started in 1886. Recently they bought two additional lots nearby at a cost of Y300 a *tsubo* for 145 *tsubo*. This was bought in February 1919 and was bought as an emergency. The board is not sure whether to enlarge or continue intensive. The plant as it now stands in one building is very compact, and Mr. Oxford thinks it makes for better contact with the young men along religious lines. They can hardly get away from it. The location of this school is fine.

Less than 1 percent of the students graduate. There are really two grades in each of the first two years and one in each of the third and fourth, making it practically a five-year course. The graduates average up with the commercial schools and colleges in their knowledge of English, which of course is the language taught. The Bible is taught.

Most of the students drop out after the third year with a very good knowledge of English, for which of course they have come to the school primarily.

From the school, 15 to 25 are received into the church each year. The pastor of the Methodist church in Kobe assists in the religious work.

Regular teachers are paid Y3 a night for two hours a night. The pay of a foreigner is Y5 a night.

SALARIES OF THE MISSIONARIES OF THE METHODIST CHURCH SOUTH

Beginning next February, the present basic salary of $1,400 is to be raised as follows: for 1 to 8 years of service, $1,550; 9 to 16 years, $1,650; 17 to 25, $1,800; beyond 25 years, $1,900.

Children's allowances are at present 1 to 10 years, $100; 11 years up, $150. They are expecting the children's allowances to be raised.

Medical bills are allowed up to 4 percent of the salary. This is done as a lump appropriation for this to the mission. If there is a balance at the end of the year, it is divided among those whose bills have been heavier than the 4 percent allowance.

Term of service is seven years but will be changed to five for the first term and seven thereafter.

Salary of single missionary is $900.

The membership of the Methodist Church South in America is $3,000,000. They have mission work in Africa, Cuba, Mexico, South America, Japan, Korea. Cuba and Mexico are administered by the home mission board. The foreign board has also started work in Belgium and France. They have 45 missionaries in Japan and are calling for more.

I learned here that an old friend of MBI days, Mr. N.S. Ogburn, is located here as evangelistic missionary for the So. Methodist church but that at present he is on furlough at Monroe, North Carolina. He can be reached through 810 Broadway, Nashville, Tennessee. He is scheduled to come back next year and teach in the Kwansei Gakuin but wishes to continue the evangelistic work instead. He has married an old sweetheart, but recently.

From Palmore Institute, we hunted up Mr. Kagawa*, who is the most noted slum worker in Japan. We found his office right near the slum district, but he was in Osaka, so we did not see him. We hope to be able to go through the slums with him in the morning, as the Kobe slums are said to be the worst in the world. What little we saw of it today was terrible. The street was being used as a public closet and sewer without regard to passersby. This was particularly true of the men and children. The houses are filthy-looking places, very small and swarming with children. Dirt and squalor and poverty abound. Little shops line the streets, with the living room in the rear. We saw any number of people cooking different articles of food right out in the street.

We walked back to the hotel, which is anything but attractive. It has a side entrance only and way back from the street. It seems to be run by Norwegians, or Scandanavians, and most of the guests at tiffin were such, many being seamen.

We noticed, however, that Dr. W.E. Lampe stopped here overnight, and that gave us courage. The food at tiffin seemed all right, but the rooms are rather shabby-looking. We have two rooms, adjoining. The price, as I mentioned before, is Y7.00 a day, American plan.

As we returned to the hotel, we saw an occasional streetcar trimmed in pretty colors and remembered that there is a big sale on in Kobe and special cars are being run for women only.

Thursday, November 18 ———— ◆ ————————

At breakfast this morning, the hotel boy, who is Japanese, told us that he learned most of his English from the guests at the hotel. He did quite well.

After breakfast, we started for the slums. Mr. Tohohiko Kagawa, the slum worker, was in his office, which is right at the edge of the slum district. He was in and invited us to come upstairs. He has a nice little office and a delightful study upstairs.

Mr. Kagawa is a young man of about 35 and one of the finest-looking men I have seen. He has a remarkable face full of fine expression, showing the traces of Christianity all over it. He is a devout Christian.

A major figure in Japanese history, see page v.

T. Kagawa, greatest slum worker in Japan, at his office, with the author.

He has three secretaries, one doctor, two nurses and one office boy. He is an ordained pastor of the Southern Presbyterian church and receives support from three sources for his work. The Presby. Church South pays him Y55 a month; six friends, half of whom are Christian, give him Y180 a month; and he receives an income from the sale of his books, etc.

He pays the doctor Y120 a month for full-time and the nurses Y30 each.

He has published thus far 11 books, two in the past year, receiving Y5,000 a year from the sale of them. He was in America two years and took postgraduate work at Princeton. From boyhood, he determined to work in the slums.

Two of his secretaries handle two cooperative unions for buying goods for the poor. He runs two dispensaries, has connections with five different trade unions, and expects in this way to prevent poverty.

He says Y5,000 a year thus spent prevents poverty, while Y5,000 spent in the dispensary heals for the time what poverty has caused.

Mr. Kagawa is president of the Printers' Union of Osaka, with a membership of 1,200. He plans to enlarge the industrial work. He is secretary of the union, which interprets moving pictures to Japan audiences. Also president of the Steel and Iron Workers, with a membership of 700. Editor of *Labor News*, a periodical.

He plans to publish another, called *Printers' News*. He spends four nights a week working in labor unions.

He says he gets many Christians through his industrial work. He does not speak so directly, but they come to his evangelistic services and are converted there. He preaches two nights a week and conducts a Bible class at 6:00 A.M. every Sunday. He says people came from all around as far as Osaka to this early-morning Bible class.

One of the achievements of Kagawa in Kobe, another industrial center, has been the establishment of these community restaurants such as pictured here. The clock indicates why the tables are empty.

The doctor examines from 70 to 90 cases a day and gives medicine accordingly. It costs Y5,000 a year to conduct the dispensary.

He has one SS every Sunday and another every other Saturday. One has an attendance of 100 and the other 30.

Mr. Kagawa finances his labor unions himself. He spent Y600 for them last year, besides giving his time. If he would not give his time to this and could spend more time writing religious novels and books on economic problems, he said he could earn Y50 a day.

He was fined twice for writing the truth about social and especially labor situations. At one time he was in China, and his friend who was publishing his paper published a labor song of the IWW. When he returned, he was arrested and fined $100. At another time he said in his paper that he "honored the laborer as a king." The courts took it as "*the* king" and fined him Y100.

In his evangelistic work he uses the language of the street because, he says, he can better reach the people that way.

There are 11,000 in this slum, which is called Shinkawa ("new river") and 6,000 in the other called Nagata ("long field"). This latter is the "eta class," or social outcasts.

The office is in the Shinkawa slum. Next door is a kindergarten conducted by a Miss Thompson of the Baptist mission. There are no slum children in this kindergarten, owing to disease among them that makes such work impossible.

There are 81 houses in this section, with from 16 to 24 rooms in each and only two mats to a room. This means that each room is six feet square. The average family living in each of these rooms is two and a half persons, but some of these single rooms have as many as nine persons living in them. The rooms are in double rows with from 8 to 12 rooms in a row and a family living in each room. These houses of from 16 to 24 families have only one water closet for each group of rooms. It is usually located at one end of the section, and the rooms nearest it are rented at a slightly lower rent.

These people live in these single rooms and do their washing at the public hydrant at the corner and their cooking in front of the room in the narrow, alley-like street.

Out of every 1,000 babies born, half die annually.

Those in this section of two-mat rooms are engaged in making clothing for the lower half of the body only, such as *geta*, *tobi*, leggings, etc. Some are also scavengers.

Other sections have three-, four-, five- and six-mat rooms, but usually a block of eight or ten rooms this size under one roof. Those in the five-mat section are mostly dockhands. Those in the six-mat rooms are dockhands or work in the match factories or shoe shops, etc.

The average rental is five sen a night for the two-mat rooms, the rent being collected daily. The three-mat rooms cost seven sen a day, four-mat 10 sen and five-mat 15 sen.

These people have somehow worked out a sort of mutual-aid society that has done wonders in taking them out of these places. It is called a *tanomoshiko* (helping-one-another club). These people soon learn who of their neighbors are trustworthy, and a trustworthy man is called *komoto*. If such a man gets into debt, a group of his friends will band together under a sort of written contract they use, and they agree to pay into a common fund, say, five sen a day for a month at a time. If the man's debt is, say, Y200, they contribute equal amounts to cover the debt at the end of the first month.

At the end of the month, the amount is turned over to him, and he pays off his debt. But instead of dissolving the organization, these 40 or so friends stick together, the man who has just been helped with them, and they determine which one is next needy, and the second month's combined contribution goes to the next needy man, and so on until every man has thus been helped. By this system, a man may borrow Y1,000 and buy a home. The amount is paid at the end of the first month of the club's existence, thus saving the interest on the money. He continues to contribute to the club for the next needy, etc., and thus each one is helped. Mr. Kagawa said he had been in these clubs for several years and had never lost a cent by it yet. He stated that beggars have become rich in this manner. Those who buy these tenements (for they usually begin by buying the house they have rented) move out into better quarters and rent to their less fortunate neighbors. The system was started by the Buddhists.

The man who owns the house across from Mr. Kagawa's was a beggar and a leper. Now he is worth Y40,000, and he got it by this kind of a start.

Before Mr. Kagawa came to this work, there was an average of ten murders in this section annually. Now there are none. He said that while he was in America, the number increased.

He calls his little band of Christian workers "The Jesus Band." He says the number is always small because when they become Christians, they get better jobs and move into more respectable communities. I wish you could have seen the smile on his face as he told me this.

Mr. Kagawa also lectures in three seminaries, the Kobe Girls' Bible School, the Methodist Bible School, and the Osaka Seminary (Presbyterian). He gives lectures on labor problems for laboring people every Monday evening from seven to nine. He handles subjects that touch every phase of the labor situation. He charges Y2.00 a season. The attendance is about 100.

He also publishes a number of tracts—*Prohibition, Alcoholism, Spiritual Regeneration, The Destructive Power of Prostitution.* These he sells in the public meetings at five sen each. The titles of some of his 11 published books are *The Psychology of the Poor; A Movement, Spiritual and Social; Human Pain and Character Building; Principles of Subjective Economics.* The latter is written in direct opposition to the materialistic socialism of Karl Marx and upholds Christian socialism as the only kind. One of his religious novels is *Beyond the Death Line.*

After this conference with Mr. Kagawa, he took us into Shinkawa, said by a Mr. Wood, a noted slum worker and worldwide slum investigator, to be the worst slum in the world. Mr. Wood is from Boston but has visited the slums of London, I am told.

How anything could be worse than this one I cannot conceive. In six blocks of it, 8,100 people live in the worst squalor I have ever witnessed. I took a number of pictures, which I hope will show something of the real conditions.

We walked through one of the narrow streets after another and found them more narrow than a common sidewalk. Several times I could put my arms akimbo, and my elbows would touch the houses on either side. On what were considered the wider lands one could easily touch both sides by stretching out the arms. We looked into a number of the homes and found in some a veritable roomful of children all belonging to one family. Many of these houses have only two-mat rooms in them, with a family to each room.

In many of them we found men, women or children lying in the corner, sick and unable to move. There were all kinds of skin diseases shown in the faces and bare parts of the bodies. Often one would see a man or a woman trying to do some kind of work in the one room with the children playing around. The rooms are dark, and such work is hard on the eyes. One old woman was making matchboxes by hand. The ground was muddy. The sewer usually ran right in front of the entrances to the rooms and was in most instances wide open and teeming with filth. The children were playing around this death trap. The water closets at the end of each section were filthy beyond description. We had to keep dodging to escape rubbing our heads in the family washings hung on bamboo poles in front of the doors or to avoid stepping on some of the countless children that thronged around the "foreigners."

When we passed the woman making the matchboxes, Mr. Garman told of a lady missionary who when she came to Japan for the first term of seven years brought enough matches to last the entire seven years, not realizing that she was coming to perhaps the most important match-producing country in the world.

A large group of Japanese, mostly children, surrounding a Western gentleman.

At one place I took a picture of a man with his family, including a lot of other children who crowded around. When I had snapped it, one of the girls about 12 years old asked in Japanese to see the picture at once. I could not explain to her and had difficulty keeping the children from taking the Kodak out of my hands. This girl finally persisted so that I held the Kodak open and let her look into the lens. Her face beamed, and she declared in Japanese that the picture was there. The poor child had never seen a Kodak before, no doubt, and upon seeing her reflection, thought it was the picture.

At another spot I was about to take a picture of three women doing the family washing at the miserable hydrant on the corner of a block of these rooms. Just before I snapped it, one of them saw me (though I was not attempting to keep it secret).

Quick as a flash, she sprang to her feet and rushed into one of the rooms, calling to the other women to get away or they would get their picture taken. I snapped the picture of what was left, and we started away. One of the other women followed us with angry looks and told us to take our pictures in some other spot. The children, of whom there were "millions," took it up and followed us some distance, talking and gesticulating. Garman said they did not like it, and rather than cause difficulty, we slipped away as fast as we could.

This picture was taken after Mr. Kagawa had left us. We had no difficulty when he was along. Everywhere he went the people showed their great love for him. He would pat the dirty diseased little children on the heads and speak kind words to the weary women and old people, and they always responded with a cheery reply. One young woman persisted in telling him a lot of things. He listened patiently, and then we went on. As we left her, he told us she was a very bad girl and was living a

A slum with a dirt road between the buildings.

life of awful sin. I was glad indeed to see the show of anger on the part of those women, for it showed a sense of pride that had not been entirely lost.

Mr. Kagawa took us to his own living apartment right in the heart of the slum. He has three rooms of five mats each, and he is keeping besides himself and wife two old people who are sick with rheumatism. We met Mrs. Kagawa at the office. She is said to have about lost the sight of one eye from disease contracted among these lowly people. But in spite of this and many other hardships, these two people are devoted to their work and enjoying it to the full. As Mr. Oxford of Palmore Institute told us, "We are playing at Christian service here in Palmore, but Mr. Kagawa is really working at it."

This place must be a fright when it rains. The roofs are poor, and the water must drip off the houses. There are no gutters, and the houses are close to the ground. The smells were terrible now, but they must be infinitely worse when it rains, especially in the hot summer. I wonder how these people stand the heat in the summer.

Our missionaries have to leave Tokyo for two or so months in the summer because of the intense heat. It must be unbearable in these slums. Mr. Kagawa's policy, as you have noticed, is to get the people to help themselves by giving them some start.

We next went to the docks that line the shore around Kobe. It was a most interesting sight. I took a picture of a great bevy of freight boats. We next visited the passengers' pier, and Mr. Garman helped two ladies find the launch that was to take them to their ship in the harbor preparatory to continuing their voyage of another month to India, where they go for their first term as missionaries. At this pier we saw one of the humiliating sights one sees once in a while in Japan, and I fancy in

Angie Crew and a Japanese friend.

other countries too—an American or Englishman dead drunk in a ricksha, being pulled hither and thither by the bewildered ricksha man.

The two ladies mentioned before are of the Disciple church and are to continue their voyage on the SS *Japan* for Calcutta.

We went back uptown and took lunch at another hotel. Cost us Y2 each, the same as the other was charging for meals.

We then climbed the hill to the Tor Hotel and turning to the left, climbed a long flight of stone steps leading to Suwayama Park. This park offers a fine view of the city and the bay full of busy craft of all descriptions. To our right we could faintly see the entrance to the famous inland sea with its numerous island spots. To the right and behind us arose the mountains that fringe the bay. Kobe lies between these mountains and the water. It is quite long as it stretches around the circle of the bay, but it is not very wide, between the mountains and the docks.

We visited Kobe College, a school for girls run by the Congregational women. Miss DeForest heads it. They have most beautiful grounds lying on the side of a hill well laid out, and the buildings are in fine condition. There were a happy lot of girls around the campus and drumming at the pianos in the halls. The main building is a large brick affair just back of which is the neat-looking home for the foreign teachers. There are also dormitories and other buildings. There are a high school course and a full college course, offered together with special courses.

We next went to the Southern Womens' Bible Training School where there are 15 women in training.

As we went along, we passed one house with the accompanying sign on a paper tacked at the entrance, which Mr. Garman explained was a death sign corresponding to our crepe.

We took dinner at the same hotel we visited this noon. After sauntering up and down the streets awhile, we went to the depot. I bought a pair of *geta* for each of the girls and some postcards. Left at nine o'clock on a second-class express for Tokyo. Garman and I had a section. In this car the seats run lengthwise part of the way, and there are also several seats in the middle running sidewise like our sleepers. It happened that ours ran lengthwise. I had the lower berth and Garman the upper. He said he wanted me to have the experience of riding in one lower berth before I left.

VI. More of Tokyo

Awoke several times in the night but had a good night's rest in spite of it.

One of the first things I saw in the morning was the sight of Mt. Fuji towering to my right. With the rising sun upon its snow-capped head, the clouds playing about its girdle, it made a glorious picture. We passed many rice paddies terraced up the hills and also a great many tea gardens. At one place I noticed an old woman watering or fertilizing the plants by hand with a bucket and dipper.

Mount Fuji comes into view closer and closer as we ride. It is the most striking single mountain peak I have yet seen, rising more than 12,000 feet from a long, rather gentle slope until near the top where it becomes more steep. I snapped a picture but discovered later to my sorrow that I had held my Kodak so as probably to cut off the top of the peak.

As we wind in and out among the hills, Mt. Fuji appears in a constantly changing aspect. For a long time it was to our right and ahead of us, while a wide bay extending in from the Pacific was to our direct right with a range of mountains standing beyond the bay. The latter was beautiful as the little fishing craft dotted the surface of the bay with open sails unfurled to the light springlike breeze.

As we went into the dining car for breakfast, we rounded a curve that placed Fuji directly to our left so that we were running between the bay and the mountains. The sun and clouds create a beautiful effect as they play about the peak with its massive height. It is covered with snow for a third of the way down the sides and looks much like a great ice-cream cone resting in chocolate syrup. Its cone-shaped summit is cut off flat just as the erupting fire and lava decapitated it several hundred years ago. As I remember it, it seems to me Fuji has much the appearance of Mt. Rainier in Washington, which I often viewed from my bedroom window in Seattle. Rainier always appeared like a big chocolate sundae.

The farmers in this section are busy putting in wheat. South of Tokyo, two crops are raised annually, though farther north it cannot be done. The farmers down here plant their wheat in November after having taken off the rice crop. There is little snow or cold weather, so the wheat grows rapidly and can be harvested in May. Then the rice fields are planted, and they are cut in November.

Another rather remarkable fruit grown here is the *nikon*, or Japanese orange. It is quite like our tangerine. We passed a number of groves of them as we rode along.

Arrived in Tokyo at twelve noon, and after taking lunch downtown, Garman took my traveling bag home while I went around to Kinjo Shokai on the Ginza with

259

A river runs through this valley. Note the mulberry bushes in the foreground.

some film to be developed. Found some letters from home when I finally reached
Kasumi cho.

Saturday, November 20 ───── ◆ ──────────

The SS teachers and kindergarten teachers of Naka Shibuya had planned an
outing to see the maple trees today and wanted me to go with them. Since I shall
not have another opportunity, I decided to go, as much as I wanted to spend the
day writing up my notes.

Miss Stacy and I had an early breakfast and with our *bento* under our arms,
started for the car at about 6:30. After a long ride with several changes of cars, we
arrived at the railroad station where we met Mr. Oishi and Miss Watanabe and
Miss Nakai of the Shibuya church. The station is called Shinjuku Station. We just
missed the train in discussing whether to attempt to go or not, owing to the threat-
ening weather, so we had an hour and a half to wait.

We decided to try to go on in spite of the weather and went out to walk around
until train time. We strolled over past the Christian Women's College and on to the
waterworks plant that supplies water for the city of Tokyo. The water is taken from
the Tama River.

It is brought to the central plant by means of a canal. At the central plant it is
first run into great reservoirs called settling beds. Here the coarser sediments drop to
the bottom. At certain intervals these beds, of which there are many, are emptied
and the sand scraped off the cement bottom. From the settling station, the water
goes through a large filter of sand, gravel and brick, after which it can be pumped

to the city mains. There is a splendid model of the entire plant on a somewhat large scale open to the public.

From the waterworks we went to a kindergarten for poor children run by Miss Noguchi, who teaches in the primary department of the Peer's School. She is a Christian and does this for the sake of helping the poor. She has two such schools. In this one there are 71 children. They bring two sen a day, and of this amount one sen is placed to their credit in the bank and the other applied on their tuition. There is a primary school in connection with this kindergarten for the older children of the poor. They pay just as the others do. They sing Christian songs and are taught Christian truth. It is interesting to note that three out of the five teachers come from Mrs. Fry's school.

The building is fitted with a dispensary for the treatment of skin diseases and eye diseases of the children. Some of the children are pitifully marred. One little girl of about 10 or 12 was especially marked with disease and indications of inferior intellect.

The school has a bathroom so that the children can be bathed properly at regular intervals. The upstairs is fitted up with a room for each of the five teachers, opening into a common room. There is also a kitchen. Beautiful pictures adorn the walls, and it is very homelike.

Took the 9:18 train, and after an hour's ride got off to change cars, only to find that we had missed all connections and must wait another hour or so. So we walked through the village and out the country road. Saw wheat growing. Some is sown in rows and others in hills. We also saw an old woman weaving cloth on an old-fashioned loom. She said she could make about ten feet a day and sold it at about Y1.00. It is very hard work.

We took the 11:29 train for Ome, arrived at 12:30, and walked through the town and out among the hills to the Tama River where we sat down on the sand near the river and ate our lunches. On the way to the river, we passed a number of homes where they were dyeing silk. It was in large strands and was being put into small vatlike containers with the dye; black, brown, yellow, blue, etc. In these vats the native would work the strands back and forth in an effort to work it thoroughly into every tiny thread of the strand. Then it is hung up to dry, being pulled out at certain intervals to keep it even. This is done by inserting a round stick in the center of the strand and then flattening the silk out and giving it a sharp jerk. We saw many different kinds of silk being dried. I took some pictures.

After lunch we strolled over a large bridge where I took a picture of a large waterwheel, many of which are lined along the bank of the river. A little wall is built out, diverting temporarily the rushing water as it dashes down the mountain. After it has fulfilled the industrious native's purpose in turning the waterwheel and furnishing the power for his ancient machinery, it is allowed to join the main body of the river again.

Coming through the town again, we noticed a flour mill, which consisted of a number of bowl-like receptacles in which the grain is placed while a heavy wooden cylinder suspended above is so operated by waterpower as to pound the grain into flour.

We also passed silk-weaving mills in a number of houses. I noticed especially that

A step in the dyeing process.

the young girl who was doing the winding in one of the homes was showing the effects of the work with a flushed face and nervous hand. She was weaving a vari-colored piece of silk, and the crude wooden loom kicked her cruelly as it swung back and forth.

At another home we saw two girls and an old woman winding silk by hand. A large wooden wheel turned by hand served as belt wheel, and by use of a small stout cord as belt the spindle was turned. The girls, who were scarcely more than 10 or 12 years old, turned the belt wheel with one hand and held the tiny silk thread with the other. It required very close application so that the tiny thread would be wound smoothly and to catch it if perchance it should break. Thousands of girls all over Japan are engaged in this work, and little thought is given to their mental or physical development and none to the spiritual. We returned home in a driving rain.

Sunday, November 21 ◆

Remained at home all morning and wrote a couple of family letters. Went to the Union church service this afternoon and attempted to see the Rev. Ukai, the ME native pastor, after the service in regard to the Japan Forward movement, but he was not in. We had a sing at Kasumi cho this evening.

Monday, November 22 ◆

Spent the morning checking up the contents of my trunks and getting them in shape for inspection at San Francisco. Also checked up a lot of Japanese writing, with Oishi-san interpreting for me. Wrote a number of cards.

Another step in the dyeing process.

This evening a number of young people from the Azabu borrowed our parlor to give a farewell reception for Mr. Uchida, one of their number who leaves soon to serve his term of two years in the army.

This was a most interesting meeting. The CE society of Azabu church gave the reception. It was to begin at seven o'clock, but at six o'clock several arrived, explaining that they knew it was a little early. Usually the Japanese announce a church meeting for an hour earlier than they expect to begin, and by this means they get part of the people out on time. By seven o'clock, most of them were here, and in 15 or 20 minutes the young man in charge called them to order and started the program. A hymn was sung, and the president of the CE society read the Scripture lesson, and another led in prayer. Then there were several talks by different ones present, including the young Mr. Uchida.

Following the program, refreshments were served, consisting of a package of cakes of various kinds and tea. There were also *nikons*. During the refreshments they called on different ones to play a piano solo or sing, and in this way an hour or so went by. The daughter of the Rev. Matsuno has just completed a course in music, and she rendered a very fine solo. Mr. Uchida also played a fine piano solo; Mr. McKnight and I were forced to sing solos; and Miss Stacy and Miss Okina sang a duet. This was followed by the old-fashioned American game of spinning the plate. It was great fun to watch the Japanese scramble for the plate, with their flowing garments and *zori*, or house slippers. Some of them had great difficulty keeping their feet, and others were unusually alert and active. I got into the game and managed to learn two or three numbers quite well after a time. This social evening has helped me to see that these people enjoy a good time of the right kind as well as anyone if they are given a chance to have it. Their laughter and bright faces were evidence of the fun they were having.

Tuesday, November 23 ——————— ◆ ——————————————————

Spent the morning writing as hard as I could. Made a trip downtown in the afternoon. Wrote as many postcards as I could today, trying to get a card to every key pastor in the United States in order to boost the mission work. The last boat before the one I sail on leaves Saturday.

Wednesday, November 24 ——————— ◆ ——————————————————

Mr. Garman and I visited Mr. Benninghoff, of the Baptist church, this morning. He is in charge of a dormitory near Waseda University with his home next door to the dormitory building, and he has been doing a very fine work with these boys. The work began in 1908 in a rented building with 30 students. This building was nearer the university than the present site. The present building was built in 1911.

Mr. Benninghoff got into touch with the university through a Bible class he had. Prof. Abe, of the university, a Christian professor, made it possible for the officials of the university to invite Mr. Benninghoff to lecture two hours a week in the university. This has made it possible for him to work freely among the students. He gave a course of lectures, "The Philosophy of Religion," first and is now giving a course, American Institutions. He is taking them up under three heads: beginnings, political parties and educational institutions. He receives no salary from the university, though he said he supposed he could draw a salary if he asked for one. He prefers to work without it. The Baptist board pays his salary.

His work lies in the Department of Political Science. Waseda has a three-year preparatory course similar to a college course in America. This course is adapted to prepare for the three-year university course following, which is mostly in foreign reference books. The school course of Japan is at present undergoing a change. Under the old system, there was a six-year primary course, with two more years added for those who did not intend to go to the middle school but wanted a little more than the primary school. For those who went from the sixth year of the primary school to the full course of the middle school, five years were given. Following the five-year middle school course were three years' college work and three years' university work. Under the new system, the six-year primary course is still supplemented by two years additional for those who cannot go to middle school. But for those planning on middle school, the six-year primary course leads straight into a four-year middle school course. Those who cannot go to college are given an extra or fifth year in the middle school if they desire, but for those going to college, the four-year middle school course is sufficient, after which they enter the three-year classical course of the college, upon completion of which they can take three years' university work, which tapers into a period of research work leading to the Ph.D. degree.

The present dormitory of Mr. B. accommodates 21. The boys pay Y7 a month room rent. Mr. Benninghoff hires one servant to care for the building, sweeping, etc., and he also makes small repairs out of the fund. The boys hire a cook and a servant, and get board on the club plan at Y18 a month each. It is a self-governing institution. Mr. B. directs the work, however, and has the final say on all matters.

The present building cost Y10,000, the land Y20 a *tsubo*. Now land is selling next door at Y60 unimproved.

They have ten months of school a year, and the boys go home or elsewhere for the two remaining months.

The present site includes the home of Mr. B., and the total amount of land in it is 760 *tsubo*. The home of Mr. B. cost Y6,000 in 1911.

The dormitory is practically a fraternity, though Mr. B. can decide each case for himself. The boys are always consulted regarding the acceptance of a new boy, however. They have a constitution covering life in the dormitory. Mr. B. thinks it is not a good place to make scholars because the social life is apt to take more time than it should from the studies. But he is convinced that it is a good place to make men. Twenty percent of the boys from the dorm go to American universities.

He plans to put up a guildhall near the university as soon as possible. They recently bought land near the university, paying Y39 a *tsubo* for 2,300 *tsubo*. The plan is to put up Y100,000 building to use for social and religious work. The dormitory at present is 15 minutes from the university.

The boys have morning prayer meetings, conducted by themselves. Mr. B. meets the boys one hour a week in two groups. This is demanded by Mr. B., and the boys are expected to be present. At these meetings they discuss problems of the boys, etc. They have a monthly business meeting for problems of dormitory life.

Four men have charge of the housekeeping, library, meetings and boarding club, respectively. At the monthly meetings, these men report the money they have handled, etc. They receive no salary for this work and serve short terms. Two are chosen by the boys in the quarterly meetings for three months' service, and the other two are chosen by Mr. B. There is a board of faculty advisers, too, for the officials of the university are back of this work.

A boy had a woman stenographer in his room for three evenings in succession doing some copying for him. Mr. B. told him it could not be allowed. The boy was angry and said he did not trust him. Mr. B. stuck to his point on the principle involved and would have dismissed the boy had he not come and straightened the matter out.

The dormitory is democratic, but Mr. B. is court of last appeal. He can dismiss or accept a boy in spite of opposition from the others, and this is clearly understood by each boy before he enters. He lays down the governing principles. It is really a school of democracy. The boys have to believe in him and have confidence in his ability to give them the principles of democracy.

Boys of all classes are admitted, but at their entrance they are told that they must accept the Christian principles by which the dormitory is governed. Mr. B. makes it a personal question with each boy. When a boy comes for admittance, he is first thoroughly questioned by Mr. B., and only after he is pretty sure that the boy can be admitted does he give him the application blank, which the boy is asked to fill out and present. Mr. B. spends from 30 minutes to an hour going over the little constitution with the boy. But he emphasizes that this is only a guide and that the spirit of the dormitory life is what counts. The boys must declare his confidence in Mr. B.'s ability to conduct the dormitory along the lines suggested. Then he is given the application. When this is accepted, he is brought in and introduced to the boys at one of the prayer meeting services. Not until after the second monthly meeting is he formally received into the brotherhood. This is a formal ceremony. A hymn is sung, and prayer is offered. Then one of the boys reads the dormitory chapter, and the boy is permitted to sign his name on the *oriho*, with all the names of all the boys ever received into membership. Since all the details of dormitory life have been explained beforehand, the danger of misunderstanding is minimized.

After the name is signed, the boys give speeches telling of their hopes and aspirations in dormitory life. Mr. B. seeks to get a man in his first year who expresses his desire to stay the full six years. He doesn't like to take in an older university man. The six years of growth from the first year are thoroughly planned. There are some exceptions to this rule, however. He doesn't especially care to take in just Christians but prefers to make Christians of them.

In addition to the dormitory life, they have a regular Sunday morning church service for all boys who want to come. Have four English classes a week. Also four English Bible classes a week and one prayer meeting. A special lecture about once a week. Mr. B. has an assistant to help in this work. He is a regular professor in the university but lives with Mr. B. He is in a three-year contract with the Baptist board and was recommended to the school by Mr. B.

A SS of 100 is conducted in the dorm, the classes being taught by the boys of the university. A Japanese assistant for Mr. B. is also supported by the Baptist board. He is pastor of the church also. The Baptist board gives Y2,500 toward this work, including the enlarged plans now afoot. The board sent a man to America for three years' study. Will become full professor in the university. The board paid his way over and back, but he is working his way while there. He will also help Mr. B. when he returns. The new building will be equipped for social service. The first floor will contain office, dining rooms, committee rooms, etc. The second floor will contain a large auditorium; the third floor, offices and reception parlor.

The YMCA has made Mr. B. a proposition that he take over all the religious work of the university. Some of the men change their life plan when they become Christians and take up definite Christian work. Six men have done so at least. Three others have become university professors. Another is at Doshisha as a professor. Many of the men go out as influential Christian businessmen.

The personal contact is the big thing. Again the personality of the man at the head looms up. He says he never holds a *sodan* (conference) with a boy but what he aims to sow seed of Christian teaching.

Mr. B. believes his board is doing far more to influence educational life in Japan that it would by having a school of its own.

I took a picture of the entrance to the dormitory with Mr. Benninghoff standing in front.

We went next to the national YMCA where we had an appointment to luncheon with Mr. Phelps, the national secretary for Japan.

He took us in the YMCA car to his home where we enjoyed a delightful visit. Mr. Phelps believes strongly in giving the Japanese a chance to run the Christian work of the island as rapidly as that is possible. The YMCA plans to send no more general secretaries to the island but will send out specialists who will train native workers to become specialists. Mr. Phelps says this is necessary if leaders are to be developed.

He believes that missionary societies should aim at the same thing, though he admits that it may be slower in coming to pass.

Mr. Phelps told me that he spent 19 months in Siberia during the war, doing relief work, etc. He then went to New York where he made his report and at the same time told the committee of the distress of their workers in Japan because of the great increase in living costs. The board then made a new ruling for Japan salaries, as follows: The basic salary has not been changed yet, but to that 115 percent has been added. Basic salary $1,200 plus 115 percent. For every five years of service, add $100 to the basic salary plus 115 percent. Children's allowances: 1–5 years, $75 plus 115 percent; 6–11, $100 plus 115 percent; 12–18, $125 plus 115 percent, or $200 if the child is off the field.

The YMCA staff here has appointed a special committee to watch living costs, and they are to report if prices fall, so the 115 percent may be reduced. They hope to see it reduced shortly. The basic salary of $1,200 has not been changed, but it is the intention to change it soon.

On the question of land buying, Mr. Phelps said they had $40,000 on hand to buy land for homes for workers but that they were not able to do so at present. They have several homes now in good locations, but he said available land near there was priced at Y300 a *tsubo*. He said the land was not worth that much but the Japanese who owned it needed about that much money and therefore asked that for the land.

He said they had gone outside the city, and even there the best price they could find was Y55 a *tsubo*.

We were taken from Mr. Phelp's to the city YMCA where we had an appointment to meet Mr. Merle Davis, who has recently come back from furlough to become superintendent of the social and industrial work of Tokyo. He is a fine chap, born of missionary parents here in Japan. He is deeply in earnest and definitely committed to winning the industrial and lower classes to Christ. It was a great pleasure to talk with him.

Some friends of his gave him the money to buy a car, and in it (a Hupmobile) he took us to the slums of Tokyo. I shall never forget this trip. The section into which we went is divided from the remainder of the city by a river and embraces a population of 700,000 in 18 square miles of territory. And in this territory factories of all sizes and descriptions are found in great numbers. They are located at every conceivable place, among the miserable homes or off to themselves, and in many, many instances they are the home itself, where the husband, together with the help of as many of the members of the family as can be of help, seeks to turn out by hand or by means of crude machinery the product that may be sold for a pittance in an effort to keep the wolf from the door.

We rode first to the Honjo Ward, where we left the machine and began to walk through the crowded section; 210,000 people live in this ward. It had been raining for a day or two, and we found the mud almost impassable. This section is scarcely a foot above sea level, and time and again the tide from the nearby beach rises above the level of the ground and floods the floors of these miserable houses. When this happens, as it frequently does, the suffering of these people is terrible. We rolled up our trousers and waded into one street after another (if you can call these

River running through one of the slums of Tokyo. (All of this was destroyed by the earth-quake in 1923.)

miserable alleys streets). Mr. Davis said there were 17,000 families in this section liv-ing in rooms of four mats (a mat is three by six feet) or less. Counting five to a family, it would mean something over 70,000. They pay from 70 to 90 sen a mat per month, which is really very high rent, considering what homes rent for.

At one place they were raising the ground by filling in with ashes after having raised the house up. We noticed here a woman stealing some of the ashes her neigh-bor had laboriously brought to fill under his house. She kept glancing about, and from her looks one could judge that she considered herself not guilty of wrongdoing unless the owner should catch her.

After wading through several of the sloppy, narrow alleys, we came to a wider street running along a canal leading to the bay. The water in the canal was ab-solutely stagnant and stood right by a row of houses on one side and a street and another row of houses on the other. There is no sewer system in Tokyo, the people depending solely upon the farmers to gather the human waste from their water closets for fertilizing their rice fields. These closets are either located right in the houses with an outside opening, or they have none at all, in which case the street or gutter along the street becomes the sewage system. These gutters usually, but not always, have running water in them, and in this case they empty into this stagnant canal. One can scarcely imagine a more ill-smelling disease-breeding place than this, and I could not help but wonder what it must be like in the terribly hot summers in Tokyo. I took a picture here of men with long hooks pulling refuse, rags, etc. out of this canal. It was one of the most sickening sights I have seen in Japan. Little children in uncountable numbers were playing about the canal and the unstable wooden bridges that crossed it.

Cross section of a long building in Tokyo's slum showing inhabitants of two rooms.

From here we entered another narrow street and worked our way among the thick groups of children. Mr. Davis would talk to them occasionally as we went along. In these narrow streets one would see at one place a little counter with fruits or cakes for sale, the woman of the household in this way seeking to help out the meager living of her husband. Or perhaps the one room of the house would be turned into a miniature manufacturing establishment, with husband and wife and the older children making toys or matchboxes or other small handmade articles while the younger children rolled about on the floor. I counted as many as nine in one such little room, and the filth is indescribable.

One of the streets led to what is called the tunnel house, which Mr. Davis was especially anxious for me to see. We finally found it. It looked like a barn—a long shedlike affair with an entrance at each end, but that was all. We went inside, and I found a narrow alley, so narrow that I could easily touch both sides at once with my hands. On each side of this alley was lined a row of 10 rooms (20 in all) under one roof. There was a tiny window in each room, which was a three-mat room, and the door from each room led into the narrow alley, which in turn led to the exit or entrance at each end of the shedlike affair. The rooms were so small that the family cooking had to be done in the alley, and you can imagine the crowded condition and the filthy circumstances under which the cooking for 20 families was done, shut off from the sunlight and with no stoves or pipes to carry the smoke away.

As we passed through, I noticed in one room a man lying on a mat with a

Entrance, also exit, of the Tunnel House in Tokyo's slum. This building was doubtless destroyed by the earthquake. This building contained ten rooms on each side, each 6 × 9 feet with a family in each.

deathly sick pallor over his face. In the next room a man and a little child lay in the same condition seemingly. In another room a nearsighted old lady was trying to do a little sewing by the dim light of the one narrow window. There were children everywhere. At one end of this long shed, in which 20 families were trying to exist in as many three-mat rooms, there was the only sanitary closet for the entire group of perhaps 100 or 125 people. And what a filthy place it was! The entire place reeked with the odor of its contents. Outside the building ran a polluted gutter stream, also full of sewage. On the corner outside the building, the women of this death trap gathered at intervals to do the family washing at the miserable-looking water pipe.

As we left the section, Mr. Davis said that he hoped within five years to be able to come down and build a little Japanese house right among these people and live there. He said Mrs. Davis was with him in the desire to do so and that they were just waiting until their children were big enough to undertake it. He said his idea would be to build a nice little Japanese house, unpretentious on the outside, and then make it strictly modern within for the sake of health. From this vantage point he meant to give himself to bettering conditions among these people.

After wading through more mud and water, we came again to the automobile and were taken to the edge of Fukagawa Ward, with 190,000 inhabitants. This is the lodging-house ward.

Families with four or five children of their own take in boarders or roomers at

Typical scene in the slum districts of Tokyo.

seven sen a night. Many of the children do not know who their own parents are, and the moral conditions in this section are terrible. There are something like 3,000 roomers lodged here. Little evil-looking hotels everywhere and also the little shops, which are legion. It was getting well on in the afternoon, and the narrow streets were becoming crowded with men just off from their work in the nearby factories. When one thinks of the crowded conditions and the large number of idle men that are often found there, one can imagine just what the social and moral life must be. As we went through one of the streets, we noticed what both Mr. Davis and Mr. Garman said they had rarely seen in Japan—namely, a woman trying to entice a man in broad daylight right on the street, which was full of people looking on. The man seemed to be drunk, and the woman with a vicious look was doing her best to persuade him or drag him into her miserable room.

At another place in this ward, we came to the edge of the canal. And by investigation we found that the water was less than three inches from the level. A little girl was washing her hands in the polluted stream. Nearby a man was working in a sort of blacksmith shop, the water almost ready to flow into it. I attempted to take several pictures, but the day was cloudy, and I fear for the results.

The Kobe slum is no doubt the worst because of the conditions extending over a larger territory, but the tunnel house, for its size, was the worst thing I have ever witnessed.

From this ward we took the car again and went over to the island ward of

The Rev. Kagawa and the Rev. Garman in the heart of Kobe slum where Kagawa began his Christian service.

Tsukijima ("made island") where the great flood of four years ago carried away many houses and destroyed the lives of hundreds of unfortunates.

There are 35,000 people in this ward, of whom one half are laborers.

We passed the naval training station and later on stopped at the Salvation Army headquarters. They have a dormitory accommodating 122 men. Twice a week they hold meetings in the little assembly room, and every other night they hold meetings in the street. The dormitory is especially for men who have just come to the city and have no work yet. The aim is to try to get them work and to get them into different quarters within six months at most. The charge for a room is 15 sen a day. There are usually eight in a room. They make some converts. Five Salvation Army captains have been made from men here. The Episcopal church is the only other holding services on this island.

The dormitory has a bath with two large tubs. A 12-mat room accommodates eight to ten men.

After visiting this section, we rode back to Hibiya Park and took the car for Kasumi cho. It was a most interesting trip, but the sight of so much filth and dirt and so many innocent little children seeking to succeed in the battle of life against such odds was extremely depressing.

Thursday, November 25 ——— ◆ ———

Spent most of the day getting out some letters and checking my work since coming to Japan. We had our Thanksgiving dinner together at Kasumi cho and enjoyed a nice day. I made a trip downtown in the afternoon. At eight in the evening, Dr. and Mrs. Woodworth came to spend a week. Dr. Woodworth is to relieve Mr. Garman in seeing me to several points yet, and they will also stay for a board meeting next week.

Friday, November 26 ———— ◆ ————————

Dr. Woodworth and I went out to Oji today to visit a factory or two in that section. We went first to the Oji church where I took a picture of the kindergarten.

We then went to the Oji branch of the Tokyo Ke Ori Kaisha (Wool Weaving Stock Co.). The company employs about 1,600 people, who receive from one to two yen a day for ten hours' work. Some of the more skillfull receive as high as Y6. These workers are fairly well educated, having as much as two years above the primary school.

The man who showed us around proved to be a Christian and said he belonged to the M.E. church. Dr. Woodworth suggested that since there was no Methodist church in Oji, he might come into our church and find plenty to do. We were served with the best tea and very fine apples. Then we went through the factory. We were first shown the raw wool as it comes to the factory. There were also scraps of cloth that were to be reworked into cloth. The raw wool and the scraps of cloth were thrown into separate machines that tore them to shreds, then into other machines where they were torn still finer until the whole was a fluffy mass. Then the wool was put into great vats where it was washed thoroughly with running water, a weak solution of carbolic acid used in the washing process. After the washing it is pressed and dried by great hot-air drying machines.

At this time they were making the wool cloth for soldiers' uniforms, and for this purpose brown and white wool were being mixed together by carrying out large baskets of each and promiscuously throwing them together. This great mass was then put into another machine in which it was pressed together and the long threads formed by tightly rolling the wool together. Great machines did this automatically. The threads were wound and rewound until they were small and quite strong. One room was given over to machines containing as many as 400 spindles, and upon these the thread was stretched and wound. These spindles were then taken to the weaving room where the cloth was woven on immense looms. After being woven, it was taken to another room where it was subjected to the process of shrinking. It was then thoroughly dried and prepared for shipping. (I was unable to take any notes and consequently have to give all this from memory.)

From the wool-weaving factory we went to a factory where they were making Japanese paper. This was a very interesting place. The paper is made of wood pulp, great piles of which we saw. It is cut up together with scraps of paper of all kinds and rags, and is thoroughly mixed and washed in great vats. It comes out white and clean after undergoing this process a number of times. It is then pressed out and stretched by machinery until it is dry and at the proper thickness and width. From here it goes to the cutting machine where it is cut to the size required. The young man who took us around gave me samples of the paper.

We next visited a paper mill making newspaper stock. The process for preparing the wood pulp was about the same as before. In the final process, the wide long sheets of newly made paper were dried by passing them through a long and intricate series of rollers of the finest type of up-to-date make. There were 16 of these rollers in one machine, and there were several such machines in the plant. It was most interesting to attempt to follow the paper as it wound in and out among the flying rollers.

Taking a car, we finally reached Ueno Station at about 2:00 P.M. and went into a *gunabi* shop for lunch. The room was on the second floor and proved to be a very large one, full of patrons even at this late hour. We picked our way among the sitting Japanese, who looked at us in mild wonderment, and finally settled ourselves at the far corner of the room in about the only available space. We ordered our *gunabi* and were soon watching the little pieces of beef sizzling over the charcoal fire which the ever-attentive Japanese girl had quickly brought. The *gunabi* is cooked in a kind of reddish oil called *shoyu*, and to this is added onions if you like. There is usually a side dish of *daikon* and the ever-present rice. This meal is one of my favorite Japanese meals.

During the process of the meal, the Japanese who sat next to us became quite stirred up through influence of *sake* of which he had taken a great deal, evidenced by the empty bottles before him. *Sake* does its work quickly, and the flaming face and sparkling eye and rapid speech soon manifest themselves in the victim. This man seemed very anxious to talk with us and asked the waitress to find someone who could talk English. Dr. Woodworth waited a few minutes and then addressed him in his native tongue. You should have seen the expression on his face. He talked loud and long, telling of the wonderful effects of *sake*. I found that Dr. Woodworth could not make out what he said, but from his motions I deducted that he was telling how accurate and quick *sake* made one in plying his trade, which I guessed from his motions might be that of a tailor. He boasted that he could drink two *sho* of *sake* a day. I think this means about two and a half quarts, perhaps three quarts.

Following the meal, we hurried on out to the house, and Mr. Garman and I went to take dinner in the evening with Mr. Ichijuro Sato and his charming family. Mr. Sato has spent some four years in London as the agent for his company and speaks English very well, as do all the members of his family, consisting of his wife and two daughters. We went to his home in a downpour of rain and were ushered into a beautifully appointed Japanese room with a great *hibachi* in the center and beautiful cushions on the floor. Here we waited until our hosts put in an appearance a quarter hour later. The Rev. Matsuno also came in, being an invited guest. When Mr. Sato came in, he announced that dinner was ready, and he led the way to the dining room.

I was prepared for a good Japanese meal, and you can imagine my surprise when I sat down to one of the finest foreign meals I have ever tasted anywhere. To be sure, we sat on the floor before a low-standing table, but other than that, the meal was strictly foreign in every particular. There were some five or six courses served on finest of china and with the best of silverware and cut glass. There was first a course of soup with relishes, then fish, then meat pie and potatoes, then two or three different kinds of dessert and fruit and tea. The grace and charm of this entire family was exquisite. Mrs. Sato presides at the table like a queen, and the two girls are as fine English conversationists as one would care to talk with. We had a most delightful time during the meal, and I almost forgot how cramped I was until I started to rise. Alas, the agony came all at once, for my rheumatic knee could not stand the cramping.

After the dinner, we were conducted to the music room, which to my surprise was foreign-style, with a fine little piano, a table and several chairs. Here we sang some church songs while Miyo, the older daughter, played for us.

During this time I asked Mr. Sato for the story of his life, and we slipped to another room while he told me the following. He became a Christian at the age of 27 seventeen years ago at the Azabu Christian Church when Dr. Woodworth and Miss Penrod were missionaries of our church. Mr. Sato, at the same time, was an officer of the railroad company and used to drink much and smoke. He told me that it had injured his health so that he became ill, from which he has never fully recovered. His home at that time was opposite Kasumi cho. Many of his friends tried to urge him to go to chuch. Dr. Woodworth was conducting a mission school at Kasumi cho then, and several students were studying the Bible there.

Mr. Sato finally attended the meeting once and says he believes this was where he got his first inspiration to become a Christian. Many young people talked about Christ and read the Bible, and it stirred him to know more about this religion. The next Sunday, he attended church at Azabu, and Mr. Takahashi preached a good sermon that again stirred him. He said he thought the sermon was preached especially for himself. Then, he said, it seemed so long until the next Sunday. He wanted to go again and asked his wife to go with him. She did, and he was stirred again.

About a month passed, and one day he met Dr. Woodworth on the street. Dr. Woodworth asked him whether he wanted to become a Christian and be baptized or not. He answered that he wanted to be baptized as soon as possible. Dr. Woodworth baptized him the very next Sunday, November 6, 1903. After being baptized, Mr. Takahashi asked him to give his testimony. He began to tell his story but broke down and had to stop. He told me in his quaint way, "I broke my heart, and I stopped."

After the service, Miss Penrod gave him a nice verse found in the OT, Joshua 1:6–9. He showed it to me marked in his own Bible, which I noticed was well marked throughout. He said he stopped his old sins of drinking and smoking, and that the appetite was entirely taken away. He began to work among his friends to get them to become Christians and to stop drinking.

When Mr. Takahashi changed to Ichinoseki, there was no pastor for the church at Azabu for two years, and during that time Mr. Sato and Mr. Tajima, another early Christian, worked for the church, helping Dr. Woodworth and Miss Penrod as much as they could. Then God sent Mr. Matsuno. Later, January 1, 1904, Mrs. Sato was baptized and also a younger sister of Mr. Sato's. She became a good SS worker.

Mr. Sato was then supt. of the SS and continued such until he went to England ten years later for the Kuhara Co., which company he had joined in 1905. He gradually went higher in his work because his employers learned that they could trust him. The Kuhara Co. is one of the biggest copper-mining companies in Japan. They have holdings in Korea, China and Japan.

Mr. Sato is now managing director of the trading department. He was the pioneer of the company in opening an office in a foreign land, London. He lived with an English family who proved to be good Christians, and during the year and a half he lived with them, he grew as a Christian.

He gave me the names of the family as follows: Mr. Ichijuro Sato, Mrs. Umeno Sato, Miss Miyo Sato and Miss Hoshino Sato. He explained that the last named means "star in the field." She was born on Christmas day 12 years ago, 1908, both parents being Christians at the time.

After my conference with Mr. Sato, we returned to the music room where Mrs. Sato served us delicious coffee and cakes. After a short season of prayer, we bade them goodbye, realizing that here was a Japanese family demonstrating the fact that Christianity and the culture going with it can do great things with the lowly of this land as well as our own. Mr. Sato now has a very fine position and has a large income.

Saturday, November 27 ———————— ◆ ————————————————

Dr. Woodworth and I went to Yokohama this morning. I did a little shopping and went to see Mr. C. Jan Yong, the Chinese who had made some shirts for me. He would not listen to my advice to follow the pattern shirt I had brought before and declared he knew how to make the shirts by measuring me. I trusted him, with the result that they were too small across the chest. He was not in this morning, and I had to leave the shirts, with the understanding that they would fix them up. It was amusing to see how they intended to do it at first. The young Chinese said they would fix them by putting in a whole new front. That sounded very plausible, but I remembered that I had some of the goods sent from Korea. I asked him where he would find goods to do it with. He replied, of course, it would have to be different goods. But he finally said he would try to find the right kind.

While in Yokohama, we visited the first Protestant church building built in Japan. It is a little old-style church known by some now as the Dog-kennel church. This title came to it through some one who was antagonistic to the builder, Dr. Ballagh. The latter secured the money from America and built the church and also a new home for himself. Someone, I have forgotten who, became on the outs with him and seeing the little church and the big house, took pictures of them and sent them back to America, calling attention to the contrast between the home and the "Dog-kennel church."

I took a picture of the church inside and out, and also the home of Dr. Ballagh, the founder. In the new building, which stands near, I found a tablet engraved as follows:

American Mission Memorial Church. To commemorate the arrival in Yokohama of the Rev. Samuel R. Brown, D.D., Nov. 1, 1859 and the Rev. James H. Ballagh, D.D., Nov. 11, 1861. Representatives of the Board of Foreign Mission of the Reformed Church in America. Through whose efforts this property was secured and the First Japanese Protestant Church was organized on this site to the glory of Almighty God. March 10, 1872.

Dr. Woodworth and I paused for prayer together.

We next climbed the bluff to the home of Mr. R.H. Fisher, head of the Baptist School in Yokohama. He was not at home, but we talked with Mrs. Fisher. They have a middle school and commercial school. The aim is to make Christian businessmen for Yokohama. Best leaders of the Baptist mission come from the North. Foreign teachers and businessmen are so ungodly that their influence is demoralizing on the Japanese. The Baptists are just starting the school. There are 241 enrolled at present in two classes. Plan is for the full five-year middle school course and the commercial school. Tuition is Y3.50. Dormitory has been started. The principal is a Japanese and receives Y175 plus Y25 for entertainment.

The plans when completed will accommodate 600 students. Land belonged to the province and was sold to the mission at Y10 a *tsubo* through the efforts of the governor of the province, who is favorable to Christian education.

The Baptist compound on the bluff was built by the Rev. Goble. He also invented the *jinrikisha*. He had an invalid wife and invented the *jinrikisha* for her. Japan took it up, and it became the principal means of conveyance.

After our visit to Mr. Fisher's, we hurried back to the train and started for Tokyo. It was dark when we arrived at the station, and Dr. Woodworth was not up-to-date on the present streetcar system. Consequently, we lost our way and went many miles beyond where we should have gone. Finally we reached home ready for a good supper. Remained at home this evening.

Sunday, November 28 ———————— ◆ ————————————————

Mr. Garman and I started out this morning to visit Mr. Sato in order to get a picture of the family, which we did. We then went past the Azabu church in an effort to find Mr. Tajima, the treasurer, whom we wished to interview as to his life and conversion. He was not there, but we saw the Sunday school in session and met Mr. Matsuno, the pastor, who asked if I would preach. We explained that we intended to go to the Ginza M.E. church in order to have an interview with the Rev. Ukai, the pastor, regarding the Forward movement of the Japan M.E. church. I noticed also that Mr. Matsuno's subject was announced and that it was in keeping with the special celebration of Bible Day.

The matter was left undecided while we went on to Mr. Tajima's. I told Mr. Garman that I felt it would be wrong to speak in Mr. Matsuno's place since he had already announced his subject. Mr. Tajima was not at home, having gone to the church another way. We rode back to the church, intending to stay a few minutes and then go to the Ginza M.E. church. Arrived just as SS was being dismissed, and at the last minute Mr. Garman decided that we had better stay here and go to the Ginza some other time.

We stayed without telling Mr. Matsuno of our change in plans, but in the midst of the service he announced that I would preach. I was completely dumbfounded as I was not expecting to be there for the service at all. I spoke about 25 minutes in an effort to lead up to the subject Mr. Matsuno had announced for himself and then turned the meeting over to him. Instead of speaking as I thought he would, he called on Dr. Woodworth, who spoke a few minutes, after which the service was dismissed.

Went to the Ginza M.E. church early after lunch and met Dr. Ukai, the pastor, who has had so much to do with the Japan Methodist Forward movement. He is a very fine gentleman and was very glad to tell us the story of the movement.

It was started by the inspiration of the M.E. centennial movement in America. In March 1919 the matter was presented to the East and West Japan conferences. A special committee of ten was appointed from each of the two conferences, but without instructions. Each committee appointed five from each committee to meet at Nagoya to decide on a plan. They met and named the movement the Dai Sei Undo, the Great Accomplishment movement.

A year ago in November, the committee met again for more carefully studying the plan of the work. They decided to call all the district superintendents and one layman from each district. This assembly met at Kamakura September 15–17 for prayer and conference. On the second evening, when the question of raising money came up, the meeting came to a standstill. Prayed that night in small groups in hotels, church, seashore, among trees, etc. Next morning they came together and held a wonderful meeting. One layman said he prayed all night. "We have twenty thousand members," he said, "of which eighty-six hundred are resident members in the Japan Methodist church. It seems to me that one-half of that number ought to be able to give fifty yen a year for three years. That would make two hundred thousand yen a year for three years. I believe it can be done." The assembly agreed that it could be done.

One member said it was a big thing and that those present should agree to give one-tenth of their income or it could not be done. They prayed together and agreed to it. A man at once offered Y5,000, and in a half hour, Y20,000 was raised right there. A program of education followed. A large poster showing the map of Japan was made. Upon it were placed the words *To Christianize Japan.*

The following goals were made: Bible living; "Each one win one" (to double the membership); stewardship; *zai san sei betsu* (how the money will be used): Y150,000 permanent fund for supporting retired ministers. Pensioning system. Y100,000 endowment to educate young people. Y80,000 current fund to help support weaker churches, salary of bishop and mission boards. Y100,000 to help build churches and parsonages in country. Y20,000 for evangelistic work in Formosa and Manchuria. Y50,000 for Loan Church Extension Fund. Y5,000 for woman's work. Y5,000 for CE work. Y10,000 for SS work. Y30,000 for social service. The money campaign began this last September, and on November 25 the committee met and found they had raised Y615,400 for the three-year period.

Mr. Ukai's church raised Y53,390 with a membership of 300 members. It has led the movement in giving.

This Sunday a Thanksgiving service was held in M.E. churches all over the country, and today the spiritual work of the movement is to begin in earnest. Some said the spiritual work must come first and then get the money, but they have found that the giving of money awakened dead churches to new life, demonstrating that where the money is, there the heart will be also.

They have a SS poster showing that from 1907 to 1918, the SS was doubled. They want 20 percent increase in number of schools and officers and 30 percent in the number of scholars by 1923.

The quota given in the financial campaign was 115 times half the church membership. They set the amount for each member, and the committee called on them and told them what they expected. If they gave more or less, no questions were asked. The Rev. Ukai is enthusiastic over the results thus far.

I asked him about his own church, the Ginza M.E. With 300 members, the annual budget is Y6,000 plus Y1,100 benevolences. Twenty-four years ago, when Dr. Ukai came, the church paid Y5 a month toward the pastor's salary. Since then, they have become self-supporting, and two new churches have started from this mother church.

After the morning service at Azabu, Mr. Tajima told me the story of his life. At the age of 7, he lost the sight of one eye in an accident flying a kite. After this, he became a devout follower of the Nichiien sect of Buddhism in the hope of getting back the sight of the eye. He came to Iigura (Azabu) at the age of 17. When we opened a preaching place at Iigura (Azabu), Mr. Jones was in charge. Tajima began to come at the age of 24. Came not to listen but to disturb. The people of that street tried to stop the meeting. They thought Christianity was against God and country. Mr. Tajima stood outside at first. This was his first contact with Christianity.

When the people knew the mission was to open, they were determined to break it down. He went the first night to help do it and heard the preaching. When they found the house was owned by the mission instead of rented, they were disappointed. Mr. Tajima went three nights and stood outside, but on the third night, through the efforts of Mr. Ota, our first convert, who was helping Mr. Jones, he went in.

Mr. Ota was so kind, Mr. Tajima said, he could not resist. So Mr. Tajima became one of the first listeners of the gospel in our mission. He began to come regularly and was baptized seven months later, July 7, 1889 (the same Sunday that Mr. Matsuno was baptized in San Francisco).

At the time he was baptized, he was working in one of his relative's stores but was expelled from the house because he became a Christian. Had to shift for himself.

Mr. Tajima was so young, it was hard for him. Next year he opened his own store (pickle and spice store) at Mita, Shiba ku, where he is now. He made a small beginning, but the store has grown through hard work and perseverance. Now he is the head of the Sukemono, sho Kumiai (Pickle Merchants Association). If he continues, he will someday be the Heinz of Tokyo.

The church struggled on, and Mr. T. has stood by it all these years. When he was converted, his relatives persecuted him and continued so for years. When he opened the store, the people of the community decided to oppose him. He continued steadfast, and now his relatives trust him and seek his help in time of need. The community also trusts him in many ways. He is a representative of the community in public affairs, treasurer of the public school, etc. He receives letters of thanks from the Tokyo government for the service he renders in a small way. He holds many minor titles, which is exceptional since he is not wealthy or educated. Is thankful for the confidence they have in him.

Mr. Tajima is treasurer of the church and also a deacon. When he converted, he

Mr. Tajima, left, treasurer, Azabu Christian Church; the person at right is not identified.

wished to become a preacher, but knew he had no education so could not; therefore, he decided to be a strong Christian layman.

After our interview with the Rev. Ukai in the afternoon, Mr. Garman and I
went to the Union church service. After the service, we walked with Mr. Herzil to
Kasumi cho, three miles, in 37 minutes and part of the way uphill.

Remained at home in the evening and had a fine prayer meeting together. It was
worthwhile and one of the things I have missed most in Japan. I had hoped that
there would be many such meetings in the Kasumi cho household but found them
rather few. It seems that every one is too busy. Woodworths have them more frequently.

Monday, November 29 ——————— ◆ ————————————————

Mrs. Fry came this morning, and a mission meeting was held all day. There was much discussion but not much actual accomplishment. It seems to take so much time to do so little. The meeting continued all day. Tonight we rested.

The morning was given over to a prayer service and the fixing of the time for my message and also the communion service. After lunch, we discussed especially the matters pertaining to the joint meeting to be held with the Japanese brethren the next day.

Tuesday, November 30 ——————— ◆ ————————————————

Mr. Matsuno, Mr. Kitano, Mr. Irokawa, Mr. Tajima and Mr. Nikaido are the Japanese members of the consultation committee. The meeting was scheduled for nine o'clock. Mr. Kitano arrived at 9:50, Mr. Tajima at 9:40, Mr. Irokawa at 10:05, and Mr. Matsuno at 10:35.

I was asked to give a message and did so, stressing the fact that "we are workers together with God." I spoke of the value of the trip in the new acquaintances I had formed and the information I had received, and emphasized the purpose of it all to advance the work of the kingdom.

I urged that we are to promote the work by:

1. A program of intensive work. For the pastors, so many books read, so much Bible study, so much personal work, etc. For the churches, a certain number of baptisms each year, a certain SS and church attendance, an added emphasis on the stewardship of money, time and life.

2. A program to develop leaders. Putting members to work, getting them to adopt definite Bible study and prayer and soulwinning, seeking recruits for the ministry.

3. A program of more thorough cooperation with the mission, with the office at Dayton, by monthly reports, by conferences for prayer and Bible study, by a real forward movement in 1921.

We had lunch together. After lunch, Mr. Matsuno spoke at some length, stating that he thinks it wise to make Sendai one center and to establish a dormitory there. Wants Mrs. Fry to turn over the girls' school, kindergarten and church at Utsunomiya to us and let us employ a Bible woman there. In Tokyo we have no church building, of which we need not be ashamed. Therefore, we cannot have a forceful pastor. We are known still less than the small Friends church. Everywhere, he is taken for a Disciple when he goes into the country. Friends have concentrated in Mita Ward and have girls' school. In the country they have work in limited districts. Their missionary, Mr. Bordes, centers his effort in Peace Society work. And everywhere he is known, and the Friends church is known through him. Like to concentrate work in Sendai and in Utsunomiya, and in one place in Tokyo. If we are to build in Naka Shibuya, let us concentrate there. Azabu church is small and unattractive, and people come two or three times, then stop. Dr. Fukazawa's children came to SS from the neighborhoods but recently discontinued. Don't go anywhere. Doubt the usefulness of the SS. One thing—suitable SS rooms are not found. The most easy work for us to attempt is the dormitory rather than a middle school. If the dormitory is easier in Sendai than in Tokyo, so is the middle school easier there.

Bekkwa students can never become conference members, and in some way the organization must be revised to admit them. Does not know how it will come about. Treatment of *bekkwa* men is a problem to be dealt with. Shall we admit such men to our ministry as Mr. Taraha or only *honkwa* men? We must decide definitely. Wants all to cooperate.

Mr. Kitano says he would like both dormitory and middle school at Sendai if possible. Would like to see a good church built in Tokyo either at Azabu or Shibuya. Would like Mrs. Fry to turn over school to us.

Mr. Tajima says Azabu church shakes when heavy vehicles pass on the street. Expected it to fall few years ago. Wants American brethren to help build church. Not firmly built and cost only Y2,000. Outward appearance not so bad, but interior bad.

Mr. Matsuno says he thinks we understand the reason for slow growth toward self-support. Comes from poor selection of our field of work. West of Tokyo self-support comes easy, but east of Tokyo it is slow. East of Tokyo, Sendai, for example, has only self-supporting churches, excepting in progressive Hokkaido. UB has growing churches, but mostly between Tokyo and Kyoto. Not fault of pastors, but location responsible for slow results. But Japan is changing. Recently cabinet members for the first time came from East Japan. Azabu church member's father is treasurer of big firm. He says his high-priced goods are not sold east of Tokyo except in Hokkaido. Sendai self-support churches have not the best men but low-priced men. If all would practice tithing, self-support would be easy. Most money comes from families where all are Christians. Azabu church contributes about Y50 to Y60 a month, but recently expenses increased above the income. Have exact budget, but all has been coming in according to expectations. Several people are in financial straits.

Could you get all Christians to try tithing for three months, it would be a worthwhile experiment.

Hereafter, under the new plan of cooperation, the *nenkwai* (consultation committee) may be given new powers now wielded by the mission, as is being done in other churches.

Irokawa says if we would have a theological school again, it would greatly help. But if we have a school, it must be up to standard. Dr. Woodworth says other such schools are without students. Irokawa says a Bible school such as Dr. Woodworth proposes would be fine for beginners. Dr. Woodworth says he means it only as the beginning and that those who study there should go on to the theological school.

I took a number of facts from my notebook to show that our churches have men of sufficient ability to give largely to our work if they would tithe. I read the names of the men and the salaries they receive. The entire group joined in this, and it uncovered some valuable information.

One of the kindergarten groups at Narugo, Japan with Pastor Kitano and wife in the new building.

The entire day was spent in discussion, and among other things agreed to was the formation of a committee to attempt to work out some form of closer cooperation between the Japanese and the mission. We had no evening session.

Wednesday, December 1 ─────── ◆ ─────────────────

I led the morning devotions, after which the mission settled down for another day of work. Dr. Woodworth and the Rev. Kitano were asked to visit Narugo and ascertain the advisability of securing rented land from the RR for a church building and what the cost of such a building would be.

A committee of four was appointed, consisting of Mr. Garman, Mr. Fry, Mr. Matsuno and Mr. Tajima, to investigate the possibilities of revising the plan of cooperation between the Christian Mission of Japan and the Japanese Christian Conference. This committee is to suggest in the report the standard of representation to the cooperating body and define the limits of such cooperation.

It was moved that Mr. Takahashi Zendo be employed as assistant in one of our churches for the remainder of the year, at Y35 a month.

Brother McKnight conducted the communion service at eleven o'clock. Mrs. Fry did not remain in the room for the communion because, she says, it should be conducted on the day when the Japanese brethren are present. This is done at the Japan conference, but at this meeting the missionaries wish to have communion alone. The whole thing looks rather childish.

Miss Yoshie Matsuno, an accomplished pianist, second daughter of the Rev. K. Matsuno, D.D., pastor of Azabu church.

Moved that the bills for one-third of the cost of the two religious volumes bought by pastors be paid by the mission. Moved that Mr. Fry be made treasurer of the mission upon his return and during the absence of Mr. Garman.

I did not succeed in getting any further notes. The entire missionary force went to the Rev. Matsuno's for dinner tonight. A very fine combination American-Japanese meal was served, after which the daughter played for us. We talked over some of the problems of the work and then returned home.

I sat up late and endeavored to get together some of the things that had been left undone in the meeting. Mr. Garman was not himself at all during the entire session and was not dependable at all. He was not sleeping at night and seems to be under a very heavy mental strain. I have tried to stir him to do something, but to no avail. I fear I have hindered rather than helped. He speaks constantly of what should have been done but has not been done. He says this and that was planned for, but that the plans did not carry, etc. It looks as though it would have been infinitely better for the work and for him had he stayed in America when he was there. He has done practically nothing since his return. I fear the strain of being away from his family is telling on him. I went over the agenda carefully after recalling the tentative decisions that were made today, though no votes were cast. I drew up resolutions to cover the items in the hope that they might be presented tomorrow and be passed.

Thursday, December 2 ——————— ◆ ———————————————

Inasmuch as the present church property at Naka Shibuya is being menaced by the building of an increasing number of houses of ill repute on land adjoining our lot and in the immediate vicinity thereto, thus changing the moral tone of the community and consequently necessitating a change in our location or a change in our program of service there, resolved that we recommend to the mission board the advisability of seeking a new location for the church in Naka Shibuya in a community more suitable to our type of work and that the present property be sold when suitable arrangements for the continuance of the work can be made. This motion presumes that the mission board will permit the mission to appropriate temporarily the money now on hand for the mission home lot for this purpose, with the understanding that fund will be reimbursed as soon as the present church lot is sold.

Resolved that the future erection of a mission home in Naka Shibuya must of necessity be contingent upon whether it is the purpose of the board to enter into a more extensive program of service for that community, requiring the presence of a missionary in the field.

Resolved that it is the sense of this mission that regardless of what advance work our church may decide to undertake in Japan, we must continue to supplement the advance work with the steady development of the present lines of activity, namely: (1) The evangelistic work, embracing at the present time not an extension of our present field but the intensive work of developing the present work in every preaching place by a more earnest effort to gain converts and by the teaching and training of the new converts and church members in the things pertaining to the Christian life. This is to be done through the pastor and each department of Sunday school and Christian Endeavor and regular church. (2) The laying of steady emphasis upon the kindergarten work and the normal extensive of the same. (3) The securing of land and building of new churches in our present field wherever practical. (4) The constant effort to cultivate promising young men for the ministry. (5) The conduct of Bible classes by the various members of the mission, the same growing out of personal contact with young people through the churches and through teaching English in the various schools where such opportunities can be accepted. (6) The acceptance of our responsibility's share in the various interdenominational activities conducted on the mission field. (7) The development of the building project for a mission home, a new church, kindergarten and night school building at Naka Shibuya as already voted by the board.

In addition to the above-mentioned normal work, it is the sense of this mission that the board can with great profit adopt one of the following suggested programs for an enlarged work: (1) A middle school of our own. (2) Middle school and theological school in connection with the Disciple school, possibly on a larger scale than at present undertaken by them alone. (3) Two dormitories, one at Tokyo and one at Sendai, together with a Bible training school. (4) A social service institution at Shibuya or Oji or both, together with a larger program for kindergarten work.

With the exception of the second named, special provision would have to be made for the training of theological students with some existing theological school through the supplying of a missionary teacher and the payment of a certain sum each year to the school. This would entitle us to admit students to the school at regular rates and would give us the advantage of having our men in personal supervision of the students enrolled from our church.

Inasmuch as the proposed new system of cooperation will of necessity involve the question of advance steps in self-support and increased membership on the part of our churches, resolved that Mr. Matsuno and Mr. Kitano, with Mr. Garman and Dr. Woodworth, be constituted a committee to work out a definite plan whereby the churches may be helped and encouraged to make marked progress along the lines mentioned before the proposed new plan of cooperation becomes effective. The plan to be known as the Christian Workers' League of the Japan Mission and to embrace the securing of definite pledges from missionaries, pastors and lay members to consecrate their money, their time and their lives to the service of God through the church of which they are members. It is the understanding that this plan is to comprehend first of all a quiet campaign for the enlistment of every missionary and every pastor to give one-tenth of his income to the service of God, to covenant to pray daily for the work of the kingdom, especially through our church to devote themselves fully to the work of the kingdom to which they have been set aside. It is further to comprehend a plan by which pastors, with the help of the missionaries, shall quietly but diligently seek out men and women of their congregations who will sign a similar pledge to give one-tenth of their income to the Lord, to read the Bible, to pray daily for the work, and as frequently as possible to lead young persons to dedicate their lives to the ministry.

Resolved that beginning January 1, 1921, the pastors be furnished with suitable report blanks covering the general activities of the church, upon which they shall on the first day of each month make a report of the activities suggested for the month just past. This report is to be made out in triplicate, one copy to be retained by the pastor and the other two to be forwarded to the treasurer of the mission each month, one copy of which shall in turn be forwarded by him to the mission office at Dayton, Ohio. The purpose of this is to check up on the work being accomplished and to furnish information to the backers of the work in America.

Resolved that the missionaries in each district shall work out a suitable plan by which the pastors in their fields may be brought together once every two months for conference, Bible study, and prayer, aiming to deepen the personal spiritual life of each pastor and to confer in the solution of problems.

Resolved that the missionaries in each field assume responsibility for getting at least one article a month to the mission secretary.

After these items were read, it was decided to take them up one at a time. The first one was reread, and Mr. McKnight offered a counterresolution seeking to fix the amount the board should send for the purchase of the new lot, thus misunderstanding the entire resolution. A great deal of discussion came out of this that clouded the point at issue and led to the statement that the mission board had not kept its word in sending the mission orders to go ahead with the night school building and mission home in Shibuya, inasmuch as they had not sent the money following the order to go ahead. This confused the point concerning the securing of permission to use the money in hand for the new church lot and led me to believe that the money was not in hand. The entire group stuck to their point that their hands had been tied by the lack of funds from America. I declared that the board should be held responsible for the matter. At this point, the Woodworths rose to catch the noon train, and nothing else was done.

After they left, I continued to question Mr. Garman, who finally stated that he had Y23,000 on hand for the mission home and some Y11,000 for the night school building and church; Y10,000 of this is borrowed, but even then, he has plenty to buy the new church lot. I urged him to reconcile this with the statement that the board had not sent funds, and he frankly admitted that he had not attempted to use the money for the mission home lot because of the feeling he had arrived at that the church would have to be changed. I told him my resolution was aimed at that very thing, and he admitted that I was right. I agreed that the board was wrong not to have sent additional money needed for the home, but it was not right to accuse them of holding up the proposition to buy at this time for the home, for the money for that purpose is actually in hand.

After lunch, Mr. Garman, Miss Stacy and I went out to visit the Shibuya kindergarten. We found our suspicions confirmed that there will soon be *geisha* houses practically on two or three sides of our church lot and the hopes for continuing the work there are very poor. The kindergarten is doing great work and needs to be encouraged, but in a different location. The problem is to find a suitable place. Miss Stacy is fitting in to the work in fine shape here. She conducts two classes, usually on Wednesday afternoon, and it was intensely interesting to see the way the children responded in English. It was a dark day, but I attempted several pictures.

After this, we inspected several lots. One on the main street in a good location seems too small. Later we found it was not available. We walked over to a location near the Imperial University agricultural department where the first lot I saw when coming to Shibuya several weeks ago was again looked at. I still feel, as I did then, that this lot should be bought. It has 300 *tsubo* and would be suitable for either a church or a home. Mr. Garman felt that it was too far away from the kindergarten, but as we walked over, Miss Stacy discovered a number of her children going home in that very neighborhood. The lot, we learned later, can be bought at Y60 a *tsubo*, and Mr. Taizumi, who has been looking for land for us, says that the lot of our present site is worth Y150. There is a house on this one, however, and not on the other. Even then, it looks like a good exchange.

The Azabu church gave me a farewell reception tonight. There were not many present, but we had a most enjoyable time. Those present gave their testimonies, and I gave a closing message. The church presented me with a dozen beautiful handkerchiefs in four different colors.

Friday, December 3   ◆

Went over some financial figures with Mr. Garman in the morning and continued packing. In the afternoon we went downtown to finish some shopping and to get money, etc. It was a long, tiresome trip with so many little things to think about.

When we arrived home, it was quite late in the afternoon, and I had but little

Miss Stacy and her Japanese friend.

time to finish up my packing and get my trunks off to the station. While I was downtown, Mrs. Sato and her maid had come and left three beautiful presents for my wife and children—two handbags for the girls and a beautiful silk picture for Mrs. Minton. Miss Watanabe called with a package to be delivered to Mr. Taizumi at Defiance, and Mrs. Taizumi also called with a package for the boy. Miss Watanabe also left two beautiful Japanese dolls for my two girls, and Mrs. Taizumi left a beautiful lacquer cake set of three pieces and a doll and cradle. The latter was in glass, and I could not take it, so gave it to Alice Elizabeth. Mr. Kitano left a package for Mrs. McCord with me Wednesday. Mrs. Woodworth gave me a beautiful lacquer box; Mrs. McKnight, two little boxes for the girls. Miss Stacy also gave me two little handkerchiefs for the girls, and Mr. Garman gave me a fine damascene stickpin, which I prize very highly. I have received so many things that it is difficult to remember them all.

We hurriedly got the trunks off, three of them, Mr. Garman sending one full of bedclothes for his family. After this, we talked somewhat of the work and had prayer together before retiring. After the others had retired, I sat up as usual and worked on some final reports, etc. I got a copy of all the matters mentioned in the mission meeting, so far as that was possible, and left a copy of my proposed resolutions with Mr. Garman in the hope that somehow he might get them into the recorded action of the mission, since practically everything in them had been agreed upon by the mission, though no formal action was taken.

It was nearly 2:00 A.M. when I retired for a short rest, though little sleep.

VII. The Return Home

Was up early and busily engaged in final preparations for the homeward trip. Mr. Garman, Mr. and Mrs. McKnight and Miss Stacy went to Yokohama with me to see me off. Mr. Takahashi went ahead to see that the trunks were put on board, etc. Mr. Oishi, Mr. Matsuno, Mr. Ishigaki, Miss Watanabe, Mrs. Taizumi, Mr. Tajima, Mr. and Mrs. Takahashi of Oji, and I do not remember how many more, went to Yokohama with us. Mr. Taizumi called very early in the morning dressed in full frock suit and apologized for being unable to go to the boat because he was sick.

I left an envelope with a little money in it for each of the servants at the house, and at 8:20 we took the car for the station and from there by electric car to Yokohama.

I had left my shirts to be remade at Yokohama and had heard nothing further from them, so when we reached the station, we took rickshas and started for Mr. C. Jan Yong's to see about them. He seemed surprised that I was leaving, though I had left word to that effect. Said they had not told him, but if we would wait a few minutes, he would get the shirts ready. After a wait of some 15 or 20 minutes, he brought them in, explaining that he had put new backs in the silk shirts and had let the other one out a half inch on either side. I had to take his word for it, and hustling into the ricksha after making a few final purchases, we rushed to the dock. Many of the party were there ahead of us, and we were soon on board, the friends being allowed on board for about 30 minutes but compelled to leave at 11:30 since the boat sailed at noon.

We found my cabin a very fine large one, with Mr. Delara and Mr. L.J. Griffen, Yokohama businessmen, as fellow passengers. It developed that Mr. Delara has his wife and two children in the next cabin, and he is intending to remain there except in case of emergency, so Mr. Griffen and I have the cabin practically to ourselves. It is one of the best on the boat with a nice writing desk and chair, two washstands, and a good-size clothes closet besides many hooks on the walls. It is on the port side and nicely fitted up with electric lights and electric fan, etc. I judge it to be almost half as large again as the one I had on the *Korea* coming over.

But to return to my story. My friends came to see my cabin, and the Kasumi cho bunch left a large box with me, which is not be opened until we get out to sea. From the message on the outside, I judge it is food for the fishes. They read: *To be taken in doses according to the condition of the patient. Warranted to contain no honey.* (We had honey every day at Kasumi cho, and I am fond of it.) *All worms found carefully removed before packing.* (Miss Stacy, Mr. Garman and I had bought some wormy peanuts one night in Juban and had eaten some before we discovered their nature.) *When this you see remember me, and how you always picked on me.* (That is from Miss Stacy, I am sure.) *Uncle Sam's in small quantities only.* (That's from Garman. He had bought a huge amount of a breakfast food called Uncle Sam's Breakfast Food, and it was the most unappetizing stuff I have ever attempted to eat. No one else would eat it, so he was bravely undertaking to eat the entire lot a little each morning when Woodworths came to the rescue and took several packages off his hands.) *The contents should be taken with a grain of salt.*

I took a picture of the group on deck. At 11:30, they had to leave the ship. They went to the dock just below where I stood, and then I was introduced to one of the pretty customs of departing vessels at Yokohama. Rolls of colored-paper ribbon (used for string in Japan) were given me, and just as the vessel started, I threw these to the friends on the dock, retaining one end in my hand. Scores of other passengers did likewise, and with these great streamers lengthening as we proceeded, we held off the final separation as long as possible, if only by means of the slender cord. Mrs. Mc-Knight, Miss Stacy, Mr. Garman and Mr. McKnight held them on shore while I held them on the ship. They walked to the extreme end of the dock, and our strings were among the last to break. Finally they gave way, and we were separated "until we meet again." It is a most beautiful way to observe the departure of friends and also helps break the strain incident to separation. With many *sayonaras* from my Japanese friends and goodbyes from the missionaries who are so bravely holding the fort, I was off. I waved the remains of the strings and my handkerchief as long as I could see people at the dock, even standing on the deck rail so that I might be seen if they were still there. One of the most impressive things I have seen is the departure of a great ocean liner. One never forgets the sight.

Went to tiffin at one o'clock and found that we were anchored in the harbor where we remained for three hours, not sailing until three o'clock. I do not know the cause of the delay, but I think it was for the purpose of inspecting the steerage passengers. We have 244 first-class passengers, 70 second-class and 702 in the steerage.

The *Shinyo* is a very fine ship of 22,000 tons and speed of 21 knots. She has triple-screw turbines and for this reason does not have the trembling that I noticed on the twin-screw *Korea*. She is said to be a trifle top-heavy, causing her to sway more than the *Korea*, but as yet I have not noticed it. She is elegantly furnished with a lounge for women and another for men, a palm garden, a social room, and many other features of luxury. The decks are a trifle narrower than those of the *Korea*, but this is more than made up by the additional space in the staterooms.

At four o'clock, I received my assignment to table sitting, chosing the first sitting, which is not quite so high class in point of dress as the second. Meals are breakfast, 7:30, tiffin, 12:00; and dinner, 6:00 P.M. This suits me fine. At my table on my right I find a Dr. Van Leauwen, who is director of the Botanical Gardens of Java. He is making a five-month trip in the interests of his work and, though Dutch, talks quite good English. There are three other Dutch people at this table—a husband and wife and another single gentleman. To my left I find Miss K.M. Kinsley, who for three years had been in charge of kindergarten work in northern Japan for the Episcopal church. She was out under a four-year contract with her sister but became so disgusted with the life and people of Japan that she gave up after three years' work, and leaving her sister to continue the fourth year alone, she has started for home. Next to her is Mr. Harvey, who professes to have been in Japan on a business trip but who in reality does not seem to be doing much of anything but having a good time.

This afternoon, soon after we started, Miss M.C. Bell, whom Mr. Garman and I had met at the Cobb's in Kyoto, hailed me in the corridor and told me an awful tale of woe about her stateroom. She said there was a woman and two children in her stateroom and she simply could not stay there. She liked children, but that was too much, and she had asked to be changed to some other room. She was also trying to rent a deck chair and a steamer rug, and the poor deck boy was doing his best to satisfy her. She had the usual number of questions to ask, most of which I could not answer, of course. I left her and a little later engaged a deck chair for myself. As the boy was about to place it on the starboard deck, I happened to glance at the name on the chair next to it, and lo and behold, it read *M.C. Bell.* Without betraying my emotions, I asked the deck boy to move my chair to the opposite side of the ship at once. He did so, none the wiser. How heartless and cruel I am becoming!

As night came on, Yokohama gradually faded not only in the approach of evening but in the lengthening distance. We were traveling along the shore of Japan, whose lights glimmered cheerfully as I retired for the night. I noticed as we left the harbor three fortified positions in the harbor itself, aiming at stopping any enemy vessel, but I could not help but think how inadequate such positions would be in the present system of warfare.

Fuji was not visible as we left the bay, the low-hanging clouds completely shutting her off from view. Other mountain peaks were seen, however, and I remembered again that Japan is seven-eighths mountains.

It has been a most interesting trip, and I have seen many things. Some things about our work were not so pleasant to face, and yet I guess we have wrought as well as possible with our limited means. As I went to bed, I prayed that the trip might not have been in vain and that our workers might be filled with new zeal and earnestness in the work with the prospect of larger resources in the future.

Sunday, December 5   ⸻   ◆   ⸻

I arose at 6:40 for my bath. As we expected, the night was somewhat rough, and the boat pitched and rolled a great deal. Despite it all, though, I had a fine night's sleep and got up feeling tip-top. But I had not been up long before I began to feel somewhat upset. I managed to get through with my breakfast, though I lost part of it soon after. However, I was not sick very long and attribute it not entirely to the motion of the vessel but to an overdose of medicine taken last night. I was one of only about a dozen or so at breakfast this morning, the balance of the passengers being unable to come from their rooms because of the roughness and seasickness. I negotiated tiffin without trouble and found only a few more present than in the morning. Dinner was a little better, but not much, as we are still rolling. After breakfast, I sat on the deck for sometime and am anticipating no more trouble from seasickness. The weather all day was cold and clammy with an overcast sky and a tossing sea. The boat seems much steadier than the *Korea* despite the sea, and the absence of the sickening tremble found on the *Korea* is very noticeable. After tiffin, I determined to catch up on some of the sleep lost in Japan and enjoyed an afternoon of real rest. Retired early tonight.

Monday, December 6   ——— ◆ ————————————

Bath, as is becoming usual, at 6:40. Find that we are advancing our watches about 25 to 35 minutes a day. The sea was somewhat calm this morning, but by noon we had headed straight into a regular gale with a driving rain and strong wind that lashed the sea and caused the boat to plunge and career almost as if she were drunk. Few people were on deck all day, many still suffering from the effects of seasickness, but I managed to take a mile or two around the deck during the day besides putting in about four hours' hard work on my notes. Am rapidly becoming regulated to my new mode of life, though it be but temporary. Want to get as much done as possible but find it difficult to do my typewriting anywhere else than in my cabin. Hope to get the bulk of it done before it gets too warm, as I fear it will be difficult to work here when it is warm. There is a fine little Japanese orchestra of five pieces aboard that plays during meals, and I am forming the habit of slipping up to the social room right after meals to listen to the music while folks at the second table have their meals. As I retire tonight, the sea is very rough, but I am anticipating a good night's sleep as usual. Mr. Delara has found that his wife and family have ample room for him in their cabin next to ours, so he has not been in to occupy his berth as yet. Says he thinks he will not need it. Pretty nice for Griffen and me.

Tuesday, December 7   ——— ◆ ————————————

Still rather rough this morning, but the sky seems to be somewhat clearer. Had about the usual routine today with some five hours or better of very hard work on my machine. Have to get at it whenever I can find the room empty so as not to disturb my cabinmate. Griffen is a typical businessman—a good mixer and straightforward in every particular. I like him, though he has no use for Christianity at all and thinks Christian missions in Japan absolutely idiotic. Says the Japanese go to the missionaries just for the English they can get, which is largely true, but even in this way, many get something besides English. He is on his way to New York on business for the Arthur and Bond silk shirt company of Yokohama. Will stop at Los Angeles en route where he has two boys preparing for Harvard. His wife and younger child are in Yokohama.

The monotony of the day was broken by Miss Kinsley coming to the tiffin table to say that a new roommate had come to her cabin, and that was a fright. She complained at everything and was a regular bore. A few questions from me brought out the fact that the new cabinmate is Miss M.C. Bell. She has succeeded in getting changed. Miss Kinsley said she was fearful for the harmony of the cabin. So am I.

At supper tonight, Miss Kinsley stated that they were having a time of it. All three in her cabin have been assigned to the first table, and they cannot get ready at the same time. Someone will have to change.

There were moving pictures tonight, but after the last one I saw on the *Korea*, I swore off, and I refuse to go again unless I have positive proof that the pictures are something else than the blood-and-thunder kind.

Did a little writing tonight and retired about ten.

Wednesday, December 8

We made 355 miles from Saturday afternoon until Monday noon and 308 from Monday to Tuesday noon. Up to noon today, we had made 346 miles. Miss Kinsley transferred to the second sitting today, and Mr. Harvey transfered to another table of the first sitting. I am finding my Dutch friends very agreeable and will stick, I think. They talk Dutch a great deal, but since the other two have left me, they have shown their ability to talk very excellent English. Besides Dr. Leauwen, who is director of the Botanical Gardens of Bruitenjoy, Java, there is a Mr. and Mrs. Meese (Maize), a wealthy banker of Holland, and a sea captain and wife whose names I have not yet learned. The wife of the sea captain has been quite sick with bronchitis ever since we started and has not been to meals.

Deck sports began today, but I kept at my work. Sea is smooth, but there is a rising wind tonight. Have written a lot of postcards and kept at my notebook.

Thursday, December 9

Made 332 miles to noon today. The weather is fine, with the exception of a very strong wind. Deck sports continue. I played a few games of shuffleboard and quoits, but just enough for exercise. I am making about two miles a day about the decks. Kept at my work, except when disturbed by my cabinmate bringing in some of his friends for a few drinks. Hope he doesn't overdo it. He is a might good fellow and very agreeable to have around. He is a good mixer and the type of man that would make a strong Christian worker if he would set himself to it. He is taking quite an active interest in the deck sports. I should have gone to see them this afternoon, at least for his sake, but I did want to get some of the work caught up, so missed it.

There is a moving-picture show and a dance on alternating nights. I have missed all of them so far and rather think I shall continue so.

Retired at about the usual time—ten o'clock.

Friday, December 10

We are slowly closing the gap between us and Honolulu. Made 348 miles today. Tomorrow is Meridian Day, which means it will be December 10 again. We are due

to arrive at Honolulu Monday sometime. The sooner the better for me, as I am getting anxious to get home. Saw the deck sports this afternoon. They were fine. The
Japanese had what they call cockfighting. Three of them would raise a fourth to
their shoulders, the latter having a cloth tied about his head. Another group would
prepare likewise, and then they would come together, the idea being to see which
man could pull the cloth from the head of the other. It was very exciting. And they
took it all in such fine shape.

Then there were the potato races, the three-legged race, thread-the-needle race,
and necktie-and-cigarette race. I stayed out of them all this time.

Have been having some long talks with Mr. Leauwen. He believes in no religion
whatsoever. I find it a little hard to talk with him as his English is a trifle peculiar,
but I am trying to impress him somehow. He said today he was sorry he could not
talk on religion better but that his vocabulary was small along that line. He has not
talked English to speak of until two months ago when he started this trip, though
he has studied it for a number of years. He says they begin to study it at 5 years of
age. Also had a good talk with Mr. Meece today and find him very interesting. He
seems to me to be a Christian, though I have not had opportunity to find out
definitely as yet.

More drinks in my cabin this afternoon after the sports. Griffen seems to need
them after the fray. He makes a mighty good manager of the games. Mr. Kitazawa
borrowed my music book tonight, explaining that a quartet is to sing Sunday morning. On inquiry, I find that the quartet is to consist of two Japanese and Mr. Griffen
and Mr. Harvey. I wonder if the last two will fit into the religious service as well as
they have been fitting into everything else.

Am all caught up on my notes and will now begin to index them. This will be
some task, but I will not have to do it in my cabin, and it will be much more enjoyable, I feel sure. Retired at ten as usual.

Meridian Day, Dec. 10 —————— ◆ ——————

Wrote several letters and a number of postcards. The day was given over to the
children on deck, and they had a great time of it. In the morning there were games
and contests, such as egg-and-spoon race, peanut race, potato race and a number of
games. This afternoon they had "placing the donkey's tail" and a contest in songs.
One little Japanese girl was by far the best, giving two motion songs in Japanese to
perfection. After the contest, I inquired and found that she had learned the songs at
a kindergarten. At four o'clock there was a tea party for the children.

Tonight the Japanese crew gave a wrestling contest that was very exciting. They
were all given names of various Japanese and American cities, and there was great
fun watching them. Some of them are very good wrestlers, as this is a favorite sport
in Japan.

We traveled 341 miles today and are about 1,065 miles out from Honolulu. We
should reach there around noon Monday. There has been a very heavy swell on the
sea for several days, and we are running directly into a head wind that tends to slow
up our pace.

Epilogue

by Ruth Minton Carstetter

The diary ends abruptly because it was nearing the Christmas season and Dad wanted to get home for Christmas Day. So his days on the boat returning home were spent with his trusty Royal portable. He made lists of every item in every suitcase, from his toothbrush to the small ceramic treasures and the yards of white silk he bought for dresses for his girls. He was hoping this would get him through Customs faster and it worked.

We were never allowed to see the tree or presents until Christmas morning. So Mother had us waiting in an upstairs bedroom, eyes glued to the window watching for Dad.

Finally a bright yellow taxi drew up at the curb. There was Dad, complete with Panama hat, camera strapped to his shoulder and all the bags and "grips" as he called them.

Then as the cab pulled away, Mother gave the signal and we all *flew* down the stairs. I'm sure none of us touched steps on the way down. What a Homecoming and what a Christmas!

We got dolls (one very old one from my Aunt) and desks, I believe. And then the Japanese presents. Two little girls in Japan had dressed a doll for each of us. Beautiful little Japanese dolls. How we loved them. But the presents were nothing of course compared to having Dad home.

April 1991

Appendix
Tokyo Sunday School Convention: Messages and Pageants

1. Marion Lawrence, "The Worldwide Progress of the SS Movement." He said there were three epochs in the development of the Sunday school movement:

> 1. The Rabbinical School—from the beginning of the Jewish race to the coming of Christ.
> 2. The Church founded by Jesus Christ—from the coming of Christ to the middle of the eighteenth century.
> 3. The Robert Raikes movement, 1780–1880. Raikes popularized the SS. As he went about the streets with the children, he was called "Bobbie Wildgoose and his ragged regiment." It is said that Raikes never conceived the idea of putting his own children in the SS.

2. Bishop George H. Bickley, of Singapore, who spoke on "The Necessity of a World Savior." This world is the organized constitution of the things in which we live. It includes all that interests or affects man. Wherever sin is found there is a need of a World Savior. World salvation means a regeneration of social conditions. It brings spiritual life to the individual. A part of the necessity for a Savior lies in human nature itself. It has the same fundamental characteristics the world over. A Savior who meets the needs of any group meets the need of all. The frailty of humanity calls for the Savior. He cannot save himself. God's righteousness shows His attitude toward sin. God's love shows His desire to save man from sin. Love found a way to do this. Love sent the followers of Christ to the world.

3. Mr. Trumbull spoke on "The Living Christ as the Life of the Individual," changing the one word *in* to *as* the life. Christ is not only in the life of the individual but He *is* the life of every believer. Phil. 1:21 contains a text from which Mr. Trumbull heard a preacher in London preach ten years ago and that changed his life. "To me, to live is Christ." Not to serve Christ, not to be like Christ, but "to me, to live is Christ." There is a vast difference between the life that is Christ's and the life that is Christ. Ill.: Pencil belongs to me, but is not a part of me. Hand belongs to me and is part of me.

What is it to be a Christian? Not doing the best we can. Not trying to do His teaching; not trying to live as He lived. It means to believe on Jesus Christ as Savior and let his Holy Spirit regenerate the life. The great danger today is the accepting of Christianity as a system and not accepting Jesus Christ as Savior. Christ is not the life of all men. John 5:11–12; Eph. 2:1 and 12; Rev. 20:14, 15. John 3:16 is the center of it all.

There are three tenses to our salvation: past, present and future. The past has to do with the first moment we believed. We were saved from the first and second death at that time. The future has to do with that which we shall receive when he comes. The blessed hope of the Christian. The present has to do with salvation from the power of sin. Rom. 6:4. Living in this present relationship to Jesus Christ, we are known as living epistles, known and read of all men.

Results from the life, that is Christ. The sustaining fellowship of Christ with God

299

becomes ours. Col. 2:6. Not by struggle but by faith. This is Christ's finished work but never-finished workings.

It means a new prayer life. The prayer life of Christ becomes ours.

4. The Rev. M. Uimura spoke on the "Sufficiency of Christ for the New Day, for the Orient." He said Christianity is not an ideal; neither is it a system of ideals. Many cults inculcated the ideals of Christ. But Christianity is the living Christ. In the personality of Christ we find the complete revelation of God to the world. Pres. D. Webster Kurtz of McPherson College, Kansas, continued on the topic. John 14:16. The true way of life is to live as sovereign over nature, brother to man and child of God. Man is to rule nature according to the plan of God. Jesus taught man his right relation to his fellow man. We are brothers, and God is our father. Jesus' gospel is a social gospel. The present world crisis is due to hate and greed. Jesus taught that man is a child of God. This means obey God, to be in tune with God. Life has no meaning or value unless grounded in a personal God.

5. Bishop S.S. Waltz, spoke on "The Bible as a Record of God's Revelation of Himself." There is a universal search after God. God is evident everywhere. The soul of man cries out for the living personal God. God has chosen only one way to reveal Himself to the human heart. In nature He is the God of power, in history the God of justice, but in the Bible we have all these combined for the soul of man. God gives us a record of his dealings with sin. A record of His plan of redemption from sin, a record of Christ not only as a Savior from sin but as a friend, a guide, a shepherd.

6. A pageant was given, entitled "The SS from Bethlehem to Tokyo." It was very well rendered. The first scene was the manger of Bethlehem, with the coming of the three Magi who presented gifts to the newborn king. In the next, the spirit of Christianity sends the light of the gospel to all the world through the SS. There came to this spirit of Christianity first an ambassador as a SS teacher who impersonated the convention topic "The Bible, God's Revelation to the World." Then followed an ambassador as the SS kindergarten teacher, impersonating the convention theme "The Christian Heritage of the Child." An ambassador as the SS evangelist, impersonating "The SS and the World Evangelism." An ambassador as religious education teacher, impersonating "The SS and Religious Education." An ambassador as the businessman as a SS worker, impersonating "The SS and Community Life." An ambassador as the SS scholar and patriot, impersonating "The SS and National Life." An ambassador as the World SS representative, impersonating "The SS and the New World." As these seven ambassadors had their torches lighted by the Spirit of Christianity, they went forth and returned, bringing in their order boy students singing "Break Thou the Bread of Life," primary children singing "Jesus Loves Me," burdened souls needing the evangelist and singing "Just As I Am," schoolgirls singing "Lord, Speak to Me That I May Speak," businessmen singing "Rise Up, O Men of God," children and adults representing the national life of Japan singing "Jesus Calls Us, O'er the Tumult," people of many nations singing "Let Every Kindred, Every Tribe."

7. Prof. Henry E. Dosker, of Louisville, then spoke on "The Bible as a Social Force." In the beginning he said, "You need not be afraid that I am going to be a nightcap for you. I have done many wrong things in my life, but never a long thing. I have excellent terminal facilities, which I will prove to you now." He then launched into a most excellent address and closed as he said he would.

8. Dr. H. Kosaki spoke on "Childhood in the Orient." The great problem since the war is reconstruction. The object and ideal of the SS is religious education, and to attain this, the SS has the cradle roll, the primary department, etc. The child is the great central fact in the SS life. Give me the first seven years of a child's life, and I will shape the entire life. These are the important years. Those who accept the faith in middle life find it is easily lost or cooled. In Japan we find such slipping out of the church, thus weakening the ranks of church life. Hence the time to secure the life is in childhood. As a child grows up, he begins to manifest the traits of his nationality. One is heredity, another is environment and a third is education. Education is easy in the earlier years. One of the great needs of Japan SS is organization. If properly handled, the SS of Japan should mount to a million or even millions. The coming of the kingdom on earth depends upon the winning of the child.

9. The Rev. Alvaro Dos Reis, of Brazil, was introduced to speak on "Childhood in Latin America." He invited the next convention to Brazil. The SS has exalted womanhood and childhood. The place of woman as a mother in Christendom is one of blessedness and honor and power. Physical culture alone will not save the woman and the child. Intellectual culture alone will not do it. These two together, even though wisely combined, will not do it. There must be the spiritual life that comes from God through faith in Jesus Christ. A description of the darkened condition of Latin America was then given.

10. The Rev. J.W. Butcher followed with a message on "Childhood in War-torn Europe." In Europe there is a great dearth of the essentials of life. Bread in Germany is black and saturated with sawdust. In parts of Poland, no bread has been seen for months, and other food is equally bad. Milk, so essential to child life, is scarce. In Germany no child over six is allowed milk. Millions of children are in war-torn Europe. Thousands contract tuberculosis and other diseases. Children are deformed because of years of slow starvation. Conditions in Poland are the worst. Weeds not known as human food are now eaten. Very little land is under cultivation. What is being done to help? The American relief work under Mr. Hoover has given meals daily to thousands of children between 6 and 14. Holland, Switzerland and Sweden have taken thousands of children into their homes and nursed them back to health. Italy has taken hundreds of children of her old enemy Austria. England has taken many. This makes for friendship between these nations.

11. Bishop Welch gave a strong message on "The Bible's Crowning Fact." 1 Cor. 15:3-6, 17. The great outstanding unifying fact about the Bible is that it reveals a World Savior. The center of the Bible is Christ. The supreme fact about Christ is his Resurrection. The two great things about which the preaching of the early apostles centered were the Crucifixion and the Resurrection. Jesus Christ is alive *now* and *forevermore*. What this means: (1) The miraculous is evident. (2) We are now the free children of a great God who holds the world in his Hand. (3) God does manifest Himself in the affairs of every day. The Resurrection of Christ opens the door of faith to the supernatural in human affairs. (4) The disciples, after His resurrection, knew they were living in the presence of a living Christ. (5) The relation of the Resurrection to the victory of goodness. Killed in innocence, Christ emerged a victor from the tomb. The apparent defeat was only a delay in God's plans for righteousness to conquer sin. (6) Now we live in a world in which nothing is too big to be believed, nothing too big to be achieved, because we are backed by the power of God in Christ.

12. The title of the second pageant was "The Rights of the Child." The first scene was religious education in the home. The Spirit of Religious Education enters the home and lights the four candles of helpfulness, fidelity, service and love to God. A Christian family enters and takes position around the study table. Father and mother renew their pledges to child life. The pageant choir sings:

> O happy home, where thou art loved the dearest,
> Thou loving friend and Saviour of our race,
> And where among the guests there never cometh,
> One who can hold such high and honored place.

The second scene: Evil spirits enter the home. Religious Education and the family are driven out by the Arch Destroyer of homes and her kindred spirits—Neglect, Falsehood, Temper, Cruelty, Intolerance and Selfishness. "We are the spirits of family hatred and neglect. We purpose breaking up every home."

Third scene: Evil spirits are driven from the home, and the family reenters to the music of "Home, Sweet, Home." The Spirit of Religious Education again lights the homefires. Scene closes with the family at prayer.

Fourth scene: Religious Education in the community. Enter Religious Education in the community, attended by heralds. Twenty-five enslaved children, representing the neglected children of any community, mutely appeal to Religious Education for help. Three Magi enter while the choir sings:

Christian, lo, the star appeareth;
Lo, 'tis yet messiah's day;
Still with tribute treasure laden
Come with the wise men on their way;
Where a life is spent in service,
Walking where the Master trod,
There is scattered myrrh most fragrant
For the blessed Christ of God.

Twenty-five Easter children, representing children loved and cared for in every community, enter singing:

Christ the Lord is risen today!
Alleluia!

Enter Spirits of Child Welfare, Education and Supervised Play, who appeal to Religious Education in behalf of enslaved children. Enslaved children are redeemed, and the Easter hymn is again sung. The Spirit of community service now leads to the platform representative of Tokyo organizations—the Mitsukoshi Band, the Boy Scouts, the Junior Red Cross, etc. The choir sings:

We are builders of that City,
All our joys and all our groans
Help to rear its shining ramparts;
All our lives are building stones.

For that City we must labor,
For its sake bear pain and grief;
In it find the end of living
And the anchor of belief.

Recessional.

13. World's SS Convention Demonstration Principal song:

1. Behold the shining garden of our Emperor,
   Of pure exalted teaching, banners upwaving.
   Behold earth's many peoples assembled from afar.
   How worthy transcendant, the glory of our God.
2. Hearken the swelling chorus voices of our children.
   To make this world thy kindgom, self-dedicating
   Body and soul we offer—Oh, listen as they sing.
   How gentle, how peaceful, the people of our God.
3. Awaken now ye kingdom, ye peoples of the earth:—
   Let the image of Jesus be formed in your hearts,
   Build the kingdom of righteousness and of holy love,
   How admirable, inspiring the Kingdom of our God.

14. Pres. D.W. Kurtz, of McPherson College, Kansas, on "Winning the World Through Its Childhood." He gave some fundamental facts:

1. The child of today is the adult of tomorrow. The culture of tomorrow depends on the training of today.
2. No culture, language or civilization is inherited by the child. These must come through education. Education is the supreme task of humanity.
3. God has provided for education by giving the human being a long childhood. Most animals mature quickly, but it takes a human being 25 or 30 years to mature. The mind must be developed while young. The high-water mark of conversion is 16. After 20, only 1 of 100 is converted. After 30, only 1 out of 1,000. The child is free from prejudice. Acts form habits, habits form character and character destiny.

4. Humanity is not in the grip of a relentless determinism. Whole nations have been changed in a generation by education. Ideas presented with emotion are the greatest dynamics in the world.

5. What we need for the winning of the world through its childhood is a vision of Christ as our only means of salvation. We need vision, consecration, loyalty, preparation. Teachers must teach the Bible so they may know the will of God, do the will of God. The teacher, to do this, must know God's word, the Bible. He must know how to teach. We must have organization. It is a means to the end of the kingdom of God. This is the epoch of the child. The Christian character is the supreme value and Christian education the supreme business. The highest patriotism is Christian education, since it builds an enduring nation.

15. Address by Dr. W.C. Poole, pastor Christ Church, London, England, "Healing and Helping a Wounded World." As a result of the World War, we have a wounded world, leaving her problems not less stupendous than the war itself. The first paroxysm of pain is over, but the dull ache of continuous anguish grips the world tonight: 60,000,000 are dead, and many times that number are incapacitated in their homes as a result of it. The very tissue of human life has been injured. The old question of Jeremiah is asked again: "Is there no balm in Gilead? Is there no physician near?" A convalescent patient is apt to be irritable, petulant, restless—the world after two years of convalescence is petulant, irritable, restless. The picture of the Good Samaritan reminds us that the Christian is the type of man who ministers to the man who falls among thieves, but Christianity is engaged in a bigger job tonight—the job of ridding the road of thieves, so that men can travel from Jerusalem to Jericho in safety. Ill.: The most stubborn case at the sheep gate, which Christ faced and healed. Typical of the case of the world tonight. It is a difficult task, but Christ can meet the need. Since Peter and John gave healing through Christ at the beautiful gate of the temple, the philanthropies of the world have come from the beautiful gate of the temple. Of course there have been philanthropies outside, but when we see the rainbow in the mud puddle, we give credit to the sun and not the puddle. Childhood is the medium for the reconstruction of the world through our Lord Jesus Christ.

The dream of a thornless world is as practical as any proverb. Who is to make real the dream? The Bible says, "Instead of the thorn shall come up the fir-tree." The Bible says, "*instead of*"—it means, "*instead of.*" Not trimming down a bad temper but getting rid of it. A thornless world is possible when we get thornless men and women.

16. The Rev. John T. Faris, D.D., on "Possible Cooperation Between Secular and Religious Education Agencies." He praised the education system of Japan. The United States spends $28 yearly on each pupil in the universities and colleges, while only 50 cents is spent by the United States on religious education. The present aim is to increase the half-hour-a-week Bible study in the SS by vacation Bible schools' cooperation with the public schools on the Gary plan. Many things done in America on these lines can be duplicated in Japan. Opportunities are offered for primary school work in Japan. The rules laid down are severe, but the effort is worthwhile. Japan has withdrawn the order of 1915 that religious instruction shall not be prohibited in private schools in Korea.

17. Bishop Welch spoke on Matt. 20:20, 28. If the greatest reality with which we have to deal is God, and Christ is the only true revelation of God, what is the reasonable life we should attempt to live? A life of intelligence, of course. The religion of Christ is the religion of light. The question of a trained Japanese woman botanist who could pick the flowers to pieces but wondered what was back of it all. Found that in a Christian school. "This is what I have been hunting." The great red thread running through the Bible is sacrifice and service. The path of service is that of the One who said, "I am as one who serves." Ill.: Jesus washing feet. Such was Christ's life all the time.

There are two great principles in human life—the principle of mastery and the principle of service. The first has done much, but the second lies at the very heart of civilization, and without it there is no civilization.

Bishop Welch said he dreamed once that a man was falling down an open elevator shaft.

Could have reached out and saved him, but he did not. Then his dream changed, and he thought he was falling instead of the other. "So he that would save his life shall lose it and he only that would lose his life in service shall save it."

The belief that a man is in the world to make money is the worst form of modern atheism. The characters whom we love in fiction and history are not the great masters of men but those who lost themselves in service to others.

18. The Rev. W.E. Chalmers, D.D., education secretary of the American Baptist Publication Society. His subject was "The SS Program for Religious Education." Every Christian must be a soldier. He must be garbed in the helmet, breastplate, and girdle that holds the others together.

He mentioned a threefold truth:

> Truth of the knowledge of God,
> Truth of the law of God,
> Truth of the grace of God.

He described a primary teacher teaching by acting the story of the Good Shepherd to children. This is illustrating the truth of the knowledge of God.

The truth of the law of God. There is a feeling of independence in early life. Ill.: Father hiding from him as he looked into a shop window on a busy street. The relief when Dad steps out from [behind] the telephone pole. Time comes when a boy loses that feeling of dependence. At that place the junior boy needs us most, but he then most easily slips from us. He must be given the law of God.

The truth of the grace of God. The greatest educational fact is not the spoken word but the life lived. Ill.: Looking through cracks into prayer meeting to see if *she* was there. Same old crowd every week; same old long prayers; but he as a boy knew those people lived as they prayed. Ill.: Father and mother of boy in city, having family worship on the old farm.

19. Miss Magaret Slattery, "The Full Achievement of Personality, the True Aim of Education." It takes great courage to look out upon the world today that we have presented to the childhood of this age. We need to apologize to them for the world we have given to them. Description of desolate Europe where Miss Slattery worked. France and Armenia—not a sound of laughter, not a smile on a child's face. That is what we have given to the childhood of Europe. Ill.: Machine perfected just before close of the war that could by the length of vibrations register the approach of an airplane and determine whether it was an enemy or an Allied plane. Miss Slattery saw this on the banks of the Marne among the tombstones of countless killed. Man could make that—but man had not learned to make a society that could keep them from killing each other. Ill.: Telephone 3,000 miles. Cable from Shanghai to Boston. Man can do anything. And he can make a world that will give freedom to children. The war is not over, it has just begun. War is the clash of ideas, and in every nation there is the clash of the idea of *getting* and the idea of *giving*.

We must fit the mind, body and soul of the childhood of today to meet the clash that is on. We are beginning to train the mind and body. Germany did this, but she failed to touch the soul. And Germany failed as a nation. If we would fit the childhood properly, we must touch the soul. We must not cheat their souls. We must teach them that those who give their lives to the making of things and not to the making of men shall surely die.

Thousands of factories in America with thousands of girls. Japan, you are just beginning to use your girls in your factories to make things. God help you to make girls with your things. As I hear the tramp of little feet over all the world, I say to them, "We will give you that which will save you from the errors we have made by giving you that purpose and that program of Jesus which is to make of all nations one brotherhood. Thou shalt love thy neighbor as thyself." It meant a cross to Him to set up such a purpose and program, and we must give it to the children, even though it be a cross to us—that a new world may be born in them through that purpose and program.

20. Bishop Welch spoke on "The Love of Righteousness." The interests of Christ are as wide as human welfare. Hence the interests of the SS must be as wide as human welfare.

Questions of social import, play, work, sanitation, wages, etc. are not alien to the Sunday school. Those who think the Christian should not meddle with these things I will not argue with. I leave them to face Jesus Christ Himself on this question. Ill.: The extreme spiritual needs of Peter on the morning following the night of toil in fishing was followed by the miraculous draught of fishes. Jesus did not upbraid Peter for betraying him at the crisis of His life; instead, Jesus recognized the fact that they were worn and hungry, and He prepared food for them. Then after they were warmed and fed, He asked Peter, "Simon, lovest thou me?" Jesus met him on his physical plane first and then on the higher plane. So must the SS do as a ministering agency in His name. But don't forget that Jesus did not stop when he fed the body. His greatest service to Peter was to change his heart. That is the supreme service of the SS to the community—to lead it to the righteousness. This is to be done not by forcing but by drawing from within.

Christianity is not a matter of mechanism. There is a place for form and ritual, but they are subordinate to the great service of practical ministration to a needy world. If a man merely crosses the boundary line of Christian faith, he is a Christian, even though his Christian life is but in the embryonic state. But there are for such a man great and far-reaching experiences in the Christian life. Name it what you will, it is possible for a Christian to reach that plane where he loves righteousness and hates sin, not because of public opinion but because of a right heart. There is a point where earthly gravitation ceases and heavenly gravitation becomes a reality.

21. Address, the Rev. Rufus Miller, SS secretary, Reformed church, "The Community School as a Social Force," The church and community are responsible for religious education. The spirit of community service goes not farther up toward God than it goes out toward man. A plea for a community service by the SS, touching all phases of community life, based upon the teaching of the Bible.

22. Pageant, "The City Beautiful." It is a pageant of the historical type, having for its central idea "The Redeemed City." The first two scenes are biblical. One, by the realistic interpretation of Hebrew dramatic literature, depicts the triumphal entry of David into Jerusalem. The other visualizes to the audience Christ's entrance on Palm Sunday. The third scene deals with the heroic attempts of the Crusaders to wrest the Holy City from the hands of the infidel. The fourth shows the forces of evil at work among the children of the modern city. The fifth reveals the power of Christianity to overcome these forces of evil—cruelty, ignorance and crime. The last looks forward to the ideal, the New Jerusalem, where the streets shall be full of happy children and where justice, righteousness, and love shall prevail.

Musical themes:

1st Scene—The Jews enter Jerusalem under King David:
Lift up your heads, O ye gates
and be ye lifted up, ye everlasting
doors, and the King of Glory
shall come in.

2nd Scene—Children Singing "Hosanna," on Palm Sunday:
From out the peaceful village,
Along the sunlit way,
The Prince of Peace leads onward

A Pilgrim band this day,
Then, lo! with shout triumphant
They hear the hillside ring,
With shouts of crowds that hasten
To greet their Prophet King, Hosanna!

3rd Scene—(a) The Holy City under the Mohammedans.
          (b) Conquered by the Crusaders.
Mohammedan call to prayer: God is great!
                    Alla-hu-ak-bar!

The cry of the Crusaders and their attack upon the city.

4th Scene — A modern city — a street in Tokyo — buying and selling, and children playing. The forces of evil enter to *Prelude* in C-sharp minor — Rachmaninoff.

5th Scene — The City of the New World Order. The ringing of chimes scatters the evil forces and ushers in the Bell Ringers:
Ring out old shapes of foul disease;
Ring out the manowing lust of gold;
Ring out the thousand wars of old;
Ring in the thousand years of peace.
Ring in the valiant man and free,
the larger heart, the kindlier hand;
Ring out the darkness of the land;
Ring in the Christ that is to be.
The city beautiful with her allies now enters. She sings:
I am the City Beautiful
Where all the children play.
The prophet's vision of the ideal city. The Allies — Church, Playtime, Child Rights, speak. All pageant participants:
We are no more strangers and foreigners,
We have been brought near by the death of Christ.
Our city is built upon the foundations of the apostles and prophets —
Jesus Christ himself being the cornerstone.
All sing. Coronation. Recessional.

23. Address by the Rev. J. Williams Butcher, of London, on "The SS as a Builder of True Citizenship." The citizenship of tomorrow depends upon the education of the children of to-day. Individual religion and community religion are not antagonstic — they are complementary. Selfishness is the seed of all sorrow. There is not only selfishness of the individual but of the class of the community and of the nation. The kind of service needed is that which cares for every brother's well being instead of my own welfare.

Salvation and service stand related. The true solution of the strife between capital and labor is found only in the acceptance by both sides of the ethics of Christianity.

24. Address, the Rev. F.W. Langford, "The SS as a Teacher of True Patriotism."

1. The worship program of the SS.
2. The instruction it may give in patriotism.
3. The service program of the SS.

1. Singing right kinds of hymns inspires patriotism. National anthems. Hope that jingoistic songs may be kept out. Public prayers in SS offer an opportunity for developing the spirit of patriotism. Matters of state and national interest should be mentioned in the SS prayers.

2. Old Testament is a literature of the most intensely nationalistic people. The lesson material of the SS comes largely from the Bible. Isaiah, Ezra, Nehemiah, etc. were great patriots. NT teaching of Jesus, emphasizing purity, love, service, etc., builds up patriotism. Jesus teaches people to love righteousness and so makes for true patriotism. Missionary instruction in SS leads to patriotism by showing the good and bad, the strength and weakness, of our own as well as other people.

3. The program of service activity of the SS provides means for the promotion of patriotism. Carrying flowers to the sick, etc. No one can be a true Christian without being a true patriot.

25. Address, Bishop Herbert Welch, "The Basis of Fellowship." 1 Pet. 2:11–17. The whole course of development of natural history has been toward mutual regard. Among men it is the same: (1) the individual; (2) family; (3) class; (4) nation. Self-regard is instinctive, family

regard easy. The family can serve as a training school for learning the rights of others. In the larger groups there must be certain forces to bind men together. The finest type of fellowship is that which is based on a faith, a common ideal. Christianity offers that faith. Other nations, it is true, accepted Christianity with some misgivings as a foreign religion. The Greeks and Romans saw it as a Jewish religion, the Japanese as an Anglo-Saxon religion, etc. But Christianity affords the soundest basis for nationality. Three forces hold nations together:

1. An effort to the common defense. Fear. Ill.: France.
2. The appeal to conquest, national pride. Greed. Ill.: Germany.
3. The idealistic motive. The desire to raise the national life to the highest for others.
Ill.: China nine years ago in establishing a republic. Another illustration is found in Russia—Bolshevism—but it is this case working through the wrong means.

In the effort to establish national unity, the appeal to fear and defense is abnormal. It implies conquest in the offending nation. The spirit of conquest is just as abnormal because it creates a spirit of fear and defense in the defending nation.

The only motive left to which we can safely appeal is the idealistic motive that helps us to shape the enthusiasm of a people. The weakness of the idealistic motive in the past has been too transcendent. When the enthusiasm dies away, the idealism has been lost. If the idealistic motive could be maintained, it is the proper motive. It can be maintained by the Bible faith. It is righteousness that exalteth a nation, but sin is a reproach to any people. Our pride is not to be in our banks, our stores, our factories, but in those idealistic aims that build permanently. It you would be the builder of a new world order, "Seek ye first the kingdom of God and His righteousness and these things shall be added."

It is only when God reigns that a government can live to preserve the peace and safety of its people.

26. Speech sent by Mr. Shibusawa.

"Delegates to the Eighth World's SS Convention: Ladies and Gentlemen: I consider it a great honor to have your presence here today and to be given an opportunity of expressing my sincere interest and sympathy with the great movement, which has brought you from the different quarters of the globe to this metropolis. It is a world movement aiming at the gradual betterment of human society through moral and religious education inculcated in the minds and hearts of those who in future will bear the burden of world's responsibilities.

"It is not a mere Christian propoganda; it is part of that greater propoganda of the Religion of Humanity, which makes us feel that all the world is akin and inspires us with universal longing for higher and nobler standards of life.

"That this historic gathering from thirty-three different nationalities should be held in this country at this juncture is both opportune and significant. It may be said to be an epoch-making event in the history of Japan. We can not, therefore, help looking forward to great and good results from it, to the hastening of that time when through its indirect influence clouds and misunderstandings in human affairs may be dispelled like mist by the rays of the Rising Sun, and men may be more and more guided by wisdom and righteousness in their dealings with individual and national as well as international relations, and the League of Nations may find its place not only in treaties but also in the hearts of all the peoples of the world.

"In closing let me assure you that Japan shares with all nations you represent the noble sentiment, Peace on earth, good will toward men."

27. Pageant, "The Court of Christianity."

1st scene—Prophecy of the coming of Christ into all the world.

Prolucutors and Pageant Choir.
Sargent's *Frieze of the Prophets*.

2nd Scene—The Court of Christianity. Christianity and her four attendants enter to the music of

Wonderful Counsellor, the Mighty God,
The everlasting Father, Prince of Peace.

Education and her attendants enter to the music

Send out thy light and thy truth,
Let them lead me.
And let them bring me to thy holy hill.

Church and her Crusaders enter to music:

Lovely appear over the mountains,
The feet of them that preach,
And bring good news of peace.

3rd Scene—The Vision of Isaiah. Isaiah takes position before the altar and speaks: "I saw the Lord sitting upon a throne, high and lifted up, and His train filled the temple. And I heard the voice of the Lord saying, 'Whom shall I send and who will go for us?' Then I said, 'Here am I send me.'"

4th Scene—All nations accept Christianity. Consecration of the four attendants to missionary service. They move out to bring back with them the League of Nations of the world with national flags and costuming. The stacking of colors and the presentation of palms of victory.

5th Scene—The Burden Bearers of Earth. The peoples in darkness are represented by man, woman and child who cry out in the night for help. Help and comfort come from Christianity, Education and Church in action and songs:

Come unto me, ye weary,
And I will give you rest.
O ye beneath life's crushing load
Whose forms are bending low.

6th Scene—The Cross of Christ.

The Cross of white—Bethlehem—"Good Will."
The Cross of red—Calvary—"Sacrifice."
The Cross of gold—Coronation—"Jesus Reigns."

Processional of convention singers and "Hallelujah Chorus" from the *Messiah*.
28. Imperial Rescript.

Know Ye, Our Subjects:

Our Imperial Ancestors have founded Our Empire on a basis broad and everlasting and have deeply and firmly implanted virtue; Our subjects, ever united in loyalty and filial piety, have from generation to generation illustrated the beauty thereof. This is the glory of the fundamental character of Our Empire, and herein also lies the source of Our education. Ye, Our subjects, be filial to your parents, affectionate to your brother and sisters; as husbands and wives, be harmonious, as friends, true; bear yourselves in modesty and moderation; extend your benevolence to all, pursue learning and cultivate arts, and thereby develop intellectual faculties and perfect moral powers; furthermore advance public good and promote common interests; always respect the Constitution and observe the laws; should emergency arise, offer yourselves courageously to the State; and thus guard and maintain the prosperity of Our Imperial Throne, coeval with heaven and earth. So shall ye not only be Our good and faithful subjects, but render illustrious the best traditions of your forefathers.

The Way here set forth is indeed the teaching bequeathed by Our Imperial Ancestors, to be observed alike by Their Descendants and the subjects, infallible for all ages and true in all places. It is Our wish to lay it to heart in all reverence, in common with you, Our subjects, that we may all thus attain to the same virtue.

The 30th day of the 10th month of the 23rd year of Meiji.

Oct. 30, 1890
[Imperial Sign Manual, Imperial Seal]

Index

Note: The Japanese method for writing persons' names is to put the surname or family name first followed by the given or individual name. Thus, the English-language's John Doe, if he were Japanese, would write his name as Doe John. Throughout this book, the English language custom has been used in writing all names, including Japanese, with the result that the Japanese names appear with the surname or family name at the end of the name. Conversely, in the index, all names, English or Japanese, are shown with the surname or family name listed first.